PENGUIN CLASSICS

THE DIVINE COMEDY
VOL. I: INFERNO

DANTE ALIGHIERI was born in Florence in 1265 and belonged to a noble but impoverished family. He followed a normal course of studies, possibly attending university in Bologna, and when he was about twenty, he married Gemma Donati, by whom he had several children. He had first met Bice Portinari, whom he called Beatrice, in 1274, and when she died in 1290, he sought distraction by studying philosophy and theology and writing *La Vita Nuova*. During this time he became involved in the strife between the Guelfs and the Ghibellines; he became a prominent White Guelf, and when the Black Guelfs came to power in 1302, Dante, during an absence from Florence, was condemned to exile. He took refuge first in Verona, and after wandering from place to place—as far as Paris and even, some have said, to Oxford—he settled in Ravenna. While there he completed *The Divine Comedy*, which he began in about 1308. Dante died in Ravenna in 1321.

MARK MUSA is a graduate of Rutgers University (B.A., 1956), the University of Florence (Fulbright, 1956–58), and the Johns Hopkins University (M.A., 1959; Ph.D., 1961). He is a former Guggenheim fellow and the author of a number of books and articles. Best known for his translations of the Italian classics (Dante and the poetry of the Middle Ages), he is Distinguished Professor of French and Italian at the center for Italian Studies, Indiana University. Mr. Musa has also translated and edited *The Portable Dante* and, with Peter Bondanella, *The Portable Machiavelli*, both published in Penguin Books.

DANTE ALIGHIERI

The Divine Comedy
Volume I: Inferno

Translated with an Introduction,
Notes, and Commentary by
MARK MUSA

PENGUIN BOOKS

PENGUIN BOOKS

Published by the Penguin Group

Penguin Putnam Inc., 375 Hudson Street, New York, New York 10014, U.S.A.
Penguin Books Ltd, 80 Strand, London WC2R 0RL, England
Penguin Books Australia Ltd, 250 Camberwell Road,
Camberwell, Victoria 3124, Australia
Penguin Books Canada Ltd, 10 Alcorn Avenue, Toronto, Ontario, Canada M4V 3B2
Penguin Books India (P) Ltd, 11 Community Centre,
Panchsheel Park, New Delhi – 110 017, India
Penguin Books (N.Z.) Ltd, Cnr Rosedale and Airborne Roads,
Albany, Auckland, New Zealand
Penguin Books (South Africa) (Pty) Ltd, 24 Sturdee Avenue, Rosebank,
Johannesburg 2196, South Africa

Penguin Books Ltd, Registered Offices:
Harmondsworth, Middlesex, England

This translation first published in the United States of America
by Indiana University Press 1971
Edition with an introduction by Mark Musa published in Penguin Classics 1984
This edition published in Penguin Books 2003

5   7   9   10   8   6   4

Copyright © Indiana University Press, 1971
Introduction copyright © Mark Musa, 1984
All rights reserved

LIBRARY OF CONGRESS CATALOGING IN PUBLICATION DATA
Dante Alighieri, 1265–1321.
The divine comedy.
(Penguin Classics)
Translation of: Divina commedia.
Bibliography: p.
Includes index.
Contents: v. 1: Inferno.
I. Musa, Mark. II. Series.
PQ4315.M8   1984   851'.1   83-17423
ISBN 0 14 24.3722 0

Printed in the United States of America
Set in Linotron Bembo

Diagrams and maps drawn by C. W. Scott-Giles

FOR
ISABELLA

Nel mezzo del cammin di nostra vita

The subject of this work must first be considered according to the letter, then be considered allegorically. The subject of the whole work, then, taken in the literal sense alone, is simply "The state of souls after death," for the movement of the whole work hinges on this. If the work be taken allegorically, the subject is "Man—as, according to his merits or demerits in the exercise of his free will, he is subject to reward or punishment by Justice. . . ."

The title of the work is "Here begins the Comedy of Dante Alighieri, Florentine by birth, not by character."

DANTE'S *Letter to Can Grande*

CONTENTS

LIST OF DIAGRAMS
AND MAPS

ACKNOWLEDGMENTS

I should like to acknowledge my gratitude to all the students in my Dante classes at Indiana University for the past nine years, whose comments I often found helpful in the preparation of my notes, and especially to Christopher Kleinhenz and Charles Jernigan (now professors), Denise Heilbronn and Judith Sherrington, who served in various ways as my research assistants; and to Indiana University's Office of Research and Advanced Studies for a number of very helpful grants. I am also indebted to Rudolph Gottfried and Gene Lawlis, professors in the English Department of this university, for valuable suggestions concerning the translation and the notes. And many thanks to Bernard Perry, the director of the Indiana University Press, for his courage and encouragement and for giving me an editor with the splendid talents of Dorothy Wikelund.

And to Anna Hatcher, my severest critic.

Special thanks to Georges Edelen, several of whose suggestions I have incorporated into this new Penguin edition, and to Peter Bondanella and Jim Jensen, who made suggestions for the Introduction. Thanks to Nancy Kipp Smith for her help with the Glossary and to sweet Sandy Claxon, who typed and typed and typed.

AN INTRODUCTION TO
DANTE AND HIS WORKS

NOT MUCH is known about Dante Alighieri. We know he was born in Florence sometime in late May or early June (he was a Gemini) of the year 1265 in the district of San Martino, the son of Alighiero di Bellincione d'Alighiero. His mother, Donna Bella, died when he was very young; his father, whom he seems to avoid mentioning as much as possible, remarried, and died while Dante was in his late teens. The Alighieri family may be considered noble by reason of the titles and dignities bestowed upon its members, although by the time Dante arrived on the scene the family seems to have been reduced to modest economic and social circumstances. According to Dante himself in *Inferno* XV, the family descended from the noble seed of the Roman founders of the city. This claim, however, remains largely unsubstantiated, as nothing is known of Dante's ancestors before his great-great-grandfather Cacciaguida, who was knighted by Emperor Conrad III. In the company of Cacciaguida Dante spends several emotional cantos in the final part of the great poem: they are cantos that occupy the central portion of the *Paradise*, in which important questions are answered, tragic events are revealed, and major themes running through the entire *Divine Comedy* are resolved. Cacciaguida died, or so Dante tells us in *Paradise* XV (139–48), during the Second Crusade, about 1147.

Like most of the city's lesser nobility and artisans, Dante's family was affiliated with the Guelf party, as opposed to the Ghibellines, whose adherents tended to belong to the feudal aristocracy. These two parties came into Italy from Germany, and their names represent Italianized forms of the names attached to the two rival German clans of Welf and Waibling. In Italy, the parties were at first identified with broad allegiances: to papal authority for the Guelfs, and to imperial authority in the case of the Ghibellines. Eventually, however this distinction between Church and Empire disappeared, and the two parties became less clearly defined in outlook and purpose. Local connotations became much more important, as party issues and activities were tied to neighborhood rivalries, family feuds, and private interests. Thus, the Guelfs and Ghibellines of Florence were in a sense factions peculiar to that region alone.

One year after Dante's birth the Guelfs gained control in Florence: 1266 marks the beginning of nearly thirty years of relative peace and prosperity in the city. Florence was flourishing at this time, artistically, intellectually, and commercially; according to a contemporary chronicler, Dino Compagni, Florence could even boast of a tourist trade. The city, composed of old and respectable, wealthy families as well as the nouveau riche, was certainly one of the wealthiest of its day. Founded on banking and the gold florin, it thrived on the manufacturing of silk, fur, leather, and especially wool. Another chronicler, Giovanni Villani, reports that there were as many as two hundred shops, or botteghe, belonging to the wool guild (which employed thirty thousand people) and as many as eighty banks in town. By this time the Florentine banking families, most prominent of whom were the Bardi and the Peruzzi, had become international leaders in the field of banking.

Like every good male citizen of Florence, Dante did his military service. In 1289 he joined the cavalry, the aristocratic branch of the armed forces, and in the summer of that year, when Florence and its Guelf allies were at war with the neighboring town of Arezzo, Dante took part in the battle of Campaldino, which ended in a decisive victory for Florence. Later on, in August, he was at the siege of the Pisan fortress of Caprona. He records both experiences in The Divine Comedy: Campaldino in Purgatory V, through the eyes of the courageous Buonconte da Montefeltro, who dies in that battle; and the surrender of Caprona's fortress in Inferno XXI.

If I were asked to quote a passage that best describes Dante's feelings about war in general, I might turn to the opening lines of *Inferno* XXII for their color and force and pageantry, but my final choice would be to quote the closing lines of Canto XXI, for the first five tercets of the next canto are simply a gloss on them. Malacoda, the devil-captain in charge of affairs in the Fifth *Bolgia*, which houses the corrupt souls of the Grafters, who misused public office, orders ten of his best devils to accompany the Pilgrim and his guide, Virgil, to the archway crossing the Sixth *Bolgia*. There is no archway, but only the captain and his men know that, and they are about to take advantage of the fact by having a little fun with their innocent wards; the canto ends with the black squadron of ten saluting their honorable captain just as they are about to take off:

> Before they turned left-face along the bank
>   each one gave their good captain a salute
>   with farting tongue pressed tightly to his teeth,
>
> and he blew back with his bugle of an ass-hole.

So much for war!

As far as one can tell from his writings, Dante's recollections of family life were pleasant ones. It is fairly certain that he received a careful education, although little of its content is precisely known. He may have attended the Franciscan lower schools, and later the order's schools of philosophy. The family's modest social standing did not prevent him from pursuing his studies, nor was he hindered in his effort to lead the life of a gentleman. His writings indicate that he was familiar with the ways of the country as well as with city life. He probably studied for a time under the direction of the distinguished teacher, scholar, and statesman Brunetto Latini (c. 1220–94), who was the author of an encyclopedia in French, the *Trésor*, a work well known all over Europe. At this time Dante was driven by a desire to master the techniques of style. It seems that Brunetto encouraged his keenness for study and learning, and this may account for a trip, around 1287, to Bologna, where Dante decided to pursue his study of rhetoric in the highly renowned university.

We learn from the *Vita nuova* (Chapter III) that as a young man Dante taught himself the art of writing verse. In time, he became acquainted with the best-known poets of Florence, corresponding with them and circulating his own love lyrics. For the youthful Dante, writing poetry gradually became an important occupation, nourished by his love for art and learning and his interest in the nature of genuine love courtship. Equally significant at this time was his friendship with the wealthy, aristocratic poet Guido Cavalcanti (c. 1240–1300), who exerted a strong influence on Dante's early poetic endeavors. This period was also marked by the death of his father (c. 1283), and by his marriage to Gemma, a gentlewoman of the Donati family. (The marriage had been arranged by Dante's father in 1277, well before his death.) Gemma gave Dante two sons, Pietro and Jacopo, and at least one daughter (there exist the names of two daughters, Antonia and Beatrice, but they could refer to the same person, Beatrice being a monastic name). Dante's marriage and family seem to have had little influence on him as a poet; some critics believe that during his last years of life in exile, Gemma joined him in Ravenna and was a comfort to him, but nowhere in his works does Dante make reference to his wife.

Besides his associations with Guido Cavalcanti and Brunetto Latini, Dante knew well the notary Lapo Gianni (c. 1270–1332) and became acquainted later on with the youthful Cino da Pistoia (c. 1270–c. 1336). Both of these men were poets, and Cino, like Dante, was a highly productive one. Dante was also on friendly terms with the musician Casella, who appears in *Purgatory* II (76–114), and about whom there exists little information. We are not certain, but the artists Oderisi da Gubbio (c. 1240–c. 1299) and Giotto (c. 1267–1337) may also have been among Dante's acquaintances. A comrade chosen with far less discrimination, perhaps, was Forese Donati (d. 1296), a kinsman of Dante's wife's and a regular rogue, with whom Dante exchanged at one time a series of reproaches and coarse insults in sonnet form. Dante the Pilgrim's meeting with his bon vivant friend Forese in the *Purgatory* (Canto XXIII) precedes a number of conversations in Cantos XXIV–XXVI

with the great poets Guido Guinizelli (c. 1230–75) and Arnaut
Daniel (c. 1150–?). And it is here, immediately following his
talk with Forese, that Dante the Pilgrim discusses poetry with
a not-too-distinguished poet from Lucca, Bonagiunta (c. 1220–
c. 1275), and in so doing gives a definition of the so-called
school of the *dolce stil nuovo*.

Along with his good friend Guido Cavalcanti, Dante refined
and developed his poetic skill and began to distinguish himself
from the other writers of the time. In their poetry, Dante and
Guido presented their ideas on the nature of love and its ability
to contribute to the inner perfection of man. Guido, however,
was more interested in natural philosophy and the psychology
of love than Dante, who favored the study of theology and
Latin poetic models. He particularly admired Virgil, from whom
he learned much about matters of style as well as content.
Though Dante was deeply influenced in his writing by the
example of his friend Guido, he eventually responded to his
own artistic temperament, to his study of Virgil, and to the
example provided by a great poetic master, Guido Guinizelli,
who died when Dante was just a child.

Dante's life and writings were also influenced by his ac-
quaintance with a noble Florentine woman of outstanding grace
and beauty. He casually mentions her name among the names
of sixty of the most beautiful women of Florence in one of
his early poems, but it was not until later that the poet truly
"discovered" her. This revelation proved to be an extremely
powerful force in his artistic development. According to the
testimony of Boccaccio and others, the woman was called
Bice, and was the daughter of Folco Portinari of Florence. She
later became the wife of the banker Simone dei Bardi. Dante
called her Beatrice, "the bringer of blessings," the one who
brought bliss to all who looked upon her.

Dante tells us that he met Beatrice for the first time when
he was nine. Some time later they met again, and if we are to
take the literal level of what our poet tells us in his *Vita nuova*
as true (and I see no reason not to), theirs was not an easy
relationship, for Beatrice was offended by the attention Dante
paid other women. The resulting rebuff caused Dante great

sorrow. His emotional attachment to Beatrice brought him to idealize her more and more as the guide of his thoughts and feelings, as the one who would lead him toward the inner perfection that is the ideal of every noble mind. In his poems, Dante praised his lady as a model of virtue and courtesy, a miraculous gift given to earth by God to ennoble and enrich all those who were able to appreciate her superior qualities. Such an exalted view of this woman was bound to carry with it the fear that she would not remain long in this life, and, in fact, she died at a rather early age in 1290. Dante was overcome with grief at his loss, and there followed a period of contemplating Beatrice in the full glory of Heaven. After the first anniversary of Beatrice's death, another woman (unnamed) succeeded in winning Dante's affection for a brief time. However, Beatrice soon came vividly to mind again, and, feeling guilt and remorse for having neglected her memory, Dante reaffirmed his fidelity to her. This experience prompted him to gather together all the poems he had written in her honor, in an attempt to celebrate her virtue. To this selective collection of poems (Dante chose to include thirty-one) he added a commentary on the meaning and occasion of each, and he called the little book *Vita nuova*, or the *New Life*.

This, the most elegant and mysterious of Dante's earliest works, is a masterpiece in its own right. Had Dante never written *The Divine Comedy*, he would undoubtedly still be remembered today for the *Vita nuova*. In addition to the poems, it includes one of the first important examples of Italian literary prose, which serves the purpose not only of offering a continuous narrative but also of explaining the occasion for the composition of each of the poems. The originality of the *Vita nuova* lies in the functional relationship between the poetry and the prose. The *Vita nuova* is, I believe, the best introduction to *The Divine Comedy*. From this little book the great poem is born, and in it we find Dante's early use of such techniques as allegory, dream, and symbolism.

In recent years the critics of *The Divine Comedy* have come to see more clearly the necessity of distinguishing between Dante the Poet—the historical figure, who wrote the poem in his own voice—and Dante the Pilgrim, the poet's creation, who moves in a world of the poet's invention. In the case of the *Vita nuova* it is more difficult to distinguish between Dante the Poet and Dante the Lover, because in this book the Lover, the protagonist, is himself a poet. More important, however, is the fact that the events of the *Vita nuova*, unlike those of *The Divine Comedy*, are surely not to be taken as pure fiction, and the protagonist himself is no fictional character: he is the historical character Dante at an earlier age. But we must attempt, just as we must do in the case of any first-person novel, to distinguish between the point of view of the one who has already lived through the experiences recorded and has had time to reflect upon them, and the point of view of the one undergoing the experiences at the time. What we have in the *Vita nuova* is a mature Dante, who is evoking his youthful experiences in a way to point up the folly of his youth.

Also significant is the chronological relationship between the composition of the poems and that of the prose narrative, which reflects the way in which the author adapted some of his earlier writings to a new purpose. In general, scholars will agree that sometime between 1292 (that is, two years after the death of Beatrice) and 1300, when Dante composed the *Vita nuova*, most—if not all—of the poems that were to appear in the text had already been written. The architecture of the work, it might be said, consists of selected poems arranged in a certain order, with bridges of prose that primarily serve a narrative function: to describe the events in the life of the protagonist that supposedly inspired the poems included in the text.

By giving the poems a narrative background, the author was able to clarify their meaning. For example, though its beauty is independent of its position in the work, the first *canzone* in the book, "Donne ch'avete intelletto d'amore" ("Ladies who have intelligence of love"), owes entirely to the preceding narrative its dramatic significance as the proclamation of a totally new attitude adopted by the young poet-lover at this time in the story. This is also true, though from a different point of view, of the most famous poem in the *Vita*

nuova (and probably one of the most exquisite sonnets in all
of world literature):

> Tanto gentile e tanto onesta pare
>   la donna mia quand'ella altrui saluta,
>   ch'ogne lingua deven tremando muta
>   e li occhi no l'ardiscon di guardare.
> Ella si va, sentendosi laudare,
>   benignamente d'umiltà vestuta,
>   e par che sia una cosa venuta
>   da cielo in terra a miracol mostrare.
> Mostrarsi sì piacente a chi la mira,
>   che dà per li occhi una dolcezza al core,
>   che 'ntender no la può chi no la prova·
>   e par che de la sua labbia si mova
>   un spirito suove, pien d'amore,
>   Che va dicendo a l'anima: "Sospira!"

> Such sweet decorum and such gentle grace
>   attend my lady's greeting as she moves
>   that lips can only tremble into silence,
>   and eyes dare not attempt to gaze at her.
> Moving benignly, clothed in humility,
>   untouched by all the praise along her way,
>   she seems to be a creature come from Heaven
>   to earth, to manifest a miracle.
> Miraculously gracious to behold,
>   her sweetness reaches, through the eyes, the heart
>   (who has not felt this cannot understand),
>   and from her lips it seems there moves a gracious
>   spirit, so deeply loving that it glides
>   into the souls of men, whispering: "Sigh!"

Just how much of the narrative prose is fiction we shall
never know. We can never be sure that a poem actually arose
from the circumstances outlined in the preceding prose. A few
critics believe that all of the events of the narrative reflect
biographical truth; most, fortunately, are more skeptical. But
it goes without saying that in reading the *Vita nuova* we must
suspend our skepticism and accept as "true" the events of
the narrative (as we must when we read *The Divine*

Comedy), for only by doing so can we perceive the significance that the author attributed to his poems as he placed them where he did.

In the opening chapter, or preface, of his little book, the author states that his purpose is to copy from his "book of memory" only those past experiences that belong to the period beginning his "new life"—a life made new by the poet's first meeting with Beatrice and the God of Love, who, together with the poet-protagonist, are the main characters in the story. And by the end of Chapter II of the *Vita nuova*, all the motifs that are important for the story that is about to unfold have been introduced. The first word of the opening sentence is "Nine": "Nine times already since my birth the heaven of light had circled back to almost the same point, when there appeared before my eyes the now glorious lady of my mind, who was called Beatrice even by those who did not know what her name was." The number nine will be repeated twice more in the next sentence (and it will appear another twenty times before the book comes to an end). In this opening sentence the reader finds not only a reference to the number nine of symbolic significance but also an emphasis on mathematical precision, which will appear at frequent intervals throughout the *Vita nuova*, and will become important to the poetic structure of *The Divine Comedy*. In the same opening sentence the child Beatrice is presented as already enjoying the veneration of the people of her city, including strangers, who did not know her name, and with the words "the now glorious lady of my mind" (the first of two time shifts in which the figure of the living Beatrice is described in such a way as to remind us of Beatrice dead), the theme of death is delicately foreshadowed at the beginning of the story. The figure of Beatrice, when she is seen for the first time in this chapter, appears in a garment of blood-red—the same color as her "shroud" will be in the next chapter. In the next three sentences the three main *spiriti* are introduced: the "vital" (in the heart), the "natural" (in the liver), and the "animal" (in the brain). They rule the body of the nine-year-old protagonist, and they speak in Latin, as will the God of Love in the chapter that follows (and again later on). The words of the first spirit describing Beatrice anticipate the first coming of Love in the next chapter and suggest something of the same mood of terror. The words of the second spirit suggest rapturous bliss to come (that bliss rhapsodically described in Chapter XI), and in the words of the third spirit, the spirit of the liver, there is the first of the many references to tears in the *Vita nuova*. It is only after this reference to the organ of digestion that Love is mentioned. He is mentioned first of all as a ruler, but we learn immediately that much of his power is derived from the protagonist's imagination—a faculty of which there will be many reminders in the form of visions throughout the book. We are also told that Love's power is restricted by reason, and later in the book the relation between Love and reason becomes an important problem. Two more themes are posited in this chapter, and will be woven into the narrative of the rest of the book: the godlike nature of Beatrice, and the strong "praise of the lady" motif, which sounds throughout the chapter, as the protagonist's admiration for Beatrice keeps growing during the nine years after her first appearance.

Thus, the opening chapter of the *Vita nuova* prepares for the rest of the book not only by presenting a background situation, an established continuity out of which single events will emerge, but also by setting in motion certain forces that will propel the *Vita nuova* forward—forces with which Dante's reader will gradually become more and more familiar. Dante presents in the first chapter of this book the major themes to be developed in the following chapters, as he will do again in Canto I of his *Divine Comedy*, which is not really the first canto of the *Inferno*, but rather the opening, introductory canto to the entire *Divine Comedy*. And we see here, as we will in the later work, the poet's medieval love for numbers and symmetry.

In Chapter XLII, the final chapter of the *Vita nuova*, the poet expresses his dissatisfaction with his work: "After this sonnet there appeared to me a miraculous vision in which I saw things that made me resolve to say no more about this blessed one until I should be capable of writing about her in a more worthy fashion." The earlier vision made him decide to keep on writing; this one, which is not revealed to the reader, makes him decide to stop. If the main action of the book is to be seen, as some critics believe, in the development of Dante's love from preoccupation with his own feelings to enjoyment of Beatrice's excellence and, finally, to an exclusive concern with her heavenly attributes and with heavenly matters, then the *Vita nuova* ends, in an important sense, in failure.

To understand the message of the book, to understand how the book succeeds through failure, we must go back in time and imagine the poet Dante, somewhere between the ages of twenty-seven and thirty-five, having already glimpsed the possibility of what was to be his terrible and grandiose masterpiece, *The Divine Comedy*—we must imagine him rereading the love poems of his earlier years, and reading a number of them with shame. He would have come to see Beatrice, too, as she was destined to appear in *The Divine Comedy*, and indeed, as she does appear briefly in the *Vita nuova*, specifically in that essay (Chapter XXIX) on the miraculous quality of the figure nine, which is the square of the number three, that is, of the Blessed Trinity, and which is Beatrice herself.

Having arrived at this point, he would choose from among his earlier love poems many tha exhibit his younger self at its worst, in order to offer a warning example to other young lovers and, especially, to other love poets. This, of course, would imply on Dante's part, as he is approaching "il mezzo del cammin di nostra vita" ("midway along the journey of our life"), a criticism of most of the Italian love poetry for which his century was famous, and also of the Provençal tradition of the preceding century, which gave birth to the Italian love lyric.

One might even say that the *Vita nuova* is a cruel book—cruel, that is, in the treatment of the human type represented by the protagonist. In the picture of the lover there is offered a condemnation of the vice of emotional self-indulgence and an exposure of its destructive effects on a man's integrity. The "tender feelings" that move the lover to hope or despair, to rejoice or to grieve (and perhaps even to enjoy his grief), spring from his vulnerability and instability and self-love. However

idealistically inspired, these feelings cannot, except spasmod-
ically, lead him ahead and above; as long as he continues to
be at their mercy, he must always fall back into the helplessness
of his self-centeredness. The man who would realize his poetic
destiny must ruthlessly cut out of his heart the canker at its
center, the canker that the heart instinctively tends to cultivate.
This is, I am convinced, the main message of the *Vita nuova*.
And the consistent, uncompromising indictment it levels has
no parallel in the literature of Dante's time. But, of course,
the *Vita nuova* offers more than a picture of the misguided
lover: there is also the glory of Beatrice, and the slowly in-
creasing ability of the lover to understand it, although he must
nevertheless confess, at the end, that he has not truly under-
stood it.

In the treatment of both the lover and Beatrice, Dante went
far beyond what he found at hand in the love poetry of the
troubadours and of their followers. He took up two of their
preoccupations (one might almost say obsessions) and devel-
oped each in a most original way: the lover's glorification of
his own feelings, and his glorification of the beloved. Of the
first he made a caricature. Unlike his friend Guido Cavalcanti,
who was also highly critical of the havoc wrought by the
emotions within a man's soul and who made the distraught
lover a macabre portrait of doom, Dante presented his pro-
tagonist mainly as an object of derision.

As to the glorification of the lady, all critics of the *Vita nuova*
will admit that Dante carried this idealization to a point never
reached before by any poet, a degree of idealization that no
poet after him would ever quite reach. However blurred may
be the lover's vision of the gracious, pure, feminine Beatrice,
Dante the Poet, in Chapter XXIX, probes to the essence of
her being and presents the coldness of her sublimity, reflected
by the coldness and the sublimity of the square of the number
three. Thus, the tender foolishness of the lover is intensified
by contrast with the icy perfection of the beloved. The nature
of Beatrice is destined to inspire not tender sentiments, and
certainly not weak tears, but only the stern resolution to strive
for spiritual growth. Tears the divine Beatrice could approve,

but these should be tears of deep contrition—as she herself will tell the Pilgrim in *The Divine Comedy*, when she first addresses him at the summit of the Mountain of Purgatory.

With a few exceptions, Dante's lyric poems (and not only those contained in the *Vita nuova*) are inferior as works of art to those of Cavalcanti and Guinizelli or, for that matter, to those of Bernart de Ventadorn and Arnaut Daniel. The greatness of the *Vita nuova* lies not in the poems but rather in the purpose that Dante forced them to serve. Certainly his recantation is the most original in medieval literature—a recantation that takes the form of a re-enactment, seen from a new perspective, of the sin recanted.

We will get a glimpse of the poet-lover protagonist of the *Vita nuova* once again in a similar tearful mood in *The Divine Comedy*, this time in the role of the fragile and inexperienced Pilgrim. In Canto V of the *Inferno* we find him in tears yet another time, after listening to the words of the most eloquent and charming of all the sinners he will encounter in Hell. She is the enchanting lady Francesca, who, with her lovely words, melts the Pilgrim's heart. At first glance, the Pilgrim's deep compassion for her seems easily understandable. The story of Francesca da Rimini and her lover, Paolo Malatesta, even reduced to its sober, factual details, is made to order for inspiring sympathy, and Dante the Poet allows Francesca to present herself, on the surface at least, as one of the most charming creatures in world literature. So the Pilgrim is seduced by the gracious, aristocratic, tenderly eloquent, and all-too-feminine Francesca—and this seduction has also infected most critics and readers of *The Divine Comedy*. How this all takes place I have tried to explain in the notes to my translation. Let me add, however, that the reader will do well to be on guard while reading the *Inferno*, for while Francesca is the only woman in the *Inferno* who talks to the Pilgrim, she is by no means the only sinner there who tries to sweet-talk the naïve traveler. We must keep in mind the words of Minòs, the grotesque and snarling figure who judges all sinners at the entrance to Hell proper, when he warns the Pilgrim: "Be careful how you enter and whom you trust" (*Inferno* V, 19).

But for the moment, let us return to Dante the man and citizen of Florence. During the time he was composing the *Vita nuova* in at least a first draft—that is, sometime between 1290 and 1300—Dante's passion for study continued unabated. His vision was broadened by the reading of Boethius and Cicero. The dissemination of the scientific and philosophical works of Aristotle was bringing recognition of the need to harmonize the ideas of the great guide of human reason with the truths and teachings of the Faith. Dante, by now a grown man, was attracted to many of the new schools and universities that were operating under the tutelage of the new religious orders. Among the Franciscans, Dominicans, and Augustinians were many eminent teachers and scholars. In this brisk intellectual environment of the 1290s, Dante applied his energies to philosophy with such fervor that "in a short time, perhaps thirty months," he began "to be so keenly aware of her sweetness that the love of her drove away and destroyed every other thought," as he tells us in his *Convivio* (II, xii, 7). Among Christian scholars and theologians, he certainly read Saint Thomas, Albertus Magnus, and Saint Augustine, Hugh and Richard of Saint Victor, Saint Bonaventure, Saint Bernard, and Peter Lombard. In the area of history, he took up Livy and Paulus Orosius, among others. Evidence of this extensive course of study found its way into his poetry, as he became interested in the glorification of philosophy as mistress of the mind. Dante also treated questions of moral philosophy, such as nobility and courtship, in a number of beautifully composed *canzoni*. Nevertheless, in spite of his ardent pursuit of philosophical matter, he retained his view of love as the most important force behind noble actions and lofty endeavors. To his appreciation of the Latin poets he added his admiration for the Provençal troubadours, and this encouraged him to attempt new poetic techniques, which would serve him well in his later writings.

In Canto IV of the *Inferno* the Pilgrim and his guide, Virgil, who are now in Limbo, see a hemisphere of light glowing in the distance, and as they move toward it they are met by four great pagan poets. Virgil explains to his ward:

"Observe the one who comes with sword in hand,
    leading the three as if he were their master.

It is the shade of Homer, sovereign poet,
    and coming second, Horace, the satirist;
    Ovid is the third, and last comes Lucan."

(86–90)

Together with Virgil these four non-Christians are the classical poets whom Dante most admired and from whom he drew much of the material for his poem. It must be said, however, that while Homer was known in the Middle Ages as the first of the great epic poets, the author of the *Iliad* and *Odyssey*, few people, including Dante, could read Greek; thus, Homer's great epics were known almost entirely secondhand, through the "revised" versions of Dares and Dictys, who told the tales of the Trojan War in a way that exalted the Trojans and often disparaged the Greeks, or through Virgil's use of Homeric material in the *Aeneid*. Dante, then, admired Homer more for his reputation than through any intimate knowledge of the Greek's works. The second of the four is Horace, whom Dante calls the "satirist" but whom he must have thought of mainly as a "moralist," since Dante was familiar only with the *Ars Poetica*. Ovid, who comes next, was the most widely read Roman poet in the Middle Ages, and he was Dante's main source for the mythology in *The Divine Comedy*. Dante, however, seems to have been acquainted with only the *Metamorphoses* of Ovid. Coming last is Lucan, author of the *Pharsalia*, which deals with the Roman civil war between the legions of Pompey and those of Caesar. The book was one of Dante's important historical sources. But among all the poets of antiquity it was Virgil who had the greatest influence on Dante. Virgil mentions, in Canto XX of the *Inferno*, that his ward knows all of his *Aeneid*, every word of it. Not only did Dante consider the great Roman poet a master of classical verse, but he also identified him with the legend of Rome itself. The Augustan Age, the time of Virgil, represented for Dante the high point of civilization: it was the time of the Coming of

Christ, the Christian savior. Dante also found Virgil attractive because of a particular passage in his *Fourth Eclogue* that was interpreted generally in Dante's time as a prophecy of the birth of Christ. Virgil, then, would serve Dante well as the guide for man on his own before the First Advent, before the coming of grace; he would stand for the highest achievement of human reason unenlightened by the word of God, the Pilgrim's guide to divine revelation.

Along with his spiritual and intellectual activities, Dante began an active public life. There is evidence that he served as a member of the People's Council of the Commune of Florence (1295), on the council for election of the priors of the city (1295), and on the Council of the Hundred (1296), a body that dealt with finance and other important civic matters.

This was a time of political ferment and instability. Between 1215 and 1278, the Guelfs and Ghibellines of Florence had engaged in a bitter struggle for power, with numerous reversals of fortune on both sides, countless plots and conspiracies, and frequent expulsion orders issued against whoever was on the losing side. The Guelfs finally prevailed. Around 1300, however, the Guelf party split into two hostile factions: the Blacks and the Whites. The Blacks, who were staunch Guelfs, led by the Donati, a family of old wealth with banking interests all over Europe and very concerned with Florentine imperialism, remained in control of the commune. The Whites, led by the rich and powerful family of the Cerchi, were prosperous merchants, who wanted peace with their neighbors so that trade could flourish. The party eventually became associated with the Ghibellines. Dante, meanwhile, was fighting to preserve the independence of Florence, and repeatedly opposed the schemes of Pope Boniface VIII, who sided with the Blacks, since he depended on the Florentine bankers of that party for most of his financial support, and who wanted to place Florence and all of Tuscany under the control of the Church. Boniface attempted to take advantage of the unrest in the city and to undermine his opponents by promising protection to those who displayed sympathy with his cause. He met with firm opposition from the six priors, or magistrates, of Florence, of whom Dante was one in the summer of 1300. To show his displeasure, Boniface moved to excommunicate the members of the priorate. Dante was spared this fate only because his term as a prior was soon due to expire (he served for the two months from June 13 to August 15). Obviously, none of this improved Dante's opinion of the pontiff. He made no secret of his opposition to the pope's ambitious policy; he regarded Boniface as an enemy of peace and later would reserve a place for him among the damned of *Inferno* XIX.

In 1301, Boniface summoned Charles of Valois and his army to Italy to help in the reconquest of Sicily. But the pope also had other plans for Charles: he hoped to use him to neutralize antipapal forces in Florence. It was at this time, as Charles approached the city, that Dante was sent, as one of three envoys of the commune, to the pope at Anagni, to request a change in papal policy toward the city and to protest the intrigues of the Blacks. After the initial talks, the other envoys were dismissed, but Dante was detained. During his absence from Florence, Charles of Valois entered the city, and the Blacks staged a revolution and gained complete control of the commune. Dante found himself sentenced to two years of exile and permanent exclusion from public office on trumped-up charges of graft, embezzlement, opposition to the pope and his forces, disturbance of the peace of Florence, and a number of other transgressions. Dante always felt that his difficulties had been brought on by the trickery of Boniface, and this aggravated his already pronounced hatred for the pontiff and his methods. When Dante failed to appear to answer the charges against him, and when, on March 10, 1302, he did not pay the fine levied against him for his "crimes," a second sentence was imposed upon him: should he ever return to the commune, he would be seized and burned alive. There is no evidence that Dante ever saw his beloved Florence again.

Shortly after his banishment, Dante conspired with his fellow exiles, most of them Whites, to regain admission to Florence. However, disapproving of their machinations and possibly in danger of his life because of their violence, he abandoned them and set off on his own to lead the life of an exiled courtier. It appears that he first took refuge with the Scala family at Verona. He is also believed to have visited the university at Bologna, where he had been known since 1287. This visit probably occurred after the death in 1304 of his generous patron, Bartolommeo della Scala. It is generally thought that Dante traveled extensively in Italy, particularly in the north. He may have been in Padua in 1306. During that same year he appeared in Lunigiana with the Malaspina family, and it was probably then that he went to the mountains of Casentino, on the upper Arno. It has also been suggested that he may have visited Paris sometime between 1307 and 1309.

In 1310, Henry VII of Luxembourg, emperor from 1308 to 1313, descended into Italy in an effort to reunite Church and State, restore order, and force various rebellious cities to submit to his authority. His coming caused a great deal of excitement and conflict. Florence generally opposed him, but Dante, who attributed the woes of Florence and all of Italy to the absence of imperial guidance, welcomed Henry as a savior. (His state of great exaltation is documented in three letters that he wrote in 1310 and 1311.) However, Henry's invasion proved fruitless; he met opposition from all sides, including the very pope, Clement V, who had sent for him in the first place. Just as the situation for Henry and his supporters began to improve, the emperor died, near Siena in 1313. With him went Dante's best hope of restoring himself to an honorable position in his city. Thus, in 1314 he took shelter with Can Grande della Scala in Verona.

Dante did not totally abandon his quest to return to his native city of Florence. He wrote letters to individual members of the government, attempting to appease those who ruled, and even sent a *canzone* to the city of Florence, praising her love for justice and asking that she work with her citizens on his behalf. Dante strove to be politically acceptable to the Florentines, but the public associated him with the Ghibellines, and no matter how he tried to free himself of suspicion, he did not succeed. He also tried to appeal to them on the grounds of his poetic ability, and sought to show that if he had cultivated poetry in the vernacular, it was not for lack of skill or study in Latin. Feeling compelled to display his love for learning and his great respect for philosophy and matters having to do with civic education, he composed two treatises (both left incomplete), the *De vulgari eloquentia* and the *Convivio*; in them one senses his longing to reestablish himself in the good graces of his city, and to find consolation for his wretchedness in the study of matters useful to man's well-being and to his art.

Thus, in the years between the *Vita nuova* and *The Divine Comedy*, Dante's studies were essentially of a philosophical and artistic nature. The *Convivio* is often acknowledged as the key to his philosophical researches, while the *De vulgari eloquentia* is viewed as the key to his artistic inquiries.

Though he desperately hoped to restore his reputation as a Florentine and resume his life in the city that had turned against him, Dante refused to compromise his principles and turned down more than one opportunity to return to Florence because returning would have involved answering the false charges made against him. Such unwillingness to dishonor himself earned him yet another sentence of death, this one extending to his sons as well. The last years of the poet's life were spent at Ravenna, where he was offered asylum by Guido Novella da Polenta, a nephew of the famous Francesca da Rimini. These years seem to have been serene ones. In Ravenna he was greatly esteemed, and he enjoyed a very pleasant social life and an eager following of pupils, for he was already well known for his lyrics, and especially for the *Convivio*, the *Inferno*, and the *Purgatory*. Shortly before his death, he was sent by Guido on a mission to Venice. Although Florence still rejected him, Bologna very much valued his presence, and his friendship with the Ghibelline captain Can Grande della Scala in Verona remained intact—it is to him that he dedicated the *Paradise*. Ravenna remained Dante's home until his death, on September 13 or 14, 1321.

Sometime between 1304 and 1308 Dante began the *Convivio*. It is an unfinished piece of work. His purpose in writing it is explained in the opening sentence, which is a quotation from

Aristotle's *Metaphysics*: "All men by nature desire to know."
The reader is invited to a "Banquet" consisting of fourteen
courses (only three were completed); the "meat" of each course
is a *canzone* concerning love and virtue, while the "bread" is
the exposition of the ode. To his banquet Dante invites all
those worthy people who, because of public duties, family
responsibilities, and the like, have not been introduced to the
science of philosophy, for it is through philosophy, he believes,
that men may attain the temporal goal of happiness. The
poems—apparently mere love poems, written to a beautiful
woman of flesh and blood, and motivated by the poet's sensual
passion—are essentially meant for the "mistress of his mind,"
Philosophy, and are motivated by virtue.

The *Vita nuova* is Dante's monument to his first love, the
lady Beatrice; the *Convivio* is a monument to his "second
love," Lady Philosophy. That this Lady Philosophy is the same
as the lady who offers to console Dante a year after the death
of Beatrice in the *Vita nuova* we learn in Chapter 2, Book II,
of the *Convivio*:

> To begin with, then, let me say that the star of Venus had already
> revolved twice in that circle of hers which makes her appear at
> evening or in the morning, according to the two different pe-
> riods, since the passing away of that blessed Beatrice who dwells
> in Heaven with the angels and on earth with my soul, when that
> gentle lady of whom I made mention at the end of the *Vita nuova*
> first appeared to my eyes, accompanied by love, and occupied a
> place in my mind.

What attracted the poet-protagonist to this lady in the *Vita
nuova* was her offer of consolation, but his love for the lady
at the window lasts only a short time, and he refers to it as
"the adversary of reason" and "most base." It should be re-
membered, however, that it is not the *donna gentile* who is
"the adversary of reason," but rather the love for this lady;
for Philosophy in the *Vita nuova* tries to make the young
protagonist forget the fact that he has lost Beatrice—and some-
thing of this earth (such as philosophy) cannot replace the love

of Beatrice. After the vision in Chapter XXXIX of the *Vita nuova*, after grasping the true significance of his lady, he returns to Beatrice, and never again will he stray. In doing this, he is not to be thought of as rejecting philosophy but rather as rejecting the ideal of replacing Beatrice with philosophy. Never in the *Convivio* does he consider such a possibility, although he calls his love for the Lady Philosophy "most noble."

The *Convivio* exalts learning and the use of reason, for only through knowledge can man hope to attain virtue and God. The *Convivio* can be seen as a connecting link between the *Vita nuova* and *The Divine Comedy*, in that love at first seems to have earthly associations but then acquires religious significance. Furthermore, Dante's praise of reason in this work is developed in *The Divine Comedy*, where reason in the pursuit of knowledge and wisdom is man's sole guide on earth, apart from the intervention of Divine Grace.

In Book I of his *Convivio* Dante suggests the revolutionary idea that the vernacular might be suitable for ethical subjects as well as amorous ones. He was a leader in considering the vernacular a potential medium for all forms of expression, and his impassioned defense and praise of Italian manifests his awareness of its value in scientific studies as well as in poetry. Book II sets forth his view that writings should be expounded in four senses: the literal, the allegorical, the moral, and the anagogical. The literal level of a story or poem need not be true. For example, when Ovid tells his reader that Orpheus moved both animals and stones with his music, what he is signifying is the power of eloquence over what is not rational. If the story is not true on the literal level, it is expounded on the second level as an allegory of poets; if the literal level is taken to be the truth, the story is understood as an allegory of theologians (so called because the literal level of the scriptures was considered to be true). The third level, the moral, has a didactic purpose; for example, the fact that Christ took only three of his disciples with him on the occasion of the Transfiguration is a way of saying that "for those things which are most secret we should have little company." The fourth sense is the anagogical, by which scripture signifies eternal things. When we read, for example, that the people of Israel came out of Egypt and Judea was made free, we must take the statement to be literally true, but it also signifies the spiritual truth that when a soul turns away from sin it becomes holy and free. The literal level of a work must always be exposed first, for it is impossible to delve into the "form" of anything without first preparing the "subject" upon which the form is to be stamped—you must prepare the wood before you build the table. Dante proposes, then, to expound first the literal level of his *canzone* and then the allegorical, bringing into play the other levels or senses when it seems appropriate. There are very few passages in Dante's work where all four senses are at work; in fact, of the three *canzoni* in the *Convivio*, the author manages to treat only the first two poems on two levels and the third only on the literal level. We must bear in mind, however, especially in regard to *The Divine Comedy*, that it is the literal sense of the great poem that contains all its other possible meanings.

In the third book of the *Convivio* Dante expounds the *canzone* "Amor che ne la mente mi ragiona" ("Love that converses with me in my mind"). It is this same poem that Casella, in *The Divine Comedy*, will sing to the newly arrived souls on the shores of Purgatory. In discussing the literal level of this ode Dante gives most of his attention to the meaning of "amor" ("love").

Dante begins the fourth book, which treats the third and final *canzone*, "Le dolci rime d'amor ch'i' solìa" ("Those sweet rhymes of love that I was wont"), by stressing the fact that his love of philosophy has led him to love all those who pursue the truth and to despise those who follow error. He tells us that in order to achieve the utmost clarity, he will discuss the poem only on the literal level. The lady involved, however, is still philosophy.

Dante never tells us why he completed only four of the projected fourteen books of the *Convivio*. In any case, whether he cut short his work on the *Convivio* for personal, political, or other reasons, if this meant he could get on with *The Divine*

Comedy and complete his masterpiece, then we should be grateful that he did.

In all his works Dante shows his concern for words and the structure of language—we can see this in Chapter XXV of the *Vita nuova*, where he takes time to explain and illustrate the use of personification, as well as in the early chapters of the *Convivio*, where he defends the use of Italian rather than Latin. But this concern is most evident in his Latin treatise, *De vulgari eloquentia*, a scholarly treatment of a vernacular language, for which there existed no precedent. Dante completed only the first and second books, but he refers to a fourth, and it is not known whether that one was to be the last.

The first book deals with the origin and history of the language. The first five chapters present basic definitions of human speech, and much of the rest is given over to a discussion of dialects and the principles of poetic composition in Italian, which Dante calls the "illustrious" vulgar tongue, the language of Guido Guinizelli, Guido Cavalcanti, Cino da Pistoia, and Dante himself.

The second book of *De vulgari eloquentia* is devoted to a more thorough discussion of the Italian tongue, which, Dante asserts, is just as appropriate for works of prose as for poetry. Early in this book (Chapter 2) he discusses what subjects are worthy of this illustrious language and concludes that only the most elevated subjects are suitable: war (or prowess of arms), love, and virtue (or direction of the will). He states that the greatest writers using a vulgar tongue wrote only on these three subjects, and cites the Provençal poets Bertran de Born, who wrote about war, Arnaut Daniel, whose subject was love, and Guiraut de Bornelh, who treated virtue. Among Italian poets he mentions that Cino da Pistoia wrote about love, and "his friend" about virtue, citing an example of verse from each poet, including one of his own, but he admits that he can find no Italian poet who has written on war. Chapter 3 presents the view that, although poets have used a variety of forms (*canzoni*, *ballate*, sonnets, and others), the most excellent form remains the *canzone*, and it is this form that is most suited for lofty subjects. The remaining chapters of Book II discuss style, and the rules and form of the *canzone*, and the work ends abruptly with the incomplete Chapter 14, in which he intended to treat the number of lines and syllables in the stanza.

Most scholars will agree that the *De vulgari eloquentia* is an unfinished first draft. There are three basic reasons for this belief: the paucity of manuscripts (there are only three), the way the work breaks off in Chapter 14, and the fact that references to points the author promises to discuss in coming chapters are never followed up. Marigo, the editor of the standard edition of the *De vulgari eloquentia* (Florence, 1938), suggests that Dante stopped writing because he was not certain of his direction. There is an obvious difference between the broad humanistic scope of the first book and the dry, manualistic approach of the second. The date of composition of the *De vulgari eloquentia* has not been definitively resolved. Boccaccio claims that it was written in Dante's old age. Marigo dates it between the spring of 1303 and the end of 1304. And the fact that in the *Convivio* Dante makes an allusion to this work in progress forces us to assume that he at least had the project in mind during this time.

It is also difficult to assign a date of composition to Dante's *De monarchia* (*On Monarchy*), primarily because it contains no references to the author's contemporaries or to events taking place at the time. Some say that it was written before Dante's exile, since the work makes no mention of it; others think that it was written even later than the *Convivio*, since a number of ideas appearing in an embryonic stage in that work are fully developed in the *De monarchia*. Nevertheless, it is most likely that it was written between 1312 and 1313, sometime before or after the coronation of Henry VII, to commemorate his advent into Italy.

The treatise is divided into three parts. The first book attempts to prove that for the welfare of the world, temporal monarchy is necessary. And temporal monarchy, or empire, means a single command exercised over all persons—that is, in those things that are subject to time, as opposed to eternal matters. In the opening sentence of the *De monarchia*, the author pays tribute to both God and Aristotle while he establishes the reason for undertaking the present work: "All men whom the higher Nature has imbued with a love of truth should feel impelled to work for the benefit of future generations, whom they will thereby enrich just as they themselves have been enriched by the labors of their ancestors." According to Dante (and we find the idea throughout his writings) the man who does not contribute to the common good fails sadly in his duty.

There is nothing new in Dante's ideas of justice, freedom, and law—they were very much in line with the philosophy of his day. The originality of the *De monarchia* rests in its main premise: the justification of a single ruler for all the human race. It is in his concern with founding a "universal community of the human race" (*universalis civilitas humani generis*) that the poet is new and even daring. In Dante's day the idea of a universal community existed only as a religious concept, that is, the Church. Dante's universal community was to take its shape from universal Christendom; it was, in a sense, to be an imitation of it, worked out from a philosophical point of view. Starting with the Averroistic concept of the "possible intellect," Dante affirms that the particular goal of mankind as a whole is to realize to the fullest all the potentialities of intellect (to have all the intellectual knowledge it is capable of having); and this can happen only under the direction of a single ruler, under one world government, because the most important essential, if we are to secure our happiness and if the human race is to fulfill its proper role, is universal peace.

In the closing paragraph of the first book we hear the desperate voice of Dante the Poet, warning all humanity. Rarely do we hear the poet's voice in his Italian or Latin prose works, where his intention is to remain as objective as possible. This passage is a preview of what is to come, for Dante will make frequent and effective use of the device of authorial intervention in *The Divine Comedy*. After he has presented his case for the necessity of a monarch in a logical and scholastic fashion, as Saint Thomas or Aristotle might have done, Dante the Poet bursts forth:

O humanity, in how many storms must you be tossed, how many shipwrecks must you endure, so long as you turn yourself into a many-headed beast lusting after a multiplicity of things! You are ailing in your intellectual powers, as well as in your heart. You pay no heed to the unshakeable principles of your higher intellect, nor tune your heart to the sweetness of divine counsel when it is breathed into you through the trumpet of the Holy Spirit: "Behold how good and pleasant it is for brethren to dwell together in unity."

Book II is primarily concerned with showing that the Romans were justified in assuming imperial power. Dante establishes his thesis first by a number of arguments based on rational principles and then attempts to establish it on the principles of the Christian faith. This book reveals Dante's debt to Virgil and for the most part tells us more about the intricate functioning of a brilliant mind than about Dante's political ideas.

In Book III the author poses the question he has from the start wanted to ask and can ask only now, having prepared the way in Books I and II: Is the authority of the Roman monarch directly dependent on God, or does his authority come indirectly from another, a vicar or minister of God (meaning the pope)? First Dante must refute the scriptural arguments based on Genesis I:16 ("And God made two great lights; the greater light to rule the day, and the lesser light to rule the night"), which were used to show the dependence of the emperor on the pope. Having done this, he turns to other historical arguments that must be refuted. The main one he must deal with is the very one that up to this point in his treatise he has been able to cope with only in a rather subjective, emotional, even poetic way: the painful reality of the Donation of Constantine. He proceeds by means of his two preferred sources: scripture (the Gospel of Matthew) and philosophy (on this occasion, Aristotle).

Man is the only being that participates in two natures: one corrupt (the body), the other incorruptible (the soul). Therefore, God, who never errs, has given man two goals: the first is happiness in this life (*beatitudinem huius vitae*) and the second is happiness in the eternal life (*beatitudinem vitae eterne*). With regard to temporal matters, the pope leads mankind in accordance with philosophical teaching. The monarch, who must devote his energies to providing freedom and peace for men as they pass through the "testing-time" of this world, receives his authority directly from God.

A dangerous conclusion can easily follow from Dante's arguments in this treatise, although he himself does not draw it: Intellectual perfection, the happiness of this world, can be attained without the Church. With proper guidance from the universal monarch, man can regain the happiness of the earthly paradise. Needless to say, the book was condemned.

Unfortunately, what Dante wished for in the *De monarchia* did not come about, and it is for this reason that the poet's political focal point shifted from the empire to the Church when he was writing his *Divine Comedy*. With the death of Henry VII, Dante's hopes for the empire and the universal monarch began to fade; he was forced to put aside his ideal and face reality: not the empire but the Church, not the monarch but the pope, would dominate Italian politics of his day. Many passages in his masterpiece lament this sad fact. To cite one of the more famous, in *Purgatory* XVI, Marco Lombardo tells the Pilgrim why the world has gone bad (". . . la cagion che 'l mondo ha fatto reo," 106–12):

> On Rome, that brought the world to know the good,
>   once shone two suns that lighted up two ways:
>   the road of this world and the road of God.
>
> The one sun has put out the other's light,
>   the sword is now one with the crook—and fused
>   together thus, must bring about misrule,
>
> since joined, now neither fears the other one.

Dante undoubtedly wrote many letters. Unfortunately, however, only ten considered to be authentic have survived; all ten are written in Latin, and none is of a personal or intimate nature. To the student of *The Divine Comedy* the most inter-

esting is the one addressed to Can Grande della Scala in which
the author sets forth, in part, his purpose and method in writ-
ing his *Divine Comedy*. The letter is extant in six manuscripts
(all sixteenth-century copies), three of which contain the letter
in its entirety. In it Dante speaks of the different meanings
contained in the work:

> For the clarity of what will be said, it is to be understood that
> this work [the *Comedy*] is not simple, but rather it is polysemous,
> that is, endowed with many meanings. For the first meaning is
> that which one derives from the letter, another is that which one
> derives from things signified by the letter. The first is called
> "literal" and the second "allegorical" or "mystical." So that this
> method of exposition may be clearer, one may consider it in
> these lines: "When Israel came out of Egypt, the house of Jacob
> from people of strange language, Judah was his sanctuary and
> Israel his dominion." If we look only at the letter, this signifies
> that the children of Israel went out of Egypt in the time of Moses;
> if we look at the allegory, it signifies our redemption through
> Christ; if we look at the moral sense, it signifies the turning of
> the souls from the sorrow and misery of sin to a state of grace;
> if we look at the anagogical sense, it signifies the passage of the
> blessed souls from the slavery of this corruption to the freedom
> of eternal glory. And although these mystical meanings are called
> by various names, in general they can all be called allegorical,
> inasmuch as they are different [*diversi*] from the literal or histor-
> ical. For "allegoria" comes from "alleon" in Greek, which in
> Latin is *alienum* [strange] or *diversum* [different]."

This letter also tells us why Dante called his poem a comedy.
The word, he says, is derived from *comus* and *oda* and means
a "rustic song." Unlike tragedy, which begins in tranquillity
but comes to a sad end, comedy may begin under adverse
circumstances, but it always has a happy ending. The language
of comedy is humble, whereas that of tragedy is lofty. There-
fore, because his poem begins in Hell and has a happy ending
in Paradise, and because it is written in a most humble lan-
guage, the Italian vernacular, it is called the *Commedia*. The
letter goes on with a meticulous, almost word-by-word ex-

amination of the verses of the opening canto of the *Paradise* up to the invocation to Apollo. The letter is thought by many to be an important piece of literary criticism in the framework of Dante's time and tradition, and as such, it certainly is worth reading.

No one knows when Dante began composing his great poem, *The Divine Comedy* (the word *Divina* was added to *Commedia* by posterity)—some say perhaps as early as 1307. In any case, the *Inferno* was completed in 1314, and it is probable that the final touches to the *Paradise* were made, as Boccaccio states, in 1321, the year of Dante's death. *The Divine Comedy* is to some degree a result of the poet's determination to fulfill the promise he made at the close of his *Vita nuova*: ". . . if it be the wish of Him in whom all things flourish that my life continue for a few years, I hope to write of her that which has never been written of any lady." But the moving purpose of the poem, as Dante reveals in his epistle to Can Grande, is "to remove those living in this life from their state of misery and lead them to the state of felicity."

The poem consists of one hundred cantos, divided into three major sections: *Inferno*, *Purgatory*, and *Paradise*. The *Purgatory* and the *Paradise* contain thirty-three cantos each, while the *Inferno* has thirty-four, the opening canto serving as an introduction to the work as a whole. The structural formula for the great masterpiece is, then, 1 + 33 + 33 + 33. For his *Divine Comedy* Dante invented a rhyme scheme known as *terza rima* (tertiary rhyme: aba/bcb/cdc), thus continuing to display the fascination with the number three that was so much on his mind when he was composing the *Vita nuova* many years earlier. And he divides each canto into three-line stanzas called *terzine*, or tercets, in which the first and third lines rhyme while the second line rhymes with the first and third of the next *terzina*, and so forth. The basic metrical unit of the verse is the hendecasyllabic line, quite common in Italian poetry: it is an eleven-syllable line in which the accent falls on the tenth syllable. I will have more to say about this later on when I discuss my translation.

The drama of the poem centers on one man's journey to

God, and its main action is the movement of the soul toward its final goal: to become one with the Universal Will. This action, as we know from the closing verses of the *Paradise*, ends successfully:

> but as a wheel in perfect balance turns,
> I felt my will and my desire impelled

> by the Love that moves the sun and the other stars.

The poet tells how God drew him to salvation through the agency of Beatrice; and the moral Dante wishes his reader to keep in mind is that what God has done for one man He can do for Everyman, if Everyman is willing to make this journey. True, it is the journey of one man, Dante, but we need read no further than the opening verse of the *Inferno* to learn that it is *our* journey as well: "Nel mezzo del cammin di nostra vita" ("Midway along the journey of our life"). Immediately his journey becomes our journey. Dante the Pilgrim becomes Everyman, who is his reader.

The Divine Comedy, like the Bible, pronounces God's judgment on man. In fact, Dante invites us to read his poem as he expects us to read the Bible, that is, to believe in the historical truth of the literal level. And this extends to the figural symbolism of the main characters in the allegory of the poem. We are not dealing with consistent or typical allegory, like that in *Pilgrim's Progress* or the *Romance of the Rose*. Dante does not call his characters by symbolic names, such as Reason or Revelation or Sodomy. His is a much more sophisticated symbolic allegory. With the exception of his mythological characters, his sinners and saints and guides are above all flesh-and-blood figures, historical characters who really existed at one time or another. And because a Virgil, a Beatrice, or a Brunetto Latini had a literal existence, we trust them in the poem all the more.

The characters do not always represent single qualities. Virgil is not always human Reason; he can shift roles: there are moments when he is merely a traveling companion of the Pilgrim's (especially in the *Purgatory*), or simply Virgil, the great poet of antiquity. There is even a time when he is unreasonable, during the mysterious medieval drama in front of the gates of Dis (*Inferno* IX). The beautiful Beatrice, too, can have different meanings. For example, at the top of the Mountain of Purgatory in the Earthly Paradise, she is Divine Revelation, but sometimes she embodies Wisdom, or simply the attributes of that lovely lady in the *Vita nuova* whom the poet loved so tearfully on earth.

As I mention in my opening note to *Inferno* I, the reader of the poem would do well to distinguish from the very beginning of *The Divine Comedy* between the two uses of the first person singular: one designates Dante the Pilgrim, the other, Dante the Poet. The first is a character in a story invented by the second. The events in the narrative are represented as having taken place in the past; the writing of the poem and the memories of these events, however, are represented as taking place in the poet's present. For example, we find references to both past and present and to both Pilgrim and Poet in verse 10 of the introductory canto of the *Inferno*: "How I entered there I cannot truly say" ("Io non so ben ridir com'io v'entrai"). There will be times in the poem when the fictional Pilgrim (Dante the Pilgrim) will embody many of the characteristics of his inventor (Dante the Poet), for *The Divine Comedy*, the journey of Everyman to God, is in many ways a personal, autobiographical journey. We must keep in mind that from the opening verse of the poem Dante begins to construct his allegory of the double journey: that is, his own personal experience in the world beyond, and the journey of Everyman, or the reader, through life.

In the *Purgatory*, Dante's Pilgrim seems to identify with many of the penitents on the seven rounds of the Mountain of Purgatory; in the *Inferno*, I believe, the Pilgrim participates in sin (symbolically or otherwise) in every circle of Hell. The poet has his Pilgrim experience each sin by means of what I call imitation of action. Let us turn for a moment to Canto XIX of the *Inferno* and examine it for evidence of the Pilgrim's "participation" in sin.

Very early in the canto, while comparing a special feature

of the infernal topography with the Baptistry of San Giovanni
in Florence, Dante introduces an autobiographical reference:
a few years earlier he had been forced to break a baptismal
font or stall in order to save a child trapped inside:

> I saw along the sides and on the bottom
>   the livid-colored rock all full of holes;
>   all were the same in size, and each was round.
>
> To me they seemed no wider and no deeper
>   than those inside my lovely San Giovanni,
>   in which the priest would stand or baptize from;
>
> and one of these, not many years ago,
>   I smashed for someone who was drowning in it:
>   let this be mankind's picture of the truth!
>
> (13–21)

This allusion to a rescue act is not a pretext for launching a
statement of self-exoneration: it was not Dante's desire to clear
himself that made him construct the topography of the Third
Bolgia of Hell in imitation of a part of the Baptistry of San
Giovanni. Why does Dante in line 20 feel he must mention
and even stress the rather incidental detail of the breaking of
a receptacle in the Baptistry? What he did was to save a human
life, but because the words "I smashed" (*"rupp' io"*) come at
the beginning of the verse, the act of breaking seems to take
precedence over the act of saving—and even over the plight
of the child. When we reach a later passage in the canto we
will make the connection and see the "participation."

The Pilgrim, brought by Virgil to the bottom of the *bolgia*
of the Simonists, addresses the twitching, upraised legs of
Nicolas III in lines 46–48:

> "Whatever you are, holding your upside down,
>   O wretched soul, stuck like a stake in ground,
>   make a sound or something," I said, "if you can."

The pope answers, to the bewilderment of the Pilgrim (52–
57):

. . . "Is that *you*, here, already, upright?
Is that you here already upright, Boniface?
By many years the book has lied to me!

Are you fed up so soon with all that wealth
for which you did not fear to take by guile
the Lovely Lady, then tear her asunder?"

In the bitter rhetorical question that Pope Nicolas intended for Boniface VIII there is an implicit description of simony, offered by one simonist to another, more infamous one. The simony of Boniface, according to this description, would consist of three offenses, greed, guile, and breaking, and the one enjoying the climactic position is *breaking*: ". . . then tear her asunder." Dante, here, takes the bold step of presenting his own act (the breaking of church property) as a technical parallel to the crimes of Boniface (the breaking up of the church). The difference between the two acts of breaking, however, rests in the fact that the simonist's sin of breaking is committed out of lust for treasure and by means of deceit, while Dante's destructive act was performed out of love for his fellow man. This is the Pilgrim's participation in the sin of Simony, and it is made all the more effective by turning the Pilgrim (though only in a brief metaphor) into a priest (like every other sinner in this *bolgia*) in the tercet 49–51, which comes immediately before the two tercets quoted above:

I stood there like a priest who is confessing
some vile assassin who, fixed in his ditch,
has called him back again to put off dying.

It is not always a simple matter to point to an example of the Pilgrim's participation in a particular sin. It is easy enough to see it in *Inferno* III, when the Pilgrim and his guide have just passed through the gate of Hell and are in the vestibule, where the souls of those who would not take a stand in life suffer their hectic torments. Virgil says concerning them in the tercet 49–51:

> "The world will not record their having been there;
> Heaven's mercy and its justice turns from them.
> Let's not discuss them; look and pass them by."

The Pilgrim (and in this case his guide, too) participates in this sin, the sin of non-participation in life, by refusing to have anything to do with the tormented souls—that is, by not participating. But how will the poor Pilgrim participate in a sin such as murder (*Inferno* XII)? I assure you that he does, as he does in Lust, Gluttony, Avarice, Wrath, straight down to the complex fraud represented by the traitors frozen in the ice surrounding the gigantic figure of Lucifer. I will not say here how he does it, nor will I talk about "participation" as such in my notes. I leave the pleasure of these discoveries to the reader.

The reader will soon see that not much is said about particular sins in any circle or *bolgia* of the *Inferno*. Most of the time there is simply a description of the state in which the sinners find themselves, after which the sinner will usually talk about himself (or herself, in the case of Francesca da Rimini, the only woman who speaks in the *Inferno*), or about something that appears to have nothing at all to do with the sin being punished there. What the reader discovers, however, is that the torments suffered by the sinners represent, in one way or another, the sins themselves. The headless figure of Bertran de Born in Canto XXVIII of the *Inferno* is a good example of what is known as a *contrapasso*, or the law of divine retribution, which Saint Thomas Aquinas talks about in his *Summa theologica*. The canto closes with Bertran holding his severed head up by its hair, "swinging it in one hand just like a lantern" (122); the head, talking to the Pilgrim and his guide, says:

> . . . "Now see the monstrous punishment,
> you there still breathing, looking at the dead,
> see if you find suffering to equal mine!
>
> And that you may report on me up there,
> know that I am Bertran de Born, the one
> who evilly encouraged the young king.

> Father and son I set against each other:
> Achitophel with his wicked instigations
> did not do more with Absalom and David.
>
> Because I cut the bonds of those so joined,
> I bear my head cut off from its life-source,
> which is back there, alas, within its trunk.
>
> In me you see the perfect *contrapasso*!"
>   (130–42)

In most cases the punishment of the sin involves a process that either resembles the sin or contrasts with it. In Canto III of the *Inferno*, for example, the *contrapasso* is a retribution for the sin of neutrality, or inactivity: these souls, who when alive on earth followed no leader, took no action in life, now are forever running behind a banner. And since on earth they were untouched and unmoved by any care, now they are stung again and again by hornets and wasps.

The entire action of *The Divine Comedy* takes place in one week's time. It is on the night of April 17, 1300, the Thursday before Good Friday, that Dante the Pilgrim comes to his senses in the *selva oscura*, the dark wood (the worldly life of sin). All of the following day he spends trying to find his way out of the place; he attempts to climb a sunlit mountain and is forced back down by three beasts—a leopard, a lion, and a she-wolf—that block his ascent. Then, all of a sudden, when all seems lost, the shade of a man suddenly appears on the scene, introduced in the mysterious verse 63 of the opening canto as "chi per lungo silenzio parea fioco," which I translate as "one grown faint, perhaps from too much silence." (This, like many other lines in the *Comedy*, has been interpreted in a number of different ways.) The figure is the shade of Virgil, who offers to lead the Pilgrim out of the dark wood by another way. The Pilgrim learns from Virgil that he has been sent to guide him to safety by none other than the blessed Beatrice herself, who left her seat in Heaven to seek Virgil's help in Hell. The only way to escape from the dark wood is to descend into Hell; the only way up that mountain lit by the rays of the sun is to go down. Man must first descend in humility before he can raise himself to God. Before man can hope to climb the mountain of salvation, he must first know what sin is. The purpose of the Pilgrim's journey through Hell is precisely this: to learn all there is to know about sin, as a necessary preparation for the ascent to God. In fact, from the opening canto of the *Inferno* to the closing one of the *Paradise*, Dante the Poet presents his Pilgrim as continuously learning, although his progress is slow and there are even occasional backslidings. His spiritual development is the main theme of the entire poem.

So then, at sunset on the eve of Good Friday, Virgil and his ward enter the Gate of Hell, and all that night and the next day they descend, circling always to the left, until they reach the gigantic figure of Lucifer, fixed in ice at the center of the earth. They climb down his hairy sides and in a matter of minutes they are in the opposite hemisphere, the midpoint of which is Purgatory. Once the travelers pass the center of the earth they gain twelve hours. All of that new Saturday as well as the next night they use in climbing up the long passageway leading to the other side of the earth. This ascent is as long as the descent was from the dark wood, wherever that was, all the way down to Lucifer's navel. But in less than three tercets, the voyage from Lucifer's tomb at the center of the universe back to the surface of the earth on the opposite hemisphere is completed·

> My guide and I entered that hidden road
>   to make our way back up to the bright world.
>   We never thought of resting while we climbed.
>
> We climbed, he first and I behind, until,
>   through a small round opening ahead of us
>   I saw the lovely things the heavens hold,
>
> and we came out to see once more the stars.

This is an elegant ending, indeed, not only because Dante manages to close all three canticles of *The Divine Comedy*— the *Inferno*, the *Purgatory*, and the *Paradise*—with the word *stelle* (stars), but also because he manages with such ease to ascend in so few verses the same distance it took him thousands of verses to descend.

Finally, on Easter Sunday morning, Virgil and the Pilgrim emerge at the foot of the Mountain-Island of Purgatory, and we are invited to remember that other mountain, in Canto I of the *Inferno*, which the Pilgrim at that point in his spiritual development was unable to climb. This mountain tells us what that earlier mountain meant. This is Virgil's first time outside the confines of Hell, and the two strangers on the Mountain of Purgatory spend three days and three nights climbing it. The Pilgrim leaves his guide, his beloved Virgil, at the edge of another wood, this one at the top of a mountain, the Earthly Paradise, where, of course, Virgil has no right to enter. The Pilgrim spends six colorful and, at times, heavily allegorical hours in that happy place before he is taken by his next guide, the Beatrice of the *Vita nuova*, up into Paradise at noon on the Wednesday after Easter. He rises through all ten heavenly spheres, circling the world with Wednesday, until he passes the meridian of Jerusalem and the day changes to Thursday. It is in the Empyrean at sunset on Thursday that he has the Beatific Vision; there the sacred journey and his poem come to an end. The circle h s been completed.

The literal level of Dante's poem unfolds many meanings to the reader which we are not expected to comprehend fully until we are well into the poem. For example, what is the meaning of the three beasts that block the Pilgrim's way up the mountain to salvation in the opening canto of the *Inferno*? Not until Canto XVI is the true meaning of the leopard revealed to us, in the tercet 106–108, where the Pilgrim is commenting on the cord that he wears around his waist and that Virgil has asked him to remove and give to him:

> I wore a cord that fastened round my waist,
>   with which I once had thought I might be able
>   to catch the leopard with the gaudy skin.

The mention of the leopard here, just when the Pilgrim is about to enter the third and final division of Hell, is certainly an indication that, of the three beasts on the mountainside, it is the leopard that we must associate with the sins of Fraud, for such sins are punished here. Other clues to the meanings of the three beasts occur before this, especially in connection with the *lupa*, or she-wolf, but *Inferno* XVI sheds the most light.

There are many other examples that one might cite to demonstrate how the poem reveals its meaning to the careful reader, but none is more significant, I feel, than the theme of the Advents of Christ. The Church Fathers—especially Saint Bernard, whom Dante uses as his Pilgrim's final guide to the Beatific Vision at the end of the *Paradise*—talk much about a Threefold Coming, the *triplex adventus* of Christ. Saint Bernard tells us that in addition to the First Coming of Christ for the salvation of mankind and the Final Coming for the judgment of mankind, there is the Intermediary Advent, when Christ comes into the hearts of individuals, of the elect, in order to protect them from temptation and to insure their salvation. Whereas in the First Advent He came once and in the Third Advent He will come once, the Intermediary Advent takes place habitually, daily (*"quotidie ad salvandas animas singulorum in spiritu venit"*). There is no series of events in the Christian cosmos more important than that represented by the Advents of Christ.

Not until one reaches Canto XXX of the *Purgatory* and observes that Beatrice comes to the Pilgrim at the top of the Mountain of Purgatory in the Earthly Paradise as a Christ figure does one begin, perhaps, to think in terms of a larger pattern, of other "Comings." By means of the imagery, costuming, and staging, the poet prepares the reader in this canto to think in terms of the Final Coming of Christ. Beatrice comes to judge her lover here as Christ will come at the end of the world to judge all mankind. If the Advent of Beatrice, then, is a representation of the Final Coming, the Last Judgment, where are the other Comings?

Other Comings? Other Advents of Christ? Of course, there must be. How could Dante resist the pattern of the *triplex adventus*? Reading backward, as it were, from the end of the *Purgatory* and thinking in terms of Advent, we can remember reading about another singular coming: someone who descends from above early on in the *Inferno* (IX), in that mysterious and very dramatic scene during which Virgil finds himself totally confused and helpless in front of the gates of Dis. This is another unique event, a one-time happening. A "messenger" from above descends to save the Pilgrim (or Everyman), just as, in the First Advent, Christ descended to save mankind.

There can only be one place for the Second Advent, the coming of Christ into the hearts of Christians every day. We see it at precisely the point in the *Purgatory*, Canto VIII, that corresponds to the point at which we witnessed the First Advent in the *Inferno*, Canto IX, for if we keep in mind that the opening canto of the *Inferno* is the introduction to the whole *Commedia*, then it is clear that *Inferno* IX = *Purgatory* VIII. The two angels who descend to take their places, one on either side, to guard the Valley of the Princes, come from the "*grembo di Maria*," from "Mary's bosom." They are two who come as one Christ figure, and they are two only because the valley they come to protect has two sides; and they come *every day*. The reader will see all this for himself, but he will see it clearly and be able to enjoy it fully only when he reaches Canto XXX of the *Purgatory*. While there are a number of patterns to be traced through the poem (and the reader, I hope, will discover one or two for himself), I feel there is none more brilliant than this one of the Advents.

It would be wrong for the reader to stop reading when he comes out to see the stars again at the end of the *Inferno*. It would be, as Dorothy Sayers once put it, like judging "a great city after a few days spent underground among the cellars and sewers." We must climb the hard Mountain of Purgatory to reach the great city of Paradise. The reader will find that Purgatory is a place of repentence, regeneration, conversion. Though the punishments inflicted on the penitents here are often more severe than those in Hell, the atmosphere is totally different: it is one of sweet encounters, culminating with Dante's reunion with Beatrice in the Earthly Paradise and Virgil's elegant disappearance. Brotherly love and humility reign here, necessary qualities for a successful journey of man's mind to God. Everyone here is destined to see God eventually; the predominant image is one of homesickness (especially in the antepurgatory), a yearning to return to man's real home in the heavens. Toward the close of the *Purgatory* the time comes for Beatrice (Divine Revelation) to take charge of the Pilgrim; human reason (Virgil) can take man only so far; it cannot show him God or explain His many mysteries.

In the *Paradise* Dante attempts to describe the religious life, one in which man centers his attentions wholly on God, His divine truths, and ultimate happiness. Only in perfect knowledge of the True Good can man have perfect happiness. Unlike Hell and Purgatory, Heaven in Dante's poem does not exist in a physical sense. The celestial spheres through which he and his guide, Beatrice, ascend and in which the souls of the Blessed appear to the wayfarer are not part of the real Paradise. That place is beyond the spheres and beyond space and time: it is the Empyrean, and Beatrice takes pains to explain this to the Pilgrim early in the *Paradise* (Canto IV, 28–36), while they are in the first sphere of the moon:

> Not the most God-like of the Seraphim,
>   not Moses, Samuel, whichever John
>   you choose—I tell you—not Mary herself
>
> has been assigned to any other heaven
>   than that of these shades you have just seen here,
>   and each one's bliss is equally eternal;
>
> all lend their beauty to the Highest Sphere,
>   sharing one same sweet life to the degree
>   that they can feel the eternal breath of God.

The dominant image in this realm is light. God is light, and the Pilgrim's goal from the very start was to reach the light (again we are reminded of the casual mention of the rays of the sun behind that mountain in the opening canto of the poem).

The formal beauty of *The Divine Comedy* should not be

dissociated from its spiritual message. The universal appeal of the poem comes from a combination of the two: poetry and philosophy. For Dante, ultimate truth was known; in principle, it was contained in the *Summa* of Saint Thomas Aquinas, and the doctrine of *The Divine Comedy* comes largely from the writings of Saint Thomas and the other Church Fathers.

Dante was in accord with Hugh of Saint Victor, who, in his *Didascalia*, says: "Contemplating what God has done, we learn what is for us to do. All nature speaks God. All nature teaches man." Dante, with his special kind of allegory, tries to imitate God: the symbolic world he creates in his poem is, in principle, a real mirror of the actual world created by God himself.

M. M.
August 1983
Bloomington, Indiana

TRANSLATOR'S NOTE:
ON BEING A GOOD LOVER

——————

To WHAT extent should the translator of Dante's *Inferno* strive to be faithful to the original? Ezra Pound distinguishes between what he calls "interpretative translation," which is what most translators are after, and a more creative, original type of paraphrase—the translator using the original mainly as an inspiration for writing his own poem. But even those who attempt an interpretive rendering differ greatly in the degree and manner of their faithfulness to the original. The question has been raised and debated: should it be the poet's voice that is heard, or the voice of the one who is making the poet accessible in another language? This is obviously a delicate, sophisticated, and complicated problem.

Surely much depends on what it is that is being translated. A principle that might apply to a sonnet or perhaps any short poem, especially a lyrical one, would not be appropriate to a lengthy narrative with theological and encyclopedic underpinnings such as *The Divine Comedy*. I should say that anyone who attempts to translate this massive poem must try, with humility and flexibility, to be as faithful as possible. He should do what Jackson Mathews recommends to the guild of translators in general—"be faithful without seeming to be"—and he adds in regard to this type of faithfulness: "a translator should make a good lover."

Perhaps it must always be the voice of Dante's translator that we hear (if we have to hear an intervening voice at all), but he should have listened most carefully to Dante's voice before he lets us hear his own. He should not only read and reread what he is translating, in order to know what it is about (know a whole canto thoroughly before translating a line), but he should also read Dante aloud, listening to the rhythm and movement within the lines and the movement from line to line. Consider, for example, line 63 of the famous Canto V of the *Inferno* (Paolo and Francesca's canto), where Virgil points out to the Pilgrim the figure of Cleopatra among the lustful souls of Dido's band, and characterizes her with one word that caps the line:

> Poi è Cleopatràs lussuriosa
> (And there is Cleopatra, who loved men's lusting)

This epithet, epitomizing the whole career of the imperial wanton, serves to remind us of the technical nature of the sin being punished in the second circle, the circle of the lustful: *i lussuriosi*. And in the movement of the word *lus-su-ri-o-sa* (Dante forces us to linger over the word this way; otherwise the verse would be a syllable short) there is an important anticipation of a movement in the second part of the canto: the dovelike movement that starts with the actual descent of Francesca and Paolo, a gentle movement that becomes the movement of the entire second half of this canto and offers such a contrast to the wild buffetings of the winds we hear in the first half, where we see the damned dashed along by the tempestuous storm. The sensitive translator must stop to question (then to understand) the rhythm of *lussuriosa* at this point in the canto: to sense how this diaphanous word in this melodious line stands out against the howling noises in the background. This seductive rhythm applied to Cleopatra's sin anticipates not only the gentle movements but the seductive atmosphere of the second half of the canto, when Francesca is on stage and melting the Pilgrim's heart. No translator I have read seems to have made any attempt to reproduce the effect intended by the line in the original: the simplicity of the first half of the line (*Poi è Cleopatràs* . . .) and the mellifluous quality of the epithet (*lussuriosa*) in final position, with its tapering-off effect.

Again, the translator should study Dante's use of poetic devices such as enjambment and alliteration. This does not mean that the translator should always use such devices when Dante does and only when he does, but that he should study the effects Dante has achieved with these devices—and his economical use of them. Dante is a greater poet than any of his translators have been or are likely to be. A translator using the English iambic pentameter may even learn from Dante's flowing lines to use better the meter he has chosen. It is true that Dante's hendecasyllabic verse is quantitative and not accentual; still, the words of the Italian language have their own natural accent. In reading aloud Dante's lines with their gentle stress, one can hear the implicit iambs and trochees and dactyls and anapaests. And one may learn to achieve the same effect of "implicitness" to counterbalance the natural tendency of English meters to have too insistent a stress.

Finally, there is the matter of diction. Here the translator must be *absolutely* faithful, choosing words and phrases that have the same tone as those of the poet. They must obviously suggest solemnity when he is solemn, lightness when he is light; they must be colloquial or formal as he is colloquial or formal. But, most of all, the diction should be simple when Dante's is. And this is where the translators have sinned the most. There are two ways to sin against simplicity of diction: one concerns only the matter of word material and syntax— for instance the use of stilted or over-flowery language and of archaic phraseology. Most translators would not agree with me; some feel free to use any word listed in the *O.E.D.* after A.D. 1000: *to girn, to birl, to skirr, scaling the scaur, to abye the fell arraign*—to say nothing of syntactical archaisms.

A more subtle sin against the simplicity of Dante's diction is the creation of original striking rhetorical or imagistic effects where Dante has intended none. Dante himself saves spectacular effects for very special occasions. Most of his narrative, if we make an exception of the elaborate similes, is composed in simple, straightforward style. Occasionally one finds an immediately striking effect in a line or phrase, and when this does happen, it is magnificent. Consider line 4 of Canto V (so different from line 63, quoted earlier, with its muted, inconspicuous effect):

> Stavvi Minòs orribilmente e ringhia
> (There stands Minòs grotesquely and he snarls)

Surely Dante meant to startle his reader with this sudden presentation (after the sober explanation of the opening three lines) of the monster-judge. The line ends with the resounding impact of the verb *ringhia*—it ends with a snarl that sounds like the lash of a whip (or tail). And we are made to feel the horror of Minòs by the key word in the middle of the line, the slow-moving *orribilmente*, which points both backward and ahead: *Stavvi orribilmente, ringhia orribilmente*. Grammatically, of course, the adverb modifies the opening word, the static verb, *Stavvi*. This construction, in which an adverb of manner modifies a verb of presence, is most unusual: Minòs was present horribly!

Usually, however, one comes to realize only at the end of several tercets that a certain effect has been achieved by the passage as a whole, one to which each single line has been quietly contributing. Dante's effects, then, are mainly of a cumulative nature. And often there are no "effects," only simple, factual, narrative details. In fact, sometimes Dante's style (and not unfortunately!) is purely prosaic. An adventurous, imaginative translator is easily tempted to speed up the movement of Dante's tranquil lines, to inject fire and color into a passage of neutral tone. Even if he carries it off successfully, I would tend to question his goal. And when the translator fails, when he falls, great is the fall thereof.

If the translator had to choose in general between a style that strives for striking effects, sometimes succeeding and sometimes failing, and one less colorful but more consistent, the choice could be merely a matter of personal taste. But when it is a question of translating a poet who himself is so economical in his use of conspicuous effects, then, I believe, it is no longer a wide-open choice. I have set as my goal simplicity and quiet, even, sober flow—except when I feel that the moment has come to let myself go, to pull out the stops: to be flamboyant or complicated instead of simple, to be noisy instead of quiet, to be rough instead of smooth—or to be deliberately mellifluous. Except for those rare occasions, I have consistently tried to find a style that does not call attention to itself. And I might add that, in translating, this requires a great deal of effort. To the extent that I have succeeded, those readers who admire the fireworks of some recent translations of the *Inferno* will find my own less exciting—as little exciting as Dante himself often is.

My desire to be faithful to Dante, however, has not led me to adopt his metrical scheme. I do not use *terza rima*, as, for example, Dorothy Sayers does, or even the "dummy" *terza rima* of John Ciardi. My medium is rhymeless iambic pentameter, that is, blank verse. I have chosen this, first, because blank verse has been the preferred form for long narrative poetry from the time of Milton on. It cannot be proved that rhyme necessarily makes verse better: Milton declared rhyme to be a barbaric device, and many modern poets resolutely avoid it. Karl Shapiro, an enthusiast for rhyme, is considering only shorter poems when he speaks of the five main qualities that rhyme gives to verse: the musical, the emphatic, the architectural, the sense of direction one feels in a well-turned stanza, and, finally, the effect of the rests that come between the stanzas. Three of these qualities could apply only to stanzaic poetry, where rhyme is much more necessary in establishing structure than in a poem with the dimensions of *The Divine Comedy*, whose only large subdivision is the canto. Only two of the qualities of rhyme he mentions might apply to Dante's poem: the musical and the emphatic.

But my main reason for avoiding rhyme has been the results achieved by all those who have used rhyme in translating *The Divine Comedy*: they have shown that the price paid was disastrously high. I believe that all those who have offered rhymed translations of Dante could have produced far better poems if they had not used rhyme. There are two reasons for the crippling effects of rhyme in translating a lengthy poem. First of all it is apparently impossible always to find perfect rhymes in English for a long stretch of lines—and if good rhyme gives a musical effect, bad rhyme is cacophonous; it is a reminder (and with some translators we are being constantly reminded) that the search for rhyme has failed. I have found at least six kinds of bad rhyme in translations of Dante: vowels that do not match, consonants that do not match, stresses that do not match, plus combinations of these. Especially when there is a pause at the end of a line or the line ends with a stressed syllable, so that the cacophonous element is put into relief, the result can be most painful. One can be more faithful to Dante (without seeming to be) by avoiding rhyme than by introducing imperfect rhyme into the rendition of his lines, whose rhymes are always acoustically perfect.

Shapiro, speaking of the power of rhyme to draw us into the movement of a poem, says that our expectation is thereby being continually raised and then satisfied; ideally, rhyme helps pull us through, and pull us in deep, as we anticipate the scheme. But, when the translator uses a mixture of perfect and imperfect rhyme—when, that is, we never know whether our expectation will be satisfied—the effect is quite different. In every tercet the reader with a sensitive ear will always be wondering "Will he make it this time?" and may often look ahead to see the result, thus breaking the movement of the poem

But the rhymed translations of the *Inferno* reveal, all of them, a second disadvantage, and a far greater one than the difficulty of matching sounds. Because of the difficulty imposed by the continuous mechanical necessity of finding rhyme, good or bad, the translator is often forced to use a diction that is aesthetically unacceptable, or even contrary to the spirit of the language (and once a translator has agreed to distort the English language for the sake of rhyme, the result could well be an increasing insensitivity to the requirements of natural diction). To be forced to think, with every line, in terms of the sound of the final stressed syllable has resulted, far too often, in lines that sound like a translation. And the first of the Capital Sins in translating is for a translation to sound like one!

For the poet creating original verse in his own language, the search for rhyme also, of course, imposes limitations, but these limitations themselves may be a help in the creative process, and the rhyme, when found, as Shapiro says, may bring an image or idea that will suggest a new line of development. At its best, rhyme leads the poet into discoveries. And since he is in the process of creation, he can afford at any moment to change the course of his poetic fluidity. But for the translator, who is faced from the beginning with an existing structure whose shape has been forever fixed, rhyme constitutes a crippling burden.

But if I feel such horror at the paralyzing potentiality of rhyme when used to translate *The Divine Comedy*, why have I chosen to bind myself to the mechanical device of meter? Five beats in every line—no more and no less. Why not choose free verse? Free verse, I feel, is more appropriate for purely creative composition than for translation; and it is more suitable for verse deeply charged with emotion than for narrative. The irregular rhythms, the modulations, of free verse must be determined by the writer's own moods, which will direct the ebbing and flowing of his verse. For this he needs space; as a translator such a writer would need to get as far away as possible from the original!

Moreover, the requirements of iambic pentameter can be very flexible if one is ready to avail oneself of the alternations possible. One need not limit oneself continually to the sequence: ˘´/˘´/˘´/˘´/˘´/. The last foot, for example, may be given, when desired, an extra unstressed syllable (feminine ending; in Italian this is the norm):

> Whĕn thóse/ŏffén/dĕd soúls/hăd tóld/*thĕir stórў* . . .

For an iamb one may substitute its opposite, a trochee (´˘):

> *Hátefŭl*/tŏ Gód/ănd tó/Hĭs eń/ĕ/miĕs . . .

Or a further extension of itself, the anapaest (˘˘´):

> Iň thĕ wořld/thĭs mán/wăs fílled/wĭth af/rŏgańce . . .

(The reader sensitive to rhythm should be on the alert for such opening anapaests.)

Or the opposite of this, the dactyl (´˘˘):

> Ĭ saíd/tŏ hím,/bówĭng/mў heád/*módeštlў* . . .

And I have often used a substitution that some translators seem to avoid, the amphibrach (˘ ˉ ˘; the final foot is always an amphibrach when there is a feminine ending):

> Ĭ saíd,/"Frăncéscă,/the tór/mĕnt thát/yŏu súffĕr . . ."

(Compare this with Dorothy Sayers's and John Ciardi's translations of the same line, in which the natural rhythm of the name *Francesca* is not echoed in an amphibrach foot: "[*Thy dreadful fate,*] *Frăncés/că, mákes/mĕ wéep,/ĭt só/ĭnspíres* [*pity*]"; "*Ĭ saíd:/'Frăncés/că whát/yŏu súf/fĕr heŕe . . .'* ")

Finally, one may let just one syllable count as a foot when the stress is very heavy:

> Loŕe,/thăt kín/dlĕs quíck/ĭn the gén/tĬe heárt . . .

And there may be gradation in degrees of stress. Iambic pentameter is a beautiful, flexible instrument, but only when the translator is freed from preoccupation with rhyme.

Because I am free of this tyranny I have had time to listen carefully to Dante's voice, and though the result is far from being a miracle of perfect translation, still, I believe I can promise that my reader seldom, if ever, will wince or have his teeth set on edge by an over-ambitious attempt to force the language into the unnatural tensions almost never felt in poetry other than translations.

THE DIVINE COMEDY
VOLUME I
INFERNO

———

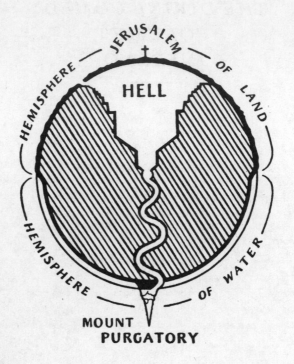

CANTO I

HALFWAY through his life, DANTE THE PILGRIM wakes to find himself lost in a dark wood. Terrified at being alone in so dismal a valley, he wanders until he comes to a hill bathed in sunlight, and his fear begins to leave him. But when he starts to climb the hill his path is blocked by three fierce beasts: first a LEOPARD, then a LION, and finally a SHE-WOLF. They fill him with fear and drive him back down to the sunless wood. At that moment the figure of a man appears before him; it is the shade of VIRGIL, and the Pilgrim begs for help. Virgil tells him that he cannot overcome the beasts which obstruct his path; they must remain until a "GREYHOUND" comes who will drive them back to Hell. Rather by another path will the Pilgrim reach the sunlight, and Virgil promises to guide him on that path through Hell and Purgatory, after which another spirit, more fit than Virgil, will lead him to Paradise. The Pilgrim begs Virgil to lead on, and the Guide starts ahead. The Pilgrim follows.

Midway along the journey of our life
  I woke to find myself in a dark wood,
    for I had wandered off from the straight path.   3

How hard it is to tell what it was like,
  this wood of wilderness, savage and stubborn
    (the thought of it brings back all my old fears),   6

a bitter place! Death could scarce be bitterer.
  But if I would show the good that came of it
    I must talk about things other than the good.   9

How I entered there I cannot truly say,
  I had become so sleepy at the moment
    when I first strayed, leaving the path of truth;   12

but when I found myself at the foot of a hill,
    at the edge of the wood's beginning, down in the valley,
    where I first felt my heart plunged deep in fear,   15

I raised my head and saw the hilltop shawled
    in morning rays of light sent from the planet
    that leads men straight ahead on every road.   18

And then only did terror start subsiding
    in my heart's lake, which rose to heights of fear
    that night I spent in deepest desperation.   21

Just as a swimmer, still with panting breath,
    now safe upon the shore, out of the deep,
    might turn for one last look at the dangerous waters,   24

so I, although my mind was turned to flee,
    turned round to gaze once more upon the pass
    that never let a living soul escape.   27

I rested my tired body there awhile
    and then began to climb the barren slope
    (I dragged my stronger foot and limped along).   30

Beyond the point the slope begins to rise
    sprang up a leopard, trim and very swift!
    It was covered by a pelt of many spots.   33

And, everywhere I looked, the beast was there
    blocking my way, so time and time again
    I was about to turn and go back down.   36

The hour was early in the morning then,
    the sun was climbing up with those same stars
    that had accompanied it on the world's first day,   39

the day Divine Love set their beauty turning;
    so the hour and sweet season of creation
    encouraged me to think I could get past   42

that gaudy beast, wild in its spotted pelt,
    but then good hope gave way and fear returned
    when the figure of a lion loomed up before me,   45

and he was coming straight toward me, it seemed,
with head raised high, and furious with hunger—
the air around him seemed to fear his presence.   48

And now a she-wolf came, that in her leanness
seemed racked with every kind of greediness
(how many people she has brought to grief!).   51

This last beast brought my spirit down so low
with fear that seized me at the sight of her,
I lost all hope of going up the hill.   54

*defeated
(but honestly
sure)*

As a man who, rejoicing in his gains,
suddenly seeing his gain turn into loss,
will grieve as he compares his then and now,   57

so she made me do, that relentless beast;
coming toward me, slowly, step by step,
she forced me back to where the sun is mute.   60

While I was rushing down to that low place,
my eyes made out a figure coming toward me
of one grown faint, perhaps from too much silence.   63

And when I saw him standing in this wasteland,
"Have pity on my soul," I cried to him,
"whichever you are, shade or living man!"   66

"No longer living man, though once I was,"
he said, "and my parents were from Lombardy,
both of them were Mantuans by birth.   69

I was born, though somewhat late, *sub Julio*,
and lived in Rome when good Augustus reigned,
when still the false and lying gods were worshipped.   72

I was a poet and sang of that just man,
son of Anchises, who sailed off from Troy
after the burning of proud Ilium.   75

But why retreat to so much misery?
Why not climb up this blissful mountain here,
the beginning and the source of all man's joy?"   78

"Are you then Virgil, are you then that fount
  from which pours forth so rich a stream of words?"
  I said to him, bowing my head modestly.   81

"O light and honor of the other poets,
  may my long years of study, and that deep love
  that made me search your verses, help me now!   84

You are my teacher, the first of all my authors,
  and you alone the one from whom I took
  the noble style that was to bring me honor.   87

You see the beast that forced me to retreat;
  save me from her, I beg you, famous sage,
  she makes me tremble, the blood throbs in my veins."   90

"But you must journey down another road,"
  he answered, when he saw me lost in tears,
  "if ever you hope to leave this wilderness;   93

this beast, the one you cry about in fear,
  allows no soul to succeed along her path,
  she blocks his way and puts an end to him.   96

She is by nature so perverse and vicious,
  her craving belly is never satisfied,
  still hungering for food the more she eats.   99

She mates with many creatures, and will go on
  mating with more until the greyhound comes
  and tracks her down to make her die in anguish.   102

He will not feed on either land or money:
  his wisdom, love, and virtue shall sustain him;
  he will be born between Feltro and Feltro.   105

He comes to save that fallen Italy
  for which the maid Camilla gave her life
  and Turnus, Nisus, Euryalus died of wounds.   108

And he will hunt for her through every city
  until he drives her back to Hell once more,
  whence Envy first unleashed her on mankind.   111

And so, I think it best you follow me
    for your own good, and I shall be your guide
    and lead you out through an eternal place   114

where you will hear desperate cries, and see
    tormented shades, some old as Hell itself,
    and know what second death is, from their screams.   117

And later you will see those who rejoice
    while they are burning, for they have hope of coming,
    whenever it may be, to join the blessèd—   120

to whom, if you too wish to make the climb,
    a spirit, worthier than I, must take you;
    I shall go back, leaving you in her care,   123

                            who is emperor
because that Emperor dwelling on high
    will not let me lead any to His city,
    since I in life rebelled against His law.   126

Everywhere He reigns, and there He rules;
    there is His city, there is His high throne.
    Oh, happy the one He makes His citizen!"   129

And I to him: "Poet, I beg of you,
    in the name of God, that God you never knew,
    save me from this evil place and worse,   132

lead me there to the place you spoke about
    that I may see the gate Saint Peter guards
    and those whose anguish you have told me of."   135

Then he moved on, and I moved close behind him.

NOTES

1–10

The reader must be careful from the beginning to distinguish
between the two uses of the first person singular in *The Divine
Comedy*: one designating Dante the Pilgrim, the other Dante

the Poet. The first is a character in a story invented by the second. The events are represented as having taken place in the past; the writing of the poem and the memories of these events are represented as taking place in the poet's present. We find references to both past and present, and to both pilgrim and poet, in line 10: "How *I entered* there *I cannot* truly say."

1. *Midway along the journey of our life*: In the Middle Ages life was often thought of as a journey, a pilgrimage, the goal of which was God and Heaven; and in the first line of *The Divine Comedy* Dante establishes the central motif of his poem— it is the story of man's pilgrimage to God. That we are meant to think in terms not just of the Pilgrim but of Everyman is indicated by the phrase "the journey of *our* life" (*our* journey through sin to repentance and redemption).

The imaginary date of the poem's beginning is the night before Good Friday in 1300, the year of the papal jubilee proclaimed by Boniface VIII. Born in 1265, Dante was thirty-five years old, which is one half of man's Biblical life span of seventy years.

8–9. *But if I would show the good*: Even though the memory of this "wood" brings back his "old fears" (6), Dante must talk about "things other than the good," which led to the final "Good" (his salvation) by contributing to the learning process of the Pilgrim.

13–15. *but when I found myself at the foot of a hill*: Once we leave Canto I, which is the introduction to the whole of *The Divine Comedy*, the topography of the various regions of Hell will be described with elaborate carefulness. But in this canto all is vague and unprepared for; the scene is set in a "nowhere land"—the region of undifferentiated sin. Suddenly the Pilgrim awakes in a forest (which is not described except in terms that could apply to Sin itself: "wilderness, savage and stubborn"); suddenly, as he is wandering through it, there is a hill—whereupon the forest becomes a valley. Other suggestions of this dreamlike atmosphere (which, under the circumstances, must be that of a nightmare) will be found throughout this canto.

17-18. *morning rays of light*: The time is the morning of Good Friday.

30. *I dragged my stronger foot and limped along*: A literal translation of this line which has puzzled all Dante critics would be "So that the firm foot (*piè fermo*) was always the lower." Let the two feet represent man's loves: when Gregory the Great comments on Jacob's wrestling with the angel, he identifies one foot as love of God and the other foot as love of the world (*Homiliarium in Ezechielem*, lib. II, hom. 2, 13; *PL* 76, 955-56). The "stronger foot," then, symbolizes the love of this world, for at this point in the Pilgrim's journey, this love is obviously "stronger" than the other; if he were not more strongly attracted to the things of this world than to God there would be little reason for him to make the journey. In order to ascend (to God) the Pilgrim must exert great force to drag upward his "stronger foot" (which is always the lower because its natural tendency is always downward) and prevent himself from slipping back into the "dark wood."

32-60

The early critics thought of the three beasts that block the Pilgrim's path as symbolizing three specific sins: lust, pride, and avarice, but I prefer to see in them the three major divisions of Hell. The spotted leopard (32) represents Fraud (cf. XVI, 106-108) and reigns over the Eighth and Ninth Circles, where the Fraudulent are punished (XVIII-XXXIV). The lion (45) symbolizes all forms of Violence, which are punished in the Seventh Circle (XII-XVII). The she-wolf (49) represents the different types of Concupiscence or Incontinence, which are punished in Circles Two to Five (V-VIII). In any case the beasts must represent the three major categories of human sin, and they threaten Dante the Pilgrim, the poet's symbol of mankind.

32-36. *sprang up a leopard*: Note the sudden appearance of the colorful leopard as if from nowhere. Then the trim, swift spotted beast disappears as such to become a symbol: a force that is everywhere, blocking upward movement.

40. *the day Divine Love set their beauty turning*: It was thought that the constellation of Aries, which is in conjunction with the sun in the spring equinox, was also in conjunction with the sun when God ("Divine Love") created the universe.

46–50. Note the triple use of the verb *seem* (which is a faithful reproduction of the original), intended to blur the figures of the lion and the she-wolf—in harmony with the "nowhereness" of the moral landscape.

55–60. *As a man who . . . the sun is mute*: it must be admitted that this simile is not one of Dante's most felicitous. The Pilgrim, having gained some terrain toward his goal, is forced back by the she-wolf, thus losing all he had gained. But in the parallel imagined by the poet, we have not only the phase of gaining followed by the phase of losing, we are also told of the victim's emotional reaction to his experience—of which there is no trace in the factual narrative.

60. *she forced me back to where the sun is mute*: In other words, back to the "dark wood" of line 2.

62. *my eyes made out a figure coming toward me*: The shade of Virgil miraculously appears before Dante. The Roman poet, born 70 B.C. in the time of Julius Caesar (*sub Julio*), represents in the symbolic allegory of the poem Reason or Human Wisdom (the best that man can achieve on his own without the special grace of God), as well as poetry and art. The Pilgrim cannot proceed to the light of Divine Love (the mountain top) until he has overcome the three beasts of his sin; and because it is impossible for man to cope with the beasts unaided, Virgil has been summoned through the chain of divine command to guide the Pilgrim and help him overcome his sins by understanding and, later, repudiating them.

63. *of one grown faint, perhaps from too much silence*: Virgil is presented for the first time in the poem as "silent": *chi per lungo silenzio parea fioco*, which is to say literally that Virgil appears (to the Pilgrim's eyes) as one who is faint because he has been dead (a shade) for so long and deprived of the light of the sun (he appears in a place "where the sun is mute," 60),

deprived of the light of God. This verse, which I would place in the same category as verse 30 of this same canto ("I dragged my stronger foot and limped along"), has other levels of meaning: it could, for example, imply that the voice of Reason has been silent in the Pilgrim's ear for too long a time.

73–75. *I was a poet and sang of that just man*: In the *Aeneid* Virgil relates the *post bellum* travels and deeds of Aeneas (son of Anchises), who, destined by the gods, founded on Italian soil the nation that, in the course of time, would become the Roman Empire.

87. *the noble style that was to bring me honor*: In the years before the composition of *The Divine Comedy* Dante employed in his sonnets and *canzoni* what he calls the tragic style, reserved for illustrious subject matter: martial exploits, love, and moral virtues (*De vulgari eloquentia* II, ii, iv). His respect for the Roman poet is boundless. The reasons for Dante's selection of Virgil as the Pilgrim's guide (instead of, shall we say, Aristotle, *the* philosopher of the time) are several: Virgil was a poet and an Italian; in the *Aeneid* is recounted the hero's descent into Hell. But the main reason surely lies in the fact that, in the Middle Ages, Virgil was considered a prophet, a judgment stemming from the interpretation of some obscure lines in the *Fourth Eclogue* as foretelling the coming of Christ. In this regard Dante saw Virgil as a sort of mediator between Imperial and Apostolic Rome. Moreover, Dante's treatise *De monarchia* reflects the principal concepts of the Roman Empire found in the pages of his guide.

91. *But you must journey down another road*: Dante must choose another road because, in order to arrive at the Divine Light, it is necessary first to recognize the true nature of sin, renounce it, and do penance for it. Virgil, here in his role of Reason or Human Wisdom, is of course the means through which man may come to an understanding of the nature of sin. With Virgil-Reason as his guide, Dante the Pilgrim will come to an understanding of sin on his journey through Hell and will see the penance imposed on repentant sinners on the Mount of Purgatory.

IOI–II

This obscure forecast of future salvation has never been explained satisfactorily: the figure of the greyhound has been identified with Henry VII, Charles Martel, and even Dante himself. It seems more plausible that the greyhound represents Can Grande della Scala, the ruler of Verona from 1308 to 1329, whose birthplace (Verona) is between Feltro and Montefeltro, and whose "wisdom, love, and virtue" (104) were certainly well known to Dante. Whoever the greyhound may be, the prophecy would seem to indicate in a larger sense the establishment of a spiritual kingdom on earth, a terrestrial paradise in which "wisdom, love, and virtue" (these three qualities are mentioned again in Canto III, 5–6, as attributes of the Trinity) will replace the bestial sins of this world.

107. *the maid Camilla*: She was the valiant daughter of King Metabus, who was slain while fighting against the Trojans (*Aeneid XI*).

108. *and Turnus, Nisus, Euryalus died of wounds*: Turnus was the King of the Rutulians who waged war against the Trojans and was killed by Aeneas in single combat. Nisus and Euryalus were young Trojan warriors slain during a nocturnal raid on the camp of the Rutulians. In subsequent literature their mutual loyalty became a standard measure of sincere friendship.

117. *and know what second death is*: The second death is the death of the soul, which occurs when the soul is damned.

122. *a spirit, worthier than I*: Just as Virgil, the pagan Roman poet, cannot enter the Christian Paradise because he lived before the birth of Christ and lacks knowledge of Christian salvation, so Reason can only guide the Pilgrim to a certain point: in order to enter Paradise, the Pilgrim's guide must be Christian Grace or Revelation (Theology) in the figure of Beatrice.

124. *that Emperor dwelling on high*: Note the pagan terminology of Virgil's reference to God; it expresses, as best it can, his unenlightened conception of the Supreme Authority, that to his mind was, and could only be, an emperor.

133–35. *lead me there to the place you spoke about*: These lines are baffling. Many commentators interpret "the gate Saint Peter guards" as referring not to the gate of Heaven (in the *Paradise* no gate is mentioned) but to the gate of Purgatory, for in Canto IX of the *Purgatory* we are told that its gate is guarded by an angel whose keys have been given him by Peter. Thus the Pilgrim would be saying: "lead me to the two places you have just mentioned so that I may see those in Purgatory and those in Hell."

But it is difficult to believe that "the gate Saint Peter guards" refers to the entrance to Purgatory: neither the Pilgrim nor his guide could have known in Canto I anything about the entrance to Purgatory, nor could they have known about the absence of a gate in Paradise. Surely the Pilgrim's allusion must reflect the popular belief that the gate to Heaven is guarded by Saint Peter. But if line 134 refers to Paradise then it is difficult to make sense of the Pilgrim's words. The reference to Heaven in line 134 could follow quite easily from 133 if we interpret the two lines as meaning: "lead me to the two places you have just mentioned, Hell and Purgatory, so that ultimately I will be able to go to Heaven." But then how is the reference in line 135 to be understood? "Take me to Hell and Purgatory so that I may see (not only Heaven but) Hell" makes no sense.

But perhaps line 133 does not mean "lead me to both places you have just mentioned" but rather "lead me to the place you mentioned last," i.e., Purgatory (the literal translation of the Italian is: "lead me there where you said"). In that case the Pilgrim would be saying "take me to Purgatory so that I may see Heaven—and (since this is unfortunately necessary) Hell too." This would betray some confusion or agitation, but what would be more natural at this stage, when the Pilgrim is just about to begin his journey?

* * * *

It is impossible to understand all of the allegory in the First Canto without having read the entire *Comedy* because Canto

I is, in a sense, a miniature of the whole, and the themes that Dante introduces here will be the major themes of the entire work. Thus, this canto is perhaps the most important of all.

The moral landscape of Canto I is tripartite, reflecting the structure of *The Divine Comedy* itself. The "dark wood" suggests the state of sin in which Dante the Pilgrim finds himself, and therefore is analogous to Hell (the subject matter of the first canticle), through which Dante will soon be traveling. The "barren slope" (29) suggests the middle ground between evil and good, which men must pass through before they reach the "sunlight" of love and blessedness at the mountain's peak. It is analogous therefore to Purgatory, the subject of the second part of the *Comedy*. The "blissful mountain" (77) bathed in the rays of the sun is the state of blessedness, toward which man constantly strives, described in the third canticle, the *Paradise*.

CANTO II

---

*BUT THE PILGRIM begins to waver; he expresses to Virgil his
misgivings about his ability to undertake the journey proposed by
Virgil. His predecessors have been Aeneas and Saint Paul, and he
feels unworthy to take his place in their company. But Virgil rebukes
his cowardice, and relates the chain of events that led him to come to
Dante. The VIRGIN MARY took pity on the Pilgrim in his despair
and instructed SAINT LUCIA to aid him. The Saint turned to BEA-
TRICE because of Dante's great love for her, and Beatrice in turn
went down to Hell, into Limbo, and asked Virgil to guide her friend
until that time when she herself would become his guide. The Pilgrim
takes heart at Virgil's explanation and agrees to follow him.*

The day was fading and the darkening air
   was releasing all the creatures on our earth
   from their daily tasks, and I, one man alone,   3

was making ready to endure the battle
   of the journey, and of the pity it involved,
   which my memory, unerring, shall now retrace.   6

O Muses! O high genius! Help me now!
   O memory that wrote down what I saw,
   here your true excellence shall be revealed!   9

Then I began: "O poet come to guide me,
   tell me if you think my worth sufficient
   before you trust me to this arduous road.   12

You wrote about young Sylvius's father,
   who went beyond, with flesh corruptible,
   with all his senses, to the immortal realm;   15

but if the Adversary of all evil
    was kind to him, considering who he was,
    and the consequence that was to come from him,   18

this cannot seem, to thoughtful men, unfitting,
    for in the highest heaven he was chosen
    father of glorious Rome and of her empire,   21

and both the city and her lands, in truth,
    were established as the place of holiness
    where the successors of great Peter sit.   24

And from this journey you celebrate in verse,
    Aeneas learned those things that were to bring
    victory for him, and for Rome, the Papal seat;   27

then later the Chosen Vessel, Paul, ascended
    to ring back confirmation of that faith
    which is the first step on salvation's road.   30

But why am I to go? Who allows me to?
    I am not Aeneas, I am not Paul,
    neither I nor any man would think me worthy;   33

and so, if I should undertake the journey,
    I fear it might turn out an act of folly—
    you are wise, you see more than my words express."   36

As one who unwills what he willed, will change
    his purpose with some new second thought,
    completely quitting what he first had started,   39

so I did, standing there on that dark slope,
    thinking, ending the beginning of that venture
    I was so quick to take up at the start.   42

"If I have truly understood your words,"
    that shade of magnanimity replied,
    "your soul is burdened with that cowardice   45

which often weighs so heavily on man,
    it turns him from a noble enterprise
    like a frightened beast that shies at its own shadow.   48

To free you from this fear, let me explain
 the reason I came here, the words I heard
 that first time I felt pity for your soul: 51

I was among those dead who are suspended,
 when a lady summoned me. She was so blessed
 and beautiful, I implored her to command me. 54

With eyes of light more bright than any star,
 in low, soft tones she started to address me
 in her own language, with an angel's voice: 57

'O noble soul, courteous Mantuan,
 whose fame the world continues to preserve
 and will preserve as long as world there is, 60

my friend, who is no friend of Fortune's, strays
 on a desert slope; so many obstacles
 have crossed his path, his fright has turned him back 63

I fear he may have gone so far astray,
 from what report has come to me in Heaven,
 that I may have started to his aid too late. 66

Now go, and with your elegance of speech,
 with whatever may be needed for his freedom,
 give him your help, and thereby bring me solace. 69

I am Beatrice, who urges you to go;
 I come from the place I am longing to return to;
 love moved me, as it moves me now to speak. 72

When I return to stand before my Lord,
 often I shall sing your praises to Him.'
 And then she spoke no more. And I began, 75

'O Lady of Grace, through whom alone mankind
 may go beyond all worldy things contained
 within the sphere that makes the smallest round, 78

your plea fills me with happy eagerness—
 to have obeyed already would still seem late!
 You needed only to express your wish. 81

But tell me how you dared to make this journey
 all the way down to this point of spacelessness,
 away from your spacious home that calls you back.' 84

'Because your question searches for deep meaning,
 I shall explain in simple words,' she said,
 'just why I have no fear of coming here. 87

A man must stand in fear of just those things
 that truly have the power to do us harm,
 of nothing else, for nothing else is fearsome. 90

God gave me such a nature through His Grace,
 the torments you must bear cannot affect me,
 nor are the fires of Hell a threat to me. 93

A gracious lady sits in Heaven grieving
 for what happened to the one I send you to,
 and her compassion breaks Heaven's stern decree. 96

She called Lucia and making her request,
 she said, "Your faithful one is now in need
 of you, and to you I now commend his soul." 99

Lucia, the enemy of cruelty,
 hastened to make her way to where I was,
 sitting by the side of ancient Rachel, 102

and said to me: "Beatrice, God's true praise,
 will you not help the one whose love was such
 it made him leave the vulgar crowd for you? 105

Do you not hear the pity of his weeping,
 do you not see what death it is that threatens him
 along that river the sea shall never conquer?" 108

There never was a wordly person living
 more anxious to promote his selfish gains
 than I was at the sound of words like these— 111

to leave my holy seat and come down here
 and place my trust in you, in your noble speech
 that honors you and all those who have heard it!' 114

When she had finished reasoning, she turned
   her shining eyes away, and there were tears
   How eager then I was to come to you!   117

And I have come to you just as she wished,
   and I have freed you from the beast that stood
   blocking the quick way up the mount of bliss.   120

So what is wrong? Why, why do you delay?
   Why are you such a coward in your heart,
   why aren't you bold and free of all your fear,   123

when three such gracious ladies, who are blessed,
   watch out for you up there in Heaven's court,
   and my words, too, bring promise of such good?"   126

As little flowers from the frosty night
   are closed and limp, and when the sun shines down
   on them, they rise to open on their stem,   129

my wilted strength began to bloom within me,
   and such warm courage flowed into my heart
   that I spoke like a man set free of fear.   132

"O she, compassionate, who moved to help me!
   And you, all kindness, in obeying quick
   those words of truth she brought with her for you—   135

you and the words you spoke have moved my heart
   with such desire to continue onward
   that now I have returned to my first purpose.   138

Let us start, for both our wills, joined now, are one.
   You are my guide, you are my lord and teacher."
   These were my words to him and, when he moved,   141

I entered on that deep and rugged road.

NOTES

5. *of the journey, and of the pity*: The theme of the Pilgrim's
pity is a major motif of the *Inferno* and one that is particularly
important for the education of the Pilgrim; this is the first
mention of pity in *The Divine Comedy*.

7–9. *O Muses! O high genius! Help me now!*: Dante links his own poem to the classical epic tradition by invoking the Muses. As Canto I is an introduction to the entire *Comedy*, it is appropriate that Dante give his invocation in Canto II, the beginning of the *Inferno* itself. This passage is balanced at the beginning of the *Purgatory* and the *Paradise* by similar invocations to the Muses.

The phrase "O high genius" may refer to Dante's own poetic skill or to that of Virgil (or both).

10–48

In the first major movement of Canto II, Dante the Pilgrim expresses fear of a journey such as Virgil proposes, for he finds himself wholly unworthy beside the two who have been allowed to visit "eternal regions" before—Aeneas and Saint Paul. The comparison between Dante the Pilgrim and Aeneas and Paul is significant. For Virgil, Aeneas's journey had but one consequence: empire; for Dante, however, it signified both empire and the establishment of the Holy Roman Church, the "City of God" where all popes reside and reign. The fundamental concepts of Church and State, their government, their conflicts and internal problems, were very important to Dante, and form one of the central themes of the *Comedy*. It is also true that the Pilgrim and Aeneas are searching for perfection according to the standard of their respective ages: moral virtue obtainable in a pagan culture, spiritual comprehension in a Christian one. The comparison between Dante the Pilgrim and the Apostle Paul is also significant: by extending the simile (as was done in the case of Aeneas), the reader may consider the Pilgrim, like Saint Paul, a "Chosen Vessel," one who, granted sufficient grace for his journey, will strengthen the faith of mankind through it (by writing *The Divine Comedy*).

13–21. *young Sylvius's father*: Sylvius was the son of Aeneas by Lavinia, his second wife and daughter to Latinus.

In the *Aeneid* Virgil recounts the history of the founding of Rome. After the fall of Troy, Aeneas, the legendary hero of the epic, embarked on his divinely inspired journey, which eventually led him to the shores of Italy, where he was to establish his city and nation. Before arriving at the Lavinian shores, however, he was obliged to descend to the Underworld, when his father, Anchises, revealed the glories of the Rome that was to be.

28–30. *the Chosen Vessel, Paul*: In his Second Epistle to the Corinthians (XII, 2–4) the Apostle Paul alludes to his mystical elevation to the third heaven and to the arcane messages pronounced there. The medieval *Visio Sancti Pauli* relates his journey through the realms of the dead. Paul's vision served to strengthen the Christian faith, that same faith which is basic to the Pilgrim's (and by extension, Everyman's) salvation ("the first step on salvation's road"—which the Pilgrim took when he turned away from the "dark wood" in Canto I).

37–42. *As one who unwills what he willed, will change*: One of Dante's favorite poetic devices is to imitate the "action" stylistically. Here the Pilgrim's confused state of mind (his fear and lack of conviction) is reflected by the involved structure of the lines.

49–142

The second major movement in Canto II includes Virgil's explanation of his coming to the Pilgrim, and the subsequent restoration of the latter's courage. According to Virgil, the Virgin Mary, who traditionally signifies mercy and compassion in Christian thought, took pity on the Pilgrim in his predicament and set in motion the operation of Divine Grace. Saint Lucia, whose name means "light," suggests the Illuminating Grace sent for by the Blessed Virgin; without Divine Grace the Pilgrim would be lost. Beatrice, whose name signifies blessedness or salvation, appears to Virgil in order to reveal to him the will of God, who is the ultimate bestower of Divine Grace. The three heavenly ladies balance the three beasts of Canto I; they represent man's salvation from sin through Grace, as the beasts represent man's sins. The Pilgrim's journey, then, actually starts in Paradise when the Blessed Virgin Mary takes pity on him; thus the action of *The Divine Comedy* is in one sense a circle that begins in Heaven, as related here, and will ultimately end in Heaven with the Pilgrim's vision of God in the closing canto.

52. *I was among those dead who are suspended*: In the *Inferno* Virgil is assigned to Limbo, the dwelling place of those virtuous shades not eligible for Heaven because they either lived before Chirst's birth or remained heathen after the advent of Christianity (see Canto IV, n.34).

61. *my friend, who is no friend of Fortune's, strays*: See n. 76–78.

74. *often I shall sing your praises to Him*: Exactly what good it would do for Beatrice to sing Virgil's praises to God is not too clear, since those shades assigned to Limbo no longer have a chance to escape (see Canto IV, 41–42).

76–78. *O Lady of Grace, through whom alone mankind*: Virgil recognizes Beatrice as one who has meaning for *all mankind*. To his pagan soul, she represents the kind of contemplation that for Aristotle was perfect happiness, and by which alone man can transcend his human state. Her realm is above the lunar sphere ("the sphere that makes the smallest round"), and to that realm of permanence and happiness we may ascend through contemplation. "Within the sphere" of the moon (i.e., on earth) is Fortune's realm, the region of change and corruption. Virgil, then, recognizes Beatrice in his own perspective, according to pagan thought; and she respects his point of view when, speaking to him (61), she refers to the Pilgrim as "my friend, who is no friend of Fortune's."

In Dante's day the Ptolemaic system of astronomy was in use. All astronomical calculations were made on the basis that the Earth was a fixed point at the center of the universe. All of the planets were thought of as being transported around the Earth in a series of transparent concentric globes or "celestial spheres." Earth, then, is enclosed by a series of seven planetary spheres, one within the other: Earth enclosed by the sphere of the Moon, by that of Mercury, by that of Venus, then by those of the Sun, Mars, Jupiter, and Saturn. Beyond this and enclosing all of it is the sphere of the Fixed Stars, which in turn is enclosed by the Primum Mobile, or First Mover, which imparts movements to all it contains. Beyond the nine spheres is the Empyrean, or Tenth Heaven: it is God's true home and has no movement or duration and is endless in size and eternal in time.

94. *A gracious lady sits in Heaven grieving*: The Virgin Mary.

102. *sitting by the side of ancient Rachel*: In the Dantean Paradise Rachel is seated by Beatrice: she represents the contemplative life.

108. *along that river the sea shall never conquer*: The river has the same kind of reality as the wood and the road of Canto I—all three belong to a stage of *our* life and have their existence in time rather than space (hence, the river will never be conquered by the sea). This river flows through the heart of Everyman (cf. Canto I, 20) and may be thought of as the *concupiscentiae fluctus* of Saint Augustine: the waters of cupidity for this world that flow in the heart of man.

119–26. *and I have freed you from the beast that stood*: The Pilgrim's initial failure to climb the mountain (due to the presence of the she-wolf, I, 49–60) and his subsequent state of desperation are recalled in these lines. Freed now, however, from this peril by Virgil, and assured of success by the "three gracious ladies," he should no longer be hindered from his journey by fear or any hesitation. Virgil must make the Pilgrim move; and he accomplishes this through the purely rational arguments established by the events of the first two cantos and recapitulated in this passage.

UPPER HELL

INCONTINENCE –
THE SINS OF THE WOLF

CANTO III

As THE TWO POETS *enter the vestibule that leads to Hell itself,*
Dante sees the inscription above the gate, and he hears the screams
of anguish from the damned souls. Rejected by God and not accepted
by the powers of Hell, the first group of souls are "nowhere," because
of their cowardly refusal to make a choice in life. Their punishment
is to follow a banner at a furious pace forever, and to be tormented
by flies and hornets. The Pilgrim recognizes several of these shades
but mentions none by name. Next they come to the River Acheron,
where they are greeted by the infernal boatman, CHARON. Among
those doomed souls who are to be ferried across the river, Charon sees
the living man and challenges him, but Virgil lets it be known that
his companion must pass. Then across the landscape rushes a howling
wind, which blasts the Pilgrim out of his senses, and he falls to the
ground.

I AM THE WAY INTO THE DOLEFUL CITY,
   I AM THE WAY INTO ETERNAL GRIEF,
   I AM THE WAY TO A FORSAKEN RACE.   3

JUSTICE IT WAS THAT MOVED MY GREAT CREATOR;
   DIVINE OMNIPOTENCE CREATED ME,
   AND HIGHEST WISDOM JOINED WITH PRIMAL LOVE.   6

BEFORE ME NOTHING BUT ETERNAL THINGS
   WERE MADE, AND I SHALL LAST ETERNALLY.
   ABANDON EVERY HOPE, ALL YOU WHO ENTER.   9

I saw these words spelled out in somber colors
   inscribed along the ledge above a gate;
   "Master," I said, "these words I see are cruel."   12

He answered me, speaking with experience:
"Now here you must leave all distrust behind;
let all your cowardice die on this spot.   15

We are at the place where earlier I said
you could expect to see the suffering race
of souls who lost the good of intellect."   18

Placing his hand on mine, smiling at me
in such a way that I was reassured,
he led me in, into those mysteries.   21

Here sighs and cries and shrieks of lamentation
echoed throughout the starless air of Hell;
at first these sounds resounding made me weep: 24

tongues confused, a language strained in anguish
with cadences of anger, shrill outcries
and raucous groans that joined with sounds of hands,   27

raising a whirling storm that turns itself
forever through that air of endless black,
like grains of sand swirling when a whirlwind blows.   30

And I, in the midst of all this circling horror,
began, "Teacher, what are these sounds I hear?
What souls are these so overwhelmed by grief?"   33

And he to me: "This wretched state of being
is the fate of those sad souls who lived a life
but lived it with no blame and with no praise.   36

They are mixed with that repulsive choir of angels
neither faithful nor unfaithful to their God,
who undecided stood but for themselves.   39

Heaven, to keep its beauty, cast them out,
but even Hell itself would not receive them,
for fear the damned might glory over them."   42

And I. "Master, what torments do they suffer
that force them to lament so bitterly?"
He answered: "I will tell you in few words: 45

these wretches have no hope of truly dying,
  and this blind life they lead is so abject
  it makes them envy every other fate.   48

The world will not record their having been there;
  Heaven's mercy and its justice turn from them.
  Let's not discuss them; look and pass them by."   51

— punishment

And so I looked and saw a kind of banner
  rushing ahead, whirling with aimless speed
  as though it would not ever take a stand;   54

behind it an interminable train
  of souls pressed on, so many that I wondered
  how death could have undone so great a number.   57

When I had recognized a few of them,
  I saw the shade of the one who must have been
  the coward who had made the great refusal.   60

At once I understood, and I was sure
  this was that sect of evil souls who were
  hateful to God and to His enemies.   63

These wretches, who had never truly lived,
  went naked, and were stung and stung again
  by the hornets and the wasps that circled them   66

What does it mean to "truly live"

and made their faces run with blood in streaks;
  their blood, mixed with their tears, dripped to their feet,
  and disgusting maggots collected in the pus.   69

And when I looked beyond this crowd I saw
  a throng upon the shore of a wide river,
  which made me ask, "Master, I would like to know: 72

who are these people, and what law is this
  that makes those souls so eager for the crossing—
  as I can see, even in this dim light?"   75

And he: "All this will be made plain to you
  as soon as we shall come to stop awhile
  upon the sorrowful shore of Acheron."   78

And I, with eyes cast down in shame, for fear
   that I perhaps had spoken out of turn,
   said nothing more until we reached the river.   81

And suddenly, coming toward us in a boat,
   a man of years whose ancient hair was white
   shouted at us, "Woe to you, perverted souls!   84

Give up all hope of ever seeing Heaven:
   I come to lead you to the other shore,
   into eternal darkness, ice, and fire.   87

And you, the living soul, you over there,
   get away from all these people who are dead."
   But when he saw I did not move aside,   90

he said, "Another way, by other ports,
   not here, shall you pass to reach the other shore;
   a lighter skiff than this must carry you."   93

And my guide, "Charon, this is no time for anger!
   It is so willed, there where the power is
   for what is willed; that's all you need to know."   96

These words brought silence to the woolly cheeks
   of the ancient steersman of the livid marsh,
   whose eyes were set in glowing wheels of fire.   99

But all those souls there, naked, in despair,
   changed color and their teeth began to chatter
   at the sound of his announcement of their doom.   102

They were cursing God, cursing their own parents,
   the human race, the time, the place, the seed
   of their beginning, and their day of birth.   105

Then all together, weeping bitterly,
   they packed themselves along the wicked shore
   that waits for every man who fears not God.   108

The devil, Charon, with eyes of glowing coals,
   summons them all together with a signal,
   and with an oar he strikes the laggard sinner.   111

As in autumn when the leaves begin to fall,
   one after the other (until the branch
   is witness to the spoils spread on the ground),   114

so did the evil seed of Adam's Fall
   drop from that shore to the boat, one at a time,
   at the signal, like the falcon to its lure.   117

Away they go across the darkened waters,
   and before they reach the other side to land,
   a new throng starts collecting on this side.   120

"My son," the gentle master said to me,
   "all those who perish in the wrath of God
   assemble here from all parts of the earth;   123

they want to cross the river, they are eager;
   it is Divine Justice that spurs them on,
   turning the fear they have into desire.   126

A good soul never comes to make this crossing,
   so, if Charon grumbles at the sight of you,
   you see now what his words are really saying."   129

He finished speaking, and the grim terrain
   shook violently; and the fright it gave me
   even now in recollection makes me sweat.   132

Out of the tear-drenched land a wind arose
   which blasted forth into a reddish light,
   knocking my senses out of me completely,   135

and I fell as one falls tired into sleep.

NOTES

5–6. DIVINE OMNIPOTENCE . . . HIGHEST WISDOM . . . PRI-
MAL LOVE: These three attributes represent, respectively, the
triune God: the Father, the Son, the Holy Spirit. Thus, the
gate of Hell was created by the Trinity moved by Justice.

  18. *of souls who lost the good of intellect*: That is, those souls

who have lost sight of the *Summum Bonum*, the "Supreme Good," or God.

22–30. *Here sighs and cries and shrieks of lamentation*: Entering the Vestibule of Hell, the Pilgrim is immediately stunned by the screams of the shades in the Vestibule, borne to him in the form of an awesome tempest. In this first encounter with eternal punishment, he receives, as it were, an acoustical impression of Hell in its entirety. Bearing this in mind, the reader should note, as he follows the Pilgrim's passage through Hell, the recurrence of the descriptive elements contained here.

35–42. *who lived a life . . . with no blame and with no praise*: The first tormented souls whom the Pilgrim meets are not in Hell itself but in the Vestibule leading to it. In a sense they are the most loathsome sinners of all because in life they performed neither meritorious nor reprehensible acts. Among them are the angels who refused to take sides when Lucifer revolted. Appropriately, these souls are all nameless, for their lack of any kind of action has left then unworthy of mention. Heaven had damned them but Hell will not accept them.

52–69. *I looked and saw a kind of banner*: In the *Inferno* divine retribution assumes the form of the *contrapasso*, i.e., the just punishment of sin, effected by a process either resembling or contrasting with the sin itself. In this canto the *contrapasso* opposes the sin of neutrality, or inactivity: the souls who in their early lives had no banner, no leader to follow, now run forever after one.

Moreover, these shades, who were on earth untouched and unmoved by any care, are here "stung and stung again by the hornets and the wasps."

60. *the coward who had made the great refusal*: The difficulty of identifying this figure has plagued critics and commentators for over seven hundred years. Among the candidates suggested are the Emperor Diocletian, who in his old age abdicated the throne; Esau, who relinquished his rights of primogeniture to Jacob; Vieri dei Cerchi (incompetent head of the Florentine Whites); Giano della Bella; Frederick II of Sicily; etc. But most critics say that it is Celestine V, who renounced the papacy in 1294, five months after having been elected. However,

Celestine, considering himself inadequate to the task, resigned his office out of humility, not out of cowardice. And the fact that the ex-pope was canonized in 1313 indicates that his refusal might well have been interpreted as a pious act.

Perhaps it is most likely that this shade is Pontius Pilate, who refused to pass sentence on Christ. His role, then, would be parallel to that of the "neutral angels": as they stood by while Lucifer rebelled against God, so Pilate's neutral attitude at the trial of Christ resulted in the crucifixion of Christ. Again, it is significant that Pilate (if the identification proposed is correct) would be the first individual pointed out to us after the Pilgrim enters the Gate of Hell. The *Inferno* concludes with the climactic figure of the rebellious Lucifer; thus, a parallel would be suggested between the arch-traitor to God in Heaven and the cowardly Pilate whose irresolution amounted to a betrayal of Christ on earth.

78. *upon the sorrowful shore of Acheron*: Acheron is one of the rivers of Hell whose origin is explained in Canto XIV, 112–20; it serves as the outer boundary of Hell proper.

83. *a man of years*: This is Charon, the boatman of classical mythology who transports the souls of the dead across the Acheron into Hades.

91–93. *Another way, by other ports*: Charon, whose boat bears only the souls of the damned, recognizes the Pilgrim as a living man and refuses him passage. This tercet contains a prophecy of Dante's salvation: "by other ports" he will pass to "reach the other shore" (of the Tiber), and go to Purgatory and eventually to Paradise.

100. *But all those souls there, naked, in despair*: Though we must assume that all the damned in the *Inferno* are naked (except the Hypocrites: Canto XXIII), only occasionally is this fact pointed out.

112–17. *As in autumn when the leaves begin to fall*: Dante's great debt to Virgil's *Aeneid* includes figures of speech such as this simile (cf. *Aeneid* VI, 309–10). Dante, of course, always adapts the imagery to his own use and frequently makes it more vivid.

124–26. *they want to cross the river, they are eager*: It is perhaps a part of the punishment that the souls of all the damned are eager for their punishment to begin; those who were so willing to sin on earth are in Hell damned with a willingness to go to their just retribution.

132. *even now in recollection makes me sweat*: The reality of the Pilgrim's journey is enhanced through the immediacy of the remembrance and the effect it produces on Dante the Poet. There will be many such authorial comments in the course of *The Divine Comedy*.

136 *and I fell as one falls tired into sleep*: The swoon (or sleep) as a transitional device is used again at the end of Canto V. Note also the opening lines of Canto I, where the Pilgrim's awaking from sleep serves an introductory purpose.

CANTO IV

WAKING FROM HIS SWOON, the Pilgrim is led by Virgil to the First Circle of Hell, known as Limbo, where the sad shades of the virtuous non-Christians dwell. The souls here, including Virgil, suffer no physical torment, but they must live, in desire, without hope of seeing God. Virgil tells about Christ's descent into Hell and His salvation of several Old Testament figures. The poets see a light glowing in the darkness, and as they proceed toward it, they are met by the four greatest (other than Virgil) pagan poets: HOMER, HORACE, OVID, and LUCAN, who take the Pilgrim into their group. As they come closer to the light, the Pilgrim perceives a splendid castle, where the greatest non-Christian thinkers dwell together with other famous historical figures. Once within the castle, the Pilgrim sees, among others, ELECTRA, AENEAS, CAESAR, SALADIN, ARISTOTLE, PLATO, ORPHEUS, CICERO, AVICENNA, and AVERROËS. But soon they must leave; and the poets move from the radiance of the castle toward the fearful encompassing darkness.

A heavy clap of thunder! I awoke
   from the deep sleep that drugged my mind—startled,
   the way one is when shaken out of sleep.   3

I turned my rested eyes from side to side,
   already on my feet and, staring hard,
   I tried my best to find out where I was,   6

and this is what I saw: I found myself
   upon the brink of grief's abysmal valley
   that collects the thunderings of endless cries.   9

So dark and deep and nebulous it was,
   try as I might to force my sight below,
   I could not see the shape of anything.   12

"Let us descend into the sightless world,"
   began the poet (his face was deathly pale):
   "I will go first, and you will follow me."   15

And I, aware of his changed color, said:
   "But how can I go on if you are frightened?
   You are my constant strength when I lose heart."   18

And he to me: "The anguish of the souls
   that are down here paints my face with pity—
   which you have wrongly taken to be fear.   21

Let us go, the long road urges us."
   He entered then, leading the way for me
   down to the first circle of the abyss.   24

Down there, to judge only by what I heard,
   there were no wails but just the sounds of sighs
   rising and trembling through the timeless air,   27

the sounds of sighs of untormented grief
   burdening these groups, diverse and teeming,
   made up of men and women and of infants.   30

Then the good master said, "You do not ask
   what sort of souls are these you see around you.
   Now you should know before we go on farther,   33

they have not sinned. But their great worth alone
   was not enough, for they did not know Baptism,
   which is the gateway to the faith you follow,   36

and if they came before the birth of Christ,
   they did not worship God the way one should;
   I myself am a member of this group.   39

For this defect, and for no other guilt,
   we here are lost. In this alone we suffer:
   cut off from hope, we live on in desire."   42

The words I heard weighed heavy on my heart;
   to think that souls as virtuous as these
   were suspended in that limbo, and forever!   45

"Tell me, my teacher, tell me, O my master,"
　　I began (wishing to have confirmed by him
　　the teachings of unerring Christian doctrine),   48

"did any ever leave here, through his merit
　　or with another's help, and go to bliss?"
　　And he, who understood my hidden question,   51

answered: "I was a novice in this place
　　when I saw a mighty lord descend to us
　　who wore the sign of victory as his crown.   54

He took from us the shade of our first parent,
　　of Abel, his good son, of Noah, too,
　　and of obedient Moses, who made the laws;   57

Abram, the Patriarch, David the King,
　　Israel with his father and his children,
　　with Rachel, whom he worked so hard to win;   60

and many more he chose for blessedness;
　　and you should know, before these souls were taken,
　　no human soul had ever reached salvation."   63

We did not stop our journey while he spoke,
　　but continued on our way along the woods—
　　I say the woods, for souls were thick as trees.   66

We had not gone too far from where I woke
　　when I made out a fire up ahead,
　　a hemisphere of light that lit the dark.   69

We were still at some distance from that place,
　　but close enough for me vaguely to see
　　that honorable souls possessed that spot.   72

"O glory of the sciences and arts,
　　who are these souls enjoying special honor,
　　dwelling apart from all the others here?"   75

And he to me: "The honored name they bear
　　that still resounds above in your own world
　　wins Heaven's favor for them in this place."   78

And as he spoke I heard a voice announce:
"Now let us honor our illustrious poet,
his shade that left is now returned to us." 81

And when the voice was silent and all was quiet
I saw four mighty shades approaching us,
their faces showing neither joy nor sorrow. 84

Then my good master started to explain:
"Observe the one who comes witn sword in hand,
leading the three as if he were their master. 87

It is the shade of Homer, sovereign poet,
and coming second, Horace, the satirist;
Ovid is the third, and last comes Lucan. 90

Since they all share one name with me, the name
you heard resounding in that single voice,
they honor me and do well doing so." 93

So I saw gathered there the noble school
of the master singer of sublimest verse,
who soars above all others like the eagle. 96

And after they had talked awhile together,
they turned and with a gesture welcomed me,
and at that sign I saw my master smile. 99

Greater honor still they deigned to grant me:
they welcomed me as one of their own group,
so that I numbered sixth among such minds. 102

We walked together toward the shining light,
discussing things that here are best kept silent,
as there they were most fitting for discussion. 105

We reached the boundaries of a splendid castle
that seven times was circled by high walls
defended by a sweetly flowing stream. 108

We walked right over it as on hard ground;
through seven gates I passed with those wise spirits,
and then we reached a meadow fresh in bloom. 111

There people were whose eyes were calm and grave,
  whose bearing told of great authority;
  seldom they spoke and always quietly.   114

Then moving to one side we reached a place
  spread out and luminous, higher than before,
  allowing us to view all who were there.   117

And right before us on the lustrous green
  the mighty shades were pointed out to me
  (my heart felt glory when I looked at them).   120

There was Electra standing with a group,
  among whom I saw Hector and Aeneas,
  and Caesar, falcon-eyed and fully armed.   123

I saw Camilla and Penthesilea;
  across the way I saw the Latian King,
  with Lavinia, his daughter, by his side.   126

I saw the Brutus who drove out the Tarquin;
  Lucretia, Julia, Marcia, and Cornelia;
  off, by himself, I noticed Saladin,   129

and when I raised my eyes a little higher
  I saw the master sage of those who know,
  sitting with his philosophic family.   132

All gaze at him, all pay their homage to him;
  and there I saw both Socrates and Plato,
  each closer to his side than any other;   135

Democritus, who said the world was chance,
  Diogenes, Thales, Anaxagoras,
  Empedocles, Zeno, and Heraclitus;   138

I saw the one who classified our herbs:
  Dioscorides I mean. And I saw Orpheus,
  Tully, Linus, Seneca the moralist,   141

Euclid the geometer, and Ptolemy,
  Hippocrates, Galen, Avicenna,
  and Averroës, who made the Commentary.   144

I cannot tell about them all in full;
   my theme is long and urges me ahead,
   often I must omit things I have seen.   147

The company of six becomes just two;
   my wise guide leads me by another way
   out of the quiet into tempestuous air.   150

I come into a place where no light is.

NOTES

7. *and this is what I saw*: The passage across the Acheron, effected between cantos, remains a mystery to the Pilgrim. Unable to explain it, he can only describe the place where he now finds himself, beginning, "and this is what I saw . . ."

20. *paints my face with pity*: Virgil's expression of pity indicates that he is thinking only of the souls in Limbo (where he himself dwells), for Reason cannot feel pity for the just punishment of sin; later he will rebuke Dante for taking pity on the sinners. Those virtuous shades in Limbo, of course, are not sinners, and the absence there of the light of God is pitiable.

34. *they have not sinned*: According to Christian doctrine no one outside the Church (i.e., without baptism, the first Sacrament and thus the "gateway to the faith") can be saved. The souls suspended in Limbo, the first circle of Hell, were on earth virtuous individuals who had no knowledge of Christ and His teachings (through no fault of their own since they preceded Him) or who, after His coming, died unbaptized. Here physical torment is absent; these shades suffer only mental anguish for, now cognizant of the Christian God, they have to "live on in desire" without any hope of beholding Him.

49–50. *did any ever leave here . . . ?*: The Pilgrim, remembering the Church's teaching concerning Christ's Harrowing of Hell, attempts to verify it by questioning Virgil, who should have been there at the time. Note the cautious presentation of the question (especially in the phrase "with another's help"), by means of which the Pilgrim, more than reassuring himself about Church doctrine, is subtly testing his guide. Virgil responds to the Pilgrim's "hidden question" in the terms of his classical culture. Unable to understand Christ in Christian terms, Virgil can only refer to Him as a "mighty lord . . . who wore the sign of victory as his crown."

66. *I say the woods, for souls were thick as trees*: This wood of souls is, of course, different from the "dark wood" of Canto I (2). Nevertheless, this "woods," as well as several yet to come, should remind us of the original "dark wood" and its symbolic suggestion of loss of salvation.

69. *a hemisphere of light that lit the dark*: The "hemisphere of light" emanates from a "splendid castle" (106), the dwelling place of the virtuous men of wisdom in Limbo. The light is the illumination of human intellect, which those who dwell there had in such high measure on earth.

86–88. *Observe the one who comes with sword in hand*: Dante's inability to read Greek denied him access to Homer's works, with which he was acquainted only incidentally through Latin commentaries and redactions. Because his name was inseparably linked with the Trojan War, Homer is portrayed by Dante as a sword-bearing poet, one who sang of arms and martial heroes.

89. *Horace, the satirist*: In this limited reference to Horace, Dante probably was thinking of the Roman poet's *Epistles* as well as of his *Satires*. It is possible that his *Odes* were unknown to Dante. Or he may have wished to stress Horace's role as a moralist.

90. *Ovid is the third, and last comes Lucan*: Ovid's major work, the *Metamorphoses*, was widely read and consulted as the principal source and authority for classical mythology during the Middle Ages. Lucan provided Dante with mythological material, and with much historical information on the civil war between Pompey and Caesar (*Pharsalia*).

91–93. *Since they all share one name with me*: This "one name" is that of "poet." The phrase "they honor me and do well doing so" is actually an expression of modesty, meaning that in "honoring me" they honor the art of poetry, which they all have in common.

95–96. *the master singer of sublimest verse*: This may be Homer, since Dante referred to him in line 87 as "leading the three as if he were their master" and in line 88 as "sovereign poet." But the words "master singer of sublimest verse" also make us think of Virgil, whom Dante referred to in Canto I as "light and honor of the other poets" (82); note also the comparison to an eagle (96), which could suggest the Roman Empire.

100–102. *Greater honor still they deigned to grant me*: In this passage Dante, equating himself with the famous poets of antiquity, acknowledges his art and talent. By this it should not be assumed that he is merely indulging in self-praise; rather, the reader should also interpret these lines as an indication of Dante's awareness of his role as a poet, of his purpose in writing, and of his unique position in the literary scene of his day.

104–105. *discussing things that here are best kept silent*: This phrase is a *topos* that Dante will frequently utilize in *The Divine Comedy*.

106–11. *We reached the boundaries of a splendid castle*: The allegorical construction of the castle is open to question. It may represent natural philosophy unilluminated by divine wisdom, in which case the seven walls serving to protect the castle would be the seven moral and speculative virtues (prudence, justice, fortitude, temperance, intellect, science, and knowledge); and the seven gates that provide access to the castle would be the seven liberal arts that formed the medieval school curriculum (music, arithmetic, geometry, astronomy—the *quadrivium*; and grammar, logic, and rhetoric—the *trivium*). The symbolic value of the stream also remains uncertain; it could signify eloquence, a "stream" that the eloquent Virgil and Dante should have no trouble crossing—and indeed, they "walked right over it as on hard ground" (109).

112–44

The inhabitants of the great castle are important pagan philosophers and poets, as well as famous warriors. Three of the shades named (Saladin, Avicenna, Averroës) lived only one or two hundred years before Dante. Modern readers might wonder at the inclusion of medieval non-Christians among the virtuous pagans of antiquity, but the three just mentioned were among the non-Christians whom the Middle Ages, particularly, respected.

121. *There was Electra standing with a group*: Electra, daughter of Atlas, was the mother of Dardanus, the founder of Troy. Thus, her followers include all members of the Trojan race. She should not be confused with Electra, daughter of Agamemnon, the character in plays by Aeschylus, Sophocles, and Euripides.

122. *among whom I saw Hector and Aeneas*: Among Electra's descendants are: Hector, the eldest son of Priam, king of Troy, who after many battles was slain by Achilles; and Aeneas (cf. I, 73–75, and II, 13–24). The transition from Trojan to Roman hero is effected through the figure of Aeneas.

123. *and Caesar, falcon-eyed and fully armed*: Julius Caesar proclaimed himself the first emperor of Rome after defeating numerous opponents in civil conflicts. Dante's source for the unusual description of Caesar ("falcon-eyed") is Suetonius; at the time "falcon-eyed" was occasionally used to describe a person with luminous or fiery eyes.

124–26. *I saw Camilla*: for Camilla, see I, n. 107. Penthesilea was the glamorous queen of the Amazons who aided the Trojans against the Greeks and was slain by Achilles during the conflict. King Latinus commanded the central region of the Italian peninsula, the site where Aeneas founded Rome. He gave Lavinia to the Trojan conqueror in marriage.

127–29. *I saw the Brutus*: Outraged by the murder of his brother and the rape (and subsequent suicide) of his sister (Lucretia), Lucius Brutus incited the Roman populace to expel the Tarquins, the perpetrators of the offenses. This accomplished, he was elected first consul and consequently became the founder of the Roman Republic. The four women were famous Roman wives and mothers: Lucretia, wife of Collatinus; Julia, daughter of Julius Caesar and wife of Pompey; Marcia, second wife of Cato of Utica (in the *Convivio* Dante makes her the symbol of the noble soul); Cornelia, daughter of Scipio Africanus Major and mother of the Gracchi, the tribunes Tiberius and Caius. A distinguished soldier, Saladin became sultan of Egypt in 1174. He launched many military campaigns and succeeded in expanding his empire. Although he won scattered victories over the crusaders, he was soundly defeated by Richard the Lion-Hearted. A year after the truce he died (1193). Medieval opinion of Saladin was favorable; he was lauded for his generosity and his magnanimity. By including him among the virtuous souls in Limbo (although he is spatially isolated from the Trojan and Roman luminaries), Dante reflects this judgment of his age.

131. *I saw the master sage of those who know*: Aristotle was regarded as the "master sage" in the later Middle Ages. His widely known treatises were adapted to a Christian context by Saint Thomas Aquinas. To Dante, Aristotle represented the summit of human reason, that point that man could reach on his own without the benefit of Christian revelation. With the exception of the Bible, Dante draws most often from Aristotle.

134. *and there I saw both Socrates and Plato*: Acquainted with these Greek philosophers primarily through the works of Cicero, Dante considered them the initiators of the moral philosophy later perfected by Aristotle.

136. *Democritus, who said the world was chance*: A Greek philosopher (c. 460–c. 361 B.C.), born in Thrace, who formulated the theory that the universe was created from the random grouping of atoms.

137. *Diogenes, Thales, Anaxagoras*: Diogenes was the Cynic philosopher who believed that the only good lies in virtue secured through self-control and abstinence. Anaxagoras was a Greek philosopher of the Ionian school (500–428 B.C.). Among his famous students were Pericles and Euripides. He introduced the theory that a spiritual presence gives life and form to material things. Thales (c. 635–c. 545 B.C.), an early Greek philosopher born at Miletus, founded the Ionian school of philosophy, and in his main doctrine maintained that water is the elemental principle of all things.

138. *Empedocles, Zeno, and Heraclitus*: Empedocles (fifth century B.C.), born at Agrigentum in Sicily, maintained that the four primal elements (fire, air, earth, water) joined together

under the influence of Love to form the Universe, whose union
is then periodically destroyed by Hate, only to be formed
anew. His works in verse later served as the model for Lucre-
tius's *On the Nature of Things*. Heraclitus (fl. 500 B.C.) was
born at Ephesus; his ideas are couched in very obscure lan-
guage. According to him, knowledge is based on sense per-
ception, and man has the possibility of progressing toward the
perfect knowledge possessed by the gods. Zeno, native of
Citium in Cyprus (c. 336–c. 264 B.C.), founded the Stoic
school of philosophy. It is, however, entirely possible that
Dante was referring to Zeno of Elea (c. 490–c. 430 B.C.), one
of Parmenides' disciples.

141. *Dioscorides I mean. And I saw Orpheus*: Dioscorides was
a Greek natural scientist and physician of the first century after
Christ. His major work is *De Materia Medica*, in which he
discourses on the medicinal properties of plants. Orpheus was
a mythical Greek poet and musician whose lyrical talent was
such that it moved rocks and trees and tamed wild beasts. It
is said that he descended into the Underworld, charmed
Persephone with his song, and almost succeeded in bringing
his wife, Eurydice, back to the world of the living.

141. *Tully, Linus, Seneca the moralist*: Tully is Marcus Tullius
Cicero, celebrated Roman orator, writer, and philosopher (106–
43 B.C.). Linus was a mythical Greek poet and musician who
is credited with inventing the dirge. Lucius Annaeus Seneca
(4 B.C.–A.D. 65) followed the philosophy of the Stoics in his
moral treatises. Dante calls him "the moralist" to distinguish
him from Seneca the tragedian, who was thought (erro-
neously) during the Middle Ages to be another person.

142. *Euclid the geometer, and Ptolemy*: Euclid, a Greek math-
ematician (fl. 300 B.C.) who taught at Alexandria, wrote a
treatise on geometry which was the first codification and ex-
position of mathematical principles. Ptolemy was a Greek
mathematician, astronomer, and geographer, born in Egypt
about the end of the first century after Christ. The Ptolemaic
system of the universe (which was accepted by the Middle
Ages), so named although he did not invent it, presented the
earth as its fixed center encircled by nine spheres.

143. *Hippocrates, Galen, Avicenna*: Hippocrates was a Greek physician (c. 460–c. 377 B.C.) who founded the medical profession and introduced the scientific art of healing; his best-known work was the *Aphorisms*, used as an authority in the Middle Ages. Galen was a celebrated physician (c. 130–c. 200) who practiced his art in Greece, Egypt, and Rome; he wrote about every branch of medicine known in his time. Like Hippocrates, he enjoyed the esteem of his contemporaries and later generations. Avicenna or ibn-Sina (980–1037), an Arabian philosopher and physician, was a prolific writer; his works include commentaries on Galen and Aristotle.

144. *and Averroës, who made the Commentary*: ibn-Rushd, called Averroës (c. 1126–98), was the celebrated Arabian scholar born in Spain whose interests ranged from medicine to philosophy and law. He was widely known in the Middle Ages for his commentary on Aristotle, which served as the basis for the work of Saint Thomas Aquinas.

CANTO V

From Limbo Virgil leads his ward down to the threshold of the Second Circle of Hell, where for the first time he will see the damned in Hell being punished for their sins. There, barring their way, is the hideous figure of Minòs, the bestial judge of Dante's underworld; but after strong words from Virgil, the poets are allowed to pass into the dark space of this circle, where can be heard the wailing voices of the Lustful, whose punishment consists in being forever whirled about in a dark, stormy wind. After seeing a thousand or more famous lovers—including Semiramis, Dido, Helen, Achilles, and Paris—the Pilgrim asks to speak to two figures he sees together. They are Francesca da Rimini and her lover, Paolo, and the scene in which they appear is probably the most famous episode of the Inferno. At the end of the scene, the Pilgrim, who has been overcome by pity for the lovers, faints to the ground.

This way I went, descending from the first
   into the second round, that holds less space
   but much more pain—stinging the soul to wailing.   3

There stands Minòs grotesquely, and he snarls,
   examining the guilty at the entrance;
   he judges and dispatches, tail in coils.   6

By this I mean that when the evil soul
   appears before him, it confesses all,
   and he, who is the expert judge of sins,   9

knows to what place in Hell the soul belongs;
   the times he wraps his tail around himself
   tell just how far the sinner must go down.   2

The damned keep crowding up in front of him:
   they pass along to judgment one by one;
   they speak, they hear, and then are hurled below.   15

"O you who come to the place where pain is host,"
   Minòs spoke out when he caught sight of me,
   putting aside the duties of his office,   18

"be careful how you enter and whom you trust·
   it's easy to get in, but don't be fooled!"
   And my guide said to him: "Why keep on shouting?   21

Do not attempt to stop his fated journey;
   it is so willed there where the power is
   for what is willed; that's all you need to know."   24

And now the notes of anguish start to play
   upon my ears; and now I find myself
   where sounds on sounds of weeping pound at me.   27

I came to a place where no light shone at all,
   bellowing like the sea racked by a tempest,
   when warring winds attack it from both sides.   30

The infernal storm, eternal in its rage,
   sweeps and drives the spirits with its blast:
   it whirls them, lashing them with punishment.   33

When they are swept back past their place of judgment,
   then come the shrieks, laments, and anguished cries;
   there they blaspheme God's almighty power.   36

I learned that to this place of punishment
   all those who sin in lust have been condemned,
   those who make reason slave to appetite;   39

and as the wings of starlings in the winter
   bear them along in wide-spread, crowded flocks,
   so does that wind propel the evil spirits: 42

now here, then there, and up and down, it drives them
   with never any hope to comfort them—
   hope not of rest but even of suffering less.   45

And just like cranes in flight, chanting their lays,
  stretching an endless line in their formation,
  I saw approaching, crying their laments,   48

spirits carried along by the battling winds.
  And so I asked, "Teacher, tell me, what souls
  are these punished in the sweep of the black wind?"   51

"The first of those whose story you should know,"
  my master wasted no time answering,
  "was empress over lands of many tongues;   54

her vicious tastes had so corrupted her
  she licensed every form of lust with laws
  to cleanse the stain of scandal she had spread;   57

she is Semiramis, who, legend says,
  was Ninus' wife as well as his successor;
  she governed all the land the Sultan rules.   60

The next is she who killed herself for love
  and broke faith with the ashes of Sichaeus;
  and there is Cleopatra, who loved men's lusting.   63

See Helen there, the root of evil woe
  lasting long years, and see the great Achilles,
  who lost his life to love, in final combat;   66

see Paris, Tristan"—then, more than a thousand
  he pointed out to me, and named them all,
  those shades whom love cut off from life on earth.   69

After I heard my teacher call the names
  of all these knights and ladies of ancient times,
  pity confused my senses, and I was dazed.   72

I began: "Poet, I would like, with all my heart,
  to speak to those two there who move together
  and seem to be so light upon the winds."   75

And he: "You'll see when they are closer to us;
  if you entreat them by that love of theirs
  that carries them along, they'll come to you."   78

When the winds bent their course in our direction
  I raised my voice to them, "O wearied souls,
  come speak with us if it be not forbidden."   81

As doves, called by desire to return
  to their sweet nest, with wings raised high and poised,
  float downward through the air, guided by will,   84

so these two left the flock where Dido is
  and came toward us through the malignant air,
  such was the tender power of my call.   87

"O living creature, gracious and so kind,
  who makes your way here through this dingy air
  to visit us who stained the world with blood,   90

if we could claim as friend the King of Kings,
  we would beseech him that he grant you peace,
  you who show pity for our atrocious plight.   93

Whatever pleases you to hear or speak
  we will hear and we will speak about with you
  as long as the wind, here where we are, is silent.   96

The place where I was born lies on the shore
  where the river Po with its attendant streams
  descends to seek its final resting place.   99

Love, quick to kindle in the gentle heart,
  seized this one for the beauty of my body,
  torn from me, (How it happened still offends me!)   102

Love, that excuses no one loved from loving,
  seized me so strongly with delight in him
  that, as you see, he never leaves my side.   105

Love led us straight to sudden death together.
  Caïna awaits the one who quenched our lives."
  These were the words that came from them to us.   108

When those offended souls had told their story,
  I bowed my head and kept it bowed until
  the poet said, "What are you thinking of?"   111

When finally I spoke, I sighed, "Alas,
   all those sweet thoughts, and oh, how much desiring
   brought these two down into this agony."   114

And then I turned to them and tried to speak;
   I said, "Francesca, the torment that you suffer
   brings painful tears of pity to my eyes.   117

But tell me, in that time of your sweet sighing
   how, and by what signs, did love allow you
   to recognize your dubious desires?"   120

And she to me: "There is no greater pain
   than to remember, in our present grief,
   past happiness (as well your teacher knows)!   123

But if your great desire is to learn
   the very root of such a love as ours,
   I shall tell you, but in words of flowing tears.   126

One day we read, to pass the time away,
   of Lancelot, of how he fell in love;
   we were alone, innocent of suspicion.   129

Time and again our eyes were brought together
   by the book we read; our faces flushed and paled.
   To the moment of one line alone we yielded: 132

it was when we read about those longed-for lips
   now being kissed by such a famous lover,
   that this one (who shall never leave my side)   135

then kissed my mouth, and trembled as he did.
   Our Galehot was that book and he who wrote it.
   That day we read no further." And all the while   138

the one of the two spirits spoke these words,
   the other wept, in such a way that pity
   blurred my senses; I swooned as though to die,   141

and fell to Hell's floor as a body, dead, falls.

NOTES

1–72

The fifth canto can be divided into two equal parts with a transitional tercet. The first part concerns Minòs and his activities, the band of souls being punished in the wind for their lust, and certain shades of royal figures seen in a formation that resembles that of flying cranes. The Pilgrim has learned (evidently from Virgil) the function of Minòs, and he will learn from him the type of sin being punished, the form of the punishment, and the names of many of those who are here. Chiefly, Virgil is trying to teach the Pilgrim three lessons in the first part of this canto, and each is concerned with the nature of lust—a heinous sin even if it is the least of those punished in Hell. The first lesson should come from the sight of Minòs exercising his function: the horror of this sight should shock the Pilgrim into an awareness of the true nature of all sin. The second lesson should come from the royal figures guilty of lust. Semiramis, who legalized lust because of her own incestuous activity (and to whom Virgil devotes three tercets, more lines than anyone else in this group receives), should be a particularly significant lesson to the Pilgrim as to the nature of carnal sins. And thirdly, the Pilgrim should come to despise the lustful because they blaspheme Divine Justice, which has placed them here, and thereby show themselves to be totally unrepentant.

But the Pilgrim learns nothing, as we see in the transitional tercet (70–72). Instead, pity for these sinners seizes his senses and he is "dazed." This tercet reveals the state of the Pilgrim's mind before meeting with Francesca da Rimini. Pity is precisely that side of the Pilgrim's character toward which Francesca will direct her carefully phrased speech. The Pilgrim has not learned his lesson, and in the direct encounter with one of the lustful (Francesca), he will fail his first "test."

4. *There stands Minòs grotesquely*: Minòs was the son of Zeus and Europa. As king of Crete he was revered for his wisdom

and judicial gifts. For these qualities he became chief magistrate of the underworld in classical literature:

> Minòs, presiding, shakes the urn; it is he who calls a court of the silent and learns men's lives and misdeeds.
>
> (Virgil, *Aeneid* VI, 432–33)

Although Dante did not alter Minòs's official function, he transformed him into a demonic figure, both in his physical characteristics and in his bestial activity. Minòs condemns souls to all parts of Hell, but Dante may well have placed him at the entrance to the Second Circle so that the reader, listening to the tragic tale of the sweet Francesca, would not be tempted to forget the hideous figure of Minòs, who, with his tail, once pronounced sentence on Francesca as well as on Thaïs the whore (XVIII).

31–32. *The infernal storm, eternal in its rage*: The *contrapasso*, or punishment, suggests that lust (the "infernal storm") is pursued without the light of reason (in the darkness).

34. *When they are swept back past their place of judgment*: In Italian this line reads, "Quando giungon davanti a la ruina," literally, "When they come before the falling place." According to Busnelli (*Miscellanea dantesca*, Padova, 1922, 51–53), the *ruina* refers to the tribunal of Minòs, that is, to the place where the condemned sinners "fall" before him at the entrance to the Second Circle to be judged. Therefore I have translated *ruina* as "their place of judgment"; the entire tercet means that every time the sinners in the windstorm are blown near Minòs they shriek, lament, and blaspheme.

58. *she is Semiramis*: the legendary queen of Assyria who, although renowned for her military conquests and civic projects, fell prey to her passions and became dissolute to the extent of legalizing lust. Paulus Orosius, Dante's principal source for the story, also attributes the restoration of Babylon, built by Nimrod, to Semiramis. According to Saint Augustine (*City of God*), one of the major conflicts of Christendom stems from the presence of two opposing civilizations: the city of God (*civitas dei*, founded by Abraham) and the city of man (*civitas*

mundi, rejuvenated by Semiramis). Therefore, in a larger sense Dante conceived the Assyrian empress not only as the representative of libidinous passion in all its forms, but also as the motivating force of the degenerate society that ultimately opposes God's divine order.

60. *she governed all the land the Sultan rules*: During the Middle Ages the Sultan controlled the area that now contains Egypt and Syria.

61–62. *The next is she who killed herself for love*: According to Virgil (*Aeneid* I and IV), Dido, the queen of Carthage, swore faithfulness to the memory of her dead husband, Sichaeus. However, when the Trojan survivors of the war arrived in port, she fell helplessly in love with their leader, Aeneas, and they lived together as man and wife until the gods reminded Aeneas of his higher destiny: the founding of Rome and the Roman Empire. Immediately he set sail for Italy, and Dido, deserted, committed suicide.

63. *and there is Cleopatra, who loved men's lusting*: Cleopatra was the daughter of Ptolemy Auletes, the last king of Egypt before it came under Roman domination. She was married to her brother in conformity with the incestuous practices of the Ptolemies, but with the assistance of Julius Caesar, whose child she bore, Cleopatra disposed of her brother and became queen of Egypt. After Caesar's death her licentious charms captured Mark Antony, with whom she lived in debauchery until his death. Finally she attempted, unsuccessfully, to seduce Octavianus, the Roman governor of Egypt, and his refusal precipitated her suicide.

To the two great empires already mentioned, Assyria and Carthage, a third must be added, Egypt, which with its libidinous queen opposed the "*civitas dei.*"

64. *See Helen there, the root of evil woe*: Helen, wife of Menelaus, king of Sparta, was presented by Aphrodite to Paris in compensation for his judgment in the beauty contest of the goddesses. Paris carried Helen off to Troy and there married her, but her enraged husband demanded aid of the other Greek nobles to regain Helen. United, they embarked for Troy, and

thus began the final conflagration involving the two powerful nations.

65–66. *and see the great Achilles*: Dante's knowledge of the Trojan War came directly or indirectly from the early medieval accounts of Dares the Phrygian (*De Excidio Trojae Historia*) and Dictys of Crete (*De Bello Trojano*). In these versions Achilles, the invincible Homeric warrior, had been transformed into an ordinary mortal who languished in the bonds of love. Enticed by the beauty of Polyxena, a daughter of the Trojan king, Achilles desired her to be his wife, but Hecuba, Polyxena's mother, arranged a counterplot with Paris so that when Achilles entered the temple for his presumed marriage, he was treacherously slain by Paris.

67. *see Paris, Tristan*: Paris was the son of Priam, king of Troy, whose abduction of Helen ignited the Trojan War. The classical Latin poets and the medieval redactors of the legend of Troy consistently depicted him more disposed to loving than to fighting.

Tristan is the central figure of numerous medieval French, German, and Italian romances. Sent as a messenger by his uncle, King Mark of Cornwall, to obtain Isolt for him in marriage, Tristan became enamored of her, and she of him. After Isolt's marriage to Mark, the lovers continued their love affair, and in order to maintain its secrecy they necessarily employed many deceits and ruses. According to one version, however, Mark, growing continuously more suspicious of their attachment, finally discovered them together and ended the incestuous relationship by mortally wounding Tristan with a lance.

73–142

Having seen the shades of many "knights and ladies of ancient times" (71), the Pilgrim now centers his attention upon a single pair of lovers. The spotlight technique here employed emphasizes the essentially dramatic quality of the *Inferno*. Francesca recognizes the Pilgrim's sympathetic attitude and tells her story in a way that will not fail to win the Pilgrim's interest, even though she, like Semiramis, was the initiator in an act of incest. Her choice of words and phrases frequently reveals her gentility and her familiarity with the works of the *stilnovisti* poets (the school of poets that was contemporary with, and perhaps included, Dante). But the careful reader can see beneath the superficial charm and grace what Francesca really is—vain and accustomed to admiration. Francesca is also capable of lying, though whether her lies are intentional or the result of self-deception we do not know. For example, her reference to the love of Lancelot in line 128 shows her technique of changing facts that would condemn her. In the medieval French romance *Lancelot du Lac*, the hero, being quite bashful in love, is finally brought together in conversation with Queen Guinevere through the machinations of Galehot ("Our Galehot was that book and he who wrote it," 137). Urged on by his words, Guinevere takes the initiative and, placing her hand on Lancelot's chin, kisses him. In order to fully understand Francesca's character, it is necessary to note that in our passage she has reversed the roles of the lovers: here she has Lancelot kissing Guinevere just as she has presented Paolo as kissing her. The distortion of this passage offered as a parallel to her own experience reveals the (at best) confusion of Francesca: if the passage in the romance inspired their kiss, it must have been she, as it was Guinevere, who was responsible. Like Eve, who tempted Adam to commit the first sin in the Garden of Eden, Francesca tempted Paolo, and thus she is perhaps an example of the common medieval view of women as "daughters of Eve." Francesca attempts to exculpate herself by blaming the romantic book that she and Paolo were reading (137); the Pilgrim is evidently convinced of her innocence for he is overcome ". . . in such a way that pity blurred [his] senses," and he faints.

Many critics, taken in like the Pilgrim by Francesca's smooth speech, have asserted that she and Paolo in their love have "conquered" Hell because they are still together. But their togetherness is certainly part of their punishment. The ever-silent, weeping Paolo is surely not happy with their state, and

Francesca coolly alludes to Paolo with the impersonal "that one" (*costui*) or "this one" (*questi*). She never mentions his name. Line 102 indicates her distaste for Paolo: the manner of her death (they were caught and killed together in the midst of their lustful passion) *still* offends her because she is forever condemned to be together with her naked lover; he serves as a constant reminder of her shame and of the reason that they are in Hell ("he never leaves my side," 105). Their temporary pleasure together in lust has become their own particular torment in Hell.

74. *those two there who move together*: Francesca, daughter of Guido Vecchio da Polenta, lord of Ravenna, and Paolo Malatesta, third son of Malatesta da Verrucchio, lord of Rimini. Around 1275 the aristocratic Francesca was married for political reasons to Gianciotto, the physically deformed second son of Malatesta da Verrucchio. In time a love affair developed between Francesca and Gianciotto's younger brother, Paolo. One day the betrayed husband discovered them in an amorous embrace and slew them both.

82–84. *As doves*: Paolo and Francesca are compared to "doves, called by desire . . ." who "float downward through the air, guided by their will." The use of the words "desire" and "will" is particularly interesting because it suggests the nature of lust as a sin: the subjugation of the will to desire.

97–99. *The place where I was born*: Ravenna, a city on the Adriatic coast.

100–108. *Love . . . Love . . . Love*: These three tercets, each beginning with the word "Love," are particularly important as revealing the deceptive nature of Francesca. In lines 100 and 103 Francesca deliberately employs the style of *stilnovisti* poets such as Guinizelli and Cavalcanti in order to ensure the Pilgrim's sympathy, but she follows each of those lines with sensual and most un-*stilnovistic* ideas. For in the idealistic world of the *dolce stil nuovo*, love would never "seize" a man for the beauty of the woman's body alone, nor would the sensual delight that "seized" Francesca be appropriate to *stilnovistic* love, which was distant, nonsexual, and ideal.

107. *Caïna awaits the one who quenched our lives*: Caïna is one of the four divisions of Cocytus, the lowest part of Hell, wherein are tormented those souls who treacherously betrayed their kin.

141-42. *I swooned as though to die*: To understand this reaction to Francesca, it is necessary to remember that Dante the Pilgrim is a fictional character, who should not be equated with Dante the Poet, author of *The Divine Comedy*. Dante the Pilgrim is journeying through Hell as a man who must learn the true nature of sin, and since this is his first contact with those who are damned and punished in Hell proper, he is easily seduced into compassion for these souls. As the Pilgrim progresses he will learn the nature of sin and of evil souls, and his reaction to them will change (cf. XIX). But the extent of his failure in Canto V to recognize sin and treat it with proper disdain is symbolized here by his abject figure, unconscious (thus, without "reason") on the floor of Hell. Perhaps we should not blame the Pilgrim for being taken in by Francesca; dozens of critics, unaware of the wiles of sin, have also been seduced by her charm and the grace of her speech.

CANTO VI

—

ON RECOVERING *consciousness the Pilgrim finds himself with Virgil in the Third Circle, where the GLUTTONS are punished. These shades are mired in filthy muck and are eternally battered by cold and dirty hail, rain, and snow. Soon the travelers come upon CERBERUS, the three-headed, doglike beast who guards the Gluttons, but Virgil pacifies him with fistfuls of slime and the two poets pass on. One of the shades recognizes Dante the Pilgrim and hails him. It is CIACCO, a Florentine who, before they leave, makes a prophecy concerning the political future of Florence. As the poets move away, the Pilgrim questions Virgil about the Last Judgment and other matters until the two arrive at the next circle.*

Regaining now my senses, which had fainted
　　at the sight of these two who were kinsmen lovers,
　　a piteous sight confusing me to tears,　　　　　　3

new suffering and new sinners suffering
　　appeared to me, no matter where I moved
　　or turned my eyes, no matter where I gazed.　　　6

I am in the third circle, in the round of rain
　　eternal, cursed, cold, and falling heavy,
　　unchanging beat, unchanging quality.　　　　　　9

Thick hail and dirty water mixed with snow
　　come down in torrents through the murky air,
　　and the earth is stinking from this soaking rain.　　12

Cerberus, a ruthless and fantastic beast,
　　with all three throats howls out his doglike sounds
　　above the drowning sinners of this place.　　　　　15

His eyes are red, his beard is slobbered black,
  his belly swollen, and he has claws for hands;
  he rips the spirits, flays and mangles them.   18

Under the rain they howl like dogs, lying
  now on one side with the other as a screen,
  now on the other turning, these wretched sinners.   21

When the slimy Cerberus caught sight of us,
  he opened up his mouths and showed his fangs;
  his body was one mass of twitching muscles.   24

My master stooped and, spreading wide his fingers,
  he grabbed up heaping fistfuls of the mud
  and flung it down into those greedy gullets.   27

As a howling cur, hungering to get fed,
  quiets down with the first mouthful of his food,
  busy with eating, wrestling with that alone,   30

so it was with all three filthy heads
  of the demon Cerberus, used to barking thunder
  on these dead souls, who wished that they were deaf.   33

We walked across this marsh of shades beaten
  down by the heavy rain, our feet pressing
  on their emptiness that looked like human form.   36

Each sinner there was stretched out on the ground
  except for one who quickly sat up straight,
  the moment that he saw us pass him by.   39

"O you there being led through this inferno,"
  he said, "try to remember who I am,
  for you had life before I gave up mine."   42

I said: "The pain you suffer here perhaps
  disfigures you beyond all recognition:
  I can't remember seeing you before.   45

But tell me who you are, assigned to grieve
  in this sad place, afflicted by such torture
  that—worse there well may be, but none more foul."   48

"Your own city," he said, "so filled with envy
   its cup already overflows the brim,
   once held me in the brighter life above.   51

You citizens gave me the name of Ciacco;
   and for my sin of gluttony I am damned,
   as you can see, to rain that beats me weak.   54

And my sad sunken soul is not alone,
   for all these sinners here share in my pain
   and in my sin." And that was his last word.   57

"Ciacco," I said to him, "your grievous state
   weighs down on me, it makes me want to weep;
   but tell me what will happen, if you know,   60

to the citizens of that divided state?
   And are there any honest men among them?
   And tell me, why is it so plagued with strife?"   63

And he replied: "After much contention
   they will come to bloodshed; the rustic party
   will drive the other out by brutal means.   66

Then it will come to pass, this side will fall
   within three suns, and the other rise to power
   with the help of one now listing toward both sides.   69

For a long time they will keep their heads raised high,
   holding the others down with crushing weight,
   no matter how these weep or squirm for shame.   72

Two just men there are, but no one listens,
   for pride, envy, avarice are the three sparks
   that kindle in men's hearts and set them burning."   75

With this his mournful words came to an end.
   But I spoke back: "There's more I want to know;
   I beg you to provide me with more facts: 78

Farinata and Tegghiaio, who were so worthy,
   Jacopo Rusticucci, Arrigo, Mosca,
   and all the rest so bent on doing good,   81

where are they? Tell me what's become of them;
  one great desire tortures me: to know
  whether they taste Heaven's sweetness or Hell's gall."   84

"They lie below with blacker souls," he said,
  "by different sins pushed down to different depths;
  if you keep going you may see them all.   87

But when you are once more in the sweet world
  I beg you to remind our friends of me.
  I speak no more; no more I answer you.."   90

He twisted his straight gaze into a squint
  and stared awhile at me, then bent his head,
  falling to join his other sightless peers   93

My guide then said to me: "He'll wake no more
  until the day the angel's trumpet blows,
  when the unfriendly Judge shall come down here;   96

each soul shall find again his wretched tomb,
  assume his flesh and take his human shape,
  and hear his fate resound eternally."   99

And so we made our way through the filthy mess
  of muddy shades and slush, moving slowly,
  talking a little about the afterlife.   102

I said, "Master, will these torments be increased,
  or lessened, on the final Judgment Day,
  or will the pain be just the same as now?"   105

And he: "Remember your philosophy:
  the closer a thing comes to its perfection,
  more keen will be its pleasure or its pain.   108

Although this cursèd race of punished souls
  shall never know the joy of true perfection,
  more perfect will their pain be then than now."   111

We circled round that curving road while talking
  of more than I shall mention at this time,
  and came to where the ledge begins descending;   114

there we found Plutus, mankind's arch-enemy.

NOTES

7-21

The shades in this circle are the gluttons, and their punishment fits their sin. Gluttony, like all the sins of Incontinence, subjects reason to desire; in this case desire is a voracious appetite. Thus the shades howl like dogs—in desire, without reason; they are sunk in slime, the image of their excess. The warm comfort their gluttony brought them in life here has become cold, dirty rain and hail.

7–9. *I am in the third circle, in the round of rain*: Note the change in tense and tone from the first two tercets. Suddenly Dante is writing in the present tense and using the sharp staccato effect of one word pounding the other in order to reinforce the immediacy of the image of cold rain and hail beating down on the sinners.

13–22. *Cerberus, a ruthless and fantastic beast*: In classical mythology Cerberus is a fierce three-headed dog that guards the entrance to the Underworld, permitting admittance to all and escape to none. He is the prototype of the gluttons, with his three howling, voracious throats that gulp down huge handfuls of muck. He has become Appetite and as such he flays and mangles the spirits who reduced their lives to a satisfaction of appetite. With his three heads, he appears to be a prefiguration of Lucifer and thus another infernal distortion of the Trinity. In line 22 he is characterized as *il gran vermo* (literally, "the great worm"), as Lucifer in Canto XXXIV (108) is called *vermo reo* ("evil worm").

26–27. *he grabbed up heaping fistfuls of the mud*: With this action, Virgil imitates the action of the Sibyl who, leading Aeneas through the Underworld, placates Cerberus by casting honeyed cakes into his three throats (*Aeneid* VI, 417–23). By substituting "dirt" for the Virgilian cakes, Dante emphasizes Cerberus's irrational gluttony.

36. *their emptiness that looked like human form*: The shades in Hell bear only the *appearance* of their corporeal forms, although

they can be ripped and torn and otherwise suffer physical torture—just as here they are able to bear the Pilgrim's weight. Yet they themselves evidently are airy shapes without weight (cf. VIII, 27) which will, after the Day of Judgment, be possessed of their actual bodies once more (cf. XIII, 103).

48. *worse there well may be, but none more foul*: At this early stage of his journey the Pilgrim, who will come to see the filth of excrements and dripping guts, can imagine nothing more foul than dirty water.

50. *its cup already overflows the brim*: The image used here by Ciacco to describe the envy in Florence also reflects the sin of gluttony.

52. *You citizens gave me the name of Ciacco*: The only glutton whom the Pilgrim actually talks to is Ciacco, one of his Florentine contemporaries, whose true identity has never been determined. Several commentators believe him to be Ciacco dell'Anguillaia, a minor poet of the time and presumably the Ciacco of one of Boccaccio's stories (*Decameron* IX, 8). However, more than a proper name, *ciacco* is a derogatory Italian word for "pig," or "hog," and is also an adjective, "filthy," or "of a swinish nature."

59. *it makes me want to weep*: The Pilgrim, having learned very little from his experience in Canto V, feels pity again at the sight of Ciacco.

65–75. *they will come to bloodshed*: Ciacco's political prophecy reveals the fact that the shades in Hell are able to see the future; they also know the past, but they know nothing of the present (cf. X, 100–108). The prophecy itself can be interpreted in the following manner: in 1300 the Guelf party, having gained complete control over Florence by defeating the Ghibellines (1289), was divided into factions: the Whites (the "rustic party," 65), headed by the Cerchi family, and the Blacks ("the other," 66), led by the Donati. These two groups finally came into direct conflict on May 1, 1300, which resulted in the expulsion of the Blacks from the city (1301). However, they returned in 1302 ("within three suns," 68, i.e., within three years) and, with the help of Pope Boniface VIII, sent the Whites (including Dante) into exile. Boniface VIII, the "one now listing toward both sides" (69), for a time did not reveal his designs on Florence, but rather steered a wavering course between the two factions, planning to aid the ultimate victor. The identity of the two honest men to whom no one listens (73) has not been established. The reader must of course realize that although the fictional date of the poem is 1300, the poem itself was written some years later; therefore most of what is "prophesied" in the *Inferno* had already taken place when Dante was writing.

73. *Two just men there are, but no one listens*: Although the two individuals remain unknown, it is probable that by "two" Dante simply intends to allude to the minimal few who are honest in corrupt Florence.

79–87. *Farinata and Tegghiaio, who were so worthy*: Ciacco informs the Pilgrim only that the men about whom he had inquired (79–81) are in Hell. But the Pilgrim will learn in the course of time that Farinata degli Uberti is in the Circle of the Heretics (X, 32); Tegghiaio Aldobrandini and Jacopo Rusticucci are among the Sodomites (XVI, n. 41 and n. 44); Mosca dei Lamberti is a Sower of Discord (XXVIII, n. 106). Arrigo is not mentioned again in the *Inferno* and has not been identified.

89. *I beg you to remind our friends of me*: In the upper regions of Hell, many of the damned are concerned with their worldly fame, because the perpetuation of their memory on earth by the living is their only means of remaining "alive." But as the sins become more heinous, the sinners seem less desirous of having their stories told on earth.

91–93. *He twisted his straight gaze into a squint*: The manner in which Ciacco takes leave is certainly odd: his eyes, fixed on the Pilgrim throughout their conversation, gradually lose their power to focus and can only stare blankly. The concentration required for the prophecy seems to have exhausted him.

106–11. *Remember your philosophy*: In answer to the Pilgrim's question (103–105), Virgil reminds him of the popular doctrine that states that the closer a thing is to perfection, the more it knows what pleasure is, and pain. The perfected state of man, from a "technical" point of view, will be attained on

Judgment Day, when the soul is reunited with the body. Therefore, the damned will feel more torment later than now; similarly, the blessed in Paradise will enjoy God's beatitude more.

115. *there we found Plutus, mankind's arch-enemy*: For Plutus, see Canto VII, 2.

CANTO VII

AT THE BOUNDARY of the Fourth Circle the two travelers con-
front clucking PLUTUS, the god of wealth, who collapses into emp-
tiness at a word from Virgil. Descending farther, the Pilgrim sees
two groups of angry, shouting souls who clash huge rolling weights
against each other with their chests. They are the PRODIGAL and the
MISERLY. Their earthly concern with material goods prompts the
Pilgrim to question Virgil about Fortune and her distribution of the
worldly goods of men. After Virgil's explanation, they descend to
the banks of the swamplike river Styx, which serves as the Fifth
Circle. Mired in the bog are the WRATHFUL, who constantly tear
and mangle each other. Beneath the slime of the Styx, Virgil explains,
are the SLOTHFUL; the bubbles on the muddy surface indicate their
presence beneath. The poets walk around the swampy area and soon
come to the foot of a high tower.

"Pape Satàn, pape Satàn aleppe!"
   the voice of Plutus clucked these words at us,
   and that kind sage, to whom all things were known,   3

said reassuringly: "Do not let fear
   defeat you, for whatever be his power,
   he cannot stop our journey down this rock."   6

Then he turned toward that swollen face of rage,
   crying, "Be quiet, cursèd wolf of Hell:
   feed on the burning bile that rots your guts.   9

This journey to the depths does have a reason,
   for it is willed on high, where Michael wrought
   a just revenge for the bold assault on God."   12

As sails swollen by wind, when the ship's mast breaks,
  collapse, deflated, tangled in a heap,
  just so the savage beast fell to the ground.   15

And then we started down a fourth abyss,
  making our way along the dismal slope
  where all the evil of the world is dumped.   18

Ah, God's avenging justice! Who could heap up
  suffering and pain as strange as I saw here?
  How can we let our guilt bring us to this?   21

As every wave Charybdis whirls to sea
  comes crashing against its counter-current wave,
  so these folks here must dance their roundelay.   24

More shades were here than anywhere above,
  and from both sides, to the sound of their own screams,
  straining their chests, they rolled enormous weights. 27

And when they met and clashed against each other
  they turned to push the other way, one side
  screaming, "Why hoard?," the other side, "Why waste?" 30

And so they moved back round the gloomy circle,
  returning on both sides to opposite poles
  to scream their shameful tune another time;   33

again they came to clash and turn and roll
  forever in their semicircle joust.
  And I, my heart pierced through by such a sight,   36

spoke out, "My Master, please explain to me
  who are these people here? Were they all priests,
  these tonsured souls I see there to our left?"   39

He said, "In their first life all you see here
  had such myopic minds they could not judge
  with moderation when it came to spending;   42

their barking voices make this clear enough,
  when they arrive at the two points on the circle
  where opposing guilts divide them into two.   45

The ones who have the bald spot on their heads
   were priests and popes and cardinals, in whom
   avarice is most likely to prevail." 48

And I: "Master, in such a group as this
   I should be able to recognize a few
   who dirtied themselves by such crimes as these." 51

And he replied, "Yours is an empty hope:
   their undistinguished life that made them foul
   now makes it harder to distinguish them. 54

Eternally the two will come to blows;
   then from the tomb they will be resurrected:
   these with tight fists, those without any hair. 57

It was squandering and hoarding that have robbed them
   of the lovely world, and got them in this brawl:
   I will not waste choice words describing it! 60

You see, my son, the short-lived mockery
   of all the wealth that is in Fortune's keep,
   over which the human race is bickering; 63

for all the gold that is or ever was
   beneath the moon won't buy a moment's rest
   for even one among these weary souls." 66

"Master, now tell me what this Fortune is
   you touched upon before. What is she like
   who holds all worldly wealth within her fists?" 69

And he to me, "O foolish race of man,
   how overwhelming is your ignorance!
   Now listen while I tell you what she means: 72

that One, whose wisdom knows infinity,
   made all the heavens and gave each one a guide,
   and each sphere shining shines on all the others, 75

so light is spread with equal distribution:
   for worldly splendors He decreed the same
   and ordained a guide and general ministress 78

who would at her discretion shift the world's
    vain wealth from nation to nation, house to house,
    with no chance of interference from mankind;   81

so while one nation rules, another falls,
    according to whatever she decrees
    (her sentence hidden like a snake in grass).   84

Your knowledge has no influence on her;
    for she foresees, she judges, and she rules
    her kingdom as the other gods do theirs.   87

Her changing changes never take a rest;
    necessity keeps her in constant motion,
    as men come and go to take their turn with her.   90

And this is she so crucified and cursed;
    even those in luck, who should be praising her,
    instead revile her and condemn her acts.   93

But she is blest and in her bliss hears nothing;
    with all God's joyful first-created creatures
    she turns her sphere and, blest, turns it with joy.   96

Now let's move down to greater wretchedness;
    the stars that rose when I set out for you
    are going down—we cannot stay too long."   99

We crossed the circle to its other bank,
    passing a spring that boils and overflows
    into a ditch the spring itself cut out.   102

The water was a deeper dark than perse,
    and we, with its gray waves for company,
    made our way down along a rough, strange path.   105

This dingy little stream, when it has reached
    the bottom of the gray malignant slopes,
    becomes a swamp that has the name of Styx.   108

And I, intent on looking as we passed,
    saw muddy people moving in that marsh,
    all naked, with their faces scarred by rage.   111

They fought each other, not with hands alone,
but struck with head and chest and feet as well,
with teeth they tore each other limb from limb.   114

And the good teacher said: "My son, now see
the souls of those that anger overcame;
and I ask you to believe me when I say,   117

beneath the slimy top are sighing souls
who make these waters bubble at the surface;
your eyes will tell you this—just look around.   120

Bogged in this slime they say, 'Sluggish we were
in the sweet air made happy by the sun,
and the smoke of sloth was smoldering in our hearts;   123

now we lie sluggish here in this black muck!'
This is the hymn they gurgle in their throats
but cannot sing in words that truly sound."   126

Then making a wide arc, we walked around
the pond between the dry bank and the slime,
our eyes still fixed on those who gobbled mud.   129

We came, in time, to the foot of a high tower.

NOTES

1. *Pape Satàn, pape Satàn aleppe!*: This line, while it has never
been interpreted satisfactorily, has certainly been interpreted
variously. Critics as early as Boccaccio have noted a relation
of "pape" to *papa* (pope). Boccaccio implies that "pape" is a
word expressive of great admiration, and Plutus applies it to
Satan, "the prince of demons." Ciardi notes that "pape Satàn"
would be the "opposite number" of *il papa santo*, or the pope.
"Aleppe" has been connected with *aleph*, the first letter of the
Hebrew alphabet, either meaning "prime"—or used as an
expression of grief!

Some think that the line is addressed by Plutus to Dante;
"Satàn" then is seen as the traditional, biblical term for "en-

emy." But the main thrust of modern criticism is to accept the line as simple gibberish (cf. Nimrod's speech in XXXI, 67). However, considering the stress on the clergy throughout the canto, I think the equation "pape" = "pope" is probably most likely.

The hard sound of Plutus's voice onomatopoetically seconds the descriptive adjective "clucking" (*chioccia*).

2–15

Plutus, the god of wealth in classical mythology, appropriately presides over the Miserly and the Prodigal, those who did not use their material goods with moderation. In this canto his collapse like inflated sails "when the ship's mast breaks" (13) is interesting not only because it attests to the true, airy emptiness of wealth, but also because the simile prefigures an image Dante uses in describing Lucifer at the end of the *Inferno*: in XXXIV, 48, Lucifer's wings are compared to sails ("I never saw a ship with larger sails"). But Plutus is an empty satanic figure and his "sails" are empty.

8. *Be quiet, cursèd wolf of Hell*: Virgil's reference to the avaricious Plutus as a "cursèd wolf" recalls the She-Wolf of Canto I and lends more credence to the idea that the She-Wolf reigns over the circles of Incontinence. This opinion is further supported by Dante's words on the terrace of Avarice in the *Purgatory* (XX, 10) in reference to the sin: "Cursèd be you, age-old She-Wolf." Compare line 43 of the present canto, where the voices of the sinners are described as "barking," another wolfish trait (as in the previous canto, VI, 19).

11–12. *where Michael wrought/a just revenge*: The archangel Michael fought against and triumphed over the rebellious angels in Heaven.

22–66

The Miserly and the Prodigal, linked together as those who misused their wealth, suffer a joint punishment. Their material wealth has become a heavy weight that each group must shove against the other, since their attitudes toward wealth on earth were opposed to each other. Each of the two groups completes a semicircle (35) as they roll their weights at each other; therefore together they complete an entire circle (but whether there are many small circles or one huge one around the whole ledge is not clear). The image of a broken circle is surely related to the concept of Fortune mentioned by Virgil. Just as the Avaricious and the Prodigal believed they could outwit the turn of Fortune's wheel (cf. n. 73–96) by hoarding material goods or by wasting them on earth, so here the "short-lived mockery/of all the wealth that is in Fortune's keep" (61–62) is apparent, since part of their punishment is to complete the turn of the wheel (circle) of Fortune, against which they had rebelled during their short space of life on earth.

Because their total concern with wealth left them undistinguished in life, they are unrecognizable here, and the Pilgrim cannot pick out any one sinner in the teeming mass (49–54).

38–48. *who are these people here? Were they all priests*: The fact that most of the avaricious are tonsured priests ("the ones who have the bald spot on their heads," 46) indicates a major abuse practiced by the priesthood in Dante's time; here we have the first of many criticisms in the *Inferno* of the materialistic clergy. See n. 1 of this canto.

57. *these with tight fists, those without any hair*: There is an old Italian proverb about prodigal individuals: "they spend even the hairs on their heads" (*spendono fino i capelli*). After the Resurrection even their hair, appropriately, will be missing.

70. *O foolish race of man*: Virgil's words are addressed not only to Dante but to every man.

73–96

Virgil's digression concerns Fortune, a major theme of medieval and Renaissance writers such as Boethius, Petrarch, Boccaccio, Chaucer, and Machiavelli. Usually it was visualized as a female figure with a wheel, the revolutions of which symbolized the rise and fall of fortune in a man's life, but Dante deviates somewhat from the standard concept of Fortune (as related, e.g., in Boethius's *Consolation of Philosophy*) by assigning to her the role of an angel. In Dante's world she is a minister of God who carries out the divine purpose among men; i.e., Dante has Christianized a pagan goddess.

84. *her sentence hidden like a snake in grass*: This simile may seem comic to the reader, but it is not comic in Italian. Furthermore, it must be retained in translation because it is the pre-Christian Virgil who is speaking, and even though he knows the divine nature of Fortune for Christians, he cannot help but think of it in pre-Christian terms—as a monstrous and cunning evil force, and *not* a minister of God.

98–99. *the stars that rose when I set out for you*: The time is past midnight. The stars setting in the West were rising in the East when Virgil first met Dante on the evening of Good Friday in the "dark wood."

108. *a swamp that has the name of Styx*: The river Styx is the second of the rivers of Hell; Dante, following the *Aeneid*, refers to it here as a marsh or quagmire. Since we know from Canto XIV that all the rivers in Hell are joined, the spring (101) must be the point where the Acheron issues from an underground source.

116–26. *the souls of those that anger overcame*: The sinners in Circle Five present a problem. Virgil identifies those who are punished here as the wrathful. Yet there is evidently a difference between those on the surface of the Styx and those beneath the slime, whose sighing makes "these waters bubble at the surface." Aristotle (*Ethics* IV, 5) and Saint Thomas (both in his commentary on Aristotle and in the *Summa Theologica*) distinguish three degrees of the wrathful: the *acuti* are the actively wrathful; the *amari*, those who are sullen because they keep their wrath locked within themselves; the *difficiles*, the vindictive. The *acuti* are probably those on the surface of the marsh; as for the other two categories, many commentators assume that those beneath the surface are the *amari* and perhaps the *difficiles* also. But Virgil says of the sinners gurgling beneath the mud that in life they were *tristi* or "sluggish" and here they remain so; and the words "smoke of sloth" (123) also indicate that those beneath the mire, whom Dante never sees, are really the Slothful. Some commentators believe that those being punished in the Vestibule of Hell (Canto III) are the Slothful, but in *Purgatory* XVIII the Slothful have a terrace to themselves, and it would seem likely that, as souls guilty of one of the seven capital sins, they would be punished in Hell itself, not in the Vestibule.

Siegfried Wenzel, in his book *The Sin of Sloth: Acedia in Medieval Thought and Literature* (Chapel Hill, N.C., 1967), admits that it is difficult to reach a final conclusion concerning the identity of these sinners, but he also states that *acedia* (sloth) was equated with *tristitia* in early fourteenth-century scholastic teaching. It seems unlikely to me that Dante would have been unaware of such an equation when he had the figures beneath the mire gurgle "*tristi fummo*" ("sluggish we were," 121). Furthermore, it satisfies aesthetic balance to place both the Wrathful and Slothful in the Styx, since the early part of the canto was also concerned with two opposite groups of sinners—the Prodigal and the Avaricious. Sloth, in fact, can be seen as the other side of the coin of Wrath.

CANTO VIII

—

*BUT BEFORE they had reached the foot of the tower, the Pilgrim
had noticed two signal flames at the tower's top, and another flame an-
swering from a distance; soon he realizes that the flames are signals to
and from PHLEGYAS, the boatman of the Styx, who suddenly appears
in a small boat speeding across the river. Wrathful and irritated though
he is, the steersman must grant the poets passage, but during the cross-
ing an angry shade rises from the slime to question the Pilgrim. After
a brief exchange of words, scornful on the part of the Pilgrim, who
has recognized this sinner, the spirit grabs hold of the boat. Virgil
pushes him away, praising his ward for his just scorn, while a group
of the wrathful attack the wretched soul, whose name is FILIPPO
ARGENTI. At the far shore the poets debark and find themselves
before the gates of the infernal CITY OF DIS, where howling figures
threaten them from the walls. Virgil speaks with them privately, but
they slam the gate shut in his face. His ward is terrified, and Virgil too
is shaken, but he insists that help from Heaven is already on the way.*

I must explain, however, that before
   we finally reached the foot of that high tower,
   our eyes had been attracted to its summit   3

by two small flames we saw flare up just there;
   and, so far off the eye could hardly see,
   another burning torch flashed back a sign.   6

I turned to that vast sea of human knowledge:
   "What signal is this? And the other flame,
   what does it answer? And who's doing this?"   9

And he replied: "You should already see
   across the filthy waves what has been summoned,
   unless the marsh's vapors hide it from you."   12

A bowstring never shot an arrow off
   that cut the thin air any faster than
   a little boat I saw that very second   15

skimming along the water in our direction,
   with a solitary steersman, who was shouting,
   "Aha, I've got you now, you wretched soul!"   18

"Phlegyas, Phlegyas, this time you shout in vain,"
   my lord responded, "you will have us with you
   no longer than it takes to cross the muck."   21

As one who learns of some incredible trick
   just played on him flares up resentfully—
   so, Phlegyas there was seething in his anger.   24

My leader calmly stepped into the skiff
   and when he was inside, he had me enter,
   and only then it seemed to carry weight.   27

Soon as my guide and I were in the boat
   the ancient prow began to plough the water,
   more deeply, now, than any time before.   30

And as we sailed the course of this dead channel,
   before me there rose up a slimy shape
   that said: "Who are you, who come before your time?" 33

And I spoke back, "Though I come, I do not stay;
   but who are you, in all your ugliness?"
   "You see that I am one who weeps," he answered.   36

And then I said to him: "May you weep and wail,
   stuck here in this place forever, you damned soul,
   for, filthy as you are, I recognize you."   39

With that he stretched both hands out toward the boat
   but, on his guard, my teacher pushed him back:
   "Away, get down there with the other curs!"   42

And then he put his arms around my neck
   and kissed my face and said, "Indignant soul,
   blessèd is she in whose womb you were conceived.   45

In the world this man was filled with arrogance,
　　and nothing good about him decks his memory;
　　for this, his shade is filled with fury here.　　48

Many in life esteem themselves great men
　　who then will wallow here like pigs in mud,
　　leaving behind them their repulsive fame."　　51

"Master, it certainly would make me happy
　　to see him dunked deep in this slop just once
　　before we leave this lake—it truly would."　　54

And he to me, "Before the other shore
　　comes into sight, you will be satisfied:
　　a wish like that is worthy of fulfillment."　　57

Soon afterward, I saw the wretch so mangled
　　by a gang of muddy souls that, to this day,
　　I thank my Lord and praise Him for that sight:　　60

"Get Filippo Argenti!" they all cried.
　　And at those shouts the Florentine, gone mad,
　　turned on himself and bit his body fiercely.　　63

We left him there, I'll say no more about him.
　　A wailing noise began to pound my ears
　　and made me strain my eyes to see ahead.　　66

"And now, my son," the gentle teacher said,
　　"coming closer is the city we call Dis,
　　with its great walls and its fierce citizens."　　69

And I, "Master, already I can see
　　the clear glow of its mosques above the valley,
　　burning bright red, as though just forged, and left　　72

to smolder." And he to me: "Eternal fire
　　burns within, giving off the reddish glow
　　you see diffused throughout this lower Hell."　　75

And then at last we entered those deep moats
　　that circled all of this unhappy city
　　whose walls, it seemed to me, were made of iron.　　78

For quite a while we sailed around, until
   we reached a place and heard our boatsman shout
   with all his might, "Get out! Here is the entrance."   81

I saw more than a thousand fiendish angels
   perching above the gates enraged, screaming:
   "Who is the one approaching? Who, without death,   84

dares walk into the kingdom of the dead?"
   And my wise teacher made some kind of signal
   announcing he would speak to them in secret.   87

They managed to suppress their great resentment
   enough to say: "You come, but he must go
   who thought to walk so boldly through this realm.   90

Let him retrace his foolish way alone,
   just let him try. And you who led him here
   through this dark land, you'll stay right where you are."93

And now, my reader, consider how I felt
   when those foreboding words came to my ears!
   I thought I'd never see our world again!   96

"O my dear guide, who more than seven times
   restored my confidence, and rescued me
   from the many dangers that blocked my going on,   99

don't leave me, please," I cried in my distress,
   "and if the journey onward is denied us
   let's turn our footsteps back together quickly."   102

Then that lord who had brought me all this way
   said, "Do not fear, the journey we are making
   none can prevent: such power did decree it.   105

Wait here for me and feed your weary spirit
   with comfort and good hope; you can be sure
   I will not leave you in this underworld."   108

With this he walks away. He leaves me here,
   that gentle father, and I stay, doubting,
   and battling with my thoughts of "yes"—but "no."   111

I could not hear what he proposed to them,
  but they did not remain with him for long;
  I saw them race each other back for home.   114

Our adversaries slammed the heavy gates
  in my lord's face, and he stood there outside,
  then turned toward me and walked back very slowly   117

with eyes downcast, all self-assurance now
  erased from his forehead—sighing, "Who are these
  to forbid my entrance to the halls of grief!"   120

He spoke to me: "You need not be disturbed
  by my vexation, for I shall win the contest,
  no matter how they plot to keep us out!   123

This insolence of theirs is nothing new;
  they used it once at a less secret gate,
  which is, and will forever be, unlocked;   126

you saw the deadly words inscribed above it;
  and now, already past it, and descending,
  across the circles, down the slope, alone,   129

comes one by whom the city will be opened."

NOTES

1–6

1–6. I must explain, however, that before: The opening words
of this canto are, in the original: "Io dico, seguitando, che . . ."
Many commentators interpret *seguitando* as evidence that Dante,
having completed the first seven cantos before his exile and
now resuming work on the *Inferno*, would quite naturally
begin: "I say, to continue (my story)." But a simple compar-
ison of the opening lines with the last line of the preceding
canto makes it unnecessary to look for the proper interpre-
tation of the opening line of this canto in biographical data.
Canto VII had concluded with the arrival of Virgil and the

Pilgrim at the foot of a tower; now the flames flaring up at the top of the tower, mentioned for the first time in this canto, must have been seen while the two poets were on their way to the tower, and this is what Dante tells us ("before we reached the foot of that high tower"). That is, he must retrace his steps while continuing his story (*seguitando*) in order to establish the flames properly in the previous temporal context.

In my opinion the "biographical interpretation" is absurd for two reasons. That Dante, at the dramatic point represented by the last line of the previous canto—knowing that at the beginning of the next he must recapitulate in order to introduce the correct timing of events—that precisely at this point Dante should have to put aside his writing is something less than probable. But even if this had been the case, why should Dante wish at this crucial point in his own narrative to drop a hint that he has taken a coffee break in exile?

18. *Aha, I've got you now, you wretched soul!*: Phlegyas, the son of Mars, set fire to Apollo's temple at Delphi, furiously enraged because Apollo raped his daughter Coronis. For this Apollo killed him and sent him to Tartarus. Dante makes Phlegyas the demonic guardian of the Styx. As a personification of great wrath he is well suited not only for guarding the Fifth Circle, where the Wrathful are, but also for transporting the Pilgrim to the inner division of Hell, the City of Dis (68), whose gates are guarded by the rebellious angels (82–83).

32. *before me there rose up a slimy shape*: The befouled and indignant shade that rises from the marsh is Filippo Argenti (line 61), a member of the Adimari family.

36–63

The scene with Filippo Argenti is one of the most dramatic in the *Inferno*. The Pilgrim, who had shown such pity for Francesca, and had even felt compassion for Ciacco, the swinish glutton, bursts into rage as soon as he recognizes Argenti. Filippo's self-identification as "one who weeps" (36) reminds us of Francesca's remark that she will speak "in words of flowing tears" (V, 126); but instead of being moved to pity

(V, 117), the Pilgrim repulses Filippo with harsh words; later he expresses to Virgil his wish to see the sinner "dunked" in the mud; when he sees Filippo being attacked viciously he rejoices and thanks God for the sight. No one has been able to explain satisfactorily this new role assumed by the Pilgrim, and the extreme intensity of his anger, with its suggestion of hatred. Many commentators believe his attitude can be explained as a personal reaction to a political adversary whom he hated. But if that had been the motivation for his outburst, this would surely not have won Virgil's encomium: "Indignant soul, / blessèd is she in whose womb you were conceived . . ." (44–45). Virgil's words must mean that he has sensed a core of righteous wrath in the Pilgrim's outburst; he sees that the hatred he has expressed is primarily a hatred of the sin of wrath. It is true that this moral anger expresses itself in a most unseemly way: there is something childishly vindictive in the taunting words he addresses to Filippo at the beginning of the scene; still more childish is his wish (52–54) to see the sinner "dunked." And when Filippo is made to suffer far greater pain, the Pilgrim's words suggest a hysterical condition. But we must remember that this is only the beginning of a spiritual development in the right direction, away from pity for the sinner toward hatred of his sin. Dante the Pilgrim has not yet learned to hate and at the same time show self-control and mastery of the situation, as he will later on, in Canto XIX.

42. *Away, get down there with the other curs!*: For the reference to *curs*, cf. VI, 19; VII, 8 and 43.

45. *blessèd is she in whose womb you were conceived*: Virgil expresses his approval of the Pilgrim's righteous indignation in an unexpected way. His words carry a strong echo of the Ave Maria (Luke 1:28), and as such, they represent a Christian utterance made by a non-Christian soul. Although it would seem impossible for Virgil to be aware that his address to the Pilgrim echoes the Annunciation, he provides nonetheless the key to Dante's subsequent allegorical presentation of the three Comings of Christ. His words prepare us for (1) the arrival of the angel-messenger to open the gate of Dis in Canto IX

(the First Coming: Christ's descent into Hell); (2) the appear-
ance of the angels, with their blunted swords, in Purgatory
VIII (the Second Coming: Christ's daily arrival in the hearts
of men); and (3) the arrival of Beatrice in Purgatory XXX (the
Third Coming: the Final Judgment). See Canto IX, n. 61–105.

68. *coming closer is the city we call Dis*: Originally Dis was
the name given by the Romans to Pluto, God of the Under-
world. Dante applies the name to Lucifer, but he also applies
the name to the pit-city at the base of which Lucifer is forever
fixed. The walls of the City of Dis mark the division between
upper Hell and "lower Hell" (75), and between the sins of
Incontinence and those of Violence. In terms of the Seven
Capital Sins, we have passed through circles punishing the five
lesser ones (Lust, Gluttony, Avarice, Sloth, and Wrath); be-
yond are sins occasioned specifically by Envy and Pride.

82–83. *I saw more than a thousand fiendish angels*: These are
the rebellious angels who, with their leader Lucifer, were cast
into Hell after their abortive attempt to gain control of Heaven.

97. *more than seven times*: that is to say, many times.

105. *such power did decree it*: Virgil hopes to allay the Pil-
grim's fears by reminding him of the special nature of the
journey, whose guarantor is God—although the "power" re-
ferred to could involve the three heavenly ladies of Canto II
(Mary, Lucia, and Beatrice).

109–11. *With this he walks away. He leaves me here*: Dante's
use of the present tense in this tercet is extraordinary. The
desired effect, I believe, is to capture the reader completely,
immersing him along with the Pilgrim in this terrible aban-
doned state, making him share the same doubts and questions.
There is no longer any temporal separation between the Pil-
grim's journey and the reader's awareness of its existence; in
this tercet the two realities are joined. Then, suddenly, it is
the Pilgrim's journey once again.

115. *Our adversaries slammed the heavy gates*: The biblical des-
ignation "our adversary" for the Devil was quite common in
the Middle Ages.

125–26. *they used it once at a less secret gate*: The rebellious
angels tried to deny Christ entry into Hell by barring the

principal ("less secret") gate, but it was forced open by Him and will remain open for eternity.

127. *you saw the deadly words*: For the inscription above the gate of Hell, see Canto III, 1–9.

130. *comes one by whom the city will be opened*: the divine messenger, dispatched to open the gates of the city of Dis. See Canto IX, 61–105.

CANTO IX

THE HELP FROM *Heaven has not yet arrived; the Pilgrim is afraid and Virgil is obviously worried. He reassures his ward by telling him that, soon after his own death, he was forced by the Sorceress Erichtho to resume mortal shape and go to the very bottom of Hell in order to bring up the soul of a traitor; thus Virgil knows the way well. But no sooner is the Pilgrim comforted than the* THREE FURIES *appear before him, on top of the tower, shrieking and tearing their breasts with their nails. They call for* MEDUSA, *whose horrible face has the power of turning anyone who looks on her to stone. Virgil turns his ward around and covers his eyes. After an "address to the reader" calling attention to the coming allegory, a strident blast splits the air, and the poets perceive an* ANGEL *coming through the murky darkness to open the gates of the City for them. Then the angel returns on the path whence he had come, and the two travelers enter the gate. Within are great open burning sarcophagi, from which groans of torment issue. Virgil explains that these are* ARCH-HERETICS *and their lesser counterparts.*

The color of the coward on my face,
 when I realized my guide was turning back,
 made him quickly change the color of his own. 3

He stood alert, like one who strains to hear;
 his eyes could not see far enough ahead
 to cut the heavy fog of that black air. 6

"But surely we were meant to win this fight,"
 he said, "or else . . . but no, such help was promised!
 Oh, how much time it's taking him to come!" 9

I saw too well how quickly he amended
 his opening words with what he added on!
 They were different from the ones he first pronounced; 12

LOWER HELL

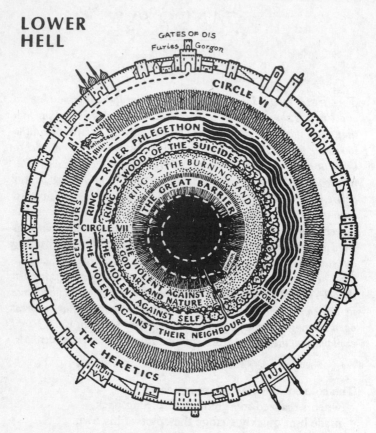

LOWER HELL

GATES OF DIS
Furies Gorgon

CIRCLE VI

CENTAURS RING 1 - RIVER PHLEGETHON RING 2 - WOOD OF THE SUICIDES
Minotaur

RING 3 - THE BURNING SAND

THE GREAT BARRIER

CIRCLE VII

THE VIOLENT AGAINST GOD ART AND NATURE

THE VIOLENT AGAINST NATURE

THE VIOLENT AGAINST SELF

FORD

THE VIOLENT AGAINST THEIR NEIGHBOURS

THE HERETICS

HERESY : VIOLENCE –
THE SINS OF THE LION

but nonetheless his words made me afraid,
   perhaps because the phrase he left unfinished
   I finished with worse meaning than he meant.   15

"Has anyone before ever descended
   to this sad hollow's depths from that first circle
   whose pain is all in having hope cut off?"   18

I put this question to him. He replied,
   "It is not usual for one of us
   to make the journey I am making now.   21

But it happens I was down here once before,
   conjured by that heartless witch, Erichtho
   (who could recall the spirit to its body).   24

Soon after I had left my flesh in death
   she sent me through these walls, and down as far
   as the pit of Judas to bring a spirit out;   27

and that place is the lowest and the darkest
   and the farthest from the sphere that circles all;
   I know the road, and well, you can be sure.   30

This swamp that breathes with a prodigious stink
   lies in a circle round the doleful city
   that now we cannot enter without strife."   33

And he said other things, but I forget them,
   for suddenly my eyes were drawn above,
   up to the fiery top of that high tower   36

where in no time at all and all at once
   sprang up three hellish Furies stained with blood,
   their bodies and their gestures those of females;   39

their waists were bound in cords of wild green hydras,
   horned snakes and little serpents grew as hair,
   and twined themselves around the savage temples.   42

And he who had occasion to know well
   the handmaids of the queen of timeless woe
   cried out to me "Look there! The fierce Erinyes!   45

That is Megaera, the one there to the left,
  and that one raving on the right, Alecto,
  Tisiphone, in the middle." He said no more.   48

With flailing palms the three would beat their breasts,
  then tear them with their nails, shrieking so loud,
  I drew close to the poet, confused with fear.   51

"Medusa, come, we'll turn him into stone,"
  they shouted all together glaring down,
  "how wrong we were to let off Theseus lightly!"   54

"Now turn your back and cover up your eyes,
  for if the Gorgon comes and you should see her,
  there would be no returning to the world!"   57

These were my master's words. He turned me round
  and did not trust my hands to hide my eyes
  but placed his own on mine and kept them covered.   60

O all of you whose intellects are sound,
  look now and see the meaning that is hidden
  beneath the veil that covers my strange verses: 63

and then, above the filthy swell, approaching,
  a blast of sound, shot through with fear, exploded,
  making both shores of Hell begin to tremble;   66

it sounded like one of those violent winds,
  born from the clash of counter-temperatures,
  that tear through forests; raging on unchecked,   69

it splits and rips and carries off the branches
  and proudly whips the dust up in its path
  and makes the beasts and shepherds flee its course!   72

He freed my eyes and said, "Now turn around
  and set your sight along the ancient scum,
  there where the marsh's mist is hovering thickest."   75

As frogs before their enemy, the snake,
  all scatter through the pond and then dive down
  until each one is squatting on the bottom,   78

so I saw more than a thousand fear-shocked souls
   in flight, clearing the path of one who came
   walking the Styx, his feet dry on the water.   81

From time to time with his left hand he fanned
   his face to push the putrid air away,
   and this was all that seemed to weary him.   84

I was certain now that he was sent from Heaven.
   I turned to my guide, but he made me a sign
   to keep my silence and bow low to this one.   87

Ah, the scorn that filled his holy presence!
   He reached the gate and touched it with a wand;
   it opened without resistance from inside.   90

"O Heaven's outcasts, despicable souls,"
   he started, standing on the dreadful threshold,
   "what insolence is this that breeds in you?   93

Why do you stubbornly resist that will
   whose end can never be denied and which,
   more than one time, increased your suffering?   96

What do you gain by locking horns with fate?
   If you remember well, your Cerberus
   still bears his chin and throat peeled clean for that!"   99

He turned then and retraced the squalid path
   without one word to us, and on his face
   the look of one concerned and spurred by things   102

that were not those he found surrounding him.
   And then we started moving toward the city
   in the safety of the holy words pronounced.   105

We entered there, and with no opposition.
   And I, so anxious to investigate
   the state of souls locked up in such a fortress,   108

once in the place, allowed my eyes to wander,
   and saw, in all directions spreading out,
   a countryside of pain and ugly anguish.   111

As at Arles where the Rhône turns to stagnant waters
   or as at Pola near Quarnero's Gulf
   that closes Italy and bathes her confines,   114

the sepulchers make all the land uneven,
   so they did here, strewn in all directions,
   except the graves here served a crueler purpose: 117

for scattered everywhere among the tombs
   were flames that kept them glowing far more hot
   than any iron an artisan might use.   120

Each tomb had its lid loose, pushed to one side,
   and from within came forth such fierce laments
   that I was sure inside were tortured souls.   123

I asked, "Master, what kind of shades are these
   lying down here, buried in the graves of stone,
   speaking their presence in such dolorous sighs?"   126

And he replied: "There lie arch-heretics
   of every sect, with all of their disciples;
   more than you think are packed within these tombs.   129

Like heretics lie buried with their like
   and the graves burn more, or less, accordingly."
   Then turning to the right, we moved ahead   132

between the torments there and those high walls.

NOTES

1. *The color of the coward on my face*: Extreme fear makes the Pilgrim pale.

17–18. *from that first circle*: Limbo, wherein are found those pagan shades who, now cognizant of the Christian God, are destined to remain in Hell, forever hoping for salvation, but in vain. See Canto IV, 34–42.

22–30. *But it happens I was down here once before*: In answer to the Pilgrim's question Virgil states that, although such a journey is rarely made, he himself accomplished it once before at the command of Erichtho, a Thessalian necromancer who conjured up dead spirits (Lucan, *Pharsalia* vi, 508–830). To retrieve a spirit for her, Virgil descended to the lowest region of Hell ("the pit of Judas"), the center of the earth and, consequently, the farthest point from the Primum Mobile ("the sphere that circles all," according to Ptolemaic astronomy). Having no literary or legendary source, the story of Virgil's descent into Hell was probably Dante's invention.

38–48

The three Furies, Tisiphone, Megaera, and Alecto, were the traditional avengers of crime in classical mythology, but here in the *Inferno*, they would appear to be antitheses of the Heavenly Ladies (Mary, Lucia, and Beatrice) who form the chain of grace in Canto II; they are, therefore, another infernal distortion of the Trinity. See n. 61–105.

44. *the handmaids of the queen of timeless woe:* The Furies are "handmaids" to Persephone (Hecate), wife of Pluto, classical god of the Underworld.

52. *Medusa, come, we'll turn him into stone:* Medusa was in classical mythology one of the three Gorgons. Minerva, furious at Medusa for giving birth to two children in one of the former's temples, changed her beautiful hair into serpents, so that whoever gazed on her terrifying aspect was turned to stone.

It should be noted that the classical environment of this canto must have struck a familiar chord in Virgil's mind. Indeed, the Roman poet (and Dante refers to him as such in 51) is quite caught up in his world and sincerely believes that the Medusa could turn Dante into stone. In fact Virgil is described as "he who had occasion to know well/the handmaids of the queen of timeless woe" (43–44). See n. 61–105.

54. *how wrong we were to let off Theseus lightly!*: Theseus, the greatest Athenian hero, descended to Hades with his friend Pirithous, king of the Lapithae, in order to kidnap Proserpina

for him. Pluto slew Pirithous, however, and kept Theseus a prisoner in Hades by having him sit on the Chair of Forgetfulness, which made his mind blank and thereby kept him from moving. Dante chooses a less common version of the myth which has Theseus set free by Hercules. See n. 61–105; also n. 98–99.

56. *for if the Gorgon comes*: The Gorgon is Medusa. See above, n. 52.

61–105

The address to the reader (61–63) is arresting; most critics have assumed that the "meaning . . . hidden/beneath the veil that covers my strange verses" refers to the preceding lines concerning the Furies and Medusa, but I believe that it refers to the lines which follow, describing the arrival of the angel at the gates of Dis. In order to fully understand the context of the address and the "meaning . . . hidden," it is necessary to compare the passage to its analogue in *Purgatory* VIII. There, as here, Dante the Poet interrupts the narrative to tell the reader to search beneath the literal level for the figurative meaning. If one accepts *Inferno* I as the introductory canto for the whole *Divine Comedy*, then *Inferno* IX is really the eighth canto dealing with Hell and therefore occupies a position parallel to the eighth canto dealing with Purgatory. Moreover, as most critics admit, the address to the reader in *Purgatory* VIII (again to direct his vision to the truth beneath a veil "which is *now* easy to penetrate" [*Purgatory* VIII, 20–21]) refers to the section that follows—and that concerns the advent of two angels at the gates of Purgatory proper. The similarities of the passages are evident: an address to the reader and a description of the descent and action of angels before the gates in Inner Hell and Purgatory proper, respectively.

Symbolically, these passages, together with the coming of Beatrice at the top of the Mountain of Purgatory, are analogous to the medieval belief in the three Advents of Christ. Saint Bernard (who appears in the *Paradise* to lead the Pilgrim to the ecstatic, beatific vision of God) expressed this concept in his *Sermons on the Advents*: there is the First Advent of Christ, which culminates in his descent into Hell; the Second Advent is the daily coming of Christ into men's hearts, which is necessary to help them combat the daily temptation of sin; and the Third Advent will be the Last Judgment, when Christ shall come to judge the living and the dead. The coming of the angel in *Inferno* IX, then, is analogous to the first coming of Christ, when He descended into Hell and opened the prime gate (Canto III) for all time in order to free the elect. That event, in fact, is referred to by Virgil at the end of the preceding canto (VIII) when he foretells the coming of the angel:

> This insolence of theirs is nothing new;
>> they used it once at a less secret gate,
>> which is, and will forever be, unlocked;
>
> you saw the deadly words inscribed above it;
>> and now, already past it, and descending,
>> across the circles, down the slope, alone,

comes one by whom the city will be opened.

The parallel between Christ's opening the gates of Hell and the angel's opening the gates of Dis is surely clear; as Christ came to free the innocent from Hell and provide salvation for Everyman, the angel comes, walking on the water of the Styx (without getting his feet wet) to free the Pilgrim (Everyman) from the powers of Hell so that he may continue his preordained journey. The Second Advent, in Purgatory, is a daily one in which the guardian angels descend at the same time every day to drive the serpent of sin back from the gates of Purgatory. It is like Christ's daily descent into the heart of the Christian. The Third Advent, the Last Judgment, is symbolized by Beatrice's coming (*Purgatory* XXX) to pass judgment on her spiritual lover, whom she then leads to Paradise.

The three Advents comprise all of Christian time, from Christ's death and descent to Hell through his daily entrance into men's lives to his eventual judgment of all men. In this respect, the three Furies and Medusa should be seen, in part at least, as a segment of the allegorical drama played out before the gates of Dis. Coming before the advent of the angel, which symbolizes the beginning of Christian time, the classical female demons symbolize pagan time; the Furies' mention of the pre-Christian descent of Theseus (54) to the Underworld and his rescue by Hercules balances the coming *Christian* descent of the Angel of God to rescue Dante. Just as Dante wants to show allegorically that the journey of *The Divine Comedy* comprises all of Christian time through the three Advents, so too he wants to suggest that the journey looks back to and takes in its sweep all of pagan time. Virgil, in fact, as the prime representative of pre-Christian time, is so sure of the power of the pagan Medusa that he shields the Pilgrim's eyes. *The Divine Comedy*, then, must be seen not only as the journey of the individual Everyman to God, but also as the entire scope of the life of mankind: from the mythological beliefs of the ancients (as well as their wisdom: Virgil is an example of both) through the life of man in the Christian age to the eventual Last Judgment.

Apart from the significance of this passage in the framework of the three Advents there is also a minor allegorical significance to be seen therein: that Reason (Virgil) can do much to instruct Everyman, but without Divine Grace (embodied in the Angel) the Pilgrim cannot hope to complete his journey and arrive at Purgatory.

94. *Why do you stubbornly resist that will*: the will of God.

98–99. *your Cerberus*: When Hercules descended into Hell to rescue Theseus, he chained the three-headed dog, Cerberus, and dragged him around and outside Hell so that the skin around his neck was ripped away.

112–17. *As at Arles where the Rhône turns to stagnant waters*: Arles, a city in Provence near the delta of the Rhône, is the site of the famous Roman (later Christian) cemetery of Aliscamps. There, as at Pola, a city in Istria (now Yugoslavia) on the Quarnero Bay also famous for its ancient burying ground, great sarcophagi cover the landscape. Interestingly, according to tradition, Christ appeared to Saint Trophimus when the latter consecrated Aliscamps as a Christian resting place, and promised that the souls of those buried there would be free from the sepulchral torments of the dead. Thus, Dante compares the sepulchers here to those at Pola and Arles, except that "the graves here served a crueler purpose" (117).

127–31. *There lie arch-heretics*: The Heretics are in a circle in Hell that is outside of the three main divisions of Incontinence, Violence, and Fraud. Heresy is not due to weaknesses of the flesh or mind (Incontinence), nor is it a form of Violence or of Fraud; it is a clearly willed sin based on intellectual pride, and because it denies the Christian concept of reality, it is punished outside of the area allocated to the Christian categories of sin. The sin of Heresy is more serious than those caused by weaknesses of the flesh but somehow less serious than willed, premeditated sins of Violence and Fraud; it is a sin of the intellect and a state of being, not a source of sinful action (Fraud, Violence). Therefore it is between Incontinence and Violence.

There is great irony in the fact that those who believed that the death of the body meant the death of the soul suffer as their punishment the entombment of their living souls.

132. *Then turning to the right, we moved ahead*: Why Dante and Virgil, who have been circling always to the left, suddenly move off to the right remains a mystery; this will happen one other time in the *Inferno*: XVII, 31.

CANTO X

THEY COME to the tombs containing the Epicurean heretics, and as they are walking by them, a shade suddenly rises to full height in one tomb, having recognized the Pilgrim's Tuscan dialect. It is the proud FARINATA, who, in life, opposed Dante's party; while he and the Pilgrim are conversing, another figure suddenly rises out of the same tomb. It is the shade of CAVALCANTE DE' CAVALCANTI, who interrupts the conversation with questions about his son Guido. Misinterpreting the Pilgrim's confused silence as evidence of his son's death, Cavalcante falls back into his sepulcher and Farinata resumes the conversation exactly where it had been broken off. He defends his political actions in regard to Florence and prophesies that Dante, like himself, will soon know the pain of exile. But the Pilgrim is also interested to know how it is that the damned can see the future but not the present. When his curiosity is satisfied, he asks Farinata to tell Cavalcante that his son is still alive, and that his silence was caused only by his confusion about the shade's inability to know the present.

Now onward down a narrow path, between
   the city's ramparts and the suffering,
   my master walks, I following close behind.   3

"O lofty power who through these impious gyres
   lead me around as you see fit," I said,
   "I want to know, I want to understand: 6

the people buried there in sepulchers,
   can they be seen? I mean, since all the lids
   are off the tombs and no one stands on guard."   9

And he: "They will forever be locked up,
   when they return here from Jehoshaphat
   with the bodies that they left up in the world.   12

The private cemetery on this side
  serves Epicurus and his followers,
  who make the soul die when the body dies.   15

As for the question you just put to me,
  it will be answered soon, while we are here;
  and the wish you are keeping from me will be granted."18

And I: "O my good guide, I do not hide
  my heart; I'm trying not to talk too much,
  as you have told me more than once to do."   21

"O Tuscan walking through our flaming city,
  alive, and speaking with such elegance,
  be kind enough to stop here for a while.   24

Your mode of speech identifies you clearly
  as one whose birthplace is that noble city
  with which in my time, perhaps, I was too harsh."   27

One of the vaults resounded suddenly
  with these clear words, and I, intimidated,
  drew up a little closer to my guide,   30

who said, "What are you doing? Turn around
  and look at Farinata, who has risen,
  you will see him from the waist up standing straight." 33

I already had my eyes fixed on his face,
  and there he stood out tall, with his chest and brow
  proclaiming his disdain for all this Hell.   36

My guide, with a gentle push, encouraged me
  to move among the sepulchers toward him:
  "Be sure you choose your words with care," he said.   39

And when I reached the margin of his tomb
  he looked at me, and half-contemptuously
  he asked, "And *who* would *your* ancestors be?"   42

And I who wanted only to oblige him
  held nothing back but told him everything.
  At this he lifted up his brows a little,   45

then said, "Bitter enemies of mine they were
    and of my ancestors and of my party;
    I had to scatter them not once but twice."   48

"They were expelled, but only to return
    from everywhere," I said, "not once but twice—
    an art your men, however, never mastered!"   51

Just then along that same tomb's open ledge
    a shade appeared, but just down to his chin,
    beside this other; I think he got up kneeling.   54

He looked around as though he hoped to see
    if someone else, perhaps, had come with me
    and, when his expectation was deceived,   57

he started weeping: "If it be great genius
    that carries you along through this blind jail,
    where is my son? Why is he not with you?"   60

"I do not come alone," I said to him,
    "that one waiting over there guides me through here,
    the one, perhaps, your Guido held in scorn."   63

(The place of pain assigned him, and what he asked,
    already had revealed his name to me
    and made my pointed answer possible.)   66

Instantly, he sprang to his full height and cried,
    "What did you say? He *held*? Is he not living?
    The day's sweet light no longer strikes his eyes?"   69

And when he heard the silence of my delay
    responding to his question, he collapsed
    into his tomb, not to be seen again.   72

That other stately shade, at whose request
    I had first stopped to talk, showed no concern
    nor moved his head nor turned to see what happened;   75

he merely picked up where we had left off:
    "If that art they did not master," he went on,
    "that gives me greater pain than does this bed.   78

But the face of the queen who reigns down here will glow
　　not more than fifty times before you learn
　　how hard it is to master such an art;　　81

and as I hope that you may once more know
　　the sweet world, tell me, why should your party be
　　so harsh to my clan in every law they make?"　　84

I answered: "The massacre and butchery
　　that stained the waters of the Arbia red
　　now cause such laws to issue from our councils."　　87

He sighed, shaking his head. "It was not I
　　alone took part," he said, "nor certainly
　　would I have joined the rest without good cause.　　90

But I alone stood up when all of them
　　were ready to have Florence razed. It was *I*
　　who openly stood up in her defense."　　93

"And now, as I would have your seed find peace,"
　　I said, "I beg you to resolve a problem
　　that has kept my reason tangled in a knot:　　96

if I have heard correctly, all of you
　　can see ahead to what the future holds
　　but your knowledge of the present is not clear."　　99

"Down here we see like those with faulty vision
　　who only see," he said, "what's at a distance;
　　this much the sovereign lord grants us here.　　102

When events are close to us, or when they happen,
　　our mind is blank, and were it not for others
　　we would know nothing of your living state.　　105

Thus you can understand how all our knowledge
　　will be completely dead at that time when
　　the door to future things is closed forever."　　108

Then I, moved by regret for what I'd done
　　said, "Now, will you please tell the fallen one
　　his son is still on earth among the living;　　111

and if, when he asked, silence was my answer,
   tell him: while he was speaking, all my thoughts
   were struggling with that point you solved for me."   114

My teacher had begun to call me back,
   so I quickly asked that spirit to reveal
   the names of those who shared the tomb with him.   117

He said, "More than a thousand lie with me,
   the Second Frederick is here and the Cardinal
   is with us. And the rest I shall not mention."   120

His figure disappeared. I made my way
   to the ancient poet, reflecting on those words,
   those words which were prophetic enemies.   123

He moved, and as we went along he said,
   "What troubles you? Why are you so distraught?"
   And I told him all the thoughts that filled my mind.   126

"Be sure your mind retains," the sage commanded,
   "those words you heard pronounced against yourself,
   and listen carefully now." He raised a finger: 129

"When at last you stand in the glow of her sweet ray,
   the one whose splendid eyes see everything,
   from her you'll learn your life's itinerary."   132

Then to the left he turned. Leaving the walls,
   he headed toward the center by a path
   that strikes into a vale, whose stench arose,   135

disgusting us as high up as we were.

NOTES

11–12. *When they return here from Jehoshaphat*: According to
the Old Testament prophet Joel (III, 2, 12), the valley of
Jehoshaphat, situated between Jerusalem and the Mount of
Olives, would be the site of the Last Judgment, when the soul

and the body would be reunited and thus returned to Heaven
or Hell for eternity.

14–15. *Epicurus and his followers*: Epicurus was the Greek
philosopher who in 306 B.C. organized in Athens the philo-
sophical school named after him. The philosophy of the Ep-
icureans taught that the highest good is temporal happiness,
which is to be achieved by the practice of the virtues. In Dante's
time Epicureans were considered heretics because they exalted
temporal happiness, and therefore denied the immortality of
the soul and the afterlife. Epicurus is among the heretics even
though he was a pagan, because he denied the immortality of
the soul, a truth known even to the ancients.

16–18. *As for the question you just put to me*: Dante's question
was in lines 7–8; as for "the wish you are keeping from me"
(18), many critics believe that it was the desire to know whether
Farinata is among the heretics. But surely it is preferable to
assume that the silent wish is rather to know the extent of the
shades' knowledge, i.e., how much of the future they can
foresee and whether they know the present. This "wish,"
which must have begun with Ciacco's prophecy in Canto VI,
will soon be the cause of Dante's silence before Cavalcante,
and will be satisfied by Farinata (100–108).

22–27. *O Tuscan walking through our flaming city*: Having
recognized Dante as a fellow Tuscan, Farinata bids him pause
a moment. Born of an old and respected Florentine family,
Farinata (Manente di Jacopo degli Uberti) took an active role
in the political life of the Commune on the side of the Ghib-
elline party, whose head he became in 1239. He died in 1264,
one year before Dante's birth.

42. *he asked, "And who would your ancestors be?"*: Farinata's
extremely proud character is reflected in these lines. The first
thing noticed by this imposing and disdainful shade is the
Pilgrim's elegance of speech (23), and his first question put to
him, delivered "half-contemptuously," concerns his lineage
(42). His haughtiness is also apparent when he completely
ignores the interruption of Cavalcante (52–72) and begins his
speech again (77) as if nothing had happened. Further, when
Dante asks him "the names of those who shared the tomb

with him" (117), he deigns to give only two names, those of an emperor and a cardinal—whose lineage meets with his approval. Such haughtiness is symptomatic of the basis for Farinata's heresy: intellectual pride. Farinata in life was so self-centered (note his emphasis on "I") and self-assured that he disdained the truth of religion. Cavalcante, too, will reflect a kind of pride in his astonishment that his son is not accompanying the Pilgrim, "If it be great genius / that carries you along" (58–59).

48–51. *I had to scatter them not once but twice*: It happens that the Pilgrim's ancestors (along with other Guelfs) were twice (in 1248 and 1260) driven from the city (note the Pilgrim's appraisal of the action, revealed by his correcting Farinata's term "scatter" to "expel") by Farinata and his kinsmen (along with other Ghibellines), but they returned after both defeats (in 1251 and 1267). Dante's gibe, "an art your men, however, never mastered," refers to the expulsion of the Uberti family and other Ghibellines, who never returned to Florence. See below, n. 84.

53. *a shade appeared, but just down to his chin*: The shade is Cavalcante de' Cavalcanti, a member of an important Florentine family and father of Guido Cavalcanti. (Boccaccio, in his commentary on *The Divine Comedy*, states that both father and son were renowned Epicureans.) Cavalcante's son Guido, born about 1255, was one of the major poets of the day and was Dante's "first friend," as he says in the *Vita nuova*. A renowned thinker, Guido cultivated a highly philosophic poetic style and influenced Dante's own poetry. The Cavalcanti were well known Guelfs, and it was the marriage of Guido to Beatrice, daughter of the Ghibelline Farinata (see above, n. 22–27 and n. 42), that sealed the peace for a time between the two factions. Guido died in August 1300.

63. *the one, perhaps, your Guido held in scorn*: Some commentators, offering a different interpretation of the syntax of these two lines (to make the line mean that Virgil was leading the Pilgrim "to her whom" Guido perhaps held in scorn), believe that it is Beatrice whom Guido scorned. Most believe, however, that the object of Guido's attitude is Virgil. I agree

with the latter critics, but not for the reasons usually offered: that Guido's pride was such that he would not submit to Reason's guidance or that he may have scorned Virgil as a symbol of classicism or of religiosity. The first hypothesis is particularly absurd: no one loved Human Reason more ardently than did Guido Cavalcanti. Perhaps it could be said that Guido, as a skeptic, refused to allow Reason to fulfill its ultimate purpose (according to the teachings of the time): that of leading man to God.

68–72. *What did you say? He* held? *Is he not living*?: The use of the preterit "held" (*ebbe*) is ambiguous and occasions the misunderstanding of the father, who assumes, upon hearing the Pilgrim's words, that his son is now dead. The Pilgrim's silence, following Cavalcante's despairing outcry (68–69), is because he was puzzled by the old man's question: the Pilgrim is not yet aware that, although the souls of the damned can see into the future, they have no knowledge of the present. And this silence confirms Cavalcante's assumption that his son is dead.

Cavalcante's misunderstanding of Dante's use of the past tense, "held," and of his subsequent silence is a part of the aesthetic structure of Canto X, which is based on interruption and misunderstanding. Farinata interrupts the conversation of the Pilgrim and Virgil (22), Cavalcante interrupts Farinata and the Pilgrim (52) and misunderstands the latter's words. Such a structure indicates the self-centeredness and lack of understanding that Dante held to be typical of heretics.

79–81. *But the face of the queen who reigns down here will glow*: Hecate, or Proserpina, the moon goddess, Queen of the Underworld (cf. IX, 44). Farinata makes the prophecy that Dante will know how difficult is the art of returning from exile before fifty months have passed. Dante was first exiled from Florence in January of 1302. The fiftieth month after Farinata's prediction (which, according to the fictional time element of the poem, took place in March of 1300) was May 1304. By this time Dante had attempted repeatedly, together with the other exiles, to return to Florence, and it was in March of 1304 that Cardinal Niccolò da Prato, sent by Benedict XI to Florence to negotiate the return of the exiles, failed in his mission.

82. *and as I hope that you may once more know*: The lofty elegance of Farinata's character is evident in this formal, involved prelude to his request (83–84).

84. *so harsh to my clan in every law they make*: The Uberti, Farinata's family, were excluded, according to Villani, from all pardons conceded to the Ghibellines, including the pardon of 1280, when most of the Ghibellines were permitted to return to Florence.

85–86. *The massacre and butchery*: The hill of Montaperti, on the left bank of the Arbia, a small stream near Siena, was the scene of the fierce battle between the Florentine Guelfs and Ghibellines (September 4, 1260), in which the Guelfs were defeated. Farinata was a leader of the Ghibellines.

88–93. *It was not I . . . But I . . . It was* I: In rebuttal, Farinata states that he was not the only Ghibelline at the battle of Montaperti, and that he had good reason to fight; but that at the Council in Empoli after the victory at Montaperti, when the Ghibellines wanted to plan the destruction of Florence, Farinata was the only Ghibelline to oppose the plan. He proudly points out that the credit for the latter action is his alone, while, on the other hand, he is not willing to accept all the blame for the bloodshed at Montaperti.

100–108. *Down here we see like those with faulty vision*: In answer to the Pilgrim's wish (the "knot" of line 96) to know the shades' capacity for knowledge of the present, Farinata states that, while they have complete knowledge of things past and future, they are ignorant of the present (except, of course, for the news of current events brought them by the new arrivals in Hell, the "others," 104). Even this knowledge will be denied them after the Day of Judgment, when all will become absolute and eternal. The door of the future will be closed (108) and their remembrance of the past will fade away, since there will no longer be any past, present, or future.

119–120. *the Second Frederick . . . , the Cardinal*: The Emperor Frederick II (1194–1250) is in the circle of the Heretics because of the commonly held belief that he was an Epicurean.

Cardinal Ottaviano degli Ubaldini, a Ghibelline, was papal legate in Lombardy and Romagna until his death in 1273. He is reported to have once said: "If I have a soul, I have lost it for the Ghibellines"; it is presumably the doubt concerning the immortality of the soul implied in these words that led Dante to condemn the Cardinal as a heretic.

129–32. *He raised a finger*: The raised finger may indicate Virgil's role of teacher admonishing his student, or he may be pointing "up" to Beatrice, to her "whose splendid eyes see everything" (131). As it happens, however, Beatrice will not be the one to unveil the course of future events to the Pilgrim; that office will be granted to his ancestor Cacciaguida in *Paradise* XVII.

CANTO XI

CONTINUING THEIR WAY within the Sixth Circle, where the heretics are punished, the poets are assailed by a stench rising from the abyss ahead of them which is so strong that they must stop in order to accustom themselves to the odor. They pause beside a tomb whose inscription declares that within is POPE ANASTASIUS. When the Pilgrim expresses his desire to pass the time of waiting profitably, Virgil proceeds to instruct him about the plan of punishments in Hell. Then, seeing that dawn is only two hours away, he urges the Pilgrim on.

We reached the curving brink of a steep bank
   constructed of enormous broken rocks;
   below us was a crueler den of pain.   3

And the disgusting overflow of stench
   the deep abyss was vomiting forced us
   back from the edge. Crouched underneath the lid   6

of some great tomb, I saw it was inscribed:
   "Within lies Anastasius, the pope
   Photinus lured away from the straight path."   9

"Our descent will have to be delayed somewhat
   so that our sense of smell may grow accustomed
   to these vile fumes; then we will not mind them,"   12

my master said. And I: "You will have to find
   some way to keep our time from being wasted."
   "That is precisely what I had in mind,"   15

he said, and then began the lesson: "My son,
   within these boulders' bounds are three more circles,
   concentrically arranged like those above,   18

all tightly packed with souls; and so that, later,
   the sight of them alone will be enough,
   I'll tell you how and why they are imprisoned.   21

All malice has injustice as its end,
   an end achieved by violence or by fraud;
   while both are sins that earn the hate of Heaven,   24

since fraud belongs exclusively to man,
   God hates it more and, therefore, far below,
   the fraudulent are placed and suffer most.   27

In the first of the circles below are all the violent;
   since violence can be used against three persons,
   into three concentric rounds it is divided: 30

violence can be done to God, to self,
   or to one's neighbor—to him or to his goods,
   as my reasoned explanation will make clear.   33

By violent means a man can kill his neighbor
   or wound him grievously; his goods may suffer
   violence by arson, theft, and devastation;   36

so, homicides and those who strike with malice,
   those who destroy and plunder, are all punished
   in the first round, but all in different groups.   39

Man can raise violent hands against himself
   and his own goods; so in the second round,
   paying the debt that never can be paid,   42

are suicides, self-robbers of your world,
   or those who gamble all their wealth away
   and weep up there when they should have rejoiced.   45

One can use violence against the deity
   by heartfelt disbelief and cursing Him,
   or by despising Nature and God's bounty;   48

therefore, the smallest round stamps with its seal
   both Sodom and Cahors and all those souls
   who hate God in their hearts and curse His name.   51

Fraud, that gnaws the conscience of its servants,
  can be used on one who puts his trust in you
  or else on one who has no trust invested.   54

This latter sort seems only to destroy
  the bond of love that Nature gives to man;
  so in the second circle there are nests   57

of hypocrites, flatterers, dabblers in sorcery,
  falsifiers, thieves, and simonists,
  panders, seducers, grafters, and like filth.   60

The former kind of fraud both disregards
  the love Nature enjoys and that extra bond
  between men which creates a special trust;   63

thus, it is in the smallest of the circles,
  at the earth's center, around the throne of Dis,
  that traitors suffer their eternal pain."   66

And I, "Master, your reasoning runs smooth,
  and your explanation certainly makes clear
  the nature of this pit and of its inmates,   69

but what about those in the slimy swamp,
  those driven by the wind, those beat by rain,
  and those who come to blows with harsh refrains?   72

Why are they, too, not punished here inside
  the city of flame, if they have earned God's wrath?
  If they have not, why are they suffering?"   75

And he to me, "Why do you let your thoughts
  stray from the path they are accustomed to?
  Or have I missed the point you have in mind?   78

Have you forgotten how your *Ethics* reads,
  those terms it explicates in such detail:
  the three conditions that the heavens hate,   81

incontinence, malice, and bestiality?
  Do you not remember how incontinence
  offends God least, and merits the least blame?   84

If you will reconsider well this doctrine
   and then recall to mind who those souls were
   suffering pain above, outside the walls,   87

you will clearly see why they are separated
   from these malicious ones, and why God's vengeance
   beats down upon their souls less heavily."   90

"O sun that shines to clear a misty vision,
   such joy is mine when you resolve my doubts
   that doubting pleases me no less than knowing!   93

Go back a little bit once more," I said
   "to where you say that usury offends
   God's goodness, and untie that knot for me."   96

"Philosophy," he said, "and more than once,
   points out to one who reads with understanding
   how Nature takes her course from the Divine   99

Intellect, from its artistic workmanship;
   and if you have your *Physics* well in mind
   you will find, not many pages from the start,   102

how your art too, as best it can, imitates
   Nature, the way an apprentice does his master;
   so your art may be said to be God's grandchild.   105

From Art and Nature man was meant to take
   his daily bread to live—if you recall
   the book of Genesis near the beginning;   108

but the usurer, adopting other means,
   scorns Nature in herself and in her pupil,
   Art—he invests his hope in something else.   111

Now follow me, we should be getting on;
   the Fish are shimmering over the horizon,
   the Wain is now exactly over Caurus,   114

and the passage down the bank is farther on."

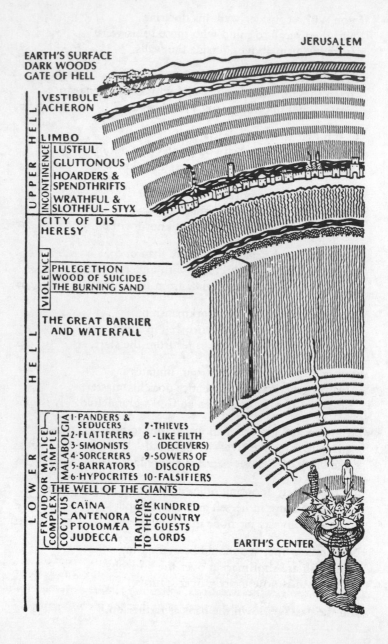

JERUSALEM

EARTH'S SURFACE
DARK WOODS
GATE OF HELL

UPPER HELL

VESTIBULE
ACHERON

LIMBO

INCONTINENCE
LUSTFUL
GLUTTONOUS
HOARDERS &
SPENDTHRIFTS
WRATHFUL &
SLOTHFUL— STYX

CITY OF DIS
HERESY

VIOLENCE
PHLEGETHON
WOOD OF SUICIDES
THE BURNING SAND

HELL

THE GREAT BARRIER
AND WATERFALL

LOWER HELL

FRAUD (OR MALICE)

SIMPLE

MALABOLGIA
1·PANDERS &
SEDUCERS
2·FLATTERERS
3·SIMONISTS
4·SORCERERS
5·BARRATORS
6·HYPOCRITES
7·THIEVES
8 – LIKE FILTH
(DECEIVERS)
9·SOWERS OF
DISCORD
10·FALSIFIERS

THE WELL OF THE GIANTS

COMPLEX

COCYTUS
CAÏNA
ANTENORA
PTOLOMÆA
JUDECCA

TRAITORS TO THEIR
KINDRED
COUNTRY
GUESTS
LORDS

EARTH'S CENTER

NOTES

8–9. *Within lies Anastasius, the pope*: Anastasius II, pope from 496 to 498, was popularly believed for many centuries to be a heretic because, supposedly, he allowed Photinus, a deacon of Thessalonica who followed the heresy of Acacius, to take communion. This heresy denied Christ's divine birth, asserting that He was begotten by a mortal man; thus Anastasius II supposedly revealed his belief in the heretical doctrine. It has been proved, however, that this pope was confused with the Byzantine Emperor Anastasius I (491–518) by Dante's probable sources. Emperor Anastasius was convinced by Photinus to accept the heretical doctrine.

14–15. *to keep our time from being wasted*: Note how the Pilgrim has become a student eager to learn. The *Inferno* consists to a great extent in action; Church doctrine is usually revealed first by the realistic panorama that confronts the student-pilgrim. But as he learns more and more by example (i.e., by action), a method any new student must use at first, he begins to hear more and more philosophical and theological doctrine from his teachers (Virgil, Beatrice, Saint Bernard, chiefly). The preponderance of doctrine increases in the *Purgatory* and grows even greater in the *Paradise*.

23. *by violence or by fraud*: The distinction between Violence and Fraud is taken from Cicero's *De Officiis* I, 13.

50. *both Sodom and Cahors*: Sodom is, of course, the Biblical city (Genesis xviii–xix) destroyed by God for its vicious sexual offenses. Cahors is a city in the south of France that was widely known in the Middle Ages as a thriving seat of usury. So notorious was Cahors for this sin that *Caorsino* came to be synonymous with "usurer" in medieval times. Dante uses the city names to indicate the Sodomites and Usurers, who are punished in the smallest round of Circle VII.

65. *at the earth's center, around the throne of Dis*: Here the name refers to Lucifer. See Canto VIII, 68.

70–75. *but what about those in the slimy swamp*: The sinners about whom Dante questions Virgil are those guilty of Incontinence. Virgil's answer (76–90) is that the Incontinent suffer a lighter punishment because their sins, being without malice, are less offensive to God.

79–84. *Have you forgotten how your* Ethics *reads?*: Virgil says "your *Ethics*" in referring to Aristotle's *Ethica Nicomachea* because he realizes how thoroughly the Pilgrim studied this work (note his reference to "your *Physics*" in line 101).

While the distinction here offered between Incontinence and Malice is based on Aristotle (Book VII, Ch. 8), it should be clear that the overall classification of sins in the *Inferno* is not. Dante's is a twofold system, the main divisions of which may be illustrated as follows:

$$\text{Sins of} \begin{cases} \text{Incontinence} \\ \text{Malice} \end{cases} \begin{cases} \text{through Violence} \\ \text{through Fraud} \end{cases}$$

Aristotle, however, has a threefold classification: Incontinence, Malice, and Bestiality (Book VII, Ch. 1), the third category having no correspondence with the outline offered by Virgil, in spite of many scholars' attempts to identify this with one of the subdivisions mentioned by him. Virgil's mention of the three sins treated by Aristotle is merely a device to introduce the work of the Greek philosopher and to indicate the exact book from which he will quote his distinction between Incontinence and Malice, for the threefold reference is found in the first sentence of Book VII of the *Nicomachean Ethics*.

It should be noted that Virgil makes no reference to the sinners in ante-Inferno, in Limbo, and in the Sixth Circle; nor is it possible to fit their sins into the system presented in this canto: the Pusillanimous, the Unbaptized, and the Heretics are guilty neither of Incontinence nor of Malice. With the last two groups we have to do with wrong beliefs rather than sinful acts; and with the first group it is the failure to act that is being punished. And Dante has indicated the tangential nature of their place within his moral system by the geographical location he has assigned them. The first two groups are not in Hell proper; the Heretics are within a kind of No-Man's-Land, between the sins of Incontinence and those of Malice, within the gates of Dis but at the top of its abyss.

101–105. *and if you have your* Physics *well in mind*: Aristotle's *Physics* (Book II, Part 2) concerns the doctrine that Art imitates Nature. Art, or human industry, is the child of Nature in the sense that it is the use to which man puts Nature, and thus is the grandchild of God. Usurers, who are in the third round of Circle VII, by doing violence to human industry, are, in effect, doing violence to God.

108. *the book of Genesis near the beginning*: Man is to draw upon both Nature and human industry if he would thrive. This principle is stated in Genesis (iii, 17, 19), where man is commanded to work and earn his bread by the sweat of his brow.

113–15. *the Fish are shimmering over the horizon*: Virgil, as always, indicates the time by referring to the stars; how he knows of their position at any given moment Dante does not explain (the stars are not visible from Hell). Pisces, the Fish, is just appearing on the horizon, while the Great Bear, the Wain, is lying completely in the northwestern quadrant of the heavens (Caurus is the Northwest Wind). The next sign of the Zodiac after Pisces is Aries; from Canto I we know that the sun is currently rising in Aries. Each sign of the Zodiac covers about two hours; thus it must be nearly two hours before sunrise.

CANTO XII

THEY DESCEND *the steep slope into the Seventh Circle by means of a great landslide, which was caused when Christ descended into Hell. At the edge of the abyss is the* MINOTAUR, *who presides over the circle of the* VIOLENT *and whose own bestial rage sends him into such a paroxysm of violence that the two travelers are able to run past him without his interference. At the base of the precipice, they see a river of boiling blood, which contains those who have inflicted violence upon others. But before they can reach the river they are intercepted by three fierce* CENTAURS, *whose task it is to keep those who are in the river at their proper depth by shooting arrows at them if they attempt to rise. Virgil explains to one of the centaurs (*CHIRON) *that this journey of the Pilgrim and himself is ordained by God; and he requests him to assign someone to guide the two of them to the ford in the river and carry the Pilgrim across it to the other bank. Chiron gives the task to* NESSUS, *one of the centaurs, who, as he leads them to the river's ford, points out many of the sinners there in the boiling blood.*

Not only was that place, where we had come
    to descend, craggy, but there was something there
    that made the scene appalling to the eye.   3

Like the ruins this side of Trent left by the landslide
    (an earthquake or erosion must have caused it)
    that hit the Adige on its left bank,   6

when, from the mountain's top where the slide began
    to the plain below, the shattered rocks slipped down,
    shaping a path for a difficult descent—   9

so was the slope of our ravine's formation.
    And at the edge, along the shattered chasm,
    there lay stretched out the infamy of Crete: 12

the son conceived in the pretended cow.
    When he saw us he bit into his flesh,
    gone crazy with the fever of his rage.   15

My wise guide cried to him: "Perhaps you think
    you see the Duke of Athens come again,
    who came once in the world to bring your death?   18

Begone, you beast, for this one is not led
    down here by means of clues your sister gave him;
    he comes here only to observe your torments."   21

The way a bull breaks loose the very moment
    he knows he has been dealt the mortal blow,
    and cannot run but jumps and twists and turns,   24

just so I saw the Minotaur perform,
    and my guide, alert, cried out: "Run to the pass!
    While he still writhes with rage, get started down."   27

And so we made our way down through the ruins
    of rocks, which often I felt shift and tilt
    beneath my feet from weight they were not used to.   30

I was deep in thought when he began: "Are you,
    perhaps, thinking about these ruins protected
    by the furious beast I quenched in its own rage?   33

Now let me tell you that the other time
    I came down to the lower part of Hell,
    this rock had not then fallen into ruins;   36

but certainly, if I remember well,
    it was just before the coming of that One
    who took from Hell's first circle the great spoil,   39

that this abyss of stench, from top to bottom
    began to shake, so I thought the universe
    felt love—whereby, some have maintained, the world   42

has more than once renewed itself in chaos.
    That was the moment when this ancient rock
    was split this way—here, and in other places.   45

But now look down the valley. Coming closer
    you will see the river of blood that boils the souls
    of those who through their violence injured others."   48

(Oh, blind cupidity and insane wrath,
    spurring us on through our short life on earth
    to steep us then forever in such misery!)   51

I saw a river—wide, curved like a bow—
    that stretched embracing all the flatland there,
    just as my guide had told me to expect.   54

Between the river and the steep came centaurs,
    galloping in single file, equipped with arrows,
    off hunting as they used to in the world;   57

then, seeing us descend, they all stopped short
    and three of them departed from the ranks
    with bows and arrows ready from their quivers.   60

One of them cried from his distant post: "You there,
    on your way down here, what torture are you seeking?
    Speak where you stand, if not, I draw my bow."   63

And then my master shouted back: "Our answer
    we will give to Chiron when we're at his side;
    as for you, I see you are as rash as ever!"   66

He nudged me, saying: "That one there is Nessus,
    who died from loving lovely Dejanira,
    and made of himself, of his blood, his own revenge.   69

The middle one, who contemplates his chest,
    is great Chiron, who reared and taught Achilles;
    the last is Pholus, known for his drunken wrath.   72

They gallop by the thousands round the ditch,
    shooting at any daring soul emerging
    above the bloody level of his guilt."   75

When we came closer to those agile beasts,
    Chiron drew an arrow, and with its notch
    he parted his beard to both sides of his jaws,   78

and when he had uncovered his great mouth
    he spoke to his companions: "Have you noticed,
    how the one behind moves everything he touches?   81

This is not what a dead man's feet would do!"
    And my good guide, now standing by the torso
    at the point the beast's two natures joined, replied: 84

"He is indeed alive, and so alone
    that I must show him through this dismal valley;
    he travels by necessity, not pleasure.   87

A spirit came, from singing Alleluia,
    to give me this extraordinary mission;
    he is no rogue nor I a criminal spirit.   90

Now, in the name of that power by which I move
    my steps along so difficult a road,
    give us one of your troop to be our guide: 93

to lead us to the ford and, once we are there,
    to carry this one over on his back,
    for he is not a spirit who can fly."   96

Chiron looked over his right breast and said
    to Nessus, "You go, guide them as they ask,
    and if another troop protests, disperse them!"   99

So with this trusted escort we moved on
    along the boiling crimson river's bank,
    where piercing shrieks rose from the boiling souls.   102

There I saw people sunken to their eyelids,
    and the huge centaur explained, "These are the tyrants
    who dealt in bloodshed and plundered wealth.   105

Their tears are paying for their heartless crimes:
    here stand Alexander and fierce Dionysius,
    who weighed down Sicily with years of pain;   108

and there, that forehead smeared with coal-black hair,
　　is Azzolino; the other one, the blond,
　　Opizzo d'Esti, who, and this is true,　　　　　　　111

was killed by his own stepson in your world."
　　With that I looked to Virgil, but he said
　　"Let him instruct you now, don't look to me."　　114

A little farther on, the centaur stopped
　　above some people peering from the blood
　　that came up to their throats. He pointed out　　117

a shade off to one side, alone, and said:
　　"There stands the one who, in God's keep, murdered
　　the heart still dripping blood above the Thames."　120

Then I saw other souls stuck in the river
　　who had their heads and chests above the blood,
　　and I knew the names of many who were there.　　123

The river's blood began decreasing slowly
　　until it cooked the feet and nothing more,
　　and here we found the ford where we could cross.　126

"Just as you see the boiling river here
　　on this side getting shallow gradually,"
　　the centaur said, "I would also have you know　　129

that on the other side the riverbed
　　sinks deeper more and more until it reaches
　　the deepest meeting place where tyrants moan:　　132

it is there that Heaven's justice strikes its blow
　　against Attila, known as the scourge of earth,
　　against Pyrrhus and Sextus; and forever　　　　135

extracts the tears the scalding blood produces
　　from Rinier da Corneto and Rinier Pazzo,
　　whose battlefields were highways where they robbed."　138

Then he turned round and crossed the ford again.

NOTES

4–10. *Like the ruins this side of Trent left by the landslide*: The way down the precipice to the Seventh Circle is here compared to a great landslide, the *Slavini di Marco*, located near Trent in northern Italy; the event, which took place about 883, diverted the Adige River from its course (6). In the *Inferno* the steep, shattered terrain was caused by the earthquake which shook Hell just before Christ descended there.

12–21. *there lay stretched out the infamy of Crete*: The Sins of Violence are also the Sins of Bestiality, and the perfect overseer of this circle is the half-man, half-bull known as the Minotaur. Called the "infamy of Crete," that creature was the result of an act of Violence against Nature (punished in the third round of this circle): Pasiphaë, wife of King Minòs of Crete, conceived an unnatural desire for a bull, which she satisfied by creeping into a wooden cow and having intercourse with the bull. The Cretan labyrinth, designed by Daedalus, was the Minotaur's home. He was finally slain by Theseus (the Duke of Athens, 17) with the help of Ariadne (Pasiphaë's human daughter and, as such, a half-sister to the beast, 20). Note the continued appearance of half-human, half-animal monsters, begun in Canto IX with the Furies.

30. *from weight they were not used to*: Compare VIII, 27–30.

35–36. *I came down to the lower part of Hell*: For the account of Virgil's earlier descent into Hell, see Canto IX, 22–30.

34–45

The "One" (38) is Christ, who, in the Harrowing of Hell, removed to Heaven the souls of the Elect (see Canto IV, 49–63). The great landslide, whose origin is explained by Virgil, is the means the poets use to descend to the Seventh Circle. Appropriately, it is described after the descent of the angel (analogous to Christ's descent) in Canto IX. Christ's life on earth, His descent into Hell, and His Resurrection were given by the grace of God to save mankind from sin and death; and here too—as in Canto IX—Dante the Pilgrim (Everyman), going to God and salvation, is aided on his journey by a phenomenon caused ultimately by the grace of God. The description of the earthquake is the last reference to the Harrowing of Hell in this part of the *Inferno* and closes the drama of the angel's advent, which began in Canto VIII.

41–43. *so I thought the universe / felt love*: According to Empedoclean doctrine, Hate, by destroying pristine harmony (i.e., original chaos), occasions the creation of all things, and Love, by reunifying these disparate elements, re-establishes concord in the universe (see Canto IV, n. 138). Virgil descibes Christ's descent into Hell in the only terms that he could conceive of, i.e., in terms of pagan philosophy.

47–48. *you will see the river of blood that boils the souls*: Phlegethon, the Virgilian river of fire, here one of boiling blood, in which are punished those shades who committed violence against their fellow men (see Canto XI, 34–39). Here are murderers and tyrants; men who through their violent deeds in life caused hot blood to flow are now themselves sunk in flowing, boiling blood.

55–56. *centaurs, / galloping in single file, equipped with arrows*: Like the Minotaur, the Centaurs who guard the murderers and tyrants are men-beasts (half-horse, half-man) and thus appropriate to the sins of violence or bestiality. Some early commentators saw them as representing foreign mercenaries, who had begun to swarm over Italy.

65. *Chiron . . .* : Represented by the ancient poets as chief of the Centaurs, he was particularly noted for his wisdom. In mythology he was the son of Saturn (who temporarily changed himself into a horse to avoid the notice and anger of his wife) and Philyra. Chiron was particularly renowned in medicine and was reputedly the tutor of Achilles (71), Aesculapius, Hercules, and many others. In the *Inferno* he is represented in a reflective pose; and since he is the chief of the Centaurs, it is naturally to him that Virgil addresses himself.

67–69. *That one there is Nessus*: the Centaur who is the first to speak to the two travelers. He is later appointed by Chiron (98–99) to accompany them; he does so, pointing out the var-

ious sinners along the way. Virgil refers to Dejanira, Hercules'
wife, whom Nessus desired. In attempting to rape her, Nessus
was shot by Hercules, but as he died he gave Dejanira a robe
soaked in his blood, which he said would preserve Hercules'
love. Dejanira took it to her husband, whose death it caused,
whereupon the distraught woman hanged herself.

72. *the last is Pholus, known for his drunken wrath*: Little is
known about Pholus except that, during the wedding of Pi
rithous and Hippodamia, when the drunken Centaurs tried to
rape the Lapithaean women, Pholus attempted to rape the bride
herself.

82. This *is not what a dead man's feet would do*: Compare Canto
VIII, 27–30, and lines 29–30 of this canto.

88. *a spirit came, from singing Alleluia*: Beatrice. See Canto
II, 53–74.

107–108. *here stand Alexander and fierce Dionysius*: The first
is possibly Alexander the Great (356–23 B.C.), who is con-
stantly referred to as a cruel and violent man by Orosius,
Dante's chief source of ancient history. But many modern
scholars believe this figure to be Alexander, tyrant of Pherae
(4th cent. B.C.), whose extreme cruelty is recorded by Cicero
and Valerius Maximus. Both of these authors link Alexander
of Pherae with the tyrant Dionysius of Syracuse, mentioned
here, who may be Dionysius the Elder, tyrant of Syracuse
(405–367 B.C.), known for his great cruelty. Or it is possible
that the reference is to his son, Dionysius the Younger, who
followed his father as a tyrant in 367 and who was also ex-
tremely cruel.

110. *Azzolino*: or Ezzelino III da Romano (1194–1259), was
a Ghibelline chief and tyrant of the March of Treviso. He was
notoriously cruel and committed such inhuman atrocities that
he was called a "son of Satan."

111–14. *Opizzo d'Esti . . .* : or Obizzo d'Esti, was Marquis
of Ferrara and of the March of Ancona (1264–93). He was a
cruel tyrant, and it is said that he was murdered by his son
Azzo, although the story is probably untrue. Dante uses the
word *figliastro* (stepson) for his murderer, possibly to show
the unnatural nature of the crime, possibly to suggest that

Azzo's mother had been unfaithful to her husband, having borne the son of another man (*figliastro* in this case would mean "bastard").

113–14. *With that I looked to Virgil*: When the Pilgrim turns to Virgil on hearing Nessus's account of the murder of Obizzo, it was probably with a look of surprise at the reference to a "stepson," since he had thought that Azzo, the son, was the murderer.

Dante the Pilgrim, who had been warned by Virgil not to waste his words (see Canto X), and who kept faithfully to matters necessary for his education in Canto XI, is completely silent here in Canto XII. He is learning to observe more objectively and to ask only the questions that a more advanced pupil might ask, for he has learned much since he plied Virgil with questions in the early cantos. Virgil has already explained to Dante (Canto XI) who the sinners in this round are, and so he has no need to ask. Moreover, he has learned (in Canto X) that Virgil knows even his unspoken questions; and therefore when Nessus begins to guide the poets, Dante does not speak but merely turns with surprise to Virgil, who answers the unspoken question with "*Questi ti sia or primo, e io secondo*" (114), literally "Let him be first for you and I second."

120. *the heart still dripping blood above the Thames*: In 1272 during Holy Mass at the church ("in God's keep") in Viterbo, Guy de Montfort (one of Charles d'Anjou's emissaries), in order to avenge his father's death at the hands of Edward I, King of England, stabbed to death the latter's cousin, Prince Henry, son of Richard, Earl of Cornwall. According to Giovanni Villani, the thirteenth-century chronicler, Henry's heart was placed in a "golden cup . . . above a column at the head of London bridge," where it still drips blood above the Thames (*Cronica* VII, xxxix). The dripping blood signifies that the murder has not yet been avenged.

124–26. *The river's blood began decreasing slowly*: The sinners are sunk in the river to a degree commensurate with the gravity of their crimes; tyrants, whose crimes of violence are directed against both man and his possessions, are sunk deeper than murderers, whose crimes are against men alone. The river is at its shallowest at the point where the poets cross; from this ford, in both directions of its circle, it grows deeper.

134. *against Attila, known as the scourge of earth*: Attila, King of the Huns (A.D. 406?–53), was called the "scourge of God" (*Flagellum Dei*) because of his tyrannical cruelty. He conquered most of Italy in 452, but Pope Leo the Great went out to meet him as he was approaching Rome and persuaded him to turn back.

135. *against Pyrrhus and Sextus*: The first named is probably Pyrrhus (318–272 B.C.), King of Epirus, who fought the Romans three times between 280 and 276 B.C. before they finally defeated him. Some of the commentators (like Boccaccio) favor the theory that Dante is referring to the famous ancestor of the King of Epirus, Pyrrhus the son of Achilles.

"Sextus" is probably the younger son of Pompey the Great. After the murder of Caesar he turned to piracy, causing near famine in Rome by cutting off the grain supply from Africa. He is condemned by Lucan (*Pharsalia* VI, 420–22) as being unworthy of his father. A few commentators believe that Dante is referring to Sextus Tarquinius Superbus, who raped and caused the death of Lucretia, the wife of his cousin.

137–38. *from Rinier da Corneto and Rinier Pazzo*: Two highway robbers famous in Dante's day. The latter, a powerful lord, was excommunicated because he particularly enjoyed robbing the clergy.

139. *Then he turned round and crossed the ford again*: The great speed of the Pilgrim's passage across the Phlegethon is evident when the reader realizes at this point that the river has already been crossed, though no mention of the crossing has been made.

CANTO XIII

NO SOONER are the poets across the Phlegethon than they encounter
a dense forest, from which come wails and moans, and which is
presided over by the hideous harpies—half-woman, half-beast, bird-
like creatures. Virgil tells his ward to break off a branch of one of
the trees; when he does, the tree weeps blood and speaks. In life he
was PIER DELLE VIGNE, chief counselor of Frederick II of Sicily;
but he fell out of favor, was accused unjustly of treachery, and was
imprisoned, whereupon he killed himself. The Pilgrim is over-
whelmed by pity. The sinner also explains how the souls of the
suicides come to this punishment and what will happen to them after
the Last Judgment. Suddenly they are interrupted by the wild sounds
of the hunt, and two naked figures, LANO OF SIENA and GIACOMO
DA SANT' ANDREA, dash across the landscape, shouting at each other,
until one of them hides himself in a thorny bush; immediately a pack
of fierce, black dogs rush in, pounce on the hidden sinner, and rip
his body, carrying away mouthfuls of flesh. The bush, which has
been torn in the process, begins to lament. The two learn that the
cries are those of a Florentine who had hanged himself in his own
home.

Not yet had Nessus reached the other side
   when we were on our way into a forest
   that was not marked by any path at all.   3

No green leaves, but rather black in color,
   no smooth branches, but twisted and entangled,
   no fruit, but thorns of poison bloomed instead.   6

No thick, rough, scrubby home like this exists—
   not even between Cecina and Corneto—
   for those wild beasts that hate the run of farmlands.   9

Here the repulsive Harpies twine their nests,
   who drove the Trojans from the Strophades
   with filthy forecasts of their close disaster. 12

Wide-winged they are, with human necks and faces,
   their feet are clawed, their bellies fat and feathered;
   perched in the trees they shriek their strange laments. 15

"Before we go on farther," my guide began,
   "remember, you are in the second round
   and shall be till we reach the dreadful sand; 18

now look around you carefully and see
   with your own eyes what I will not describe,
   for if I did, you wouldn't believe my words." 21

Around me wails of grief were echoing,
   and I saw no one there to make those sounds;
   bewildered by all this, I had to stop. 24

I think perhaps he thought I might be thinking
   that all the voices coming from those stumps
   belonged to people hiding there from us, 27

and so my teacher said, "If you break off
   a little branch of any of these plants,
   what you are thinking now will break off too." 30

Then slowly raising up my hand a bit
   I snapped the tiny branch of a great thornbush,
   and its trunk cried: "Why are you tearing me?" 33

And when its blood turned dark around the wound,
   it started saying more: "Why do you rip me?
   Have you no sense of pity whatsoever? 36

Men were we once, now we are changed to scrub;
   but even if we had been souls of serpents,
   your hand should have shown more pity than it did." 39

Like a green log burning at one end only,
   sputtering at the other, oozing sap,
   and hissing with the air it forces out, 42

so from that splintered trunk a mixture poured
   of words and blood. I let the branch I held
   fall from my hand and stood there stiff with fear.   45

"O wounded soul," my sage replied to him,
   "if he had only let himself believe
   what he had read in verses I once wrote,   48

he never would have raised his hand against you,
   but the truth itself was so incredible,
   I urged him on to do the thing that grieves me.   51

But tell him who you were; he can make amends,
   and will, by making bloom again your fame
   in the world above, where his return is sure."   54

And the trunk: "So appealing are your lovely words,
   I must reply. Be not displeased if I
   am lured into a little conversation.   57

I am that one who held both of the keys
   that fitted Frederick's heart; I turned them both,
   locking and unlocking, with such finesse   60

that I let few into his confidence.
   I was so faithful to my glorious office,
   I lost not only sleep but life itself.   63

That courtesan who constantly surveyed
   Caesar's household with her adulterous eyes,
   mankind's undoing, the special vice of courts,   66

inflamed the hearts of everyone against me,
   and these, inflamed, inflamed in turn Augustus,
   and my happy honors turned to sad laments.   69

My mind, moved by scornful satisfaction,
   believing death would free me from all scorn,
   made me unjust to me, who was all just.   72

By these strange roots of my own tree I swear
   to you that never once did I break faith
   with my lord, who was so worthy of all honor.   75

If one of you should go back to the world,
  restore the memory of me, who here
  remain cut down by the blow that Envy gave."   78

My poet paused awhile, then said to me,
  "Since he is silent now, don't lose your chance,
  ask him, if there is more you wish to know."   81

"Why don't you keep on questioning," I said,
  "and ask him, for my part, what I would ask,
  for I cannot, such pity chokes my heart."   84

He began again: "That this man may fulfill
  generously what your words cry out for,
  imprisoned soul, may it please you to continue   87

by telling us just how a soul gets bound
  into these knots, and tell us, if you know,
  whether any soul might someday leave his branches."   90

At that the trunk breathed heavily, and then
  the breath changed to a voice that spoke these words:
  "Your question will be answered very briefly.   93

The moment that the violent soul departs
  the body it has torn itself away from,
  Minòs sends it down to the seventh hole;   96

it drops to the wood, not in a place allotted,
  but anywhere that fortune tosses it.
  There, like a grain of spelt, it germinates,   99

soon springs into a sapling, then a wild tree;
  at last the Harpies, feasting on its leaves,
  create its pain, and for the pain an outlet.   102

Like the rest, we shall return to claim our bodies,
  but never again to wear them—wrong it is
  for a man to have again what he once cast off.   105

We shall drag them here and, all along the mournful
  forest, our bodies shall hang forever more,
  each one on a thorn of its own alien shade."   108

We were standing still attentive to the trunk,
    thinking perhaps it might have more to say,
    when we were startled by a rushing sound,   111

such as the hunter hears from where he stands:
    first the boar, then all the chase approaching,
    the crash of hunting dogs and branches smashing,   114

then, to the left of us appeared two shapes
    naked and gashed, fleeing with such rough speed
    they tore away with them the bushes' branches.   117

The one ahead: "Come on, come quickly, Death!"
    The other, who could not keep up the pace,
    screamed, "Lano, your legs were not so nimble   120

when you jousted in the tournament of Toppo!"
    And then, from lack of breath perhaps, he slipped
    into a bush and wrapped himself in thorns.   123

Behind these two the wood was overrun
    by packs of black bitches ravenous and ready,
    like hunting dogs just broken from their chains;   126

they sank their fangs in that poor wretch who hid,
    they ripped him open piece by piece, and then
    ran off with mouthfuls of his wretched limbs.   129

Quickly my escort took me by the hand
    and led me over to the bush that wept
    its vain laments from every bleeding sore: 132

"O Giacomo da Sant' Andrea," it said,
    "what good was it for you to hide in me?
    What fault have I if you led an evil life?"   135

My master, standing over it, inquired:
    "Who were you once that now through many wounds
    breathes a grieving sermon with your blood?"   138

He answered us: "O souls who have just come
    in time to see this unjust mutilation
    that has separated me from all my leaves,   141

gather them round the foot of this sad bush.
   I was from the city that took the Baptist
   in exchange for her first patron, who, for this,   144

swears by his art she will have endless sorrow;
   and were it not that on the Arno's bridge
   some vestige of his image still remains,   147

those citizens who built anew the city
   on the ashes that Attila left behind
   would have accomplished such a task in vain;   150

I turned my home into my hanging place."

NOTES

1–9

The Wood of the Suicides is described in a series of negatives
("No green leaves . . . no smooth branches . . . no fruit"),
and in fact the first three tercets begin with a negative. This
device anticipates the negation inherent in suicide and suggests
the atmosphere in which the action of this canto will move:
mistrust and incredulity.

8–9. *not even between Cecina and Corneto*: The vast swamp-
land known as the "Maremma toscana" lies between the towns
of Cecina and Corneto, which mark its northern and southern
boundaries. The contorted syntax of these lines is in accord
with the aesthetic pattern of the canto (cf. n. 25 and n. 68–72)
and may in particular suggest the rugged topography of the
uncultivated land.

10–15. *Here the repulsive Harpies twine their nests*: The Harpies
were the daughters of Thaumas and Electra. Because of their
malicious deeds they were banished to the Strophades Islands,
where, having encountered Aeneas and his followers from
Troy, they defiled their table and forecast future hardships for

them (11–12)—still another example of half-human, half-bestial creatures.

25. *I think perhaps he thought I might be thinking*: The Pilgrim's "bewildered" (24) state is reflected by the syntax, which imitates, in its own way, the action of a confused mind.

34. *And when its blood turned dark around the wound*: One aesthetic tie between this round and the previous one is the continuation of blood imagery.

47–49. *if he had only let himself believe*: Virgil is referring to that section of the *Aeneid* (III, 22–43) where Aeneas breaks a branch from a shrub, which then begins to pour forth blood; at the same time a voice issues from the ground beneath the shrub, where Polydorus is buried. See Canto XXX, 18.

52–54. *But tell him who you were*: Compare VI, 88–89, and XVI, 82–85.

58–78

Born in the southern Italian town of Capua (c. 1190), Pier delle Vigne studied at Bologna and, having attracted the attention of Frederick II, became attached to his court at Palermo, where he soon became the emperor's most trusted minister ("I . . . held both of the keys / that fitted Frederick's heart," i.e., Pier's counsel of "Yes" opened the emperor's heart and "No" closed it). Around 1248, however, he fell from the emperor's grace and was placed in jail, where he committed suicide. Pier delle Vigne tells how Envy ("that courtesan," 64), ever present at Frederick's court ("Caesar's household," 65), inflamed everyone against him, Frederick ("Augustus," 68) becoming influenced by the attitude of others. The dishonor of the imprisonment and the envisaged self-justification through death led him to take his own life by dashing his head against the prison wall. He concludes by declaring his innocence (73–75) and expressing the desire for re-evaluation of his deeds, which will ensure his earthly fame (76–78).

68–72. *and these, inflamed, inflamed in turn Augustus*: Pier was also a renowned poet of the Sicilian School, which flourished under Frederick's patronage and which is noted for its love of complex conceits and convoluted wordplay. Dante the Poet endows Pier with the type of poetic language for which he was well known (see particularly lines 68 and 72).

84. *for I cannot, such pity chokes my heart*: The Pilgrim feels pity for Pier because of the false accusation that precipitated his fall from favor, not because of the punishment meted out to this shade for having taken his own life. It is a completely different kind of pity from that which Dante felt for Francesca or Ciacco (V and VI). Even Pier himself recognized the justice of his punishment and the sinfulness of his suicide: "My mind . . . made me unjust to me, who was all just" (70–72).

95–108. *the body it has torn itself away from*: Having denied the God-given sanctity of their bodies on earth, in Hell the Suicides are completely denied bodily form; their souls, thrown into this round by Minòs (96) fall at random and sprout like seeds in the same careless way in which they had treated their bodies (97–100). Even after the Last Judgment, when the Suicides, like all the other shades in Hell, will return to earth to reclaim their mortal flesh, each will be denied the use of its body, which will hang "on a thorn of its own alien shade" (103–108).

Part of the *contrapasso* inflicted on these sinners is the physical torment caused by the Harpies, who rend the branches of the trees, causing "pain, and for the pain an outlet" (101–102). It is only when part of the tree or bush is torn or broken that the shade can make sounds—thus the necessity for Dante to break a branch before Pier can speak.

115–21. *then, to the left of us appeared two shapes*: The second group of souls punished here are the Profligates, who did violence to their earthly goods by not valuing them as they should have, just as the Suicides did not value their bodies. They are represented by Lano (120), probably a member of the wealthy Maconi family of Siena, and by Giacomo da Sant' Andrea (133) from Padua. Both had the dubious honor of being incorrigible self-vandalizers who squandered most of their wealth and property. The "tournament of Toppo" (121) recalls the disastrous defeat of the Sienese troops at the hands of the Aretines in 1287 at a river ford near Arezzo. Lano went into this battle to die because he had squandered his fortune; as legend has it, he remained to fight rather than escape on foot (hence Giacomo's reference to his "legs," 120), and was killed.

125–29. *by packs of black bitches ravenous and ready*: These dogs that pursue the Profligates have invited many interpretations (conscience, poverty, ruin and death, remorse, creditors), but I think that they probably represent that violent force which drove the Profligates to their end: they seem to be the dramatization of the act of violence itself. It is violence that distinguishes these Profligates from the Spendthrifts, who are linked with the Misers in the Fourth Circle (Canto VII); these were merely wasteful, not *violent* in their wasting: the figures in the Seventh Circle on the other hand seem to have been driven by violent passions to consume their possessions as fast as possible, perhaps to outdo other profligates in the expense of magnificence. In fact, Giacomo da Sant'Andrea is reported to have set on fire several houses on his estate just for "kicks."

143–50. *I was from the city that took the Baptist*: The identity of this Florentine Suicide remains unknown. The "first patron" of Florence was Mars, the god of war (thus his "art" [145] is warfare); a fragment of his statue was to be found on the Ponte Vecchio ("the Arno's bridge," 146) until 1333. The Anonymous Suicide states that if this fragment of the statue were not still there, then Florence would have been completely destroyed after "those citizens . . . built anew the city / on the ashes that Attila left behind" (148–49). The reference to Attila, king of the Huns, is erroneous; Dante must have intended Totila, king of the Ostrogoths, who razed Florence in the sixth century. The confusion of Attila with Totila was common in the Middle Ages.

The second patron of the city was John the Baptist (143), whose image appeared on the florin, the principal monetary unit of the time. It has been suggested that Florence's change of patron indicates its transformation from a stronghold of martial excellence (under Mars) to one of servile money-making (under the Baptist).

151. *I turned my home into my hanging place*: The Florentine's

anonymity corroborates his symbolic value as a representative of his city. Like the suicides condemned to this round, the city of Florence was killing itself, in Dante's opinion, through its internecine struggles (the revenge of Mars for having been abandoned as patron): she is making of herself a hanging place.

CANTO XIV

THEY COME to the edge of the Wood of the Suicides, where they see before them a stretch of burning sand upon which flames rain enternally and through which a stream of boiling blood is carried in a raised channel formed of rock. There, many groups of tortured souls are on the burning sand; Virgil explains that those lying supine on the ground are the BLASPHEMERS, those crouching are the USURERS, and those wandering aimlessly, never stopping, are the SODOMITES. Representative of the blasphemers is CAPANEUS, who died cursing his god. The Pilgrim questions his guide about the source of the river of boiling blood; Virgil's reply contains the most elaborate symbol in the Inferno, that of the OLD MAN OF CRETE, whose tears are the source of all the rivers in Hell.

The love we both shared for our native city
   moved me to gather up the scattered leaves
   and give them back to the voice that now had faded.   3

We reached the confines of the woods that separate
   the second from the third round. There I saw
   God's justice in its dreadful operation.   6

Now to picture clearly these unheard-of things:
   we arrived to face an open stretch of flatland
   whose soil refused the roots of any plant;   9

the grieving forest made a wreath around it,
   as the sad river of blood enclosed the woods.
   We stopped right here, right at the border line.   12

This wasteland was a dry expanse of sand,
   thick, burning sand, no different from the kind
   that Cato's feet packed down in other times.   15

O just revenge of God! how awesomely
   you should be feared by everyone who reads
   these truths that were revealed to my own eyes!   18

Many separate herds of naked souls I saw,
   all weeping desperately; it seemed each group
   had been assigned a different penalty: 21

some souls were stretched out flat upon their backs,
   others were crouching there all tightly hunched,
   some wandered, never stopping, round and round.   24

Far more there were of those who roamed the sand
   and fewer were the souls stretched out to suffer,
   but their tongues were looser, for the pain was greater.   27

And over all that sandland, a fall of slowly
   raining broad flakes of fire showered steadily
   (a mountain snowstorm on a windless day),   30

like those that Alexander saw descending
   on his troops while crossing India's torrid lands:
   flames falling, floating solid to the ground,   33

and he with all his men began to tread
   the sand so that the burning flames might be
   extinguished one by one before they joined.   36

Here too a never-ending blaze descended,
   kindling the sand like tinder under flint-sparks,
   and in this way the torment there was doubled.   39

Without a moment's rest the rhythmic dance
   of wretched hands went on, this side, that side,
   brushing away the freshly fallen flames.   42

And I: "My master, you who overcome
   all opposition (except for those tough demons
   who came to meet us at the gate of Dis),   45

who is that mighty one that seems unbothered
   by burning, stretched sullen and disdainful there,
   looking as if the rainfall could not tame him?"   48

And that very one, who was quick to notice me
    inquiring of my guide about him, answered:
    "What I was once, alive, I still am, dead!   51

Let Jupiter wear out his smith, from whom
    he seized in anger that sharp thunderbolt
    he hurled, to strike me down, my final day;   54

let him wear out those others, one by one,
    who work the soot-black forge of Mongibello
    (as he shouts, 'Help me, good Vulcan, I need your help,'   57

the way he cried that time at Phlegra's battle),
    and with all his force let him hurl his bolts at me,
    no joy of satisfaction would I give him!"   60

My guide spoke back at him with cutting force,
    (I never heard his voice so strong before):
    "O Capaneus, since your blustering pride   63

will not be stilled, you are made to suffer more:
    no torment other than your rage itself
    could punish your gnawing pride more perfectly."   66

And then he turned a calmer face to me,
    saying, "That was a king, one of the seven
    besieging Thebes; he scorned, and would seem still   69

to go on scorning God and treat him lightly,
    but, as I said to him, he decks his chest
    with ornaments of lavish words that prick him.   72

Now follow me and also pay attention
    not to put your feet upon the burning sand,
    but to keep them well within the wooded line."   75

Without exchanging words we reached a place
    where a narrow stream came gushing from the woods
    (its reddish water still runs fear through me!);   78

like the one that issues from the Bulicame,
    whose waters are shared by prostitutes downstream,
    it wore its way across the desert sand.   81

This river's bed and banks were made of stone,
    so were the tops on both its sides; and then
    I understood this was our way across.   84

"Among the other marvels I have shown you,
    from the time we made our entrance through the gate
    whose threshold welcomes every evil soul,   87

your eyes have not discovered anything
    as remarkable as this stream you see here
    extinguishing the flames above its path."   90

These were my master's words, and I at once
    implored him to provide me with the food
    for which he had given me the appetite.   93

"In the middle of the sea there lies a wasteland,"
    he immediately began, "that is known as Crete,
    under whose king the world knew innocence.   96

There is a mountain there that was called Ida;
    then happy in its verdure and its streams,
    now deserted like an old, discarded thing;   99

Rhea chose it once as a safe cradle
    for her son, and, to conceal his presence better,
    she had her servants scream loud when he cried.   102

In the mountain's core an ancient man stands tall;
    he has his shoulders turned toward Damietta
    and faces Rome as though it were his mirror.   105

His head is fashioned of the finest gold;
    pure silver are his arms and hands and chest;
    from there to where his legs spread, he is brass;   108

the rest of him is all of chosen iron,
    except his right foot which is terra cotta;
    he puts more weight on this foot than the other.   111

Every part of him, except the gold, is broken
    by a fissure dripping tears down to his feet,
    where they collect to erode the cavern's rock;   114

from stone to stone they drain down here, becoming
    rivers: the Acheron, Styx, and Phlegethon,
    then overflow down through this tight canal   117

until they fall to where all falling ends:
    they form Cocytus. What that pool is like
    I need not tell you. You will see, yourself."   120

And I to him: "If this small stream beside us
    has its source, as you have told me, in our world,
    why have we seen it only on this ledge?"   123

And he to me: "You know this place is round,
    and though your journey has been long, circling
    toward the bottom, turning only to the left,   126

you still have not completed a full circle;
    so you should never look surprised, as now,
    if you see something you have not seen before."   129

And I again: "Where, Master, shall we find
    Lethe and Phlegethon? You omit the first
    and say the other forms from the rain of tears."   132

"I am very happy when you question me,"
    he said, "but that the blood-red water boiled
    should answer certainly one of your questions.   135

And Lethe you shall see, but beyond this valley,
    at a place where souls collect to wash themselves
    when penitence has freed them of their guilt.   138

Now it is time to leave this edge of woods,"
    he added. "Be sure you follow close behind me:
    the margins are our road, they do not burn,   141

and all the flames above them are extinguished."

NOTES

   3. *the voice that now had faded*: that of the anonymous Florentine suicide.

   10. *the grieving forest*: the Wood of the grieving Suicides.

15. *that Cato's feet packed down in other times*: Cato of Utica (born 95 B.C.), a friend of Cicero, sided with Pompey in the Roman civil war. After Pompey was defeated at Pharsalia, Cato joined Metellus Scipio in Africa; and when it became apparent that he was about to be captured by Caesar, he killed himself (46 B.C.). The year before his death he led a march across the desert of Libya (recorded by Lucan in the *Pharsalia*)—hence the comparison between the arid plain of the Seventh Circle and the hot desert crossed by Cato.

22–24. *some . . , others . . . , some . . .* : The shades in this third round of the Seventh Circle are divided into three groups: the Blasphemers lie supine on the ground (22), the Usurers are "crouching" (23), and the Sodomites wander, "never stopping" (24). The sand they lie on perhaps suggests the sterility of their acts, just as the black leaves and lack of fruit on the trees in the Wood of the Suicides depicted their perversion of fruitful living.

33–36. *flames falling, floating solid to the ground*: Dante's source was probably Albertus Magnus's *De meteoris*. Albertus refers to an apocryphal letter from Alexander to Aristotle concerning the former's adventures in India. There, Alexander was said to have first encountered a heavy snowfall and later a rain of fire. According to the letter, Alexander had his soldiers trample the snow, but Albertus (and Dante after him) confuses the snow with the fire and has Alexander's legions trampling the flames.

41. *of wretched hands went on, this side, that side*: Note the expression "this side, that side," whose rhythm (in the original: *or quindi, or quinci*) imitates the ceaseless movements of the sinners' hands attempting to brush off the falling flames from their bodies. We will find this same effect also in line 55 ("one by one": *a muta a muta*), line 57 ("Help me . . . I need your help": *aiuta, aiuta*), and even in the next canto, line 84 ("hour after hour": *ad ora ad ora*). In fact, this leitmotiv first appears before the sinners come in view, at the moment when the travelers reach the edge of the burning sand: "We stopped *right here, right* at the border line": *a randa, a randa* (12).

44–45. *those tough demons*: The rebel angels of Canto IX who barred the travelers' entrance to the city of Dis. Note that the Pilgrim, in praising his guide, naively reminds him of his recent difficulty.

51–60. *What I was once, alive, I still am, dead!*: The representative of the Blasphemers is Capaneus, who, as Virgil will explain, was one of the seven kings who assaulted Thebes. Statius describes how Capaneus, when scaling the walls of Thebes, blasphemed against Jove, who then struck him with a thunderbolt (54). Capaneus died with blasphemy on his lips and now, even in Hell, he is able to defy Jove's thunderbolts (59–60). At Phlegra Jove defeated the Titans who attempted to storm Olympus. Vulcan and the Cyclopes, of course, were the manufacturers of the thunderbolts. *Mongibello* (56), the Sicilian name for Mt. Aetna, was supposed to be Vulcan's furnace.

68–69. *one of the seven / besieging Thebes*: Thebes, the capital of Boeotia, was the scene of a great struggle for sovereignty between Eteocles and Polynices, the sons of Oedipus. Adrastus, King of Argos, on Polynices' behalf led an expedition of seven kings (including Capaneus) against Thebes and Eteocles. See the above note, 51–60.

79–80. *like the one that issues from the Bulicame*: Near Viterbo there was a hot spring called the Bulicame, whose sulphurous waters transformed the area into a watering place. Among the inhabitants were many prostitutes, who were required to live in a separate quarter. A special stream channeled the hot spring water through their section, since they were denied use of the public baths. Here Dante compares the stream which flows from the river in Canto XII to the hot, steamy flow channeled for the prostitutes from the Bulicame—whose mineral-rich waters undoubtedly had a reddish cast.

86–87. *from the time we made our entrance through the gate*: The principal gate of Hell. Compare Canto III, 1–11, and Canto VIII, 125–26.

94–119. *In the middle of the sea there lies a wasteland*: The island of Crete is given as the source of Acheron, Styx, and Phlegethon, the joined rivers of Hell whose course eventually leads to the "pool," Cocytus (119), at the bottom of Hell. Crete was probably chosen by Dante because, according to Virgil, it was the birthplace of Trojan—therefore Roman—civilization, the Trojan Aeneas being the founder of Rome (cf. I, 73–75, and II, 13–24). Crete was also at the center of the known world, the continents of Asia, Africa, and Europe. According to mythology, Mt. Ida on Crete was the place chosen by Rhea to protect her infant son, Jupiter, from his father, Saturn, who usually devoured his sons when they were born. Rhea, to keep him from finding Jupiter, "had her servants scream loud when he cried" (102) to drown out the infant's screams.

Within Mt. Ida Dante places the statue of the "Old Man of Crete" (certainly one of the most elaborate symbols in the *Inferno*), with his back to Damietta and gazing toward Rome (104–105). Damietta, an important Egyptian seaport, represents the East, the pagan world; Rome, of course, the modern, Christian world. The figure of the Old Man is drawn from the book of Daniel (II, 32–35), but the symbolism is different, and more nearly (though not absolutely) reflects a poetic symbol utilized by Ovid (*Metamorphoses* I). The head of gold represents the Golden Age of man (that is, in Christian terms, before the Fall). The arms and breast of silver, the trunk of brass, and the legs of iron represent the three declining ages of man. The clay foot (the one made of *terra cotta*) may symbolize the Church, weakened and corrupted by temporal concerns and political power struggles. Through the fissure that cracks every part of the figure but the golden head flow the Old Man's tears, the sins and sorrows of man through all ages except the Golden Age of Innocence. The tears bore their way down through the mountain, and eventually their course forms the rivers of Hell, which are joined, evidently, by tributary streams (as we see here), since they are all circular. The Old Man, imprisoned in the darkness of Mt. Ida, certainly symbolizes from the neck down the fallen state of man due to the original sin in the Garden of Eden. Mt. Ida was once like Eden, "then happy in its verdure and its streams" (98), but now, devastated like man after the Fall, it is a "wasteland"

(94). The fissure, through which flow the tears of sorrow caused by the Fall, represents an imperfection symbolic of original sin.

126. *turning only to the left*: as was pointed out in the note to Canto IX, 132, there are two exceptions to the usual procedure of circling to the left.

134–35. *that the blood-red water boiled*: To the Pilgrim's naive question (130–31) Virgil replies that he should have been able to recognize Phlegethon by its extreme heat. This property of the river is mentioned in the *Aeneid* (VI, 550–51):

> Encircled with a rushing flood of torrential flames Tartarean
> Phlegethon . . .

136–38. *And Lethe you shall see, but beyond this valley*: Dante places Lethe, the River of Forgetfulness, in the Earthly Paradise atop the mountain of Purgatory.

141. *the margins are our road, they do not burn*: The "margins" are the miraculously protected paths which run alongside the stream. See lines 82–84.

CANTO XV

THEY MOVE OUT across the plain of burning sand, walking along the ditchlike edge of the conduit through which the Phlegethon flows, and after they have come some distance from the wood they see a group of souls running toward them. One, BRUNETTO LATINI, a famous Florentine intellectual and Dante's former teacher, recognizes the Pilgrim and leaves his band to walk and talk with him. Brunetto learns the reason for the Pilgrim's journey and offers him a prophecy of the troubles lying in wait for him—an echo of Ciacco's words in Canto VI. Brunetto names some of the others being punished with him (PRISCIAN, FRANCESCO D'ACCORSO, ANDREA DE' MOZZI); but soon, in the distance, he sees a cloud of smoke approaching, which presages a new group, and because he must not associate with them, like a foot-racer Brunetto speeds away to catch up with his own band.

Now one of those stone margins bears us on
    and the river's vapors hover like a shade,
    sheltering the banks and the water from the flames.   3

As the Flemings, living with the constant threat
    of flood tides rushing in between Wissant
    and Bruges, build their dikes to force the sea back;   6

as the Paduans build theirs on the shores of Brenta
    to protect their town and homes before warm weather
    turns Chiarentana's snow to rushing water—   9

so were these walls wĕ walked upon constructed,
    though the engineer, whoever he may have been,
    did not make them as high or thick as those.   2

We had left the wood behind (so far behind,
    by now, that if I had stopped to turn around,
    I am sure it could no longer have been seen)   15

when we saw a troop of souls come hurrying
　　toward us beside the bank, and each of them
　　looked us up and down, as some men look   18

at other men, at night, when the moon is new.
　　They strained their eyebrows, squinting hard at us,
　　as an old tailor might at his needle's eye.   21

Eyed in such a way by this strange crew,
　　I was recognized by one of them, who grabbed
　　my garment's hem and shouted: "How marvelous!"   24

And I, when he reached out his arm toward me,
　　straining my eyes, saw through his face's crust,
　　through his burned features that could not prevent   27

my memory from bringing back his name;
　　and bending my face down to meet with his,
　　I said: "Is this really you, here, Ser Brunetto?"   30

And he: "O my son, may it not displease you
　　if Brunetto Latini lets his troop file on
　　while he walks at your side for a little while."   33

And I: "With all my heart I beg you to,
　　and if you wish me to sit here with you,
　　I will, if my companion does not mind."   36

"My son," he said, "a member of this herd
　　who stops one moment lies one hundred years
　　unable to brush off the wounding flames,   39

so, move on; I shall follow at your hem
　　and then rejoin my family that moves
　　along, lamenting their eternal pain."   42

I did not dare step off the margin-path
　　to walk at his own level but, with head
　　bent low in reverence, I moved along.   45

He began: "What fortune or what destiny
　　leads you down here before your final hour?
　　And who is this one showing you the way?"   48

"Up there above in the bright living life
   before I reached the end of all my years,
   I lost myself in a valley," I replied;   51

"just yesterday at dawn I turned from it.
   This spirit here appeared as I turned back,
   and by this road he guides me home again."   54

He said to me: "Follow your constellation
   and you cannot fail to reach your port of glory,
   not if I saw clearly in the happy life;   57

and if I had not died just when I did,
   I would have cheered you on in all your work,
   seeing how favorable Heaven was to you.   60

But that ungrateful and malignant race
   which descended from the Fiesole of old,
   and still have rock and mountain in their blood,   63

will become, for your good deeds, your enemy—
   and right they are: among the bitter berries
   there's no fit place for the sweet fig to bloom.   66

They have always had the fame of being blind,
   an envious race, proud and avaricious;
   you must not let their ways contaminate you.   69

Your destiny reserves such honors for you:
   both parties shall be hungry to devour you,
   but the grass will not be growing where the goat is.   72

Let the wild beasts of Fiesole make fodder
   of each other, and let them leave the plant untouched
   (so rare it is that one grows in their dung-heap)   75

in which there lives again the holy seed
   of those remaining Romans who survived there
   when this new nest of malice was constructed."   78

"Oh, if all I wished for had been granted,"
   I answered him, "you certainly would not,
   not yet, be banished from our life on earth;   81

my mind is etched (and now my heart is pierced)
    with your kind image, loving and paternal,
    when, living in the world, hour after hour   84

you taught me how man makes himself eternal.
    And while I live my tongue shall always speak
    of my debt to you, and of my gratitude.   87

I will write down what you tell me of my future
    and save it, with another text, to show
    a lady who can interpret, if I can reach her.   90

This much, at least, let me make clear to you:
    if my conscience continues not to blame me,
    I am ready for whatever Fortune wants.   93

This prophecy is not new to my ears,
    and so let Fortune turn her wheel, spinning it
    as she pleases, and the peasant turn his spade."   96

My master, hearing this, looked to the right,
    then, turning round and facing me, he said:
    "He listens well who notes well what he hears."   99

But I did not answer him; I went on talking,
    walking with Ser Brunetto, asking him
    who of his company were most distinguished.   102

And he: "It might be good to know who some are,
    about the rest I feel I should be silent,
    for the time would be too short, there are so many.   105

In brief, let me tell you, all here were clerics
    and respected men of letters of great fame,
    all befouled in the world by one same sin: 108

Priscian is traveling with that wretched crowd
    and Franceso d'Accorso too; and also there,
    if you could have stomached such repugnancy,   111

you might have seen the one the Servant of Servants
    transferred to the Bacchiglione from the Arno
    where his sinfully erected nerves were buried.   114

I would say more, but my walk and conversation
   with you cannot go on, for over there
   I see a new smoke rising from the sand: 117

people approach with whom I must not mingle.
   Remember my *Trésor*, where I live on,
   this is the only thing I ask of you."   120

Then he turned back, and he seemed like one of those
   who run Verona's race across its fields
   to win the green cloth prize, and he was like   123

the winner of the group, not the last one in.

NOTES

1. *Now one of those stone margins bears us on*: Note the use of the present tense. Compare VIII, n. 109–111.

4–6. *As the Flemings, living with the constant threat*: The cities of Wissant, between Boulogne and Calais, and Bruges, in eastern Flanders, were both centers of trade during the thirteenth century. Wissant was an important port city, and Bruges was famous for its extensive trade, especially with Italy.

It is not inconceivable that cities such as these, which counted a considerable number of itinerant tradesmen and sailors among their population, might have had a reputation for sodomy during Dante's time.

7. *as the Paduans build theirs on the shores of Brenta*: Although I know of no evidence that might support the theory that Padua was renowned for sodomy during the Middle Ages, it is perhaps not mere coincidence that in the journals of William Lithgow, a seventeenth-century Scottish (?) traveler and writer, we find reference made to the propensity for sodomy he had noted among the Paduans ("for beastly Sodomy . . . [is] . . . a monstrous filthinesse, and yet to them a pleasant pastime, making songs, and singing sonets of the beauty and pleasure of their Bardassi, or buggered boyes").

9. *turns Chiarentana's snow to rushing water*: The Chia-

rentana is a mountainous district situated north of the Brenta River.

11. *the engineer*: God.

16–114

The sin of sodomy being punished in this round is aesthetically mirrored in much of the imagery of the canto (the way in which the group of sodomites ogle the Pilgrim and Virgil, 17–22), and particularly in the language used by Brunetto Latini. He greets the Pilgrim with the exclamation "How marvelous!" (24), and in the metaphors of his prophecy (61–78), Dante is a "sweet fig" (66), whom "both parties shall be hungry to devour" (71); the next moment he is "grass" to be eaten by a "goat" (72). And it is difficult to be more explicit than Brunetto was in his description of Andrea de' Mozzi, who died in Vicenza, "where his sinfully erected nerves were buried" (114). The imagery used in connection with these scholarly or clerical sodomites should be compared to the more robust imagery used for the ones who were soldiers in Canto XVI, 22–27. The eternal wandering of the sodomites is comparable to the *contrapasso* of the lustful in Canto V, who are forever blown about aimlessly by a wind.

30. *I said: "Is this really you, here, Ser Brunetto?"*: The Pilgrim addresses his fellow Florentine Brunetto Latini (c. 1220–94) with the respectful pronoun form *"voi"* (cf. Dante's use of *"voi"* with Farinata and Cavalcante in Canto X). The reverent tone of Dante's words bespeaks his admiration and affection for the famous Guelf statesman and writer, whose *Trésor* (see below, n. 119–20) and *Tesoretto*, an allegorical poem in Italian, greatly influenced Dante's own life and works. Brunetto was a notary, and Dante accordingly prefixes the title "Ser" to his name. Forced into exile after the Guelf defeat at Montaperti (1260), he remained in France for six years. The Ghibelline defeat at Benevento (1266) ensured his safe return to Florence, where he took an active part in public affairs until his death.

48. *And who is this one showing you the way?*: The Pilgrim fails to answer Brunetto's second question, possibly because naming Virgil, who has become his second "teacher," might offend Brunetto.

51. *I lost myself in a valley*: The "valley" is the "dark wood" of Canto I.

54. *and by this road he guides me home again*: That is, to God, man's true home. In the Middle Ages man's earthly existence was viewed as a pilgrimage, a preparation for the after-life.

61–78. *But that ungrateful and malignant race*: During a Roman power struggle, Catiline fled Rome and found sanctuary for himself and his troops in the originally Etruscan town of Fiesole. After Caesar's successful siege of that city, the survivors of both camps founded Florence, where those of the Roman camp were the elite.

Brunetto prophesies about Florence that both political parties will become Dante's enemies (61–64), for he will be the "sweet fig" (66), among the "bitter berries" (65), who are "an envious race, proud and avaricious" (68). They must hate the plant in which "there lives again the holy seed / of those remaining Romans who survived there . . ." (76–77).

The prophecy, with its condemnation of the current state of Florence (and Italy) and its implied hope of a renascent empire, continues the political theme begun with the speech of the Anonymous Suicide in Canto XIII, and continued in the symbol of the Old Man of Crete in Canto XIV.

68. *an envious race, proud and avaricious*: Envy and pride are always the basis of the sins beyond the walls of Dis. See XXXI, n. 19–127.

85. *you taught me how man makes himself eternal*: Dante expresses his gratitude to Brunetto by saying that it was he who taught him how to become immortal through literary accomplishments.

89–90. *and save it, with another text, to show*: Again (as in X, 130–32), Beatrice is referred to as the one who will reveal to the Pilgrim his future course. She will gloss the earlier prophecies ("another text") of Ciacco (VI, 64–75) and Farinata (X,

79–81), together with the one just related by Brunetto. However, in the *Paradise* this role is given to Dante's ancestor Cacciaguida.

95–96. *let Fortune turn her wheel, . . . / . . . and the peasant turn his spade*: It is as right for Fortune to spin her wheel as it is for the peasant to turn his spade; and the Pilgrim will be as indifferent to the first as to the second.

Could there also be a suggestion in his reference to the peasant's spade of his indifference to those who might attempt to dig up the "plant . . . in which there lives again the holy seed . . ."?

99. *He listens well who notes well what he hears*: Virgil is certainly not rebuking the Pilgrim, as some think (for his supposed indifference to Brunetto's words), but rather praising him for remembering the other prophecies and for believing that they will eventually be interpreted by Beatrice. And surely, if the Pilgrim had considered himself rebuked by his guide, he would not have reacted as he did: "But I did not answer him; I went on talking."

110. *and Francesco d'Accorso*: A celebrated Florentine lawyer (1225–94) who taught law at the University of Bologna and later at Oxford at the request of King Edward I.

112–14. *you might have seen the one the Servant of Servants*: Andrea de' Mozzi was Bishop of Florence from 1287 to 1295, when, by order of Pope Boniface VIII (the "Servant of Servants": i.e., the servant of the servants of God), he was transferred to Vicenza (on the Bacchiglione River), where he died that same year or the next. The early commentators make reference to his naive and inept preaching and to his general stupidity. Dante, by mentioning his "sinfully erected nerves," calls attention to his major weakness: unnatural lust or sodomy. See n. 16–114, above.

119–20. *Remember my* Trésor, *where I live on*: The *Livres du Tresor*, Brunetto's most significant composition, was written during his exile in France, and is an encyclopedic work written in French prose.

123–24. *to win the green cloth prize*: The first prize for the footrace, which was one of the games held annually on the first Sunday of Lent in Verona during the thirteenth century, was a green cloth. Ironically, the Pilgrim's last view of his elderly and dignified teacher is the sight of him, naked, racing off at top speed to catch up with his companions in sin. This image of the race in Verona (which was, appropriately for its aesthetic function in this canto, run naked) prepares the reader for the athletic imagery of the next canto.

CANTO XVI

CONTINUING *through the third round of the Circle of Violence, the Pilgrim hears the distant roar of a waterfall, which grows louder as he and his guide proceed. Suddenly three shades, having recognized him as a Florentine, break from their company and converse with him, all the while circling like a turning wheel. Their spokesman,* JACOPO RUSTICUCCI, *identifies himself and his companions (*GUIDO GUERRA *and* TEGGHIAIO ALDOBRANDINI*) as well-known and honored citizens of Florence, and begs for news of their native city. The three ask to be remembered in the world and then rush off. By this time the sound of the waterfall is so deafening that it almost drowns out speech, and when the poets reach the edge of the precipice, Virgil takes a cord which had been bound around his pupil's waist and tosses it into the abyss. It is a signal, and in response a monstrous form looms up from below, swimming through the air. On this note of suspense, the canto ends.*

Already we were where I could hear the rumbling
   of the water plunging down to the next circle,
   something like the sound of beehives humming,   3

when three shades with one impulse broke away,
   running, from a group of spirits passing us
   beneath the rain of bitter suffering.   6

They were coming toward us shouting with one voice:
   "O you there, stop! From the clothes you wear, you seem
   to be a man from our perverted city."   9

Ah, the wounds I saw covering their limbs,
   some old, some freshly branded by the flames!
   Even now, when I think back to them, I grieve.   12

Their shouts caught the attention of my guide,
   and then he turned to face me, saying, "Wait,
   for these are shades that merit your respect.   15

And were it not the nature of this place
   to rain with piercing flames, I would suggest
   you run toward *them*, for it would be more fitting."   18

When we stopped, they resumed their normal pace
   and when they reached us, then they started circling;
   the three together formed a turning wheel,   21

just like professional wrestlers stripped and oiled,
   eyeing one another for the first, best grip
   before the actual blows and thrusts begin.   24

And circling in this way each kept his face
   pointed up at me, so that their necks and feet
   moved constantly in opposite directions.   27

"And if the misery along these sterile sands,"
   one of them said, "and our charred and peeling flesh
   make us, and what we ask, repulsive to you,   30

let our great wordly fame persuade your heart
   to tell us who you are, how you can walk
   safely with living feet through Hell itself.   33

This one in front, whose footsteps I am treading,
   even though he runs his round naked and skinned,
   was of noble station, more than you may think: 36

he was the grandson of the good Gualdrada;
   his name was Guido Guerra, and in his life
   he accomplished much with counsel and with sword.   39

This other one, who pounds the sand behind me,
   is Tegghiaio Aldobrandi, whose wise voice
   the world would have done well to listen to.   42

And I, who share this post of pain with them,
   was Jacopo Rusticucci, and for sure
   my reluctant wife first drove me to my sin."   45

If I could have been sheltered from the fire,
  I would have thrown myself below with them,
  and I think my guide would have allowed me to;   48

but, as I knew I would be burned and seared,
  my fear won over my first good intention
  that made me want to put my arms around them.   51

And then I spoke: "Repulsion, no, but grief
  for your condition spread throughout my heart
  (and years will pass before it fades away),   54

as soon as my lord here began to speak
  in terms that led me to believe a group
  of such men as yourselves might be approaching.   57

I am from your city, and your honored names
  and your accomplishments I have always heard
  rehearsed, and have rehearsed, myself, with fondness.   60

I leave the bitter gall, and journey toward
  those sweet fruits promised me by my true guide,
  but first I must go down to the very center."   63

"So may your soul remain to guide your body
  for years to come," that same one spoke again,
  "and your fame's light shine after you are gone,   66

tell us if courtesy and valor dwell
  within our city as they used to do,
  or have they both been banished from the place?   69

Guglielmo Borsiere, who joined our painful ranks
  of late, and travels there with our companions,
  has given us reports that make us grieve."   72

"A new breed of people with their sudden wealth
  have stimulated pride and unrestraint
  in you, O Florence, made to weep so soon."   75

These words I shouted with my head strained high,
  and the three below took this to be my answer
  and looked, as if on truth, at one another.   78

"If you always answer questions with such ease,"
   they all spoke up at once, "O happy you,
   to have this gift of ready, open speech;   81

therefore, if you survive these unlit regions
   and return to gaze upon the lovely stars,
   when it pleases you to say 'I was down there,'   84

do not fail to speak of us to living men."
   They broke their man-made wheel and ran away,
   their nimble legs were more like wings in flight.   87

"Amen" could not have been pronounced as quick
   as they were off, and vanished from our sight;
   and then my teacher thought it time to leave.   90

I followed him, and we had not gone far
   before the sound of water was so close
   that if we spoke we hardly heard each other.   93

As that river on the Apennines' left slope,
   first springing from its source at Monte Veso,
   then flowing eastward holding its own course   96

(called Acquacheta at its start above
   before descending to its lower bed
   where, at Forlì, it has another name),   99

reverberates there near San Benedetto
   dell'Alpe (plunging in a single bound),
   where at least a thousand vassals could be housed,   102

so down a single rocky precipice
   we found the tainted waters falling, roaring
   sound loud enough to deafen us in seconds.   105

I wore a cord that fastened round my waist,
   with which I once had thought I might be able
   to catch the leopard with the gaudy skin.   108

As soon as I removed it from my body
   just as my guide commanded me to do,
   I gave it to him looped into a coil.   111

Then taking it and turning to the right,
  he flung it quite a distance past the bank
  and down into the deepness of the pit.   114

"Now surely something strange is going to happen,"
  I thought to myself, "to answer the strange signal
  whose course my master follows with his eyes."   117

How cautious a man must be in company
  with one who can not only see his actions
  but read his mind and understand his thoughts!   120

He spoke: "Soon will rise up what I expect;
  and what you are trying to imagine now
  soon must reveal itself before your eyes."   123

It is always better to hold one's tongue than speak
  a truth that seems a bold-faced lie when uttered,
  since to tell this truth could be embarrassing;   126

but I shall not keep quiet; and by the verses
  of my *Comedy*—so may they be received
  with lasting favor, Reader—I swear to you   129

I saw a figure coming, it was swimming
  through the thick and murky air, up to the top
  (a thing to startle even stalwart hearts),   132

like one returning who has swum below
  to free the anchor that has caught its hooks
  on a reef or something else the sea conceals,   135

spreading out his arms, and doubling up his legs.

NOTES

1–3. *I could hear the rumbling / of the water*: The action of this canto begins and ends with the waterfall of the tributary of the Phlegethon; in the first tercet it is distant, and the Pilgrim hears "something like the sound of beehives humming," but by the end of the canto, when the poets stand beside the precipice, the roaring water is "loud enough to deafen us in seconds" (105).

9. *from our perverted city*: Florence. The three shades in question are all Florentines.

20–45

Dante now comes upon a group of warrior-sodomites, and the language and imagery, though changed, still reflect the sin. Jacopo Rusticucci uses bold, masculine language (in contrast to the delicate and rather precious diction of Brunetto Latini in the previous canto) to question Dante, and to identify himself and his companions (28–45). But the dancelike image of the turning wheel formed by the three shades is perfectly suited to describe these sinners (25–27).

37–39. *he was the grandson of the good Gualdrada*: The good Gualdrada was the daughter of Bellincione Berti of Florence. According to a story well known in medieval Italy, she was married to Guido Guerra IV at the suggestion of the Emperor Otto IV, who had been impressed with her great beauty, wit, and modesty. The legend is discredited by the fact that she married Guido Guerra IV in 1180, twenty years before Otto IV became emperor. Her grandson was the Guido Guerra (1220–72) mentioned here. This Guido was a Guelf leader in several battles, hence his nickname (*guerra*—"war"). His wisdom (*counsel*, 39) is exemplified by his advice to the Florentine Guelfs not to undertake the campaign against Siena in 1260; they ignored his words, and that battle destroyed the Guelf party in Florence.

41–42. *Tegghiaio Aldobrandi*: He, like Guido Guerra, was a leader of the Guelf party in Florence (d. before 1266). He, too, tried to dissuade the Guelfs from attacking the Sienese in 1260; in fact, he was the spokesman for the group of Guelf soldiers headed by Guido Guerra. The fact that his advice was disregarded probably accounts for Dante's saying that "the world would have done well to listen to" his voice.

44–45. *Jacopo Rusticucci*: Little is known of this spokesman for the three Sodomites. He is occasionally mentioned in Florentine records between 1235 and 1266 and was probably a rich merchant. The early Dante commentary of the "Anonimo Fiorentino" relates that he "was a man of the people, of lowly origin, a knight, a valorous and pleasing man." The source also states that his argumentative wife was sent home to her parents.

48. *and I think my guide would have allowed me to*: In essence Virgil gave his consent in lines 16–18.

52–54. *Repulsion, no, but grief*: It is worth noting that Dante once again feels grief (a step removed from pity) for those sinners, presumably because they were Florentines whose ". . . accomplishments I have always heard / rehearsed, and have rehearsed, myself, with fondness" (59–60). They recall the flourishing times of Florence, and Dante is grieved over their suffering.

63. *but first I must go down to the very center*: The "center" is the center of the earth and, consequently, the lowest part of Hell (Cocytus).

70–72. *Guglielmo Borsiere*: Little is known of him except that he must have died about 1300, as is evident from lines 70–71. Boccaccio says that he was a knight of the Court, a matchmaker, and a peacemaker.

73–75. *A new breed of people with their sudden wealth*: Dante attributes the ills of Florence to the infiltration by the rural population of the established Florentine gentry. His rhetorical condemnation of Florence here may be linked with his picture of Profligates (Lano and Giacomo da Sant'Andrea), with the words of the anonymous suicide in Canto XIII, with the symbolism of the Old Man of Crete in Canto XIV, and with Brunetto Latini's prophecy in Canto XV. All suggest the decay of the city and loss of its golden age through violent squandering—personally and socially—of the gifts of God: the perversion of the shades in Circle VII reflects the "perverted city" (9) from which Dante comes.

85. *do not fail to speak of us to living men*: Many of the infernal shades are concerned with their memory on earth, through which they continue to "live." Compare Ciacco's last words to the Pilgrim (VI, 88–89).

94–101. *As that river on the Apennines' left slope*: Dante compares the descent of the tributary of the Phlegethon River in Hell with the plummeting fall of the Montone River near the San Benedetto dell'Alpe monastery. Evidently, in Dante's time the river was called the Acquacheta as far as Forlì, where it became the Montone. Today the entire river is known as the Montone.

102. *where at least a thousand vassals could be housed*: According to Boccaccio one of the Conti Guidi, who ruled over this region, had planned to construct, near the waterfall, lodgings for a large number of his vassals; he died, however, before his plan could be put into effect.

If this sudden allusion to something so irrelevant, dropped, in passing, at the end of a long description of the course of a river, should seem puzzling, the reader need only remember the reference in Canto XIV (79–81) to the stream issuing from the Bulicame, whose waters, we are told, were shared by prostitutes.

106–108. *I wore a cord that fastened round my waist*: There are many interpretations for the cord that Virgil takes from the Pilgrim and throws over the edge of the steep. Some have seen in this passage evidence that Dante the Poet became a Franciscan friar, the cord being a sign of that order. However that may be, I feel that the cord here has a purely symbolic meaning. It represents self-confidence; for with that cord, he tells us here, he had once thought he could catch the leopard (whom we met in Canto I). Thus he would be deliberately confessing here the weakness of foolish self-confidence. It is at the command of his guide, Reason, that he frees himself of the cord, to rely on him fully in the coming encounter with Fraud. Fraud, personified by the monster Geryon, is naturally attracted by this symbol of confidence and comes swimming to the top; but against Reason, Fraud cannot prevail. The Pilgrim will now go without a cord until Cato in Purgatory instructs him to gird himself with a reed in order to be able to ascend the Mount of Purgatory (*Purgatory* I); the reed symbolizes humility, the opposite of self-confidence, and another step forward in the growth of the Pilgrim.

The mention of the leopard (108) at the moment when the Pilgrim is about to enter into a new division (the third and final one) of Hell is to me clear evidence that of the three great beasts belonging to the "nowhere" landscape of Canto I, it is the leopard that reigns over this last division, where Fraud is punished (some commentators believe that the leopard reigns over the circles of the Incontinent).

CANTO XVII

THE BEAST that had been seen approaching at the end of the last canto is the horrible monster GERYON; his face is appealing like that of an honest man, but his body ends in a scorpionlike stinger. He perches on the edge of the abyss and Virgil advises his ward, who has noticed new groups of sinners squatting on the fiery sand, to learn who they are, while he makes arrangements with Geryon for the descent. The sinners are the USURERS, unrecognizable except by the crests on the moneybags hanging about their necks, which identify them as members of the GIANFIGLIAZZI, UBRIACHI, and SCROVEGNI families. The Pilgrim listens to one of them briefly but soon returns to find his master sitting on Geryon's back. After he conquers his fear and mounts, too, the monster begins the slow, spiraling descent into the Eighth Circle.

"And now, behold the beast with pointed tail
    that passes mountains, annulling walls and weapons,
    behold the one that makes the whole world stink!"   3

These were the words I heard my master say
    as he signaled for the beast to come ashore,
    up close to where the rocky levee ends.   6

And that repulsive spectacle of fraud
    floated close, maneuvering head and chest
    on to the shore, but his tail he let hang free.   9

His face was the face of any honest man,
    it shone with such a look of benediction;
    and all the rest of him was serpentine;   12

his two clawed paws were hairy to the armpits,
    his back and all his belly and both flanks
    were painted arabesques and curlicues: 15

the Turks and Tartars never made a fabric
  with richer colors intricately woven,
  nor were such complex webs spun by Arachne.   18

As sometimes fishing boats are seen ashore,
  part fixed in sand and part still in the water;
  and as the beaver, living in the land   21

of drunken Germans, squats to catch his prey,
  just so that beast, the worst of beasts, hung waiting
  on the bank that bounds the stretch of sand in stone.   24

In the void beyond he exercised his tail,
  twitching and twisting-up the venomed fork
  that armed its tip just like a scorpion's stinger.   27

My leader said: "Now we must turn aside
  a little from our path, in the direction
  of that malignant beast that lies in wait."   30

Then we stepped off our path down to the right
  and moved ten paces straight across the brink
  to keep the sand and flames at a safe distance.   33

And when we stood by Geryon's side, I noticed,
  a little farther on, some people crouched
  in the sand quite close to the edge of emptiness.   36

Just then my master spoke: "So you may have
  a knowledge of this round that is complete,"
  he said, "go and see their torment for yourself.   39

But let your conversation there be brief;
  while you are gone I shall speak to this one
  and ask him for the loan of his strong back."   42

So I continued walking, all alone,
  along the seventh circle's outer edge
  to where the group of sufferers were sitting.   45

The pain was bursting from their eyes; their hands
  went scurrying up and down to give protection
  here from the flames, there from the burning sands.   48

They were, in fact, like a dog in summertime
  busy, now with his paw, now with his snout,
  tormented by the fleas and flies that bite him.   51

I carefully examined several faces
  among this group caught in the raining flames
  and did not know a soul, but I observed   54

that around each sinner's neck a pouch was hung,
  each of a different color, with a coat of arms,
  and fixed on these they seemed to feast their eyes.   57

And while I looked about among the crowd,
  I saw something in blue on a yellow purse
  that had the face and bearing of a lion;   60

and while my eyes continued their inspection
  I saw another purse as red as blood
  exhibiting a goose more white than butter.   63

And one who had a blue sow, pregnant-looking,
  stamped on the whiteness of his moneybag
  asked me: "What are you doing in this pit?   66

Get out of here! And since you're still alive,
  I'll tell you that my neighbor Vitaliano
  will come to take his seat on my left side.   69

Among these Florentines I sit, one Paduan:
  time after time they fill my ears with blasts
  of shouting: 'Send us down the sovereign knight   72

who will come bearing three goats on his pouch.' "
  As final comment he stuck out his tongue—
  as far out as an ox licking its nose.   75

And I, afraid my staying there much longer
  might anger the one who warned me to be brief,
  turned my back on these frustrated sinners.   78

I found my guide already sitting high
  upon the back of that fierce animal;
  he said: "And now, take courage and be strong.   81

From now on we descend by stairs like these.
  Get on up front. I want to ride behind,
  to be between you and the dangerous tail."   84

A man who feels the shivers of a fever
  coming on, his nails already dead of color,
  will tremble at the mere sight of cool shade;   87

I was that man when I had heard his words.
  But then I felt those stabs of shame that make
  a servant brave before his valorous master.   90

As I squirmed around on those enormous shoulders,
  I wanted to cry out, "Hold on to me,"
  but I had no voice to second my desire.   93

Then he who once before had helped me out
  when I was threatened put his arms around me
  as soon as I was settled, and held me tight;   96

and then he cried: "Now Geryon, start moving,
  descend with gentle motion, circling wide:
  remember you are carrying living weight."   99

Just as a boat slips back away from shore,
  back slowly, more and more, he left that pier;
  and when he felt himself all clear in space,   102

to where his breast had been he swung his tail
  and stretched it undulating like an eel,
  as with his paws he gathered in the air.   105

I doubt if Phaëthon feared more—that time
  he dropped the sun-reins of his father's chariot
  and burned the streak of sky we see today—   108

or if poor Icarus did—feeling his sides
  unfeathering as the wax began to melt,
  his father shouting: "Wrong, your course is wrong"—   111

than I had when I felt myself in air
  and saw on every side nothing but air;
  only the beast I sat upon was there.   114

He moves along slowly, and swimming slowly,
    descends a spiral path—but I know this
    only from a breeze ahead and one below;   117

I hear now on my right the whirlpool roar
    with hideous sound beneath us on the ground;
    at this I stretch my neck to look below,   120

but leaning out soon made me more afraid,
    for I heard moaning there and saw the flames;
    trembling, I cowered back, tightening my legs,   123

and I saw then what I had not before:
    the spiral path of our descent to torment
    closing in on us, it seemed, from every side.   126

As the falcon on the wing for many hours,
    having found no prey, and having seen no signal
    (so that his falconer sighs: "Oh, he falls already"),   129

descends, worn out, circling a hundred times
    (instead of swooping down), settling at some distance
    from his master, perched in anger and disdain,   132

so Geryon brought us down to the bottom
    at the foot of the jagged cliff, almost against it,
    and once he got our bodies off his back,   135

he shot off like a shaft shot from a bowstring.

NOTES

1–27

In classical mythology Geryon was a three-bodied giant who ruled Spain and was slain by Hercules in the course of his Twelve Labors. Here in the *Inferno* he is the personification of Fraud, whose face ("the face of any honest man," 10) deceives his victim long enough for his poisoned tail ("like a scorpion's stinger," 27) to strike. The triune nature of Geryon, as Dante presents him here, is an adaptation and modification of passages from the Bible (Revelation IX, 7–11) and from Pliny (*Historia naturalis* VIII, 30). Because of his threefold nature Geryon assumes a place alongside other Dantean monsters that are perversions of the Trinity.

We should note that, by answering Virgil's signal, Geryon himself has been deceived: the symbol of Fraud has been defrauded.

16–17. *the Turks and Tartars never made a fabric*: The Tartars and the Turks were often considered the best weavers of the Middle Ages. Their highly colored and ornate fabrics were very fashionable and much in demand.

18. *nor were such complex webs spun by Arachne*: Arachne, a legendary Lydian maiden, was so skilled in the art of weaving that she challenged the goddess Minerva to a contest. Minerva, furious because her opponent's cloth was perfect, tore it to shreds; Arachne hanged herself, but Minerva loosened the rope, turning it into a web and Arachne into a spider.

21–22. *and as the beaver*: According to medieval bestiaries the beaver, squatting on the ground at the edge of the water, catches fish with its tail hanging in the water. Geryon assumes a similar pose.

31. *down to the right*: See IX, n. 132.

35–36. *some people crouched*: The Usurers, described in Canto XI as those who scorn "Nature in herself and in her pupil, / Art" (110–111), are the last group in the third round of the Seventh Circle. Having introduced Geryon, Dante the Poet then brings in these sinners, who, crouching very close to the edge of the abyss, serve as the artistic and spatial connection between the sins of Violence and those of Fraud. Similarly Geryon, who at this moment rests partly in Circle Seven and partly (his tail, 25) in Circle Eight, links the two sins. Earlier Dante effected the transition from Incontinence to Violence via the sin of Anger (crossing the river of the Wrathful); here he accomplishes the transition to Fraud through Usury.

48. *here from the flames, there from the burning sands*: Compare

the similar construction used to describe the movement of the Sodomites' hands (XIV, 41).

55–56. *that around each sinner's neck a pouch was hung*: The identity (or rather the family connection) of the usurers, who "feast their eyes" (57) on the purses dangling from their necks, is revealed to the Pilgrim by the different coats of arms visible on the pouches. Apparently the usurers are unrecognizable through facial characteristics because their total concern with their material goods has caused them to lose their individuality. The yellow purse with the blue lion (59–60) indicates the Gianfigliazzi family of Florence; the red purse with the "goose more white than butter" (62–63), the Ubriachi family, also of Florence; the one with the "blue sow, pregnant-looking" (64–65), the Scrovegni family of Padua.

68–69. *I'll tell you that my neighbor Vitaliano*: Referred to as "my neighbor" by one of the Scrovegni family, the Vitaliano who will join the company of usurers is undoubtedly from Padua, but beyond this nothing certain is known.

70. *Among these Florentines I sit, one Paduan*: The theme of the decadence and materialism of Florence is continued to the very edge of the circle of Violence.

72–73. *Send us down the sovereign knight*: This is generally considered to be Giovanni Buiamonte, one of the Florentine Becchi family. He took part in public affairs and was honored with the title of "knight" in 1298. His business, money-lending, made his family one of the wealthiest in Florence; however, after going bankrupt he died in abject poverty in 1310.

82. *From now on we descend by stairs like these*: The Pilgrim and Virgil will descend from the Eighth Circle to the Ninth with the help of the giant Antaeus (XXXI, 130–45), and from Cocytus to Purgatory by climbing up Lucifer's legs (XXXIV, 70–87). By the phrase "stairs like these," Virgil is simply alluding to methods of getting from one circle to another, methods as terrifying as their ride on Geryon's back.

106–108. *I doubt if Phaëthon feared more—that time*: Phaëthon, son of Apollo, was told by Epaphus that Apollo was not his father. Thereupon the boy begged Apollo to allow him to drive the Chariot of the Sun for one day to prove himself the offspring of the God of the Sun. The request was granted, but Phaëthon, unable to control the Chariot, let loose the reins. The Chariot raced wildly through the heavens, burning the "streak of sky" which today we call the Milky Way, and at one point dipping so close to the Earth that it almost set the planet afire. But Jupiter, hearing the Earth's prayer, killed the youthful charioteer with a thunderbolt and hurled him to his death. The story was familiar to Dante from Ovid's *Metamorphoses* II, 1–324.

109–11. *or if poor Icarus did—feeling his sides*: Daedalus, father of Icarus, in order to escape from Crete, fashioned wings for himself and his son. Because the feathers were fastened with wax, Daedalus warned his son not to fly too close to the sun. But Icarus, ignoring his father's words, flew too high, and when the sun had melted the wax, he plunged to his death in the Aegean Sea.

The stories of Phaëthon and Icarus were often used in the Middle Ages as examples of pride, thus giving more support to the theory that Pride and Envy underlie the sins punished in Lower Hell. See Canto XXXI, n. 19–127.

136. *he shot off like a shaft shot from a bowstring*: The metaphor used to describe Geryon's rapid departure (arrow shot from the bow) is the same as that found in the description of Phlegyas's swift approach in Canto VIII (13–15). The wrath of the swiftly moving Phlegyas was clearly indicated by his words; I think we are meant to assume that the mute Geryon was also moved by anger (and had been sulking all the while), because he had been outwitted by Reason. Moreover, in the description of Geryon's descent there are two indications of his hostility: the falcon to whose descending movement his own is compared shows anger and disdain (132) toward his master; and the way in which Geryon lands, bringing the Pilgrim and his guide almost up against the jagged cliff (134), suggests a futile final gesture of sulkiness.

CANTO XVIII

THE PILGRIM describes the view he had of the Eighth Circle of Hell while descending through the air on Geryon's back. It consists of ten stone ravines called Malebolge (Evil Pockets), and across each bolgia is an arching bridge. When the poets find themselves on the edge of the first ravine they see two lines of naked sinners, walking in opposite directions. In one are the PIMPS or PANDERERS, and among them the Pilgrim recongizes VENEDICO CACCIANEMICO; in the other are the SEDUCERS, among whom Virgil points out JASON. As the two move toward the next bolgia, they are assailed by a terrible stench, for here the FLATTERERS are immersed in excrement. Among them are ALESSIO INTERMINEI and THAÏS the whore.

There is a place in Hell called Malebolge,
   cut out of stone the color of iron ore,
   just like the circling cliff that walls it in.   3

Right at the center of this evil plain
   there yawns a very wide, deep well, whose structure
   I will talk of when the place itself is reached.   6

That belt of land remaining, then, runs round
   between the well and cliff, and all this space
   is divided into ten descending valleys,   9

just like a ground-plan for successive moats
   that in concentric circles bind their center
   and serve to protect the ramparts of the castle.   12

This was the surface image they presented;
   and as bridges from a castle's portal stretch
   from moat to moat to reach the farthest bank,   15

LOWER
HELL

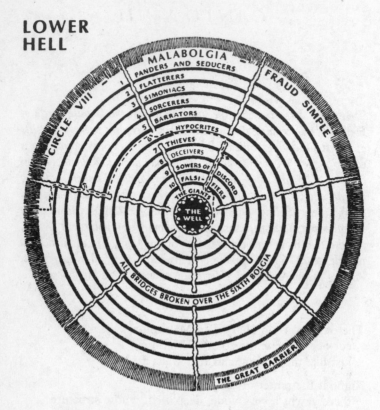

THE SINS OF THE LEOPARD

so, from the great cliff's base, jut spokes of rock,
　　crossing from bank to bank, intersecting ditches
　　until the pit's hub cuts them off from meeting.　　18

This is the place in which we found ourselves,
　　once shaken from the back of Geryon.
　　The poet turned to the left, I walked behind him.　　21

There, on our right, I saw new suffering souls,
　　new means of torture, and new torturers,
　　crammed into the depths of the first ditch.　　24

Two files of naked souls walked on the bottom,
　　the ones on our side faced us as they passed,
　　the others moved as we did but more quickly.　　27

The Romans, too, in the year of the Jubilee
　　took measures to accommodate the throngs
　　that had to come and go across their bridge:　　30

they fixed it so on one side all were looking
　　at the castle, and were walking to St. Peter's;
　　on the other, they were moving toward the mount.　　33

On both sides, up along the deadly rock,
　　I saw horned devils with enormous whips
　　lashing the backs of shades with cruel delight.　　36

Ah, how they made them skip and lift their heels
　　at the very first crack of the whip! Not one of them
　　dared pause to take a second or a third!　　39

As I walked on my eyes met with the glance
　　of one down there; I murmured to myself:
　　"I know this face from somewhere, I am sure."　　42

And so I stopped to study him more closely;
　　my leader also stopped, and was so kind
　　as to allow me to retrace my steps;　　45

and that whipped soul thought he would hide from me
　　by lowering his face—which did no good.
　　I said, "O you, there, with your head bent low,　　48

if the features of your shade do not deceive me,
  you are Venedico Caccianemico, I'm sure.
  How did you get yourself in such a pickle?"   51

'I'm not so keen on answering," he said,
  "but I feel I must; your plain talk is compelling,
  it makes me think of old times in the world.   54

I was the one who coaxed Ghisolabella
  to serve the lusty wishes of the Marquis,
  no matter how the sordid tale is told;   57

I'm not the only Bolognese who weeps here—
  hardly! This place is packed with us; in fact,
  there are more of us here than there are living tongues, 60

between Savena and Reno, saying 'Sipa';
  I call on your own memory as witness:
  remember we have avaricious hearts."   63

Just at that point a devil let him have
  the feel of his tailed whip and cried: "Move on,
  you pimp, you can't cash in on women here!"   66

I turned and hurried to rejoin my guide;
  we walked a few more steps and then we reached
  the rocky bridge that juts out from the bank.   69

We had no difficulty climbing up,
  and turning right, along the jagged ridge,
  we left those shades to their eternal circlings.   72

When we were where the ditch yawned wide below
  the ridge, to make a passage for the scourged,
  my guide said: "Stop and stand where you can see   75

these other misbegotten souls, whose faces
  you could not see before, for they were moving
  in the same direction we were, over there."   78

So from the ancient bridge we viewed the train
  that hurried toward us along the other tract—
  kept moving, like the first, by stinging whips.   81

And the good master, without my asking him,
  said, "Look at that imposing one approaching,
  who does not shed a single tear of pain: 84

what majesty he still maintains down there!
  He is Jason, who by courage and sharp wits,
  fleeced the Colchians of their golden ram.   87

He later journeyed through the isle of Lemnos,
  whose bold and heartless females, earlier,
  had slaughtered every male upon the island;   90

there with his words of love, and loving looks,
  he succceded in deceiving young Hypsipyle,
  who had in turn deceived the other women.   93

He left her there, with child, and all alone:
  such sin condemns him to such punishment,
  and Medea, too, gets her revenge on him.   96

With him go all deceivers of this type,
  and let this be enough to know concerning
  the first valley and the souls locked in its jaws."   99

We were already where the narrow ridge
  begins to cross the second bank, to make it
  an abutment for another ditch's arch.   102

Now we could hear the shades in the next pouch
  whimpering, making snorting grunting sounds.
  and sounds of blows, slapping with open palms.   105

From a steaming stench below, the banks were coated
  with a slimy mold that stuck to them like glue,
  disgusting to behold and worse to smell.   108

The bottom was so hollowed out of sight,
  we saw it only when we climbed the arch
  and looked down from the bridge's highest point: 111

there we were, and from where I stood I saw
  souls in the ditch plunged into excrement
  that might well have been flushed from our latrines;   114

my eyes were searching hard along the bottom,
and I saw somebody's head so smirched with shit,
you could not tell if he were priest or layman.   117

He shouted up: "Why do you feast your eyes
on me more than these other dirty beasts?"
And I replied: "Because, remembering well,   120

I've seen you with your hair dry once or twice.
You are Alessio Interminei from Lucca;
that's why I stare at you more than the rest."   123

He beat his slimy forehead as he answered:
"I am stuck down here by all those flatteries
that rolled unceasing off my tongue up there."   126

He finished speaking, and my guide began:
"Lean out a little more, look hard down there
so you can get a good look at the face   129

of that repulsive and disheveled tramp
scratching herself with shitty fingernails,
spreading her legs while squatting up and down: 132

it is Thaïs the whore, who gave this answer
to her lover when he asked: 'Am I very worthy
of your thanks?': 'Very? Nay, incredibly so!'   135

I think our eyes have had their fill of this."

NOTES

1–20. *There is a place in Hell called Malebolge*: This detailed
description of the Eighth Circle with its ten ditches (*Malebolge*)
may surprise the reader, coming as it does before the Pilgrim
has as much as landed at the edge of its beginning. Are we
supposed to imagine we are hearing the voice of Dante the
Poet supplying us with information that the Pilgrim himself
could not have known? Surely not: Dante the Poet never in-
tervenes for such practical (and inartistic) considerations. It is
the Pilgrim who offers the description of the Eighth Circle,

as he has seen it from the air, when descending in a slow gyre on Geryon's back (see XVII, 115–26). The picture presented here can be only an aerial view.

26–27. *the ones on our side faced us as they passed*: The first *bolgia* accommodates two classes of sinners, each filing by rapidly, but in separate directions. The Pimps are those walking toward the Pilgrim and his guide; the Seducers go in the same direction as the Pilgrim.

28–33. *The Romans, too, in the year of the Jubilee*: Dante compares the movement of the sinners in the First *Bolgia* to that of the many pilgrims who, having come to Rome for the Jubilee in 1300, were herded across the bridge, half going toward the Castel Sant'Angelo and St. Peter's and the other half going toward Monte Giordano (the "mount," 33), a small knoll on the opposite side of the Tiber River.

50–57. *Venedico Caccianemico*: This person (born c. 1228) was head of the Guelfs in Bologna from 1260 to 1297; he was at various times *podestà* (mayor) of Pistoia, Modena, Imola, and Milan. He was accused of, among other things, murdering his cousin, but he is placed in this *bolgia* because, according to popular report, he acted as a procurer, turning his own sister, Ghisolabella, over to the Marquis of Este (either Obizzo II or his son, Azzo VIII) to curry favor.

51. *How did you get yourself in such a pickle*: Dante is undoubtedly punning on the word *salse* (pickle), which characterizes the torments suffered in this *bolgia*, and also is the name of a certain ravine (a *bolgia*, if you will) near Bologna (Venedico's city) into which the bodies of criminals were thrown.

61. *saying "Sipa"*: Venedico reveals that he is not the only Bolognese punished in this *bolgia* and further states that there are more pimps here from that city than there are present-day inhabitants of the region between the Savena and Reno rivers (i.e., Bolognese), indicated by the word *sipa*, dialect for *si*, "yes." Compare XXXIII, 80, and note.

86–96. *He is Jason, who by courage and sharp wits*: Jason, leader of the Argonauts, when a child, had been deprived of the throne of Iolcus by his half-brother Pelias. When Jason grew up, Pelias promised him the kingdom if he could secure the

golden fleece of King Aeëtes of Colchis. Jason agreed to make
the attempt, and on the way to Colchis stopped at Lemnos,
where he seduced and abandoned Hypsipyle (92), the daughter
of the King of Lemnos. At Colchis King Aeëtes agreed to give
Jason the fleece if he would yoke two fire-breathing oxen to
a plow and sow the teeth of the dragon that guarded the fleece.
Medea (96), who was a sorceress and the daughter of the king,
fell in love with Jason and with magic helped him fulfill her
father's conditions and obtain the fleece. The two returned to
Greece, where Jason married her, but later he fell in love with
Creusa, daughter of Creon, King of Corinth, and deserted
Medea to marry her. Medea, mad with rage, killed Creusa by
sending her a poisoned coat as a wedding gift, and then mur-
dered her own children; Jason himself died of grief.

Hypsipyle "deceived the other women" (93) of Lemnos by
swearing that she had slain her father, Thoas, the King, when
the Lemnian women massacred all the males on that island.
Instead she hid him, saving his life.

104–105. *whimpering, making snorting grunting sounds*: The
sinners found in the excrement of the Second *Bolgia* are the
Flatterers. Note the "teeming" nature of the language, differ-
ent from that of the first *bolgia*, a change indicative of the
nature of the sin of flattery and its punishment.

122. *You are Alessio Interminei from Lucca*: The Interminei
family was prominent in the White Party at Lucca. But of
Alessio almost nothing is known save that his name is recorded
in several documents of the second half of the thirteenth cen-
tury, the last in 1295, when apparently he was still alive.

135. *Very, nay, incredibly so!*: This Thaïs is not the historical
person by the same name (the most famous courtesan of all time)
but a character in Terence's *Eunuchus*. Dante was probably un-
familiar with the play, but he knew of this Thaïs from Cicero's
De amicitia, where her reply to her lover is presented as an exam-
ple of the exaggeration used by flatterers. In the play a lover
sends Thaïs a slave, and later sends a servant to inquire if he
is worthy of her thanks. Dante attributes the exaggerated re-
ply, "Very, nay, incredibly so!" to Thaïs, although in the play
it is the servant Gnatho who thus exaggerates her response.

CANTO XIX

FROM THE BRIDGE *above the* Third *Bolgia can be seen a rocky landscape below filled with holes, from each of which protrude a sinner's legs and feet; flames dance across their soles. When the Pilgrim expresses curiosity about a particular pair of twitching legs, Virgil carries him down into the bolgia so that the Pilgrim himself may question the sinner. The legs belong to* POPE NICHOLAS III, *who astounds the Pilgrim by mistaking him for* BONIFACE VIII, *the next pope, who, as soon as he dies, will fall to the same hole, thereby pushing Nicholas farther down. He predicts that soon after Boniface,* POPE CLEMENT V *will come, stuffing both himself and Boniface still deeper. To Nicholas's rather rhetoric-filled speech the Pilgrim responds with equally high language, inveighing against the* SIMON- ISTS, *the evil churchmen who are punished here. Virgil is much pleased with his pupil and, lifting him in an affectionate embrace, he carries him to the top of the arch above the next* bolgia.

O Simon Magus! O scum that followed him!
   Those things of God that rightly should be wed
   to holiness, you, rapacious creatures,   3

for the price of gold and silver, prostitute.
   Now, in your honor, I must sound my trumpet
   for here in the third pouch is where you dwell.   6

We had already climbed to see this tomb,
   and were standing high above it on the bridge,
   exactly at the mid-point of the ditch.   9

O Highest Wisdom, how you demonstrate
   your art in Heaven, on earth, and here in Hell!
   How justly does your power make awards!   12

I saw along the sides and on the bottom
　　the livid-colored rock all full of holes;
　　all were the same in size, and each was round.　　15

To me they seemed no wider and no deeper
　　than those inside my lovely San Giovanni,
　　in which the priest would stand or baptize from;　　18

and one of these, not many years ago,
　　I smashed for someone who was drowning in it:
　　let this be mankind's picture of the truth!　　21

From the mouth of every hole were sticking out
　　a single sinner's feet, and then the legs
　　up to the calf—the rest was stuffed inside.　　24

The soles of every sinner's feet were flaming;
　　their naked legs were twitching frenziedly—
　　they would have broken any chain or rope.　　27

Just as a flame will only move along
　　an object's oily outer peel, so here
　　the fire slid from heel to toe and back.　　30

"Who is that one, Master, that angry wretch,
　　who is writhing more than any of his comrades,"
　　I asked, "the one licked by a redder flame?"　　33

And he to me, "If you want to be carried down
　　along that lower bank to where he is,
　　you can ask him who he is and why he's here."　　36

And I, "My pleasure is what pleases you:
　　you are my lord, you know that from your will
　　I would not swerve. You even know my thoughts."　　39

When we reached the fourth bank, we began to turn
　　and, keeping to the left, made our way down
　　to the bottom of the holed and narrow ditch.　　42

The good guide did not drop me from his side
　　until he brought me to the broken rock
　　of that one who was fretting with his shanks.　　45

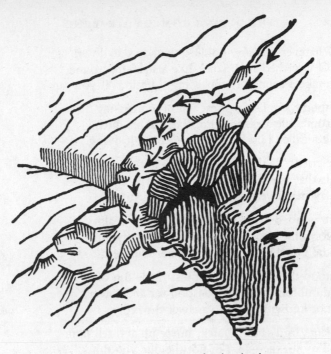

Bridge over Bolgia 3, showing path taken by the poets

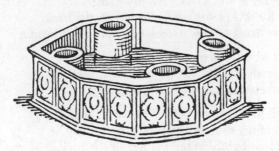

Font in the Baptistery at Pisa, showing the "holes" made for the priests to stand in or baptize from.

"Whatever you are, holding your upside down,
   O wretched soul, stuck like a stake in ground,
   make a sound or something," I said, "if you can."   48

I stood there like a priest who is confessing
   some vile assassin who, fixed in his ditch,
   has called him back again to put off dying.   51

He cried: "Is that *you*, here, already, upright?
   Is that you here already upright, Boniface?
   By many years the book has lied to me!   54

Are you fed up so soon with all that wealth
   for which you did not fear to take by guile
   the Lovely Lady, then tear her asunder?"   57

I stood there like a person just made fun of,
   dumbfounded by a question for an answer,
   not knowing how to answer the reply.   60

Then Virgil said: "Quick, hurry up and tell him:
   'I'm not the one, I'm not the one you think!' "
   And I answered just the way he told me to.   63

The spirit heard, and twisted both his feet,
   then, sighing with a grieving, tearful voice,
   he said: "Well then, what do you want of me?   66

If it concerns you so to learn my name
   that for this reason you came down the bank,
   know that I once was dressed in the great mantle.   69

But actually I was the she-bear's son,
   so greedy to advance my cubs, that wealth
   I pocketed in life, and here, myself.   72

Beneath my head are pushed down all the others
   who came, sinning in simony, before me,
   squeezed tightly in the fissures of the rock.   75

I, in my turn, shall join the rest below
   as soon as *he* comes, the one I thought you were
   when, all too quick, I put my question to you.   78

But already my feet have baked a longer time
   (and I have been stuck upside-down like this)
   than he will stay here planted with feet aflame: 81

soon after him shall come one from the West,
   a lawless shepherd, one whose fouler deeds
   make him a fitting cover for us both.   84

He shall be another Jason, like the one
   in Maccabees: just as his king was pliant,
   so France's king shall soften to this priest."   87

I do not know, perhaps I was too bold here,
   but I answered him in tune with his own words:
   "Well, tell me now: what was the sum of money   90

that holy Peter had to pay our Lord
   before He gave the keys into his keeping?
   Certainly He asked no more than 'Follow me.'   93

Nor did Peter or the rest extort gold coins
   or silver from Matthias when he was picked
   to fill the place the evil one had lost.   96

So stay stuck there, for you are rightly punished,
   and guard with care the money wrongly gained
   that made you stand courageous against Charles.   99

And were it not for the reverence I have
   for those highest of all keys that you once held
   in the happy life—if this did not restrain me,   102

I would use even harsher words than these,
   for your avarice brings grief upon the world,
   crushing the good, exalting the depraved.   105

You shepherds it was the Evangelist had in mind
   when the vision came to him of her who sits
   upon the waters playing whore with kings: 108

that one who with the seven heads was born
   and from her ten horns managed to draw strength
   so long as virtue was her bridegroom's joy.   111

You have built yourselves a God of gold and silver!
  How do you differ from the idolator,
  except he worships one, you worship hundreds?   114

O Constantine, what evil did you sire,
  not by your conversion, but by the dower
  that the first wealthy Father got from you!"   117

And while I sang these very notes to him,
  his big flat feet kicked fiercely out of anger,
  —or perhaps it was his conscience gnawing him.   120

I think my master liked what I was saying,
  for all the while he smiled and was intent
  on hearing the ring of truly spoken words.   123

Then he took hold of me with both his arms,
  and when he had me firm against his breast,
  he climbed back up the path he had come down.   126

He did not tire of the weight clasped tight to him,
  but brought me to the top of the bridge's arch,
  the one that joins the fourth bank to the fifth.   129

And here he gently set his burden down—
  gently, for the ridge, so steep and rugged,
  would have been hard even for goats to cross.   132

From there another valley opened to me.

NOTES

1–6

As related in Acts (viii: 9–24), Simon the magician, having observed the descent of the Holy Spirit upon the Apostles John and Peter, desired to purchase this power for himself. Whereupon Peter harshly admonished him for even thinking that the gift of God might be bought. Derived from this sorcerer's name, the word "simony" refers to those offenses involving the sale or fraudulent possession of ecclesiastical offices.

Note the dramatic effect achieved by the opening six-line invective following immediately upon the quiet words of Virgil with which Canto XVIII closed, and followed immediately by the calm tone of the narrative with which we might have expected the canto to open. The emotional force of this apostrophe (the words certainly are those of Dante the Poet, for the Pilgrim could neither have known what sin is being punished in the Third *Bolgia*, to which he has not as yet been formally introduced, nor could he have consciously thought in terms of the originator of the sin) has no equal in the *Inferno*; the initial position of the outburst in the canto shocks the reader and prepares him to read with greater awareness, while its passion is intended to arouse his hatred for the sin a priori.

4. *for the price of gold and silver, prostitute*: In spite of the fact that the opening invective seems to make a clear break between this canto and the previous one, the connection is aesthetically achieved through the image of prostitution. Thus the final figure of Canto XVIII, Thaïs the whore, provides the link to the simonists, who prostitute "those things of God . . . for the price of gold and silver" (2–4). Other echoes of this image are found in this canto: see 55–57, 108.

5–6. *Now, in your honor, I must sound my trumpet*: Dante, in announcing the nature of the sin being punished in the Third *Bolgia*, is comparing himself to the medieval town-crier whose announcements were preceded by a blast from his trumpet.

10–12. *O Highest Wisdom, how you demonstrate*: Again Dante the Poet interrupts his narrative, this time to praise the workings of Divine Justice (as yet unobserved in this canto!). The rapid succession of the interruptive apostrophes enhances the effectiveness of Dante's moral indignation at the sin of simony.

21. *let this be mankind's picture of the truth*: Most commentators interpret these lines as an attempt on Dante's part to exonerate himself from the charge of sacrilege, which technically could have been leveled at him in consequence of this (obviously humanitarian) act. But surely the interpolation of

such a highly personal element, completely irrelevant to the aesthetic structure of the canto, was not Dante's intention. Rather, he considered the breakage of a baptismal implement as a symbol of the practice of Simony, though the former was done out of love and the latter out of lust for material gain. Dante, then, by incorporating this simile hoped to reveal to his reader the true nature of Simony: an act that results in the destruction of Christ's Church, symbolized by the Font.

25. *The soles of every sinner's feet were flaming*: Just as the Simonists' perversion of the Church is symbolized by their "perverted" immersion in holes resembling baptismal fonts, so their "baptism" is perverted: instead of the head being moistened with water, the feet are "baptized" with oil and fire.

45. *of that one who was fretting with his shanks*: Note the pejorative word shanks (*zanche*) applied to the conspicuous legs of Nicholas. The only other appearance of this word in *The Divine Comedy* is in Canto XXXIV, 79, where it is used to refer to the legs of Lucifer.

48. *"make a sound or something," I said, "if you can"*: Confronted with the grotesque spectacle of two gesticulating legs, Dante the Pilgrim addresses them in a manner that certainly reveals his confused, uncertain state of mind. His invocation, "Whatever you are," reveals his doubts concerning the "human" nature of the soul. The closing imperative, "make a sound . . . if you can," suggests his belief that the object in front of him may not be able even to do that.

53. *Is that you here already upright, Boniface?*: From the foreknowledge granted to the infernal shades, the speaker knows that Pope Boniface VIII, upon his death in 1303, will take his place in that very receptacle wherein he himself is now being tormented. The Pilgrim's voice, so close at hand, has caused the sinner to believe that his successor has arrived unexpectedly before his time (three years, in fact) and, consequently, that the Divine Plan of Events, the Book of Fate (54), has lied to him.

Having obtained the abdication of Pope Celestine V, Boniface gained the support of Charles II of Naples and thus was assured of his election to the papacy (1294). In addition to misusing the Church's influence in his dealings with Charles, Boniface VIII freely distributed ecclesiastical offices among his family and confidants. As early as 1300 he was plotting the destruction of the Whites, the Florentine political faction to which Dante belonged (cf. VI, 67–69). Thus, he was ultimately responsible for the Poet's exile in 1302, which is mentioned in a "prophetic" passage in the *Paradise*, XVII, 49–51.

57. *the Lovely Lady*: the Church.

67–72. *If it concerns you so to learn my name*: Gian Gaetano degli Orsini (literally, "of the little bears," hence the designation "she-bear's son," and the reference to "my cubs") became Pope Nicholas III in 1277. As a cardinal he won renown for his integrity; however, in the short three years between ascent to the papal throne and his death he became notorious for his simoniacal practices. He furthered his dynastic aspirations by the ecclesiastical advancement of many relatives, the acquisition of lands, the channeling of public power into the hands of his kinsmen, and the arrangement of political marriages with other ruling families of Europe.

The famous pun in line 72 signifies Nicholas's *contrapasso*: as he "pocketed" wealth in life, in Hell he himself is in a "pocket."

74. *sinning in simony*: The Italian verb *simoneggiare* (here used in the gerund by Nicholas III—"sinning in simony"), was invented by Dante, doubtless to anticipate the parallel form *puttaneggiando* ("playing whore"), 108, employed by the Pilgrim.

77. *as soon as* he *comes, the one I thought you were*: Boniface VIII. See above, n. 53.

82–84. *soon after him shall come one from the West*: Pope Clement V of Gascony, upon his death in 1314, will join Nicholas and Boniface in eternal torment. In exchange for his election to the papacy, Clement promised to engage in numerous secret intrigues with Philip the Fair, King of France. In Philip's hands he was no more than a puppet, constrained by his pledges to carry out the king's devious plans, among them the suppression and plunder of the Templars. During

Clement's rule the Holy See was transferred from Rome to Avignon.

85–87. *He shall be another Jason, like the one*: Having obtained the high priesthood of the Jews by bribing King Antiochus of Syria, Jason neglected the sacrifices and sanctuary of the Temple and introduced Greek modes of life into his community. As Jason had fraudulently acquired his position, so had Menelaus, who offered more money to the king, supplanted Jason (II Maccabees iv:7–27). As Jason obtained his office from King Antiochus fraudulently, so shall Clement acquire his from Philip.

94–96. *Nor did Peter or the rest extort gold coins*: After the treachery and subsequent expulsion of Judas, the apostles cast lots in order to replenish their number. Thus, by the will of God, not through monetary payment, was Matthias elected to the vacated post (Acts i:15–26).

98–99. *and guard with care the money wrongly gained*: The thirteenth-century Florentine chronicler Giovanni Villani alludes to a plot against Charles d'Anjou, King of Naples and Sicily, promoted by Nicholas III and supported by the "money wrongly gained" of Michael Palaeologus, Emperor of Greece. The pope transferred his aid and influence to Giovanni da Procida in Sicily, who, it is supposed, was a motive force behind the Sicilian Vespers, a bloody insurrection in which the Sicilian people liberated themselves from French domination.

106–11. *You shepherds it was the Evangelist had in mind*: Saint John the Evangelist relates his vision of the dissolute Imperial City of Rome. To Dante, she "who sits / upon the waters" represents the Church, which has been corrupted by the simoniacal activities of many popes (the "shepherds" of the Church). The seven heads symbolize the seven Holy Sacraments; the ten horns represent the Ten Commandments.

115–17. *O Constantine, what evil did you sire*: Constantine the Great, Emperor of Rome (306–337), was converted to Christianity in the year 312. Having conquered the eastern Mediterranean lands, he transferred the capital of the Roman Empire to Constantinople (330). This move, according to tradition, stemmed from Constantine's decision to place the western part of the empire under the jurisdiction of the Church in order to repay Pope Sylvester ("the first wealthy Father") for healing him of leprosy. The so-called "Donation of Constantine," though it was proved in the fifteenth century to be a complete fabrication on the part of the clergy, was universally accepted as the truth in the Middle Ages. Dante the Pilgrim reflects this tradition in his sad apostrophe to the individual who first would have introduced wealth to the Church and who, unknowingly, would be ultimately responsible for its present corruption. Compare *De monarchia* III, 10.

The entire *Divine Comedy* is, of course, the story of the Pilgrim's learning process and spiritual development, and here in *Inferno* XIX Dante has chosen to present us with a picture of that process in miniature. Virgil tells the Pilgrim that he will carry him to the bottom of the *bolgia* so that he can learn for himself about the sinner who has stirred his curiosity (36). And the Pilgrim does learn; Nicholas becomes his teacher, describing his sin and his punishment and announcing the next two popes, who will come after him to push him deeper into his hole. The Pilgrim also learns from the lofty tone of Nicholas's discourse, and responds, for the first time in the *Inferno*, with a full-fledged rhetorical "speech":

> I do not know, perhaps I was too bold here,
>> but I answered him in tune with his own words:
>>> (88–89)

The last part of the "speech," moreover, is aimed not just at Nicholas, but at all the Simonists in this *bolgia*, a fact signified by the change in the Italian text from the singular pronoun *tu*, used when Dante is speaking only to Nicholas, to the plural pronoun *voi* from line 104 on. Dante has not only learned the nature of the sin of simony, but he recognizes that the sin is more important than is an individual sinner like Nicholas. And just as Dante the Poet had opened the canto with an authorial apostrophe-invective against Simon Magus, so Dante the Pilgrim, having reached the Poet's state of knowledge, ends the segment dealing with the Simonists with an apostrophe-invective against Constantine. Thus the Pilgrim's learning process is aesthetically "imitated" in his speech—beginning with his speechlessness.

Virgil is quite pleased by the Pilgrim's accomplishments and he takes him "with both his arms, / and when he had [him] firm against his breast, / he climbed back up the path he had come down" (124–26). When Virgil carried his ward down into the *bolgia*, he clasped him to his side (43), but now he carries him up against his breast, showing his pleasure, and bringing the circle of movement to a close.

That Dante the Poet set great importance on his Pilgrim's learning thoroughly the base nature of simony is evident not only from the didactic invectives within the canto, but also from the way the picture of the Simonists in their holes is recalled in the final canto of the *Inferno* (XXXIV, 88–90): after the two travelers have completed their journey along a portion of Lucifer's huge body, during which they have passed the midpoint of the earth, Dante pauses and looks up to see the raised legs of Lucifer protruding from the crevice in which he is frozen, like a magnification of the legs of Nicholas. Just as Nicholas defrauded God's Church, so Lucifer tried to defraud God himself.

CANTO XX

IN THE FOURTH Bolgia *they see a group of shades weeping as they walk slowly along the valley; they are the SOOTHSAYERS and their heads are twisted completely around so that their hair flows down their fronts and their tears flow down to their buttocks. Virgil points out many of them, including AMPHIARAUS, TIRESIAS, ARUNS, and MANTO. It was Manto who first inhabited the site of Virgil's home city of Mantua, and the poet gives a long description of the city's founding, after which he names more of the condemned soothsayers: EURYPYLUS, MICHAEL SCOT, GUIDO BONATTI, and AS-DENTE.*

Now I must turn strange torments into verse
   to form the matter of the twentieth canto
   of the first chant, the one about the damned.   3

Already I was where I could look down
   into the depths of the ditch: I saw its floor
   was wet with anguished tears shed by the sinners,   6

and I saw people in the valley's circle,
   silent, weeping, walking at a litany pace
   the way processions push along in our world.   9

And when my gaze moved down below their faces,
   I saw all were incredibly distorted,
   the chin was not above the chest, the neck   12

was twisted—their faces looked down on their backs;
   they had to move ahead by moving backward,
   for they never saw what was ahead of them.   15

Perhaps there was a case of someone once
   in a palsy fit becoming so distorted,
   but none that *I* know of! I doubt there could be!   18

So may God grant you, Reader, benefit
    from reading of my poem, just ask yourself
    how I could keep my eyes dry when, close by,   21

I saw the image of our human form
    so twisted—the tears their eyes were shedding
    streamed down to wet their buttocks at the cleft.   24

Indeed I did weep, as I leaned my body
    against a jut of rugged rock. My guide:
    "So you are still like all the other fools?   27

In this place piety lives when pity is dead,
    for who could be more wicked than that man
    who tries to bend divine will to his own!   30

Lift your head up, lift it, see him for whom
    the earth split wide before the Thebans' eyes,
    while they all shouted, 'Where are you rushing off to,   33

Amphiaraus? Why do you quit the war?'
    He kept on rushing downward through the gap
    until Minòs, who gets them all, got him.   36

You see how he has made his back his chest:
    because he wished to see too far ahead,
    he sees behind and walks a backward track.   39

Behold Tiresias, who changed his looks:
    from a man he turned himself into a woman,
    transforming all his body, part for part;   42

then later on he had to take the wand
    and strike once more those two snakes making love
    before he could get back his virile parts.   45

Backing up to this one's chest comes Aruns,
    who, in the hills of Luni, worked by peasants
    of Carrara dwelling in the valley's plain,   48

lived in white marble cut into a cave,
    and from this site, where nothing blocked his view,
    he could observe the sea and stars with ease.   51

And that one, with her hair loose, flowing back
   to cover both her breasts you cannot see,
   and with her hairy parts in front behind her,   54

was Manto, who had searched through many lands
   before she came to dwell where I was born;
   now let me tell you something of her story.   57

When her father had departed from the living,
   and Bacchus' sacred city fell enslaved,
   she wandered through the world for many years.   60

High in fair Italy there spreads a lake,
   beneath the mountains bounding Germany
   beyond the Tyrol, known as Lake Benaco;   63

by a thousand streams and more, I think, the Alps
   are bathed from Garda to the Val Camonica
   with the waters flowing down into that lake;   66

at its center is a place where all three bishops
   of Trent and Brescia and Verona could,
   if they would ever visit there, say Mass;   69

Peschiera sits, a handsome well-built fortress,
   to ward off Brescians and the Bergamese,
   along the lowest point of that lake's shore,   72

where all the water that Benaco's basin
   cannot hold must overflow to make a stream
   that winds its way through countrysides of green;   75

but when the water starts to flow, its name
   is not Benaco but Mencio, all the way
   to Governol, where it falls into the Po;   78

but before its course is run it strikes a lowland,
   on which it spreads and turns into a marsh
   that can become unbearable in summer.   81

Passing this place one day the savage virgin
   saw land that lay in the center of the mire,
   untilled and empty of inhabitants.   84

There, to escape all human intercourse,
  she stopped to practice magic with her servants;
  there she lived, and there she left her corpse.   87

Later on, the men who lived around there gathered
  on that very spot, for it was well protected
  by the bog that girded it on every side.   90

They built a city over her dead bones,
  and for her, the first to choose that place, they named it
  Mantua, without recourse to sorcery.   93

Once, there were far more people living there,
  before the foolish Casalodi listened
  to the fraudulent advice of Pinamonte.   96

And so, I warn you, should you ever hear
  my city's origin told otherwise,
  let no false tales adulterate the truth."   99

And I replied: "Master, your explanations
  are truth for me, winning my faith entirely;
  any others would be just like burned-out coals.   102

But speak to me of these shades passing by,
  if you see anyone that is worth noting;
  for now my mind is set on only that."   105

He said: "That one, whose beard flows from his cheeks
  and settles on his back and makes it dark,
  was (when the war stripped Greece of all its males,   108

so that the few there were still rocked in cradles)
  an augur who, with Calchas, called the moment
  to cut the first ship's cable free at Aulis: 111

he is Eurypylus. I sang his story
  this way, somewhere in my high tragedy:
  you should know where—you know it, every line.   114

That other one, whose thighs are scarcely fleshed,
  was Michael Scot, who most assuredly
  knew every trick of magic fraudulence.   117

See there Guido Bonatti; see Asdente,
  who wishes now he had been more devoted
  to making shoes—too late now for repentance.   120

And see those wretched hags who traded in
  needle, spindle, shuttle, for fortune-telling,
  and cast their spells with image-dolls and potions.   123

Now come along. Cain with his thorn-bush straddles
  the confines of both hemispheres already
  and dips into the waves below Seville;   126

and the moon last night already was at full;
  and you should well remember that at times
  when you were lost in the dark wood she helped you."   129

And we were moving all the time he spoke.

NOTES

1-3. *Now I must turn strange torments into verse*: This canto
has the most prosaic opening of all those in the *Inferno*. And
the second part (61–99) contains the prosaic description of the
founding of Mantua. Perhaps this undramatic canto is meant
to serve as a rest for the reader from the action-filled cantos
with their elaborate poetic openings that have preceded (and
that will follow). Also, the prosaic nature of this canto, with
its stress on facts and the truth, may be a device to entice the
reader to suspend his disbelief and accept the truth of the
fantastic cantos to come—in which Dante will always be at
pains to emphasize the "truthful" nature of the fiction.

15. *for they never saw what was ahead of them*: Note the ap-
propriate nature of the punishment: the augurs, who, when
living, looked into the future, are here in Hell denied any
forward vision. See lines 38–39.

28. *In this place piety lives when pity is dead*: In the original
there is a play on words: the word *pietà* means both "piety"
and "pity."

The Pilgrim has once again felt pity for the torments of the sinners, and Virgil rebukes him with some exasperation. This rebuke is the climax of the important theme of the Pilgrim's pity. Compare V, 138–42; VI, 58–59, etc.

34–36. *Amphiaraus? Why do you quit the war?*: Amphiaraus was a seer, and one of the seven kings who led the expedition against Thebes (see XIV, 68–69). He foresaw that he would die during the siege, and to avoid his fate he hid himself so that he would not have to fight. But his wife, Eriphyle, revealed his hiding place to Polynices, and Amphiaraus was forced to go to battle. He met his death when the earth opened up and swallowed him. Dante's source was Statius's *Thebaid* VII and VIII.

40–45. *Behold Tiresias, who changed his looks*: Tiresias was the famous soothsayer of Thebes referred to by Ovid (*Metamorphoses* III, 316–38). According to Ovid, Tiresias with his rod once separated two serpents which were coupled together, whereupon he was transformed into a woman. Seven years later he found the same two serpents, struck them again, and became a man once more. Later Jupiter and Juno asked Tiresias, who had had the experience of belonging to both sexes, which sex enjoyed love-making more. When Tiresias answered, "Woman," Juno struck him blind. However, Jupiter, in compensation, gave him the gift of prophecy.

46–51. *Backing up to this one's chest comes Aruns*: Aruns, the Etruscan diviner who forecast the Roman civil war and its outcome (Caesar's triumph over Pompey [Lucan, *Pharsalia* I, 584–638]), made his home "in the hills of Luni" (47), the area now known as Carrara and renowned for its white marble.

52–60. *And that one, with her hair loose, flowing back*: Manto, upon the death of her father, Tiresias, fled Thebes ("Bacchus' sacred city," 59) and its tyrant, Creon. She finally arrived in Italy and there founded the city of Mantua, Virgil's birthplace (56).

61–99

Virgil's account of the founding of Mantua seems to have been offered to provide the true version of an apparently controversial issue. In Canto XIX the Pilgrim had revealed the true nature of Simony, and the line (20) containing the first reference to "breaking" is followed by the words "Let this be mankind's picture of the truth." Now, in Canto XX, Virgil tells the "true" story of the founding of Mantua ("without recourse to sorcery," 93) and reveals the "true" nature of augury, i.e., that it is a fraudulent practice, adding "let no false tales adulterate the truth" (99). (Perhaps Virgil is here, by implication, defending himself against his medieval reputation as a magician.) Thus, Cantos XIX and XX are linked by these correlative investigations and interpretations of the true nature of the respective sins.

63. *beyond the Tyrol, known as Lake Benaco*: Lake Benaco is today Lake Garda, which lies in northern Italy at the center of the triangle formed by the cities of Trent, Brescia, and Verona (68).

64–66. *by a thousand streams and more, I think, the Alps*: Here, the "Alps" means that range between the Camonica valley, west of Lake Garda, and the city of Garda, on the lake's eastern shore, that is watered by many streams, which ultimately flow into Lake Garda.

67–69. *at its center is a place where all three bishops*: On an island in Lake Garda (Benaco) the boundaries of the dioceses of Trent, Brescia, and Verona met, thereby making it possible for all three bishops to hold services or "say Mass" there. It is quite possible that Dante, in the phrase "if they would ever visit there" (69), intends to criticize the practice of non-resident clergy's taking money from their parishes.

70–72. *Peschiera sits, a handsome well-built fortress*: The fortress of Peschiera and the town of the same name are on the southeast shore of Lake Garda.

78. *to Governol, where it falls into the Po*: Governol, now called Governolo, is twelve miles from Mantua and situated at the junction of the Mincio and the Po rivers.

82. *the savage virgin*: Manto.

93. *without recourse to sorcery*: The customs of ancient peoples dictated that the name of a newly founded city be obtained through sorcery. Such was not the case with Mantua.

95-96. *before the foolish Casalodi listened*: In 1272 Alberto da Casalodi, one of the Guelf counts of Brescia, was lord of Mantua. Having encountered public opposition, he was duped by the Ghibelline Pinamonte de' Bonaccolsi into thinking that he could remain in power only by exiling the nobles. Having faithfully followed Pinamonte's false counsel, he found himself bereft of his supporters and protectors, and consequently Pinamonte was able to take command; he banished the Guelfs, and ruled until 1291.

106-112. *That one, whose beard flows from his cheeks*: At the time of the Trojan War ("when the war stripped Greece of all its males," 108) Eurypylus, whom Dante thought to be a Greek augur (as was Calchas, 110), was asked to divine the most opportune time to launch the Greek fleet ("to cut the first ship's cable free," 111) from the port at Aulis.

113. *this way, somewhere in my high tragedy*: The "high tragedy" is, of course, the *Aeneid* (Book II, 114-19). In this work, however, Eurypylus is not an augur, but a soldier sent to the oracle to discover Apollo's predictions as to the best time to set sail from Troy.

116-17. *Michael Scot*: A Scottish philosopher attached to Frederick II's court at Palermo (see X, 119) who translated the works of Aristotle from the Arabic of his commentator Avicenna (see IV, 143). By reputation he was a magician and augur. Compare Boccaccio, *Decameron* VIII, 9.

118-20. *See there Guido Bonatti; see Asdente*: A native of Forlì, Guido Bonatti was a well-known astrologer and diviner in the service of many lords, among whom were Frederick II, Ezzelino (see XII, 110), and Guido da Montefeltro (see XXVII).

Benvenuto (or Asdente, "toothless," as he was called) was a cobbler from Parma who supposedly possessed certain magical powers. According to Dante, he would have fared better had he "been more devoted / to making shoes" (119-20). See the *Convivio* IV, xvi, 6.

124-26. *Now come along. Cain with his thorn-bush straddles*: By some mysterious power Virgil is able to reckon time in the depths of Hell. The moon (referred to as "Cain with his thorn-bush," 124, the medieval Italian counterpart of our "Man in the Moon") is directly over the line of demarcation between the Northern (land) and the Southern (water) Hemispheres and is setting on the western horizon (the "waves below Seville," 126). The time is approximately six a.m.

129. *when you were lost in the dark wood she helped you*: See Canto I, 2. The literal significance of this line defies explanation, since in the beginning of the *Inferno*, describing the Pilgrim's wanderings in the "dark wood," no mention is made of the moon. Most commentators would see an allegorical significance intended, but their interpretations vary and I find none of them convincing.

CANTO XXI

WHEN THE TWO reach the summit of the arch over the Fifth Bol-
gia, they see in the ditch below the bubbling of boiling pitch. Virgil's
sudden warning of danger frightens the Pilgrim even before he sees
a black devil rushing toward them, with a sinner slung over his
shoulder. From the bridge the devil flings the sinner into the pitch,
where he is poked at and tormented by the family of MALEBRANCHE
devils. Virgil, advising his ward to hide behind a rock, crosses the
bridge to face the devils alone. They threaten him with their pitch-
forks, but when he announces to their leader, MALACODA, that
Heaven has willed that he lead another through Hell, the devil's
arrogance collapses. Virgil calls the Pilgrim back to him. SCARMI-
GLIONE, who tries to take a poke at him, is rebuked by his leader,
who tells the travelers that the sixth arch is broken here but farther
on they will find another bridge to cross. He chooses a squad of his
devils to escort them there: ALICHINO, CALCABRINA, CAGNAZZO,
BARBARICCIA, LIBICOCCO, DRAGHIGNAZZO, CIRIATTO, GRAF-
FIACANE, FARFARELLO, and RUBICANTE. The Pilgrim's suspicion
about their unsavory escorts is brushed aside by his guide, and the
squad starts off, giving an obscene salute to their captain, who returns
their salute with a fart.

From this bridge to the next we walked and talked
    of things my Comedy does not care to tell;
    and when we reached the summit of the arch,   3

we stopped to see the next fosse of Malebolge
    and to hear more lamentation voiced in vain:
    I saw that it was very strangely dark!   6

In the vast and busy shipyard of the Venetians
    there boils all winter long a tough, thick pitch
    that is used to caulk the ribs of unsound ships.   9

Since winter will not let them sail, they toil:
   some build new ships, others repair the old ones,
   plugging the planks come loose from many sailings;   12

some hammer at the bow, some at the stern,
   one carves the oars while others twine the ropes,
   one mends the jib, one patches up the mainsail;   15

here, too, but heated by God's art, not fire,
   a sticky tar was boiling in the ditch
   that smeared the banks with viscous residue.   18

I saw it there, but I saw nothing in it,
   except the rising of the boiling bubbles
   breathing in air to burst and sink again.   21

I stood intently gazing there below,
   my guide, shouting to me: "Watch out, watch out!"
   took hold of me and drew me to his side.   24

I turned my head like one who can't resist
   looking to see what makes him run away
   (his body's strength draining with sudden fear),   27

but, looking back, does not delay his flight;
   and I saw coming right behind our backs,
   rushing along the ridge, a devil, black!   30

His face, his look, how frightening it was!
   With outstretched wings he skimmed along the rock,
   and every single move he made was cruel;   33

on one of his high-hunched and pointed shoulders
   he had a sinner slung by both his thighs,
   held tightly clawed at the tendons of his heels.   36

He shouted from our bridge: "Hey, Malebranche,
   here's one of Santa Zita's elders for you!
   You stick him under—I'll go back for more;   39

I've got that city stocked with the likes of him,
   they're all a bunch of grafters, save Bonturo!
   You can change a 'no' to 'yes' for cash in Lucca."   42

He flung him in, then from the flinty cliff
  sprang off. No hound unleashed to chase a thief
  could have taken off with greater speed than he.   45

That sinner plunged, then floated up stretched out,
  and the devils underneath the bridge all shouted:
  "You shouldn't imitate the Holy Face!   48

The swimming's different here from in the Serchio!
  We have our grappling-hooks along with us—
  don't show yourself above the pitch, or else!"   51

With a hundred prongs or more they pricked him, shrieking:
  "You've got to do your squirming under cover,
  try learning how to cheat beneath the surface."   54

They were like cooks who make their scullery boys
  poke down into the caldron with their forks
  to keep the meat from floating to the top.   57

My master said: "We'd best not let them know
  that you are here with me; crouch down behind
  some jutting rock so that they cannot see you;   60

whatever insults they may hurl at me,
  you must not fear, I know how things are run here;
  I have been caught in as bad a fix before."   63

He crossed the bridge and walked on past the end;
  as soon as he set foot on the sixth bank
  he forced himself to look as bold as possible.   66

With all the sound and fury that breaks loose
  when dogs rush out at some poor begging tramp,
  making him stop and beg from where he stands,   69

the ones who hid beneath the bridge sprang out
  and blocked him with a flourish of their pitchforks,
  but he shouted: "All of you behave yourselves!   72

Before you start to jab me with your forks,
  let one of you step forth to hear me out,
  and then decide if you still care to grapple."   75

They all cried out: "Let Malacoda go!"
  One stepped forward—the others stood their ground—
  and moving, said, "What good will this do him?"   78

"Do you think, Malacoda," said my master,
  "that you would see me here, come all this way,
  against all opposition, and still safe,   81

without propitious fate and God's permission?
  Now let us pass, for it is willed in Heaven
  that I lead another by this savage path."   84

With this the devil's arrogance collapsed,
  his pitchfork, too, dropped right down to his feet,
  as he announced to all: "Don't touch this man!"   87

"You, hiding over there," my guide called me,
  "behind the bridge's rocks, curled up and quiet,
  come back to me, you may return in safety."   90

At his words I rose and then I ran to him
  and all the devils made a movement forward;
  I feared they would not really keep their pact.   93

(I remember seeing soldiers under truce,
  as they left the castle of Caprona, frightened
  to be passing in the midst of such an enemy.)   96

I drew up close to him, as close as possible,
  and did not take my eyes from all those faces
  that certainly had nothing good about them.   99

Their prongs were aimed at me, and one was saying:
  "Now do I let him have it in the rump?"
  They answered all for one: "Sure, stick him good!"   102

But the devil who had spoken with my guide
  was quick to spin around and scream an order:
  "At ease there, take it easy, Scarmiglione!"   105

Then he said to us: "You cannot travel straight
  across this string of bridges, for the sixth arch
  lies broken at the bottom of its ditch;   108

if you have made your mind up to proceed,
　　you must continue on along this ridge;
　　not far, you'll find a bridge that crosses it.　　　111

Five hours more and it will be one thousand,
　　two hundred sixty-six years and a day
　　since the bridge-way here fell crumbling to the ground.　114

I plan to send a squad of mine that way
　　to see that no one airs himself down there;
　　go along with them, they will not misbehave.　　　117

Front and center, Alichino, Calcabrina,"
　　he shouted his commands, "you too, Cagnazzo;
　　Barbariccia, you be captain of the squad.　　　120

Take Libicocco with you and Draghignazzo,
　　toothy Ciriatto and Graffiacane,
　　Farfarello and our crazy Rubicante.　　　123

Now tour the ditch, inspect the boiling tar;
　　these two shall have safe passage to the bridge
　　connecting den to den without a break."　　　126

"O master, I don't like the looks of this,"
　　I said, "let's go, just you and me, no escort,
　　you know the way. I want no part of them!　　　129

If you're observant, as you usually are,
　　why is it you don't see them grind their teeth
　　and wink at one another?—we're in danger!"　　　132

And he to me: "I will not have you frightened;
　　let them do all the grinding that they want,
　　they do it for the boiling souls, not us."　　　135

Before they turned left-face along the bank
　　each one gave their good captain a salute
　　with farting tongue pressed tightly to his teeth,　　　138

and he blew back with his bugle of an ass-hole.

NOTES

7–15. In the vast and busy shipyard of the Venetians: During the Middle Ages the shipyard at Venice, built in 1104, was one of the most active and productive in all Europe. The image of the busy shipyard with its activity revolving around a vat of viscous pitch establishes the tone for this canto (and the next) as one of tense and excited movement. Also we once again see Dante imitating the action with his language: the busy syntax reflects the activity of the shipyard.

20–21. except the rising of the boiling bubbles: The repetition of "b" sounds (and "p's" in the Italian) audibly represents the bubbling, bursting action of the boiling pitch.

37. Hey, Malebranche: The *Malebranche* ("Evil Claws") are the overseer-devils of this *bolgia*, wherein are punished the Barrators (grafters, 41), those swindlers in public office whose sin against the state is comparable to that of the Simonists against the Church (XIX).

38–42. here's one of Santa Zita's elders for you!: Santa Zita, who lived and was canonized in the thirteenth century, is the patron saint of Lucca. The "elders" (38) are the Luccan government officials; and one of them, Bonturo Dati (41), is ironically referred to here as being guiltless when in reality he was the worst barrator of them all.

48–51. You shouldn't imitate the Holy Face!: The "Holy Face" was a wooden crucifix at Lucca. The sinner surfaces stretched out (46) on his back with arms flung wide like the figure on a crucifix—and this gives rise to the devil's remark that here in Hell one does not swim the same way as in the Serchio (a river near Lucca). In other words, in the Serchio people swim for pleasure, often floating on their backs (in the position of a crucifix). The use of a crucifixion image to suggest swimming for pleasure is in keeping with the grotesque humor of XXI—XXIII.

55–57. They were like cooks who make their scullery boys: The "cooking" imagery begun here is continued in XXII, 150, and is one of several images that unify these cantos.

76. They all cried out: "Let Malacoda go!": Malacoda is the leader of the devils in this *bolgia*. It is significant that a devil whose name means "Evil-Tail" ends this canto with a fart (139).

94–96. *I remember seeing soldiers under truce*: Dante's personal recollection concerns the siege of Caprona (a fortress on the Arno River near Pisa) by Guelf troops from Lucca and Florence in 1289. Having surrendered, the Pisan soldiers "under truce" issued forth, having to pass through the rank of the enemy. The Pilgrim's present state is similar to that of the frightened soldiers. The military imagery begun here will continue in the next canto.

112–14. *Five hours more and it will be . . . .*: Christ's death on Good Friday, A.D. 34, would in five hours, according to Malacoda, have occurred 1266 years ago yesterday—"today" being the morning of Holy Saturday, 1300. Although the bridge across the next *bolgia* was shattered by the earthquake following Christ's crucifixion, Malacoda tells Virgil and the Pilgrim that there is another bridge that crosses this *bolgia*. This lie, carefully contrived by the spokesman for the devils, sets the trap for the overly confident, trusting Virgil and his wary charge, who—at least in these cantos—appears more intelligent than his guide. See lines 127–32; also Canto XXIII, n. 140–41.

118–23. *Front and center, Alichino, Calcabrina*: The significance of the devils' names reinforces their ambivalent nature, both comic and fearful. While they inspire fear in Virgil and the Pilgrim, their words and gestures are for the most part light and playful. Many of the names could be translated, but they would lose much of their grotesque appearance. (Malacoda, for instance, means "Evil-Tail," Barbariccia means "Curly-Beard.") Some critics have suggested that Dante might be mocking Florentine or Luccan magistrates of the early 1300s through the devils. Manno Branca, for example, was mayor of Florence in 1300 and his followers might easily have been called *Male branche* ("Bad Brancas"); one of the priors of Florence at the time was named Raffacani—which is quite close to the devil-name Graffiacane.

139. *and he blew back with his bugle of an ass-hole*: The canto

closes on this vulgar but comic note, which is indicative of the essentially farcical nature of this *bolgia*, so different from the remainder of the *Inferno*. In the next canto we see the devils and sinners amusing themselves with bizarre sports, which we must assume are the rule rather than the exception.

CANTO XXII

The note of grotesque comedy in the bolgia of the Malebranche
continues, with a comparison between Malacoda's salute to his soldiers
and different kinds of military signals the Pilgrim has witnessed in
his lifetime. He sees many GRAFTERS squatting in the pitch, but as
soon as the Malebranche draw near, they dive below the surface.
One unidentified NAVARRESE, however, fails to escape and is hoisted
up on Graffiacane's hooks; Rubicante and the other Malebranche
start to tear into him, but Virgil, at his ward's request, manages to
question him between torments. The sinner briefly tells his story, and
then relates that he has left below in the pitch an Italian, FRA
GOMITA, a particularly adept grafter, who spends his time talking
to MICHEL ZANCHE.

The Navarrese sinner promises to lure some of his colleagues to
the surface for the devils' amusement, if the tormentors will hide
themselves for a moment. Cagnazzo is skeptical but Alichino agrees,
and no sooner do the Malebranche turn away than the crafty grafter
dives below the pitch. Alichino flies after him, but too late; now
Calcabrina rushes after Alichino and both struggle above the boiling
pitch, and then fall in. Barbariccia directs the rescue operation as the
two poets steal away.

I have seen troops of horsemen breaking camp,
    opening the attack, or passing in review,
    I have even seen them fleeing for their lives;   3

I have seen scouts ride, exploring your terrain,
    O Aretines, and I have seen raiding-parties
    and the clash of tournaments, the run of jousts—   6

to the tune of trumpets, to the ring of clanging bells,
    to the roll of drums, to the flash of flares on ramparts,
    to the accompaniment of every known device;   9

but I never saw cavalry or infantry
  or ships that sail by landmarks or by stars
  signaled to set off by such strange bugling!   12

So, on our way we went with those ten fiends.
  What savage company! But—in church, with saints—
  with rowdy good-for-nothings, in the tavern!   15

My attention now was fixed upon the pitch
  to see the operations of this *bolgia,*
  and how the cooking souls got on down there.   18

Much like the dolphins that are said to surface
  with their backs arched to warn all men at sea
  to rig their ships for stormy seas ahead,   21

so now and then a sinner's back would surface
  in order to alleviate his pain,
  then dive to hide as quick as lightning strikes.   24

Like squatting frogs along the ditch's edge,
  with just their muzzles sticking out of water,
  their legs and all the rest concealed below,   27

these sinners squatted all around their pond;
  but as soon as Barbariccia would approach
  they quickly ducked beneath the boiling pitch.   30

I saw (my heart still shudders at the thought)
  one lingering behind—as it sometimes happens
  one frog remains while all the rest dive down—   33

and Graffiacan, standing in front of him,
  hooked and twirled him by his pitchy hair
  and hoisted him. He looked just like an otter!   36

By then I knew the names of all the fiends:
  I had listened carefully when they were chosen,
  each of them stepping forth to match his name.   39

"Hey, Rubicante, dig your claws down deep
  into his back and peel the skin off him,"
  this fiendish chorus egged him on with screams.   42

I said: "Master, will you, if you can, find out
   the name of that poor wretch who has just fallen
   into the cruel hands of his adversaries?"   45

My guide walked right up to the sinner's side
   and asked where he was from, and he replied:
   "I was born and bred in the kingdom of Navarre;   48

my mother gave me to a lord to serve,
   for she had me by some dishonest spendthrift
   who ran through all he owned and killed himself.   51

Then I became a servant in the household
   of good King Thibault. There I learned my graft,
   and now I pay my bill by boiling here."   54

Ciriatto, who had two tusks sticking out
   on both sides of his mouth, just like a boar's,
   let him feel how just one tusk could rip him open.   57

The mouse had fallen prey to evil cats,
   but Barbariccia locked him with his arms,
   shouting: "Get back while I've got hold of him!"   60

Then toward my guide he turned his face and said:
   "If you want more from him, keep questioning
   before he's torn to pieces by the others."   63

My guide went on: "Then tell me, do you know
   of some Italian stuck among these sinners
   beneath the pitch?" And he, "A second ago   66

I was with one who lived around those parts.
   Oh, I wish I were undercover with him now!
   I wouldn't have these hooks or claws to fear."   69

Libicocco cried: "We've waited long enough,"
   then with his fork he hooked the sinner's arm
   and, tearing at it, he pulled out a piece.   72

Draghignazzo, too, was anxious for some fun;
   he tried the wretch's leg, but their captain quickly
   spun around and gave them all a dirty look.   75

As soon as they calmed down a bit, my master
    began again to interrogate the wretch,
    who still was contemplating his new wound: 78

"Who was it, you were saying, that unluckily
    you left behind you when you came ashore?"
    "Gomita," he said, "the friar from Gallura,   81

receptacle for every kind of fraud:
    when his lord's enemies were in his hands,
    the treatment they received delighted them: 84

he took their cash, and as he says, hushed up
    the case and let them off; none of his acts
    was petty grafting, all were of sovereign order.   87

He spends his time with don Michele Zanche
    of Logodoro, talking on and on
    about Sardinia—their tongues no worse for wear!   90

Oh, but look how that one grins and grinds his teeth;
    I could tell you so much more, but I am afraid
    he is going to grate my scabby hide for me."   93

But their master-sergeant turned to Farfarello,
    whose wild eyes warned he was about to strike,
    shouting, "Get away, you filthy bird of prey."   96

"If you would like to see Tuscans or Lombards,"
    the frightened shade took up where he left off,
    "and have a talk with them, I'll bring some here;   99

but the Malebranche must back up a bit,
    or else those shades won't risk a surfacing;
    I, by myself, will bring you up a catch   102

of seven, without moving from this spot,
    just by whistling—that's our signal to the rest
    when one peers out and sees the coast is clear."   105

Cagnazzo raised his snout at such a story,
    then shook his head and said: "Listen to the trick
    he's cooked up to get off the hook by jumping!"   108

And he, full of the tricks his trade had taught him,
  said: "Tricky, I surely am, especially
  when it comes to getting friends into worse trouble."   111

But Alichin could not resist the challenge,
  and in spite of what the others thought, cried out:
  "If you jump, I won't come galloping for you,   114

I've got my wings to beat you to the pitch.
  We'll clear this ledge and wait behind that slope.
  Let's see if one of you can outmatch us!"   117

Now listen, Reader, here's a game that's strange:
  they all turned toward the slope, and first to turn
  was the fiend who from the start opposed the game.   120

The Navarrese had perfect sense of timing:
  feet planted on the ground, in a flash he jumped,
  the devil's plan was foiled, and he was free.   123

The squad was stung with shame but most of all
  the one who brought this blunder to perfection;
  he swooped down, howling, "Now I've got you caught!"

Little good it did, for wings could not outstrip
  the flight of terror: down the sinner dived
  and up the fiend was forced to strain his chest   129

like a falcon swooping down on a wild duck:
  the duck dives quickly out of sight, the falcon
  must fly back up dejected and defeated.   132

In the meantime, Calcabrina, furious,
  also took off, hoping the shade would make it,
  so he could pick a fight with his companion.   135

And when he saw the grafter hit the pitch,
  he turned his claws to grapple with his brother,
  and they tangled in mid-air above the ditch;   138

but the other was a full-fledged hawk as well
  and used his claws on him, and both of them
  went plunging straight into the boiling pond.   141

The heat was quick to make them separate,
  but there seemed no way of getting out of there;
  their wings were clogged and could not lift them up.   144

Barbariccia, no less peeved than all his men,
  sent four fiends flying to the other shore
  with their equipment at top speed; instantly,   147

some here, some there, they took the posts assigned them.
  They stretched their hooks to reach the pitch-dipped pair,
  who were by now deep-fried within their crusts.   150

And there we left them, all messed up that way.

NOTES

1–12. *I have seen troops of horsemen breaking camp*: Continuing
the military imagery, Dante elaborates in mock-epic style on
the effect of the vulgar signal (the "strange bugling," 12) given
at the close of Canto XXI. The reference to the Aretines (5)
recalls Dante's presence at their defeat in the battle of Cam-
paldino (1289) at the hands of the Florentine and Luccan troops.

14–15. *But—in church, with saints*: The proverbial nature of
this phrase is characteristic of the flippant manner of speech
found throughout Cantos XXI and XXII and, moreover, is
indicative of the playful atmosphere, in which all participants
(the Pilgrim, Virgil, the devils, and the sinners) seem to operate
on the same plane as equal agents.

19. *Much like the dolphins that are said to surface*: Consistent
with the playful and grotesque nature of this canto is Dante's
use of animal imagery. The grafters are compared successively
to dolphins, frogs (25–33), an otter (36), a mouse (58), a wild
duck (130); the devils are compared to falcons (130) and hawks
(139). All of these animals are depicted in grotesque poses or
are described as playing games.

48–54. *I was born and bred in the kingdom of Navarre*: Early
commentators have given the name of Ciampolo or Giampolo
to this native of Navarre who, after being placed in the service

of a Spanish nobleman, later served in the court of Thibault II. Exploiting the court duties with which he was entrusted, he took to barratry. One commentator suggests that were it not for the tradition that attributes the name of Ciampolo to this man, one might identify him with the seneschal Goffredo di Beaumont, who took over the government of Navarre during Thibault's absence.

53. *good King Thibault*: Thibault II, the son-in-law of Louis IX of France, was Count of Champagne and later King of Navarre during the mid-thirteenth century.

58. *The mouse had fallen prey to cats*: This image, together with the references to frogs (25–33) and to the "games" of the Malebranche and Ciampolo, anticipates the reference to Aesop's fable that begins Canto XXIII (4–6).

81–87. *"Gomita," he said, "the friar from Gallura"*: Fra Gomita was a Sardinian friar, chancellor of Nino Visconti, governor of Pisa, whom Dante places in Purgatory (*Purgatory* VIII, 53). From 1275 to 1296 Nino Visconti was judge of Gallura, one of the four districts into which Sardinia, a Pisan possession during the thirteenth century, was divided. Profiting by his position and the good faith of Nino Visconti, who refused to listen to the complaints raised against him, Fra Gomita indulged in the sale of public offices. When Nino learned, however, that he had accepted bribes to let prisoners escape, he promptly had him hanged.

88–89. *He spends his time with don Michele Zanche*: Although no documents mentioning the name of Michele Zanche have been found, he is believed to have been the governor of Logodoro, another of the four districts into which Sardinia was divided in the thirteenth century (see n. 81–87) during the period when King Enzo of Sardinia, the son of Frederick II, was engaged in war. After King Enzo was captured and subsequently divorced from the queen, Michele married her and took over the government of the Sardinian provinces. Around 1275 he was murdered by his son-in-law, Branca d'Oria, whose shade Dante will see in the lowest region of Hell (see XXXIII, 134–47).

97–132

The second lie of Cantos XXI–XXII is Ciampolo's device to escape the claws of the *Malebranche*: if the devils will hide, he will whistle and thus summon his fellow sinners from below the pitch in order to get his friends into worse trouble than he himself is in. Thus he tells the devils that he will lie to his friends (by whistling to let them know that the coast is clear), but actually he is lying to the devils. They are suspicious but they agree to hide and play the game and Ciampolo escapes. In Ciampolo, for the first time in the *Inferno,* we see a sinner actually performing his sin: for the clever way in which Ciampolo constructs his lie (using Virgil and Dante), his admission that he is "tricky" (110), and his well-timed leap into the pitch all show the sin of fraud in action. Just as Malacoda joined his lie with a very minute and truthful description of the time since the bridge had fallen (XXI, 112–14), so Ciampolo leads up to his lie with a precise and truthful statement of the major facts of his life (48–54). The admixture of precise truth and falsehood gives, in both cases, an aura of unquestioned truth to what is ultimately a fraud, and that method too comes, of course, from experience in the sin of barratry. Compare XXI, 109–11; also XXIII, n. 140–41.

There is possibly a third, implicit, lie in this canto, this time perpetrated by the devils again. Cagnazzo from the start is suspicious of Ciampolo's proposal, but when Alichino cannot resist the challenge, Cagnazzo is the first to turn to go and hide ("first to turn / was the fiend who from the start opposed the game," 119–20). The Pilgrim calls this "a game that's strange" (118), and indeed it is, because each of the devils is silently "lying" to his brother by agreeing to what they must realize is a fraud on the part of Ciampolo; the real reason for their ready acceptance of Ciampolo's proposal is, of course, that when he escapes they can "pick a fight" with the responsible devil—Alichino. That is exactly what happens when Calcabrina, "furious, / also took off, hoping the shade would make it, / so he could pick a fight with his companion" (133–

35). The deceit involved in this "game" strikes the Pilgrim as "strange," but we must assume that it represents the normal daily fare in this *bolgia*, where there is a free interchange of roles between devils and sinners, and a continuous activity that is grotesquely comic.

CANTO XXIII

THE ANTICS of CIAMPOLO, the Navarrese, and the Malebranche bring to the Pilgrim's mind the fable of the frog, the mouse, and the hawk—and that in turn reminds him of the immediate danger he and Virgil are in from the angry Malebranche. Virgil senses the danger too, and grabbing his ward as a mother would her child, he dashes to the edge of the bank and slides down the rocky slope into the Sixth Bolgia—not a moment too soon, for at the top of the slope they see the angry Malebranche. When the Pilgrim looks around him he sees weeping shades slowly marching in single file, each one covered from head to foot with a golden cloak lined with lead, which weights them down. These are the HYPOCRITES. Two in this group identify themselves as CATALANO DE' MALAVOLTI and LODERINGO DEGLI ANDALÒ, two Jovial Friars. The Pilgrim is about to address them when he sees the shade of CAIAPHAS (the evil counselor who advised Pontius Pilate to crucify Christ), crucified and transfixed by three stakes to the ground. Virgil discovers from the two friars that in order to leave this bolgia they must climb up a rockslide; he also learns that this is the only bolgia over which the bridge is broken. Virgil is angry with himself for having believed Malacoda's lie about the bridge over the Sixth Bolgia (Canto XXI, 111).

In silence, all alone, without an escort,
    we moved along, one behind the other,
    like minor friars bent upon a journey.   3

I was thinking over one of Aesop's fables
    that this recent skirmish had brought back to mind,
    where he tells the story of the frog and mouse;   6

for "yon" and "there" could not be more alike
    than the fable and the fact, if one compares
    the start and finish of both incidents.   9

As from one thought another often rises,
   so this thought gave quick birth to still another,
   and then the fear I first had felt was doubled.   12

I was thinking: "Since these fiends, on our account,
   were tricked and mortified by mockery,
   they certainly will be more than resentful;   15

with rage now added to their evil instincts,
   they will hunt us down with all the savagery
   of dogs about to pounce upon the hare."   18

I felt my body's skin begin to tighten—
   I was so frightened!—and I kept looking back:
   "O master," I said, "if you do not hide   21

both of us, and very quick, I am afraid
   of the Malebranche—right now they're on our trail—
   I feel they're there, I think I hear them now."   24

And he replied: "Even if I were a mirror
   I could not reflect your outward image faster
   than your inner thoughts transmit themselves to me.   27

In fact, just now they joined themselves with mine,
   and since they were alike in birth and form,
   I decided to unite them toward one goal: 30

if the right-hand bank should slope in such a way
   as to allow us to descend to the next *bolgia,*
   we could escape that chase we have imagined."   33

He had hardly finished telling me his plan
   when I saw them coming with their wings wide open
   not too far off, and now they meant to get us!   36

My guide instinctively caught hold of me,
   like a mother waking to some warning sound,
   who sees the rising flames are getting close   39

and grabs her son and runs—she does not wait
   the short time it would take to put on something;
   she cares not for herself, only for him.   42

And over the edge, then down the stony bank
   he slid, on his back, along the sloping rock
   that walls the higher side of the next *bolgia*.   45

Water that turns a mill wheel never ran
   the narrow sluice at greater speed, not even
   at the point before it hits the paddle-blades,   48

than down that sloping border my guide slid,
   bearing me with him, clasping me to his chest
   as though I were his child, not his companion.   51

His feet had hardly touched rock bottom, when
   there they were, the ten of them, above us
   on the height; but now there was no need to fear: 54

High Providence that willed for them to be
   the ministers in charge of the fifth ditch
   also willed them powerless to leave their realm.   57

And now, down there, we found a painted people,
   slow-motioned: step by step, they walked their round
   in tears, and seeming wasted by fatigue.   60

All were wearing cloaks with hoods pulled low
   covering the eyes (the style was much the same
   as those the Benedictines wear at Cluny),   63

dazzling, gilded cloaks outside, but inside
   they were lined with lead, so heavy that the capes
   King Frederick used, compared to these, were straw.   66

O cloak of everlasting weariness!
   We turned again, as usual, to the left
   and moved with them, those souls lost in their mourning;

but with their weight that tired-out race of shades
   paced on so slowly that we found ourselves
   in new company with every step we took;   72

and so I asked my guide: "Please look around
   and see, as we keep walking, if you find
   someone whose name or deeds are known to me."   75

And one who overheard me speaking Tuscan
   cried out somewhere behind us: "Not so fast,
   you there, rushing ahead through this heavy air,   78

perhaps from me you can obtain an answer."
   At this my guide turned toward me saying, "Stop,
   and wait for him, then match your pace with his."   81

I paused and saw two shades with straining faces
   revealing their mind's haste to join my side,
   but the weight they bore and the crowded road delayed them.

When they arrived, they looked at me sideways
   and for some time, without exchanging words;
   then they turned to one another and were saying: 87

"He seems alive, the way his throat is moving,
   and if both are dead, what privilege allows them
   to walk uncovered by the heavy cloak?"   90

Then they spoke to me: "O Tuscan who has come
   to visit the college of the sullen hypocrites,
   do not disdain to tell us who you are."   93

I answered them: "I was born and I grew up
   in the great city on the lovely Arno's shore,
   and I have the body I have always had.   96

But who are you, distilling tears of grief,
   so many I see running down your cheeks?
   And what kind of pain is this that it can glitter?"   99

One of them answered: "The orange-gilded cloaks
   are thick with lead so heavy that it makes us,
   who are the scales it hangs on, creak as we walk.   102

Jovial Friars we were, both from Bologna.
   My name was Catalano, his, Loderingo,
   and both of us were chosen by your city,   105

that usually would choose one man alone,
   to keep the peace. Evidence of what we were
   may still be seen around Gardingo's parts."   108

I began: "O Friars, all your wretchedness . . ."
    but said no more; I couldn't, for I saw
    one crucified with three stakes on the ground.   111

And when he saw me all his body writhed,
    and through his beard he heaved out sighs of pain;
    then Friar Catalano, who watched the scene,   114

remarked: "That impaled figure you see there
    advised the Pharisees it was expedient
    to sacrifice one man for all the people.   117

Naked he lies stretched out across the road,
    as you can see, and he must feel the load
    of every weight that steps on him to cross.   120

His father-in-law and the other council members,
    who were the seed of evil for all Jews,
    are racked the same way all along this ditch."   123

And I saw Virgil staring down amazed
    at this body stretching out in crucifixion,
    so vilely punished in the eternal exile.   126

Then he looked up and asked one of the friars:
    "Could you please tell us, if your rule permits:
    is there a passage-way on the right, somewhere,   129

by which the two of us may leave this place
    without summoning one of those black angels
    to come down here and raise us from this pit?"   132

He answered: "Closer than you might expect,
    a ridge jutting out from the base of the great circle
    extends, and bridges every hideous ditch   135

except this one, whose arch is totally smashed
    and crosses nowhere; but you can climb up
    its massive ruins that slope against this bank."   138

My guide stood there awhile, his head bent low,
    then said: "He told a lie about this business,
    that one who hooks the sinners over there."   141

And the friar: "Once, in Bologna, I heard discussed
   the devil's many vices; one of them is
   that he tells lies and is father of all lies."   144

In haste, taking great strides, my guide walked off,
   his face revealing traces of his anger.
I turned and left the heavy-weighted souls   147

to make my way behind those cherished footprints.

NOTES

3. *like minor friars bent upon a journey*: The image of the
"minor friars" (Franciscans) who walk in single file is pre-
paratory to the presentation of the Hypocrites, whose clothing
is compared to that of monks (61–66).

4–9. *I was thinking over one of Aesop's fables*: Dante incorrectly
attributes the fable of the frog and the mouse to Aesop, to
whom during the Middle Ages all such tales were attributed.
The fable concerns a mouse who, arriving at a stream, asks a
frog to carry him across; the frog agrees and ties the mouse
to his leg, but once they are in the water the frog attempts to
drown the mouse by diving. But while the mouse is fighting
to stay afloat, a hawk swoops down and carries them away,
and (in most versions) frees the mouse and eats the frog. Dante
restricts the comparison to the "start and finish of both inci-
dents" (9). Most critics have equated the frog with Ciampolo
and the mouse with Alichino, since the former attempts to
(and does) deceive the latter, and they see the end of the fable—
the hawk swooping down on frog and mouse—as the rescue
of the two stuck devils by their fellows. Although apparently
no exact equation between the fable and the "recent skirmish"
was intended by Dante, it seems to me that the beginning of
the fable (the deception of the mouse by the frog) better sug-
gests the attempted deception of Dante and Virgil (who are
looking for a way to cross the Sixth *Bolgia*) by the *Malebranche*,
and that the end of the fable that Dante refers to (9) is not the
end of the story itself, but the moral, which was inevitably

appended to such fables in the Middle Ages: in this case that divine justice punishes the guilty (the frog is caught, and two of the *Malebranche* fall into the pitch)—and the innocent "mice," Dante and Virgil, get away.

7. *for "yon" and "there" could not be more alike*: The words *mo* and *issa* of the Italian text, which I have translated as "yon" and "there," are synonymous in the Lucchese dialect, both meaning "now."

25–27. *Even if I were a mirror*: Compare Proverbs XXVII, 19.

37–42. *My guide instinctively caught hold of me*: Note the instinctive reaction of Virgil, who, at this moment, is not acting in the capacity of Reason. Compare n. 140–41.

61–63. *All were wearing cloaks with hoods pulled low*: The vestments of the monks at Cluny were particularly famous for their fullness and elegance. Saint Bernard wrote sarcastically that if the elegance of the dress indicated holiness, he too would become a Benedictine at Cluny. Perhaps Dante is using the comparison to criticize the hypocrisy of those monks in their choice of habit.

64–66. *dazzling, gilded cloaks outside, but inside*: Dante's image of the gilded exterior concealing a leaden interior is perhaps drawn from Matthew XXIII, 27: "Woe unto you, scribes and Pharisees, hypocrites! for ye are like unto whited sepulchres, which indeed appear beautiful outward but are within full of dead men's bones, and of all uncleanness."

Probably also known to Dante was the *Magnae Derivationes* of Uguccione da Pisa, who says that *ypocrita*, coming from the Greek, meant *superauratus* or "gilded."

The "capes / King Frederick used" (65–66) refers to a mode of punishment for traitors reportedly instituted by Frederick II, grandson of Frederick Barbarossa. The condemned were dressed in leaden capes, which were then melted on their bodies. It is uncertain whether or not Frederick actually used this punishment.

103–108. *Jovial Friars we were, both from Bologna*: The Order of the Cavalieri di Beata Santa Maria was founded at Bologna in 1261 and was dedicated to the maintenance of peace between political factions and families, and to the defense of the weak and poor. However, because of its rather liberal rules, this high-principled organization gained the nickname of "Jovial Friars" (*frati gaudenti*)—which, no doubt, impaired its serious function to some degree. The Bolognese friars Catalano de' Malavolti (c. 1210–85) and Loderingo degli Andalò (c. 1210–93) were elected jointly to the office of *Podestà* (mayor) in Florence because it was thought that the combination of the former, a Guelf, and the latter, a Ghibelline, would ensure the peace of the city. In reality their tenure, short though it was, was characterized by strife, which culminated in the expulsion of the Ghibellines from Florence in 1266. Gardingo (108) is the name of the section of Florence around the Palazzo Vecchio; in this area the Uberti family, the heads of the Florentine Ghibelline party, had their palace, which was razed during the uprisings of 1266. Modern historians have proved that Pope Clement IV controlled both the election and actions of Catalano and Loderingo, in order to overthrow the Ghibellines and establish the Guelfs in power.

115–24. *That impaled figure you see there*: Caiaphas, the High Priest of the Jews, maintained that it was better that one man (Jesus) die than for the Hebrew nation to be lost (John XI, 49–50). Annas, Caiaphas's father-in-law (121), delivered Jesus to him for judgment. For their act against God these men and the other evil counselors who judged Christ were the "seed of evil for all Jews" (122); in retaliation God caused Jerusalem to be destroyed and the Hebrew people dispersed to all parts of the world. It is, then, a fitting punishment for Caiaphas, Annas, and the rest to bear the weight of all the hypocrites for their crime, and to be crucified on the ground with "three stakes" (111).

It should be noted that these crucified hypocrites are also evil counselors.

124–27. *And I saw Virgil staring down amazed*: Most commentators seem to think that Virgil's amazement at seeing the crucified Caiaphas is due to the fact that he was not there when Virgil first descended into Hell. However, many of the shades seen by Dante and Virgil were not there on Virgil's first descent and the Roman poet expresses no amazement at seeing tnem; it seems more likely that Virgil is struck by the unusual form which the *contrapasso* takes—crucifixion.

140–41. *He told a lie about this business*: Aesthetically, the action of the Fifth *Bolgia* ends here, with Virgil's recognition that Malacoda's words (XXI, 110–11) about the unbroken bridge were false. The events, in fact, of Cantos XXI–XXIII revolve around a series of lies which show the general sin of fraud in action. First Malacoda and the other *Malebranche* deceive Dante and Virgil by making them think that although the "primary" bridge over the Sixth *Bolgia* is smashed, there is another farther on which is whole; next, Ciampolo, the Navarrese, deceives Dante and Virgil into thinking that he is going to summon up Italians from beneath the pitch for them to speak with, and he tricks the *Malebranche* into leaving him free for a moment with the promise that he will call up new sinners for them to torment (XXII, 97–132); then the *Malebranche* subtly deceive each other by agreeing to Ciampolo's lying proposal so that they might have a fight among themselves should Ciampolo escape—as he does (XXII, 106–41); and finally the sin of hypocrisy, which we see in Canto XXIII, reflects all of the lies that have gone before. In fact the method of telling lies portrayed by Malacoda and Ciampolo—a precise truth followed by a false statement (see XXI, n. 112–14; XXII, n. 97–132)—is depicted in a larger sense by the punishment of the Hypocrites with their appearance of truth (gilded exterior) cloaking a false substance.

It is interesting that Virgil, too, is taken in by the lies, and is almost a weaker figure in these cantos than the Pilgrim. In XXI he belittles the Pilgrim's fear when he is suspicious of the *Malebranche* (127–35), and in XXIII he waits for his warning (21–24) before grabbing him up and sliding into the next *bolgia*. Virgil's failure to cope with the lies perhaps indicates Reason's inability immediately to recognize fraud, which is always disguised in reasonable phrases (the precise truths preceding the lies); and in this light it should be noted that Virgil's escape from the lying devils of the Sixth *Bolgia* is instinctive and not reasoned (XXIII, 37–45).

146–48. *his face revealing traces of his anger*: Virgil is angry, of course, because he had trusted Malacoda and had been deceived, and also because of the friar's slightly taunting rebuke at his naiveté (142–44). That Virgil's temporary failure has not lessened the Pilgrim's respect and love in any way is evident in the concluding line: "to make my way behind those cherished footprints" (148).

*   *   *   *

Dante shows complete mastery of the techniques that unify these last three cantos. First, of course, Barratry and Hypocrisy, the sins punished in the Fifth and Sixth *Bolge,* are closely related, and the lies told by the characters in the Fifth *Bolgia* (XXI and XXII) are revealed as falsehoods in the Sixth *Bolgia* (XXIII). The *Malebranche* figures continue through all three cantos, and the humor, often grotesque, comes through in the flippant language and Keystone Kop–like actions of the devils. The humor perhaps comes to an end with the sarcastic remark of the friar to Virgil that "Once, in Bologna, I heard discussed / the devil's many vices; one of them is / that he tells lies and is father of all lies" (XXIII, 142–44). The imagery too binds the cantos together. The opening image of XXI (the Venice shipyard) forecasts the coming busy, semi-military activity of the *Malebranche* around the pitch; the mock epic opening of XXII continues the comic military imagery in its reference back to the fart that ended XXI; and Aesop's fable, of which the Pilgrim is reminded at the beginning of XXIII by the skirmish at the end of XXII, is also foreshadowed in XXII by animal similes involving frogs, a mouse, and a hawk. Finally Dante deftly alternates speed and slowness in his poetry to reflect the activity described and to link the cantos. The rapid busyness of the Venetian shipyard simile is soon reflected in the busyness of the *Malebranche*'s speech:

> . . . "Hey, Malebranche,
> here's one of Santa Zita's elders for you!
> You stick him under—I'll go back for more . . ."
> (XXI, 37–39)

The busy language is continued through XXII, but the first tercets of XXIII are by contrast slow and ponderous:

> In silence, all alone, without an escort,
>   we moved along, one behind the other,
>   like minor friars bent upon a journey.
>   (1–3)

These lines of course foreshadow the heavy, slow movement of the Hypocrites, but soon, as Virgil and Dante escape the *Malebranche,* the pace is picked up again, and it reaches its frenetic climax as the poets' sliding down the bank is compared to water rushing down a mill-sluice (46–51). But as soon as they are safely on the ground of the Sixth *Bolgia,* they see the Hypocrites, and the pace slows to a crawl again:

> And now, down there, we found a painted people,
>   slow-motioned: step by step, they walked their round
>   (58–59)

These three cantos are linked by aesthetic devices of particular effectiveness.

CANTO XXIV

After an elaborate simile describing Virgil's anger and the return of his composure, the two begin the difficult, steep ascent up the rocks of the fallen bridge. The Pilgrim can barely make it to the top even with Virgil's help, and after the climb he sits down to catch his breath; but his guide urges him on, and they make their way back to the bridge over the Seventh Bolgia. From the bridge confused sounds can be heard rising from the darkness below. Virgil agrees to take his pupil down to the edge of the eighth encircling bank, and once they are there, the scene reveals a terrible confusion of serpents, and THIEVES *madly running.*

Suddenly a snake darts out and strikes a sinner's neck, whereupon he flares up, turning into a heap of crumbling ashes; then the ashes gather together into the shape of a man. The metamorphosed sinner reveals himself to be VANNI FUCCI, *a Pistoiese condemned for stealing the treasure of the sacristy of the church of San Zeno at Pistoia. He makes a prophecy about the coming strife in Florence.*

In the season of the newborn year, when the sun
   renews its rays beneath Aquarius
   and nights begin to last as long as days,   3

at the time the hoarfrost paints upon the ground
   the outward semblance of his snow-white sister
   (but the color from his brush soon fades away),   6

the peasant wakes, gets up, goes out and sees
   the fields all white. No fodder for his sheep!
   He smites his thighs in anger and goes back   9

into his shack and, pacing up and down,
   complains, poor wretch, not knowing what to do;
   once more he goes outdoors, and hope fills him   12

again when he sees the world has changed its face
   in so little time, and he picks up his crook
   and out to pasture drives his sheep to graze—   15

just so I felt myself lose heart to see
   my master's face wearing a troubled look,
   and as quickly came the salve to heal my sore: 18

for when we reached the shattered heap of bridge,
   my leader turned to me with that sweet look
   of warmth I first saw at the mountain's foot.   21

He opened up his arms (but not before
   he had carefully studied how the ruins lay
   and found some sort of plan) to pick me up.   24

Like one who works and thinks things out ahead,
   always ready for the next move he will make,
   so, while he raised me up toward one great rock,   27

he had already singled out another,
   saying, "Now get a grip on that rock there,
   but test it first to see it holds your weight."   30

It was no road for one who wore a cloak!
   Even though I had his help and he weighed nothing,
   we could hardly lift ourselves from crag to crag.   33

And had it not been that the bank we climbed
   was lower than the one we had slid down—
   I cannot speak for him—but I for one   36

surely would have quit. But since the Evil Pits
   slope toward the yawning well that is the lowest,
   each valley is laid out in such a way   39

that one bank rises higher than the next.
   We somehow finally reached the point above
   where the last of all that rock was shaken loose.   42

My lungs were so pumped out of breath by the time
   I reached the top, I could not go on farther,
   and instantly I sat down where I was.   45

BOLGIA V

BOLGIA VI ── *Remains of broken bridge*

Diagram to illustrate Canto XXIV, 34–35

"Come on, shake off the covers of this sloth,"
   the master said, "for sitting softly cushioned,
   or tucked in bed, is no way to win fame;   48

and without it man must waste his life away,
   leaving such traces of what he was on earth
   as smoke in wind and foam upon the water.   51

Stand up! Dominate this weariness of yours
   with the strength of soul that wins in every battle
   if it does not sink beneath the body's weight.   54

Much steeper stairs than these we'll have to climb;
   we have not seen enough of sinners yet!
   If you understand me, act, learn from my words."   57

At this I stood up straight and made it seem
   I had more breath than I began to breathe,
   and said: "Move on, for I am strong and ready."   60

We climbed and made our way along the bridge,
   which was jagged, tight and difficult to cross,
   and steep—far more than any we had climbed.   63

Not to seem faint, I spoke while I was climbing;
   then came a voice from the depths of the next chasm,
   a voice unable to articulate.   66

I don't know what it said, even though I stood
   at the very top of the arch that crosses there;
   to me it seemed whoever spoke, spoke running.   69

I was bending over, but no living eyes
   could penetrate the bottom of that darkness;
   therefore I said: "Master, why not go down   72

this bridge onto the next encircling bank,
   for I hear sounds I cannot understand,
   and I look down but cannot see a thing."   75

"No other answer," he replied, "I give you
   than doing what you ask, for a fit request
   is answered best in silence and in deed."   78

From the bridge's height we came down to the point
   where it ends and joins the edge of the eighth bank,
   and then the *bolgia* opened up to me: 81

down there I saw a terrible confusion
   of serpents, all of such a monstrous kind
   the thought of them still makes my blood run cold.   84

Let all the sands of Libya boast no longer,
   for though she breeds chelydri and jaculi,
   pharcans, cenchres, and head-tailed amphisbenes,   87

she never bred so great a plague of venom,
   not even if combined with Ethiopia
   or all the sands that lie by the Red Sea.   90

Within this cruel and bitterest abundance
   people ran terrified and naked, hopeless
   of finding hiding-holes or heliotrope.   93

Their hands were tied behind their backs with serpents,
   which pushed their tails and heads around the loins
   and coiled themselves in knots around the front.   96

And then—at a sinner running by our bank
   a snake shot out and, striking, hit his mark:
   right where the neck attaches to the shoulder.   99

No *o* or *i* was ever quicker put
   by pen to paper than he flared up and burned,
   and turned into a heap of crumbled ash;   102

and then, these ashes scattered on the ground
   began to come together on their own
   and quickly take the form they had before: 105

precisely so, philosophers declare,
   the phoenix dies to be reborn again
   as she approaches her five-hundredth year;   108

alive, she does not feed on herbs or grain,
   but on teardrops of frankincense and balm,
   and wraps herself to die in nard and myrrh.   111

As a man in a fit will fall, not knowing why
   (perhaps some hidden demon pulls him down,
   or some oppilation chokes his vital spirits),   114

then, struggling to his feet, will look around,
   confused and overwhelmed by the great anguish
   he has suffered, moaning as he stares about—   117

so did this sinner when he finally rose.
   Oh, how harsh the power of the Lord can be,
   raining in its vengeance blows like these!   120

My guide asked him to tell us who he was,
   and he replied: "It's not too long ago
   I rained from Tuscany to this fierce gullet.   123

I loved the bestial life more than the human,
   like the bastard that I was; I'm Vanni Fucci,
   the beast! Pistoia was my fitting den."   126

I told my guide: "Tell him not to run away;
   ask him what sin has driven him down here,
   for I knew him as a man of bloody rage."   129

The sinner heard and did not try to feign;
   directing straight at me his mind and face,
   he reddened with a look of ugly shame,   132

and said: "That you have caught me by surprise
   here in this wretched *bolgia*, makes me grieve
   more than the day I lost my other life.   135

Now I am forced to answer what you ask:
   I am stuck so far down here because of theft:
   I stole the treasure of the sacristy—   138

a crime falsely attributed to another.
   I don't want you to rejoice at having seen me,
   if ever you escape from these dark pits,   141

so open your ears and hear my prophecy:
   Pistoia first shall be stripped of all its Blacks,
   and Florence then shall change its men and laws;   144

from Valdimagra Mars shall thrust a bolt
   of lightning wrapped in thick, foreboding clouds,
   then bolt and clouds will battle bitterly   147

in a violent storm above Piceno's fields,
   where rapidly the bolt will burst the cloud,
   and no White will escape without his wounds.   150

And I have told you this so you will suffer!"

NOTES

1–18. *In the season of the newborn year, when the sun*: The
striking image that opens Canto XXIV has been taken by most
critics to be a *tour de force* that has little or no relation to the
canto as a whole; I believe, however, that in its shifting im-
agery it sets the tone for the fantastic metamorphoses of this
canto and the next. In the simile, a peasant, erroneously be-
lieving the hoarfrost to be snow, first becomes angry, then,
discovering that he has been deceived, regains his composure
and drives his sheep out to pasture. From one point of view
the peasant is like Dante the Pilgrim and Virgil is like the
countryside:

> just so I felt myself lose heart to see
> my master's face wearing a troubled look,
> and as quickly came the salve to heal my sore.
>
> (16–18)

So Dante, when he sees that Virgil has regained his composure, is glad, like the peasant "when he sees the world has changed its face / in so little time . . ." (13–14). But from another point of view the peasant is like Virgil, because he believed the hoarfrost to be snow, just as Virgil had believed Malacoda's lie; like the angry peasant, who recovers his composure "in so little time," so Virgil does also. The Pilgrim, in this case, is like the sheep that the peasant drives out to pasture, for Virgil, having regained his composure, urges the Pilgrim up the rocky slope.

Thus the two figures compared to the elements of the simile undergo a shifting metamorphosis, just as the thieves in the Seventh *Bolgia* will. But Dante's subtle foreshadowing of metamorphosis does not stop there; within the simile itself the countryside undergoes a metamorphosis as the white hoarfrost melts away. Even in the rhyme itself, in Italian, there are words that suggest the same process, for here Dante makes extensive use of equivocal rhyme: two words that sound alike and are spelled the same way but mean different things. One example (out of at least three instances in the first twenty-four lines) occurs in lines 11 and 13:

> Come 'l tapin che non sa che si faccia;
> . . . .
> veggendo il mondo aver cangiata faccia

"Che si faccia" in line 11 means "what to do" (from *fare*, v. "to do") while "aver cangiata faccia" in line 13 means "has changed its face" (*la faccia*, n. "face"). Thus words themselves in this passage undergo metamorphosis.

The simile is indeed a *tour de force*, but a *tour de force* foreshadowing the complex and fantastic transformations to come.

21. *at the mountain's foot*: The mountain of Canto I, a reference that reminds the reader of the entire journey.

31. *It was no road for one who wore a cloak!*: Such as the Hypocrites of the previous *bolgia*.

38. *slope toward the yawning well that is the lowest*: That is, toward Cocytus, the lowest part of Hell.

47–48. *for sitting softly cushioned*: Note the rustic, proverbial tone of Virgil's words. He is talking like the peasant to whom he is compared in the opening simile.

55. *Much steeper stairs than these we'll have to climb*: Virgil is referring to the ascent up Lucifer's legs and beyond. See XXXIV, 82–84.

85–90. *Let all the sands of Libya boast no longer*: Libya and the other lands near the Red Sea (Ethiopia and Arabia) were renowned for producing several types of dreadful reptiles. All of these mentioned by Dante were described in the *Pharsalia* (IX, 700 ff). The *chelydri*, according to Lucan, leave smoking paths; the *jaculi* dart through the air and pierce whatever they encounter. The *phareans* make paths in the earth with their tails; the *cenchres* leave a wavering course in the sand; and the *amphisbenes* have two heads, one at each end.

92. *people ran terrified and naked, hopeless*: The Thieves.

93. *of finding hiding-holes or heliotrope*: According to folk tradition, heliotrope was believed to be a stone of many virtues. It could cure snake bites and make the man who carried it on his person invisible. Boccaccio relates a tale of a man who thought himself invisible through the power of the heliotrope (*Decameron* VIII, 3).

100. *No o or i was ever quicker put*: The letter *o* and the undotted *i* can be written with one stroke of the pen; thus, the action described is very rapid.

108–11. *as she approaches her five-hundredth year*: Dante compares the complex metamorphosis of Vanni Fucci to that of the phoenix, which, according to legend, consumes itself in flames every five hundred years. From the ashes is born a worm, which in three days develops into the bird again. The "philosophers" (*savi*, which can also be translated as "poets") are probably Ovid and Brunetto Latini, both of whom wrote about the phoenix.

112–17. *As a man in a fit will fall, not knowing why*: It was a

popular belief that during an epileptic fit, the victim was pos-
sessed by the devil; in addition to this, Dante presents a more
rational explanation: that some blockage of his veins inhibits
the proper functioning of a man's body.

125–29. *like the bastard that I was; I'm Vanni Fucci*: Vanni
Fucci, the illegitimate son of Fuccio de' Lazzari, was a militant
leader of the Blacks in Pistoia. His notoriety "as a man of
bloody rage" (129) was widespread; in fact, the Pilgrim is
surprised to find him here and not immersed in the Phlegethon
together with the other shades of the Violent (Canto XII).

138–39. *I stole the treasure of the sacristy*: Around 1293 the
treasury of San Iacopo in the church of San Zeno at Pistoia
was robbed. The person unjustly accused (139) of the theft
(and almost executed for it) was Rampino Foresi. Later, the
facts came to light, and Vanni della Monna, one of the con-
spirators, was sentenced to death. Vanni Fucci, however, es-
caped, and although he received a sentence in 1295 for murder
and other acts of violence, he managed to remain free until
his death in 1300.

143–50. *Pistoia first shall be stripped of all its Blacks*: Vanni
Fucci's prophecy remains somewhat obscure, but the best ex-
planation for it seems to be as follows. Members of the White
party in Pistoia forced the Blacks to leave after May 1301. The
Pistoian Blacks fled to Florence and, together with the Flor-
entine Blacks, took over the government of the city with the
aid of Charles of Valois in November 1301; the Whites were
then banished from the city. The Valdimagra of line 145 was
the territory of Moroello Malaspina (the "bolt of lightning"),
who as captain led a force of Florentines and Lucchesi (Blacks?)
against Pistoia in 1302. The "thick, foreboding clouds" in
which he is "wrapped" are the Pistoians who surprised
Moroello and surrounded him at the battle of Serravalle, a
town near "Piceno's fields." Although surrounded, Moroello
managed to rally his forces and disperse the enemy.

The use of meteorological imagery is typical of the science
of Dante's time.

CANTO XXV

The wrathful Vanni Fucci directs an obscene gesture to God, whereupon he is attacked by several snakes, which coil about him, tying him so tight that he cannot move a muscle. As soon as he flees, the centaur CACUS gallops by with a fire-breathing dragon on his back, and following close behind are three shades, concerned because they cannot find CIANFA—who soon appears as a snake and attacks AGNÈL; the two merge into one hideous monster, which then steals off. Next, GUERCIO, in the form of a snake, strikes BUOSO, and the two exchange shapes. Only PUCCIO SCIANCATO is left unchanged.

When he had finished saying this, the thief
　　shaped his fists into figs and raised them high
　　and cried: "Here, God, I've shaped them just for you!"　3

From then on all those snakes became my friends,
　　for one of them at once coiled round his neck
　　as if to say, "That's all you're going to say,"　6

while another twisted round his arms in front;
　　it tied itself into so tight a knot,
　　between the two he could not move a muscle.　9

Pistoia, ah, Pistoia! why not resolve
　　to burn yourself to ashes, ending all,
　　since you have done more evil than your founders?　2

Throughout the circles of this dark inferno
　　I saw no shade so haughty toward his God,
　　not even he who fell from Thebes' high walls.　15

Without another word he fled, and then
  I saw a raging centaur gallop up
  roaring: "Where is he, where is that untamed beast?"   18

I think that all Maremma does not have
  as many snakes as he had on his back,
  right up to where his human form begins.   21

Upon his shoulders, just behind the nape,
  a dragon with its wings spread wide was crouching
  and spitting fire at whoever came its way.   24

My master said to me: "That one is Cacus,
  who more than once in the grotto far beneath
  Mount Aventine spilled blood to fill a lake.   27

He does not go the same road as his brothers
  because of the cunning way he committed theft
  when he stole his neighbor's famous cattle-herd;   30

and then his evil deeds came to an end
  beneath the club of Hercules, who struck
  a hundred blows, and he, perhaps, felt ten."   33

While he was speaking Cacus galloped off;
  at the same time three shades appeared below us;
  my guide and I would not have seen them there   36

if they had not cried out: "Who are you two?"
  At this we cut our conversation short
  to give our full attention to these three.   39

I didn't know who they were, but then it happened,
  as often it will happen just by chance,
  that one of them was forced to name another: 42

"Where did Cianfa go off to?" he asked. And then,
  to keep my guide from saying anything,
  I put my finger tight against my lips.   45

Now if, my reader, you should hesitate
  to believe what I shall say, there's little wonder,
  for I, the witness, scarcely can believe it.   48

While I was watching them, all of a sudden
 a serpent—and it had six feet—shot up
 and hooked one of these wretches with all six. 51

With the middle feet it hugged the sinner's stomach
 and, with the front ones, grabbed him by the arms,
 and bit him first through one cheek, then the other; 54

the serpent spread its hind feet round both thighs,
 then stuck its tail between the sinner's legs,
 and up against his back the tail slid stiff. 57

No ivy ever grew to any tree
 so tight entwined, as the way that hideous beast
 had woven in and out its limbs with his; 60

and then both started melting like hot wax
 and, fusing, they began to mix their colors
 (so neither one seemed what he was before), 63

just as a brownish tint, ahead of flame,
 creeps up a burning page that is not black
 completely, even though the white is dying. 66

The other two who watched began to shout:
 "O Agnèl! If you could see how you are changing!
 You're not yourself, and you're not both of you!" 69

The two heads had already fused to one
 and features from each flowed and blended into
 one face where two were lost in one another; 72

two arms of each were four blurred strips of flesh;
 and thighs with legs, then stomach and the chest
 sprouted limbs that human eyes have never seen. 75

Each former likeness now was blotted out:
 both, and neither one it seemed—this picture
 of deformity. And then it sneaked off slowly. 78

Just as a lizard darting from hedge to hedge,
 under the stinging lash of the dog-days' heat,
 zips across the road, like a flash of lightning, 81

so, rushing toward the two remaining thieves,
   aiming at their guts, a little serpent,
   fiery with rage and black as pepper-corn,   84

shot up and sank its teeth in one of them,
   right where the embryo receives its food,
   then back it fell and lay stretched out before him.   87

The wounded thief stared speechless at the beast,
   and standing motionless began to yawn
   as though he needed sleep, or had a fever.   90

The snake and he were staring at each other;
   one from his wound, the other from its mouth
   fumed violently, and smoke with smoke was mingling. 93

Let Lucan from this moment on be silent,
   who tells of poor Nasidius and Sabellus,
   and wait to hear what I still have in store;   96

and Ovid, too, with his Cadmus and Arethusa—
   though he metamorphosed one into a snake,
   the other to a fountain, I feel no envy,   99

for never did he interchange two beings
   face to face so that both forms were ready
   to exchange their substance, each one for the other's,   102

an interchange of perfect symmetry:
   the serpent split its tail into a fork,
   and the wounded sinner drew his feet together;   105

the legs, with both the thighs, closed in to join
   and in a short time fused, so that the juncture
   didn't show signs of ever having been there,   108

the while the cloven tail assumed the features
   that the other one was losing, and its skin
   was growing soft, the other's getting scaly;   111

I saw his arms retreating to the armpits,
   and the reptile's two front feet, that had been short,
   began to stretch the length the man's had shortened;   114

the beast's hind feet then twisted round each other
   and turned into the member man conceals,
   while from the wretch's member grew two legs.   117

The smoke from each was swirling round the other,
   exchanging colors, bringing out the hair
   where there was none, and stripping off the other's.   120

The one rose up, the other sank, but neither
   dissolved the bond between their evil stares,
   fixed eye to eye, exchanging face for face;   123

the standing creature's face began receding
   toward the temples; from the excess stuff pulled back,
   the ears were growing out of flattened cheeks,   126

while from the excess flesh that did not flee
   the front, a nose was fashioned for the face,
   and lips puffed out to just the normal size.   129

The prostrate creature strains his face out long
   and makes his ears withdraw into his head,
   the way a snail pulls in its horns. The tongue,   132

that once had been one piece and capable
   of forming words, divides into a fork,
   while the other's fork heals up. The smoke subsides.   35

The soul that had been changed into a beast
   went hissing off along the valley's floor,
   the other close behind him, spitting words.   138

Then he turned his new-formed back on him and said
   to the shade left standing there: "Let Buoso run
   the valley on all fours, the way I did."   141

Thus I saw the cargo of the seventh hold
   exchange and interchange; and let the strangeness
   of it all excuse me, if my pen has failed.   144

And though this spectacle confused my eyes
   and stunned my mind, the two thieves could not flee
   so secretly I did not recognize   147

that one was certainly Puccio Sciancato
  (and he alone, of that company of three
    that first appeared, did not change to something else),   150

the other, he who made you mourn, Gaville.

NOTES

2. *shaped his fists into figs and raised them high*: An obscene gesture still current in Italy. The gesture is made by closing the hand to form a fist with the thumb inserted between the first and second fingers. It means "Up yours!" or "Fuck you!"

10–12. *Pistoia, ah, Pistoia! why not resolve*: Pistoia was supposedly founded by the remnants of the defeated army of Catiline (cf. XV, 61–78), composed primarily of evil-doers and brigands. Note that Dante calls upon Pistoia to destroy itself in the same manner that Vanni Fucci, its native son, was destroyed in the previous canto (100–17).

15. *he who fell from Thebes' high walls*: Capaneus, whom Dante placed among the Blasphemers in the Seventh Circle (XIV, 63). Like Vanni Fucci, Capaneus continues to blaspheme and rebel against God even in Hell.

19–20. *I think that all Maremma does not have*: Maremma was a swampy area along the Tuscan coast that was infested with snakes. See Canto XIII, n. 8–9; also XXIX, n. 47–49.

25–33. *That one is Cacus*: Cacus, a centaur, was the son of Vulcan; he was a fire-belching monster who lived in a cave beneath Mt. Aventine and pillaged the inhabitants of the area. But when he stole several cattle from Hercules, the latter went to Cacus's cave and killed him. "His brothers" (28) are the centaurs who serve as guardians in the first round of the Seventh Circle (Canto XII).

43. *"Where did Cianfa go off to?" he asked*: Cianfa was a member of the Florentine Donati family. He makes his appearance in line 50 in the form of a serpent.

68. *O Agnèl!*: Besides the indication that Agnèl is Florentine (except for Vanni Fucci, the thieves in this canto are all Flor-

entines), and possibly is one of the Brunelleschi family, nothing more is known of him.

86. *right where the embryo receives its food*: The navel.

94–102. *Let Lucan from this moment on be silent*: In the *Pharsalia* (IX, 763 and 790) Lucan tells of the physical transformations undergone by Sabellus and Nasidius, both soldiers in Cato's army who, being bitten by snakes, turned respectively into ashes (cf. Vanni Fucci's metamorphosis, XXIV, 100–17) and into a formless mass. Ovid relates (*Metamorphoses* IV, 576) how Cadmus took the form of a serpent and how Arethusa became a fountain (V, 572).

In these rather boastful verses Dante declares the superiority of his art, at least in this case, to that of Lucan and Ovid. Theirs was a "one-way" transformation; his transformation will be reciprocal, and therein lies its uniqueness.

140–41. *Let Buoso run*: The identity of Buoso, the newly formed serpent, is uncertain; some commentators think him to be Buoso degli Abati and others, Buoso Donati (see XXX, 44).

142. *Thus I saw the cargo of the seventh hold*: Dante, by referring to the inhabitants of the Seventh *Bolgia* as "cargo" (*zavorra*), sets up the ship imagery for Ulysses in the next canto.

145–51

That the Pilgrim's eyes are confused and his mind is stunned at this point is easily understandable in terms merely of the spectacle he has witnessed. He has seen three types of metamorphosis undergone by the thieves in Cantos XXIV–XXV. First, a sinner (Vanni Fucci) is struck by a serpent at the base of the neck, burns to ashes, and reshapes himself from the pile of ashes; more complicated is the next transformation, caused when another sinner is attacked by a six-footed serpent—who merges with him as the two grow together into one hideous creature; finally, the attacking serpent shares again in the metamorphosis, in a still more complicated way: the snake becomes a man and the man becomes a snake. As for the symbolism

involved in these metamorphoses, I agree with Dorothy Say-
ers's interpretation: "In this canto we see how the Thieves,
who made no distinction between *meum* and *tuum* . . . cannot
call their forms or their personalities their own."

But there is still a greater reason for the Pilgrim's confusion,
given the problems of identification involved in the last two
metamorphoses. We are told beforehand that the one who
imitates the birth and death of the phoenix is Vanni Fucci; but
it takes careful reading and re-reading (and some guessing) to
establish the roles played by three of the five sinners alluded
to in this canto: Cianfa, Buoso, and "he who made you mourn,
Gaville" (Francesco Cavalcanti, see n. 151). Cianfa's name is
mentioned by one of the three thieves appearing in line 35,
who seems surprised at Cianfa's disappearance ("Where did
Cianfa go off to?" 43). But if Cianfa has disappeared we must
assume it is because he has just been transformed into the six-
footed serpent who attacks Agnèl ("O Agnèl! If you could see
how you are changing!" 68), to fuse with him into one mon-
strous form. From the words "Let Buoso run / the valley on
all fours, the way I did" (140–41), spoken after the next met-
amorphosis by the serpent-become-man about the man-become-
serpent, we learn that Buoso must have also been one of the
three thieves seen by the Pilgrim. Finally, the speaker himself
must have been Francesco Cavalcanti, alluded to in the last
line of the canto. Surely the blurry presentation of identities
offered to the reader represents an artistic device on the part
of Dante to enhance the fluctuation of identity given by met·
amorphosis itself.

148. *that one was certainly Puccio Sciancato*: Puccio Sciancato
(the only one of the original three Florentine thieves who does
not assume a new shape) was a member of the Galigai family
and a supporter of the Ghibellines. He was exiled from Flor-
ence in 1268.

151. *the other, he who made you mourn, Gaville*: Francesco
Cavalcanti, known as Guercio, was slain by the inhabitants of
Gaville, a small town near Florence in Valdarno (Arno Valley).
The Cavalcanti family avenged his death by decimating the
populace; thus, he was Gaville's reason to mourn.

CANTO XXVI

FROM THE RIDGE *high above the Eighth* Bolgia *can be perceived a myriad of flames flickering far below, and Virgil explains that within each flame is the suffering soul of a* Deceiver. *One flame, divided at the top, catches the Pilgrim's eye and he is told that within it are jointly punished* Ulysses *and* Diomed. *Virgil questions the pair for the benefit of the Pilgrim. Ulysses responds with the famous narrative of his last voyage, during which he passed the Pillars of Hercules and sailed the forbidden sea until he saw a mountain shape, from which came suddenly a whirlwind that spun his ship around three times and sank it.*

Be joyful, Florence, since you are so great
    that your outstretched wings beat over land and sea,
    and your name is spread throughout the realm of Hell!   3

I was ashamed to find among the thieves
    five of your most eminent citizens,
    a fact which does you very little honor   6

But if early morning dreams have any truth,
    you will have the fate, in not too long a time,
    that Prato and the others crave for you.   9

And were this the day, it would not be too soon!
    Would it had come to pass, since pass it must!
    The longer the delay, the more my grief.   12

We started climbing up the stairs of boulders
    that had brought us to the place from where we watched;
    my guide went first and pulled me up behind him.   15

We went along our solitary way
　　among the rocks, among the ridge's crags,
　　where the foot could not advance without the hand.   18

I know that I grieved then, and now again
　　I grieve when I remember what I saw,
　　and more than ever I restrain my talent   21

lest it run a course that virtue has not set;
　　for if a lucky star or something better
　　has given me this good, I must not misuse it.   24

As many fireflies (in the season when
　　the one who lights the world hides his face least,
　　in the hour when the flies yield to mosquitoes)   27

as the peasant on the hillside at his ease
　　sees, flickering in the valley down below,
　　where perhaps he gathers grapes or tills the soil—   30

with just so many flames all the eighth *bolgia*
　　shone brilliantly, as I became aware
　　when at last I stood where the depths were visible.   33

As he who was avenged by bears beheld
　　Elijah's chariot at its departure,
　　when the rearing horses took to flight toward Heaven,   36

and though he tried to follow with his eyes,
　　he could not see more than the flame alone
　　like a small cloud once it had risen high—   39

so each flame moves itself along the throat
　　of the abyss, none showing what it steals
　　but each one stealing nonetheless a sinner.   42

I was on the bridge, leaning far over—so far
　　that if I had not grabbed some jut of rock
　　I could easily have fallen to the bottom.   45

And my guide, who saw me so absorbed, explained:
　　"There are souls concealed within these moving fires,
　　each one swathed in his burning punishment."   48

"O master," I replied, "from what you say
    I know now I was right; I had guessed already
    it might be so, and I was about to ask you: 51

Who's in that flame with its tip split in two,
    like that one which once sprang up from the pyre
    where Eteocles was placed beside his brother?"   54

He said: "Within, Ulysses and Diomed
    are suffering in anger with each other,
    just vengeance makes them march together now.   57

And they lament inside one flame the ambush
    of the horse become the gateway that allowed
    the Romans' noble seed to issue forth.   60

Therein they mourn the trick that caused the grief
    of Deïdamia, who still weeps for Achilles;
    and there they pay for the Palladium."   63

"If it is possible for them to speak
    from within those flames," I said, "master, I pray
    and repray you—let my prayer be like a thousand—   66

that you do not forbid me to remain
    until the two-horned flame comes close to us;
    you see how I bend toward it with desire!"   69

"Your prayer indeed is worthy of highest praise,"
    he said to me, "and therefore I shall grant it;
    but see to it your tongue refrains from speaking.   72

Leave it to me to speak, for I know well
    what you would ask; perhaps, since they were Greeks,
    they might not pay attention to your words."   75

So when the flame had reached us, and my guide
    decided that the time and place were right,
    he addressed them and I listened to him speaking: 78

"O you who are two souls within one fire,
    if I have deserved from you when I was living,
    if I have deserved from you much praise or little,   81

when in the world I wrote my lofty verses,
   do not move on; let one of you tell where
   he lost himself through his own fault, and died."   84

The greater of the ancient flame's two horns
   began to sway and quiver, murmuring
   just like a flame that strains against the wind;   87

then, while its tip was moving back and forth,
   as if it were the tongue itself that spoke,
   the flame took on a voice and said: "When I   90

set sail from Circe, who, more than a year,
   had kept me occupied close to Gaëta
   (before Aeneas called it by that name),   93

not sweetness of a son, not reverence
   for an aging father, not the debt of love
   I owed Penelope to make her happy,   96

could quench deep in myself the burning wish
   to know the world and have experience
   of all man's vices, of all human worth.   99

So I set out on the deep and open sea
   with just one ship and with that group of men,
   not many, who had not deserted me.   102

I saw as far as Spain, far as Morocco,
   both shores; I had left behind Sardinia,
   and the other islands which that sea encloses.   105

I and my mates were old and tired men.
   Then finally we reached the narrow neck
   where Hercules put up his signal-pillars   108

to warn men not to go beyond that point.
   On my right I saw Seville, and passed beyond;
   on my left, Ceüta had already sunk behind me.   111

'Brothers,' I said, 'who through a hundred thousand
   perils have made your way to reach the West,
   during this so brief vigil of our senses   114

that is still reserved for us, do not deny
   yourself experience of what there is beyond,
   behind the sun, in the world they call unpeopled.   117

Consider what you came from: you are Greeks!
   You were not born to live like mindless brutes
   but to follow paths of excellence and knowledge.'   120

With this brief exhortation I made my crew
   so anxious for the way that lay ahead,
   that then I hardly could have held them back;   123

and with our stern turned toward the morning light,
   we made our oars our wings for that mad flight,
   gaining distance, always sailing to the left.   126

The night already had surveyed the stars
   the other pole contains; it saw ours so low
   it did not show above the ocean floor.   129

Five times we saw the splendor of the moon
   grow full and five times wanc away again
   since we had entered through the narrow pass—   132

when there appeared a mountain shape, darkened
   by distance, that arose to endless heights.
   I had never seen another mountain like it.   135

Our celebrations soon turned into grief:
   from the new land there rose a whirling wind
   that beat against the forepart of the ship   138

and whirled us round three times in churning waters;
   the fourth blast raised the stern up high, and sent
   the bow down deep, as pleased Another's will.   141

And then the sea was closed again, above us."

NOTES

1–6. *Be joyful, Florence, since you are so great*: Dante's invec-
tive against Florence, inspired by the presence of five of her
citizens in the *bolgia* of the thieves, also serves an artistic func-

tion. Depicted as a great bird that spreads its wings, the proud city of Florence prefigures Lucifer (cf. XXXIV, 46–48) and, more immediately, the "mad flight" (125) of Ulysses, whose ship's oars were like wings. But as Lucifer was cast down into Hell in defeat by God, so Ulysses was cast into the depths of the sea by a force he refers to as "Another's will" (141). The implication is that someday Florence, by adhering to her present course, will also be destroyed.

7–9. *But if early morning dreams have any truth*: According to the ancient and medieval popular tradition, the dreams that men have in the early morning hours before daybreak will come true.

Dante's dream-prophecy concerns impending strife for Florence and can be interpreted in several ways. It could refer to the malediction placed on the city by Cardinal Niccolò da Prato, who was sent (1304) by Pope Benedict XI to reconcile the opposing political factions, and who, having failed in his mission, decided to lay a curse on the city. Or we may have an allusion to the expulsion of the Blacks from Prato in 1309. However, it seems most plausible, given the phrase "and the others" (9), that Prato is to be interpreted here in a generic sense to indicate all the small Tuscan towns subjected to Florentine rule, which will soon rebel against their master.

34–39. *As he who was avenged by bears beheld*: The prophet Elisha saw Elijah transported to Heaven in a fiery chariot. When Elisha on another occasion cursed, in the name of the Lord, a group of children who were mocking him, two bears came out of the forest and devoured them (II Kings II, 9–12, 23–24).

52–54. *Who's in that flame with its tip split in two*: Here the attention of the Pilgrim, is captured by a divided flame, as it was in Canto XIX by the flaming, flailing legs of Nicholas III. Dante compares this flame with that which rose from the funeral pyre of Eteocles and Polynices, the sons of Oedipus and Jocasta, who, contesting the throne of Thebes, caused a major conflict known as the Seven Against Thebes (see XIV, 68–69). The two brothers met in single combat and slew each other. They were placed together on the pyre, but because of their great mutual hatred, the flame split.

55–57. *Within, Ulysses and Diomed*: Ulysses, the son of Laertes, was a central figure in the Trojan War. Although his deeds are recounted by Homer, Dictys of Crete, and many others, the story of his last voyage presented here by Dante (90–142) has no literary or historical precedent. His story, being an invention of Dante's, is unique in *The Divine Comedy*.

Diomed, the son of Tydeus and Deipyle, ruled Argos. He was a major Greek figure in the Trojan War and was frequently associated with Ulysses in his exploits.

In Italian, lines 56–57 are: ". . . e così 'nseme / a la vendetta vanno come a l'ira." Most commentators interpret the lines to mean that Ulysses and Diomed go together toward punishment ("vendetta") now, as in life they went together in anger (they fought together?). But because of the parallel construction *a la vendetta . . . a l'ira*, both parts of which depend on the verb *vanno* ("go") in the present tense, and because of the comparison Dante makes between Ulysses and Diomed and Eteocles and Polynices, I believe that these two figures in the flames are angry *now*; that it is part of their punishment, since they were close companions in sin on earth, to suffer ". . . in anger with each other" in Hell. "Togetherness" in punishment suffered by those who were once joined in sin has been suggested in the case of Paolo and Francesca (Canto V).

58–60. *And they lament inside one flame the ambush*: The Trojans mistakenly believed the mammoth wooden horse, left outside the city's walls, to be a sign of Greek capitulation. They brought it through the gates of the city amid great rejoicing. Later that evening the Greek soldiers hidden in the horse emerged and sacked the city. The Fall of Troy occasioned the journey of Aeneas and his followers ("noble seed") to establish a new nation on the shores of Italy which would become the heart of the Roman Empire. See Cantos I (73–75) and II (13–21).

61–62. *the grief / of Deïdamia*: Thetis brought her son Achilles, disguised as a girl, to the court of King Lycomedes on the

island of Scyros, so that he would not have to fight in the
Trojan War. There Achilles seduced the king's daughter Dei-
damia, who bore him a child and whom he later abandoned,
encouraged by Ulysses (who in company with Diomed had
come in search of him) to join the war. Achilles' female dis-
guise was unveiled by a "trick": bearing gifts for Lycomedes'
daughters, Ulysses had smuggled in among them a shield and
lance; Achilles betrayed his real sex by manifesting an inor-
dinate interest in the two weapons.

63. *and there they pay for the Palladium*: The sacred Palladium,
a statue of the goddess Pallas Athena, guaranteed the integrity
of Troy as long as it remained in the citadel. Ulysses and
Diomed stole it and carried it off to Argos, thereby securing
victory for the Greeks over the Trojans.

75. *they might not pay attention to your words*: No one has yet
offered a convincing explanation for Virgil's reluctance to al-
low the Pilgrim to address the two Greek warriors. Perhaps
Virgil felt that it was more fitting for him to speak because
he represented the same world of antiquity as they. (See XXVII,
n. 33.)

90–92. *When I / set sail from Circe*: On his return voyage to
Ithaca from Troy Ulysses was detained by Circe, the daughter
of the Sun, for more than a year. She was an enchantress who
transformed Ulysses' men into swine.

92–93. *close to Gaëta*: Along the coast of southern Italy above
Naples there is a promontory (and now on it there is a city)
then called Gaëta. Aeneas named it to honor his nurse, who
had died there. See *Aeneid* VII, 1ff. and Ovid's *Metamorphoses*
XIV, 441ff.

94–96. *not sweetness of a son, not reverence*: In his quest for
knowledge of the world Ulysses puts aside his affection for
his son, Telemachus, his duty toward his father, Laertes, and
the love of his devoted wife, Penelope; that is, he sinned against
the classical notion of *pietas*.

108. *where Hercules put up his signal-pillars*: The Strait of
Gibraltar, referred to in ancient times as the Pillars of Hercules.
The two "pillars" are Mt. Abyla on the North African coast
and Mt. Calpe on the European side; originally one mountain,

they were separated by Hercules to designate the farthest reach of the inhabited world, beyond which no man was permitted to venture.

110–11. *On my right I saw Seville, and passed beyond*: In other words Ulysses has passed through the Strait of Gibraltar and is now in the Atlantic Ocean. Ceuta is a town on the North African coast opposite Gibraltar; in this passage Seville probably represents the Iberian Peninsula and, as such, the boundary of the inhabited world.

125. *we made our oars our wings for that mad flight*: Note Ulysses' *present* judgment in Hell of his past action. (See XXVII, final note.)

130–31. *Five times we saw the splendor of the moon*: Five months had passed since they began their voyage:

133. *when there appeared a mountain shape, darkened*: In Dante's time the Southern Hemisphere was believed to be composed entirely of water; the mountain that Ulysses and his men see from afar is the Mount of Purgatory, which rises from the sea in the Southern Hemisphere, the polar opposite of Jerusalem. For the formation of the mountain see XXXIV, 112–26.

*   *   *   *

In the list of sins punished in the Eighth Circle of Hell (those of Simple Fraud) which Virgil offers in Canto XI, two categories are left unspecified, summed up in the phrase "and like filth." When the sins specified in this list are assigned to their respective *bolge* (and all commentators are agreed as to their localization), two *bolge* are left open: the Eighth and the Ninth—which must be those where the sins of "like filth" are punished. As for the specific variety of Fraud being punished in the Ninth *Bolgia*, the sinners there are clearly identified when we meet them in Canto XXVIII, as "sowers of scandal and schism." As for our canto, all scholars have assumed that the sin for which Ulysses and Diomed are being punished is that of Fraudulent Counseling, not because of what is said about them here but because of what is said about Guido da Montefeltro in the next canto: the Black Cherub, in claiming Guido's soul, says (XXVII, 115–16): "He must come down to join my other servants for the false counsel he gave." Since Guido is in the same *bolgia*, and suffers the same punishment as Ulysses and Diomed, critics have evidently assumed (as is only logical) that they must have committed the same sin; they also assume that the sin they share in common must be that of Fraudulent Counseling.

But as for Ulysses and Diomed, their sins are specifically mentioned and in none of the three instances involved is any act of "fraudulent counseling" recorded. If these two are not in Hell for this sin, then, in spite of the Black Cherub's words, it must follow that neither is Guido. (See final note to Canto XXVII).

CANTO XXVII

*As soon as Ulysses has finished his narrative, another flame—
its soul within having recognized Virgil's Lombard accent—comes for-
ward asking the travelers to pause and answer questions about the
state of affairs in the region of Italy from which he came. The Pilgrim
responds by outlining the strife in Romagna and ends by asking the
flame who he is. The flame, although he insists he does not want
his story to be known among the living, answers because he is sup-
posedly convinced that the Pilgrim will never return to earth. He is
another famous deceiver, Guido da Montefeltro, a soldier who
became a friar in his old age; but he was untrue to his vows when,
at the urging of Pope Boniface VIII, he counseled the use of fraud
in the pope's campaign against the Colonna family. He was damned
to Hell because he failed to repent his sins, trusting instead in the
pope's fraudulent absolution.*

By now the flame was standing straight and still,
   it said no more and had already turned
   from us, with sanction of the gentle poet,   3

when another, coming right behind it,
   attracted our attention to its tip,
   where a roaring of confusing sounds had started.   6

As the Sicilian bull—that bellowed first
   with cries of that one (and it served him right)
   who with his file had fashioned such a beast—   9

would bellow with the victim's voice inside,
   so that, although the bull was only brass,
   the effigy itself seemed pierced with pain: 12

so, lacking any outlet to escape
   from the burning soul that was inside the flame,
   the suffering words became the fire's language.　　　15

But after they had made their journey upward
   to reach the tip, giving it that same quiver
   the sinner's tongue inside had given them,　　　18

we heard the words: "O you to whom I point
   my voice, who spoke just now in Lombard, saying:
   'you may move on, I won't ask more of you.'　　　21

although I have been slow in coming to you,
   be willing, please, to pause and speak with me.
   You see how willing I am—and I burn!　　　24

If you have just now fallen to this world
   of blindness, from that sweet Italian land
   where I took on the burden of my guilt,　　　27

tell me, are the Romagnols at war or peace?
   For I come from the hills between Urbino
   and the mountain chain that lets the Tiber loose."　　　30

I was still bending forward listening
   when my master touched my side and said to me:
   "*You* speak to him; *this* one is Italian."　　　33

And I, who was prepared to answer him,
   began without delaying my response:
   "O soul who stands concealed from me down there,　　　36

your Romagna is not now and never was
   without war in her tyrants' hearts, although
   there was no open warfare when I came here.　　　39

Ravenna's situation has not changed:
   the eagle of Polenta broods up there,
   covering all of Cervia with its pinions;　　　42

the land that stood the test of long endurance
   and left the French piled in a bloody heap
   is once again beneath the verdant claws.　　　45

Verrucchio's Old Mastiff and its New One,
   who both were bad custodians of Montagna,
   still sink their fangs into their people's flesh;   48

the cities by Lamone and Santerno
   are governed by the Lion of the White Lair,
   who changes parties every change of season.   51

As for the town whose side the Savio bathes:
   just as it lies between the hills and plains,
   it lives between freedom and tyranny.   54

And now I beg you tell us who you are—
   grant me my wish as yours was granted you—
   so that your fame may hold its own on earth."   57

And when the fire, in its own way, had roared
   awhile, the flame's sharp tip began to sway
   to and fro, then released a blow of words: 60

"If I thought that I were speaking to a soul
   who someday might return to see the world,
   most certainly this flame would cease to flicker;   63

but since no one, if I have heard the truth,
   ever returns alive from this deep pit,
   with no fear of dishonor I answer you: 66

I was a man of arms and then a friar,
   believing with the cord to make amends;
   and surely my belief would have come true   69

were it not for that High Priest (his soul be damned!)
   who put me back among my early sins;
   I want to tell you why and how it happened.   72

While I still had the form of the bones and flesh
   my mother gave me, all my actions were
   not those of a lion, but those of a fox;   75

the wiles and covert paths, I knew them all,
   and so employed my art that rumor of me
   spread to the farthest limits of the earth.   78

When I saw that the time of life had come
    for me, as it must come for every man,
    to lower the sails and gather in the lines,   81

things I once found pleasure in then grieved me;
    repentant and confessed, I took the vows
    a monk takes. And, oh, to think it could have worked! 84

And then the Prince of the New Pharisees
    chose to wage war upon the Lateran
    instead of fighting Saracens or Jews,   87

for all his enemies were Christian souls
    (none among the ones who conquered Acri,
    none a trader in the Sultan's kingdom).   90

His lofty papal seat, his sacred vows
    were no concern to him, nor was the cord
    I wore (that once made those it girded leaner).   93

As Constantine once had Silvestro brought
    from Mount Soracte to cure his leprosy,
    so this one sought me out as his physician   96

to cure his burning fever caused by pride.
    He asked me to advise him. I was silent,
    for his words were drunken. Then he spoke again: 99

'Fear not, I tell you: the sin you will commit,
    it is forgiven. Now you will teach me how
    I can level Palestrina to the ground.   102

Mine is the power, as you cannot deny,
    to lock and unlock Heaven. Two keys I have,
    those keys my predecessor did not cherish.'   105

And when his weighty arguments had forced me
    to the point that silence seemed the poorer choice,
    I said: 'Father, since you grant me absolution   108

for the sin I find I must fall into now:
    ample promise with a scant fulfillment
    will bring you triumph on your lofty throne.'   111

Saint Francis came to get me when I died,
    but one of the black Cherubim cried out:
    'Don't touch him, don't cheat me of what is mine!   114

He must come down to join my other servants
    for the false counsel he gave. From then to now
    I have been ready at his hair, because   117

one cannot be absolved unless repentant,
    nor can one both repent and will a thing
    at once—the one is canceled by the other!'   120

O wretched me! How I shook when he took me,
    saying: 'Perhaps you never stopped to think
    that I might be somewhat of a logician!'   123

He took me down to Minòs, who eight times
    twisted his tail around his hardened back,
    then in his rage he bit it, and announced: 126

'He goes with those the thievish fire burns.'
    And here you see me now, lost, wrapped this way,
    moving, as I do, with my resentment."   129

When he had brought his story to a close,
    the flame, in grievous pain, departed from us
    gnarling and flickering its pointed horn.   132

My guide and I moved farther on; we climbed
    the ridge until we stood on the next arch
    that spans the fosse where penalties are paid   135

by those who, sowing discord, earned Hell's wages.

NOTES

7–15. *As the Sicilian bull—that bellowed first*: Phalaris, des-
potic ruler of Agrigentum in Sicily, commissioned Perillus to
construct a bronze bull to be used as an instrument of torture;
it was fashioned so that, once it was heated, the victim roasting
within would emit cries which sounded without like those of

a bellowing bull. To test the device, Phalaris made the artisan himself its first victim, and thus he received his just reward for creating such a cruel instrument.

20. *who spoke just now in Lombard*: Evidently the words overheard by Guido were contained in Virgil's dismissal of Ulysses (3), which means that Virgil from the beginning had spoken to him in that dialect (or possibly only with a Lombard accent). Although some commentators have suggested that "Lombard" simply means "Italian," it would be quite fitting for Virgil to speak the dialect of his native region.

28. *tell me, are the Romagnols at war or peace?*: The Romagnols are the inhabitants of Romagna, the area bounded by the Po and the Reno rivers, the Apennines, and the Adriatic Sea.

29–30. *For I come from the hills between Urbino*: Between the town of Urbino and Mount Coronaro (one of the Tuscan Apennines, where the Tiber River originates) lies the region known as Montefeltro. The speaker is Guido da Montefeltro, the Ghibelline captain whose wisdom and skill in military strategy won him fame. In a later passage (73–78) he refers to his martial talent and activity as more foxlike than lionlike.

33. You *speak to him;* this *one is Italian.*: After having prevented the Pilgrim from addressing Ulysses and Diomed (because they were Greeks?), he now, in the case of the Italian Guido, urges his ward to do the talking.

41–42. *the eagle of Polenta broods up there*: In 1300 Guido Vecchio, head of the Polenta family (whose coat of arms bears an eagle) and father of Francesca da Rimini, governed Ravenna and the surrounding territory, which included Cervia, a small town on the Adriatic.

43–45. *the land that stood the test of long endurance*: Besieged for many months by French and Guelf troops, the Ghibelline city of Forlì emerged victorious. In May 1282, her inhabitants, led by Guido da Montefeltro, broke the siege and massacred the opposing army. However, in 1300 Forlì was dominated by the tyrannical Ordelaffi family, whose insignia bore a green lion ("beneath the verdant claws," 45)

46–48. *Verrucchio's Old Mastiff and its New One*: In return for their services the city of Rimini gave her ruling family the castle of Verrucchio. Malatesta, lord of Rimini from 1295 to 1312, and his first-born son, Malatestino, are respectively the "Old" and "New" mastiffs. Having defeated the Ghibellines of Rimini in 1295, Malatesta captured Montagna de' Parcitati, the head of the party, who was subsequently murdered in prison by Malatestino.

49–51. *the cities by Lamone and Santerno*: The cities of Faenza (situated on the Lamone River) and Imola (near the Santerno) were governed by Maghinardo Pagani da Susinana, whose coat of arms bore a blue lion on a white field. He was noted for his political instability (Ghibelline in Romagna and Guelf in Tuscany).

52–54. *As for the town whose side the Savio bathes*: Unlike the other cities mentioned by Guido, Cesena was not ruled by a despot; rather, her government, although not completely determined by the people, was in the hands of an able ruler, Galasso da Montefeltro, a cousin of Guido.

67–71. *I was a man of arms and then a friar*: In 1296 Guido joined the Franciscan order. The reason for his harsh condemnation of Pope Boniface VIII ("that High Priest") is found in lines 85–111.

81. *to lower the sails and gather in the lines*: Guido's use of the metaphor of the voyage to describe his arrival at old age certainly invites us to think of Ulysses' voyage, also undertaken when Ulysses was an old man; and the two voyages underscore the nature of the central metaphor of *The Divine Comedy*, the "voyage" of Dante the Pilgrim. As a pagan, Ulysses, of course, could not have reached the Mount of Purgatory; but even in pagan terms he committed two serious sins in undertaking the voyage: he failed to honor his commitments to his family as son, husband, and father (XXVI, 94–96), and he sailed past the limits allowed to pagan man (the pillars Hercules "put up . . . / to warn men not to go beyond that point," XXVI, 108–109). This voyage could only end in failure.

Guido's "voyage" is his whole life, and when he becomes an old man, he gives the *appearance* of doing what is right in Christian terms: "repentant and confessed, I took the vows / a monk takes" (XXVII, 83–84). but his repentance could not have been sincere, since Guido breaks his vows with his sinful advice to Pope Boniface. Thus Guido's "voyage," too, can only end in failure, and in thinking that appearance is enough, he only deceives himself.

The Pilgrim, however, will be successful in his "voyage" because he undertakes it for the right reason (to learn the nature of sin, that he may repent past sins and avoid future ones, and ultimately to reach God) and because he goes in a spirit of humility and love of God; also the Pilgrim does not wait until old age to repent of his sinful past (he is "midway along the journey of . . . life," I, 1) and the success of his journey is vouchsafed by the grace of God. Unlike Ulysses and Guido, who were also men of great genius and excellence, Dante uses his *virtù* in the right way: in the service of God. See the final note to this canto.

85–90. *And then the Prince of the New Pharisees*: In 1297 the struggle between Boniface VIII ("the Prince of the New Pharisees") and the Colonna family (who lived near the Lateran palace, the pope's residence, and who did not consider the resignation of Celestine V valid) erupted into open conflict. Boniface did not launch his crusade against the traditional rivals—Saracens and Jews (87)—but rather against his fellow Christians, faithful warriors of the Church who neither aided the Saracens during the conquest of Acre in 1291 (the last Christian stronghold in the Holy Land), nor disobeyed the interdict on commerce with Mohammedan lands (89–90).

92–93 *nor was the cord / I wore*: In earlier, less corrupt times the friars of the Franciscan order ("those it [the cord] girded") were faithful to their founder's example of poverty and abstinence.

94–95. *As Constantine once had Silvestro brought*: See Canto XIX, n. 115–17.

102. *I can level Palestrina to the ground*: The Colonna family, excommunicated by Boniface, took refuge in their fortress at Palestrina (twenty-five miles east of Rome), which was able to withstand the onslaughts of papal troops. Acting on Guido's counsel (110–11), Boniface promised (but without serious in-

tentions) to grant complete pardon to the Colonna family, who then surrendered and, consequently, lost everything.

104–105. *Two keys I have*: Deceived by Boniface, who was to be his successor, Celestine V renounced the papacy ("those keys") in 1294. See Cantos III, n. 60, and XIX, n. 53.

108–109. *Father, since you grant me absolution*: Guido's principal error was self-deception: a man cannot be absolved from a sin before he commits it, and moreover, he cannot direct his will toward committing a sin and repent it at the same time (118–20).

113. *one of the black Cherubim*: Some of the Cherubim (the *eighth* order of angels) were transformed into demons for their rebellion against God; appropriately they appear in the *Eighth* Circle and the *Eighth Bolgia* of Hell.

* * * *

In the final note to Canto XXVI it was stated that there is no record of Ulysses having used fraudulent counseling in the three sins attributed to him by Virgil and that, if Ulysses is not being punished for that sin, the same must be true of Guido. But Guido confesses to having given fraudulent counsel, in one case at least, at the urging of Pope Boniface; and when the Black Cherub comes to claim his soul from Saint Francis, he says of Guido: "He must come down to join my other servants / for the false counsel he gave."

But Guido's advice to the pope was not only a sin committed at a given moment but also, and in a far more important way, a revelation about his past, his whole past: in the scene between Guido and Boniface we see that the wily strategist has not truly repented of the sins committed during his military career. Yes, Guido is in Hell because he gave the fraudulent counsel— that is, because he was capable of such an act; and he was capable of it because he had not repented for the sins committed during his life as a soldier, sins which we have no reason to believe were those of counseling ("I was a man of arms," 67). His "repentance" itself was fraudulent: "believing with the cord to make amends" (68).

If, then, both Ulysses and Guido are in Hell for having committed a sin other than that of fraudulent counseling, what is that sin? The only clear-cut subdivision of simple fraud that could fit the two sinners would be that of military fraud, since both of them were men of arms who were famous for their guile. Perhaps military fraud could be on a level with simony, which is ecclesiastical fraud: one would involve the abuse of a noble profession, the other of a sacred office. But there is something else in common between Ulysses and Guido which is far more important than the profession they shared in life, and that is their exceptional sharpness of intellect and powers of invention. And so, instead of a clear-cut subdivision, determined by the professional goal toward which the fraud is directed, I prefer to think, in a more general way, of fraud unspecified—except in terms of the talents that characterize its practitioners. While all fraud involves in some way the abuse of the intellect, the intellect that Ulysses and Guido abused was exceptionally brilliant. If all men are endowed with reason, they had received a special gift from God, but they had used it—these brilliant sinners who shine in flames—for deception and the creation of snares.

CANTO XXVIII

—————

IN THE NINTH Bolgia the Pilgrim is overwhelmed by the sight
of mutilated, bloody shades, many of whom are ripped open, with
entrails spilling out. They are the SOWERS OF SCANDAL AND SCHISM,
and among them are MAHOMET, ALI, PIER DA MEDICINA, GAIUS
SCRIBONIUS CURIO, MOSCA DE' LAMBERTI, and BERTRAN DE
BORN. All bemoan their painful lot, and Mahomet and Pier da
Medicina relay warnings through the Pilgrim to certain living Italians
who are soon to meet terrible ends. Bertran de Born, who comes
carrying his head in his hand like a lantern, is a particularly arresting
example of a Dantean contrapasso.

Who could, even in the simplest kind of prose
    describe in full the scene of blood and wounds
    that I saw now—no matter how he tried!   3

Certainly any tongue would have to fail:
    man's memory and man's vocabulary
    are not enough to comprehend such pain.   6

If one could bring together all the wounded
    who once upon the fateful soil of Puglia
    grieved for their life's blood spilled by the Romans,   9

and spilled again in the long years of the war
    that ended in great spoils of golden rings
    (as Livy's history tells, that does not err),   12

and pile them with the ones who felt the blows
    when they stood up against great Robert Guiscard,
    and with those others whose bones are still in heaps   15

at Ceprano (there where every Puglian
  turned traitor), and add those from Tagliacozzo,
  where old Alardo conquered, weaponless—   18

if all these maimed with limbs lopped off or pierced
  were brought together, the scene would be nothing
  to compare with the foul ninth *bolgia*'s bloody sight.   21

No wine cask with its stave or cant-bar sprung
  was ever split the way I saw someone
  ripped open from his chin to where we fart.   24

Between his legs his guts spilled out, with the heart
  and other vital parts, and the dirty sack
  that turns to shit whatever the mouth gulps down.   27

While I stood staring into his misery,
  he looked at me and with both hands he opened
  his chest and said: "See how I tear myself!   30

See how Mahomet is deformed and torn!
  In front of me, and weeping, Ali walks,
  his face cleft from his chin up to the crown.   33

The souls that you see passing in this ditch
  were all sowers of scandal and schism in life,
  and so in death you see them torn asunder.   36

A devil stands back there who trims us all
  in this cruel way, and each one of this mob
  receives anew the blade of the devil's sword   39

each time we make one round of this sad road,
  because the wounds have all healed up again
  by the time each one presents himself once more.   42

But who are you there, gawking from the bridge
  and trying to put off, perhaps, fulfillment
  of the sentence passed on you when you confessed?"   45

"Death does not have him yet, he is not here
  to suffer for his guilt," my master answered;
  "but that he may have full experience,   48

I, who am dead, must lead him through this Hell
    from round to round, down to the very bottom,
    and this is as true as my presence speaking here."   51

More than a hundred in that ditch stopped short
    to look at me when they had heard his words,
    forgetting in their stupor what they suffered.   54

"And you, who will behold the sun, perhaps
    quite soon, tell Fra Dolcino that unless
    he wants to follow me here quick, he'd better   57

stock up on food, or else the binding snows
    will give the Novarese their victory,
    a conquest not won easily otherwise."   60

With the heel of one foot raised to take a step,
    Mahomet said these words to me, and then
    stretched out and down his foot and moved away.   63

Another, with his throat slit, and his nose
    cut off as far as where the eyebrows start
    (and he only had a single ear to show),   66

who had stopped like all the rest to stare in wonder,
    stepped out from the group and opened up his throat,
    which ran with red from all sides of his wound,   69

and spoke: "O you whom guilt does not condemn,
    whom I have seen in Italy up there,
    unless I am deceived by similarity,   72

recall to mind Pier da Medicina,
    should you return to see the gentle plain
    declining from Vercelli to Marcabò,   75

and inform the two best citizens of Fano—
    tell Messer Guido and tell Angiolello—
    that, if our foresight here is no deception,   78

from their ship they shall be hurled bound in a sack
    to drown in the water near Cattolica,
    the victims of a tyrant's treachery;   81

between the isles of Cyprus and Mallorca
   so great a crime Neptune never witnessed
   among the deeds of pirates or the Argives.   84

That traitor, who sees only with one eye
   and rules the land that someone with me here
   wishes he'd never fed his eyes upon,   87

will have them come to join him in a parley,
   then see to it they do not waste their breath
   on vows or prayers to escape Focara's wind."   90

And I to him: "If you want me to bring back
   to those on earth your message—who is the one
   sated with the bitter sight? Show him to me."   93

At once he grabbed the jaws of a companion
   standing near by, and squeezed his mouth half open,
   announcing, "Here he is, and he is mute.   96

This man, in exile, drowned all Caesar's doubts
   and helped him cast the die, when he insisted:
   'A man prepared, who hesitates, is lost.' "   99

How helpless and bewildered he appeared,
   his tongue hacked off as far down as the throat,
   this Curio, once so bold and quick to speak!   102

And one who had both arms but had no hands,
   raising the gory stumps in the filthy air
   so that the blood dripped down and smeared his face,   105

cried: "You, no doubt, also remember Mosca,
   who said, alas, 'What's done is over with,'
   and sowed the seed of discord for the Tuscans."   108

"And of death for all your clan," I quickly said,
   and he, this fresh wound added to his wound,
   turned and went off like one gone mad from pain.   111

But I remained to watch the multitude,
   and saw a thing that I would be afraid
   to tell about without more evidence,   114

were I not reassured by my own conscience—
    that good companion enheartening a man
    beneath the breastplate of its purity.   117

I saw it, I'm sure, and I seem to see it still:
    a body with no head that moved along,
    moving no differently from all the rest;   120

he held his severed head up by its hair,
    swinging it in one hand just like a lantern,
    and as it looked at us it said: "Alas!"   123

Of his own self he made himself a light
    and they were two in one and one in two.
    How could this be? He who ordained it knows.   126

And when he had arrived below our bridge,
    he raised the arm that held the head up high
    to let it speak to us at closer range.   129

It spoke: "Now see the monstrous punishment,
    you there still breathing, looking at the dead,
    see if you find suffering to equal mine!   132

And that you may report on me up there,
    know that I am Bertran de Born, the one
    who evilly encouraged the young king.   135

Father and son I set against each other:
    Achitophel with his wicked instigations
    did not do more with Absalom and David.   138

Because I cut the bonds of those so joined,
    I bear my head cut off from its life-source,
    which is back there, alas, within its trunk.   141

In me you see the perfect *contrapasso*!"

NOTES

7–12. *If one could bring together all the wounded*: In order to
introduce the great number of maimed and dismembered shades
that will present themselves in the Ninth *Bolgia*, Dante "piles"

together references to a number of bloody battles which took place in Puglia, the southeastern section of the Italian peninsula. The first of the series, in which the Pugliese "grieved for their life's blood spilled by the Romans" (9), is the long war between the Samnites and the Romans (343–290 B.C.). The next, "the long years of the war / that ended in great spoils of golden rings" (10–11), is the Second Punic War, which Hannibal's legions fought against Rome (218–201 B.C.). Livy writes that after the battle of Cannae (where Hannibal defeated the Romans, 216 B.C.), the Carthaginians gathered three bushels of rings from the fingers of dead Romans.

14. *when they stood up against great Robert Guiscard*: In the eleventh century Robert Guiscard (c. 1015–85), a noble Norman adventurer, gained control of most of southern Italy and became duke of Apulia and Calabria, as well as Gonfalonier of the Church (1059). For the next two decades he battled the schismatic Greeks and the Saracens for the Church in the South of Italy. Later he fought for the Church in the East, raised a siege against Pope Gregory VII (1084), and died at the age of seventy, still engaged in warfare. Dante places him with the warriors for the Faith in the Heaven of Mars (*Paradise* XVIII, 48).

15–18. *and with those others whose bones are still in heaps*: A further comparison between bloody battles in Puglia and the Ninth *Bolgia*: in 1266 Charles of Anjou marched against the armies of Manfred, King of Sicily. Manfred blocked the passes leading to the south, but the pass at Ceprano was abandoned by its traitorous defenders. Charles then advanced unhindered and defeated the Sicilians at Benevento, killing Manfred. In reality, then, the battle did not take place at Ceprano, but at Benevento.

The final example in the lengthy series of battles was a continuation of the hostilities between Charles of Anjou and the followers of Manfred. In 1268 at the battle of Tagliacozzo Charles adopted the suggestions of his general Érard de Valéry (*Alardo*) and won the encounter. Although Érard's strategy was one of wit rather than force (a "hidden" reserve troop entered the battle at the last minute, when Manfred's nephew

Conradin seemed to have won), it can hardly be said that "old Alardo" conquered without arms.

31. *See how Mahomet is deformed and torn!*: Mahomet, founder of the Mohammedan religion, was born at Mecca about 570 and died in 632. His punishment, to be split open from the crotch to the chin, together with the complementary punishment of Ali, represents Dante's belief that they were initiators of the great schism between the Christian Church and Mohammedanism. Many of Dante's contemporaries thought that Mahomet was originally a Christian and a cardinal who wanted to become pope.

32. *In front of me, and weeping, Ali walks*: Ali (c. 600–61) was the first of Mahomet's followers, and married the prophet's daughter Fatima. Mahomet died in 632, and Ali assumed the Caliphate in 656.

45. *of the sentence passed on you when you confessed*: That is, confessed before Minòs. Compare V, 8.

56–60. *tell Fra Dolcino*: Fra Dolcino (d. 1307), though not a monk, as his name would seem to indicate, was the leader of a religious sect banned as heretical by Pope Clement V in 1305. Dolcino's sect, the Apostolic Brothers, preached the return of religion to the simplicity of apostolic times, and among their tenets were community of property and sharing of women. When Clement V ordered the eradication of the Brothers, Dolcino and his followers retreated to the hills near Novara, where they withstood the papal forces for over a year until starvation conquered them. Dolcino and his companion, Margaret of Trent, were burned at the stake in 1307. Mahomet's interest in Dolcino may stem from their similar views on marriage and women.

73. *recall to mind Pier da Medicina*: Although nothing certain is known about the life of this sinner, we do know that his home was in Medicina, a town in the Po River Valley ("the gentle plain" that lies between the towns of Vercelli and Marcabò, 74) near Bologna. According to the early commentator Benvenuto da Imola, Pier da Medicina was the instigator of strife between the Polenta and Malatesta families.

77–90. *tell Messer Guido and tell Angiolello*: Guido del Cassero and Angiolello di Carignano, leading citizens of Fano, a small town on the Adriatic, south of Rimini, were invited by Malatestino (the "traitor, who sees only with one eye," 85) to meet on a ship off the coastal city of Cattolica, which lies between Rimini and Fano. There Malatestino, Lord of Rimini from 1312 to 1317, ordered them thrown overboard in order that he might gain control of Fano. Already dead, the two victims of Malatestino's treachery will not have to pray to escape "Focara's wind," (90), the terribly destructive gale that preyed on vessels passing by the promontory of Focara near Cattolica.

92–93. *who is the one / sated with the bitter sight?*: The Pilgrim refers to what Pier da Medicina said earlier about "someone" who "wishes he'd never fed his eyes upon" Rimini (86–87).

97–102. *This man, in exile, drowned all Caesar's doubts*: Caius Scribonius Curio wishes he had never seen Rimini, the city near which the Rubicon River empties into the Adriatic. Once a Roman tribune under Pompey, Curio defected to Caesar's side, and, when the Roman general hesitated to cross the Rubicon, Curio convinced him to cross and march on Rome. At that time the Rubicon formed the boundary between Gaul and the Roman Republic; Caesar's decision to cross it precipitated the Roman civil war.

106–108. *You, no doubt, also remember Mosca*: Mosca, about whom the Pilgrim earlier had asked Ciacco (VI, 80), was a member of the Lamberti family of Florence. His counsel ("What's done is over with," 107) was the cause of the division of Florence into the feuding Guelf and Ghibelline parties. As tradition has it, Buondelmonte de' Buondelmonti was engaged to the daughter of Lambertuccio degli Amidei; however, Aldruda, of the Donati family, offered him her daughter and promised to pay the penalty for the broken engagement. Buondelmonte accepted, thus enraging Oderigo, who demanded revenge. The powerful Uberti family, at the instigation of Mosca, declared that Buondelmonte should be killed (and he was), because a milder form of revenge (a simple beating, for example) would incur as much hatred as the most severe form (murder).

134–36. *know that I am Bertran de Born, the one*: One of the greatest of the Provençal troubadours, Bertran de Born lived in the second half of the twelfth century. His involvement in the politics of the time is reflected in his poetry, which is almost entirely of a political character. He suffers here in Hell for having caused the rebellion of Prince Henry (the "young king," 135) against his father, Henry II, King of England.

137–38. *Achitophel with his wicked instigations*: Dante compares Bertran de Born's evil counsel with that of Achitophel. Once the aide of David, Achitophel the Gilonite provoked Absalom's rebellion against David, his father and king. See II Samuel, 15–17.

142. *In me you see the perfect* contrapasso!: The decapitated figure of Bertran de Born perhaps best illustrates the law of divine retribution, the *contrapasso*, at work in the Dantean *Inferno*. In a manner of speaking, it is identical with the Old Testament God's form of vengeance: "An eye for an eye, a tooth for a tooth." Bertran de Born's *contrapasso* may have been suggested to Dante by a passage in the Provençal *vida* (biography) affixed to Bertran's poetry. Having once boasted to King Henry that he had more intelligence than he needed, he was later reminded of this boast after the death of the "young king" and after his own imprisonment by Henry. In the *vida* we read that "when King Henry took him prisoner he asked him whether he had not need of all his wits then; and Bertran answered that he lost all his wits when the young king died." In this canto, of course, Bertran's "wits" are physically separated from his body.

Bertran's most famous poem, in fact, was a lament (*planh*) for the death of the young Henry, the first stanza of which may well have suggested the opening imagery of this canto, with its piling up of the miseries of war:

> If all the grief and bitterness and woe
> And all the pain and hurt and suffering
> That in this world of misery men know,
> Were massed in one, it would seem but a light thing
> Beside the death of the Young English King.

So Dante says:

> If one could bring together all the wounded
> who once upon the fateful soil of Puglia
> grieved for their life's blood . . .
>
> . . . .
>
> . . . the scene would be nothing
> to compare with the foul ninth *bolgia*'s bloody sight

Dante knew Bertran's poetry well, and in the *De Vulgari eloquentia* II, ii, 9, he asserts that Bertran was the paragon of martial poets.

CANTO XXIX

WHEN THE PILGRIM is rebuked by his mentor for his inappropriate interest in these wretched shades, he replies that he was looking for someone. Virgil tells the Pilgrim that he saw the person he was looking for, GERI DEL BELLO, pointing a finger at him. They discuss Geri until they reach the edge of the next bolgia, where all types of FALSIFIERS are punished. There miserable, shrieking shades are afflicted with diseases of various kinds and are arranged in various positions. Sitting back to back, madly scratching their leprous sores, are the shades of GRIFFOLINO DA AREZZO and one CAPOCCHIO, who talk to the Pilgrim, the latter shade making wisecracks about the Sienese.

The crowds, the countless, different mutilations,
    had stunned my eyes and left them so confused
    they wanted to keep looking and to weep,   3

but Virgil said: "What are you staring at?
    Why do your eyes insist on drowning there
    below, among those wretched, broken shades?   6

You did not act this way in other *bolge*.
    If you hope to count them one by one, remember,
    the valley winds some twenty-two miles around;   9

and already the moon is underneath our feet;
    the time remaining to us now is short—
    and there is more to see than you see here."   12

"If you had taken time to find out what
    I was looking for," I started telling him,
    "perhaps you would have let me stay there longer."   15

My guide was moving on, with me behind him,
  answering as I did while we went on,
  and adding: "Somewhere down along this ditch   18

that I was staring at a while ago,
  I think there is a spirit of my family
  mourning the guilt that's paid so dear down there."   21

And then my master said: "From this time on
  you should not waste another thought on him;
  think on ahead, and let him stay behind,   24

for I saw him standing underneath the bridge
  pointing at you, and threatening with his gesture,
  and I heard his name called out: Geri del Bello.   27

That was the moment you were so absorbed
  with him who was the lord of Altaforte
  that you did not look his way before he left."   30

"Alas, my guide," I answered him, "his death
  by violence, which has not yet been avenged
  by anyone who shares in his disgrace,   33

made him resentful, and I suppose for this
  he went away without a word to me,
  and because he did I feel great piety."   36

We spoke of this until we reached the start
  of the bridge across the next *bolgia*, from which
  the bottom, with more light, might have been seen.   39

Having come to stand above the final cloister
  of Malebolge, we saw it spreading out,
  revealing to our eyes its congregation.   42

Weird shrieks of lamentation pierced through me
  like arrow-shafts whose tips are barbed with pity,
  so that my hands were covering my ears.   45

Imagine all the sick in the hospitals
  of Maremma, Valdichiana, and Sardinia
  between the months of July and September,   48

crammed all together rotting in one ditch—
   such was the misery here; and such a stench
   was pouring out as comes from flesh decaying.   51

Still keeping to our left, we made our way
   down the long bridge onto the final bank,
   and now my sight was clear enough to find   54

the bottom where the High Lord's ministress,
   Justice infallible, metes out her punishment
   to falsifiers she registers on earth.   57

I doubt if all those dying in Aegina
   when the air was blowing sick with pestilence
   and the animals, down to the smallest worm,   60

all perished (later on this ancient race,
   according to what the poets tell as true,
   was born again from families of ants)   63

offered a scene of greater agony
   than was the sight spread out in that dark valley
   of heaped-up spirits languishing in clumps.   66

Some sprawled out on others' bellies, some
   on others' backs, and some, on hands and knees,
   dragged themselves along that squalid alley.   69

Slowly, in silence, slowly we moved along,
   looking, listening to the words of all those sick,
   who had no strength to raise their bodies up.   72

I saw two sitting, leaning against each other
   like pans propped back to back against a fire,
   and they were blotched from head to foot with scabs.   75

I never saw a curry-comb applied
   by a stable-boy who is harried by his master,
   or simply wants to finish and go to bed,   78

the way those two applied their nails and dug
   and dug into their flesh, crazy to ease
   the itching that can never find relief.   81

THE DIVINE COMEDY: INFERNO

They worked their nails down, scraping off the scabs
   the way one works a knife to scale a bream
   or some other fish with larger, tougher scales.   84

"O you there scraping off your scabs of mail
   and even making pincers of your fingers,"
   my guide began to speak to one of them,   87

"so may your fingernails eternally
   suffice their task, tell us: among the many
   packed in this place is anyone Italian?"   90

"Both of us whom you see disfigured here,"
   one answered through his tears, "we are Italians.
   But you, who ask about us, who are you?"   93

"I am one accompanying this living man
   descending bank from bank," my leader said,
   "and I intend to show him all of Hell."   96

With that each lost the other back's support
   and each one, shaky, turned to look at me,
   as others did who overheard these words.   99

My gentle master came up close to me
   and said: "Now ask them what you want to know,"
   and since he wanted me to speak, I started: 102

"So may the memory of you not fade
   from the minds of men up there in the first world,
   but rather live on under many suns,   105

tell me your names and where it was you lived;
   do not let your dreadful, loathsome punishment
   discourage you from speaking openly."   108

"I'm from Arezzo," one of them replied,
   "and Albert of Siena had me burned,
   but I'm not here for what I died for there;   111

it's true I told him, jokingly, of course:
   'I know the trick of flying through the air,'
   and he, eager to learn and not too bright,   114

asked me to demonstrate my art; and only
    just because I didn't make him Daedalus,
    he had me burned by one whose child he was.   117

But here, to the last *bolgia* of the ten,
    for the alchemy I practiced in the world
    I was condemned by Minòs, who cannot err."   120

I said to my poet: "Have you ever known
    people as silly as the Sienese?
    Even the French cannot compare with them!"   123

With that the other leper who was listening
    feigned exception to my quip: "Excluding,
    of course, Stricca, who lived so frugally,   126

and Niccolo, the first to introduce
    the luxury of the clove for condiment
    into that choice garden where the seed took root,   129

and surely not that fashionable club
    where Caccia squandered all his woods and vineyards
    and Abbagliato flaunted his great wit!   132

That you may know who this is backing you
    against the Sienese, look sharply at me
    so that my face will give you its own answer,   135

and you will recognize Capocchio's shade,
    betrayer of metals with his alchemy;
    you'll surely recall—if you're the one I think—   138

how fine an ape of nature I once was."

NOTES

10. *and already the moon is underneath our feet*: The sun, then,
is directly overhead, indicating that it is midday in Jerusalem.

27–35. *and I heard his name called out: Geri del Bello*: Geri del
Bello was a first cousin of Dante's father. Little is known about
him except that he was among those to whom reparation was

made in 1269 for damages suffered at the hands of the Ghibellines in 1260, and that he was involved in a blood feud with the Sacchetti family. It was probably one of the Sacchetti who murdered him. Vengeance by kinsmen for a slaying was considered obligatory at the time, and apparently Geri's murder was still unavenged by the Alighieri in 1300.

29. *the lord of Altaforte*: Bertran de Born. See XXVIII, 130–42 and n.142.

40. *Having come to stand above the final cloister*: Cantos XXVIII–XXX seem to be all part of one unit, indicating perhaps that the frauds are becoming more difficult to separate from each other the deeper the Pilgrim goes. Links between *Bolge* Nine and Ten include the similarities in the punishment (dismembered, diseased, and disfigured bodies and minds), and the fact that the Ninth *Bolgia* is carried over into Canto XXIX (the Tenth *Bolgia* actually begins here, at line 40).

47–49. *of Maremma, Valdichiana, and Sardinia*: Valdichiana and Maremma are swampy areas in Tuscany. Along with the swamps of Sardinia they were famous for breeding malaria and other diseases. Dante mentioned Maremma in XXV, 19, in connection with the snakes that infested the swamp. The "hospital" image introduces the diseased shades of the Tenth *Bolgia*.

58–66. *I doubt if all those dying in Aegina*: This comparison with the sufferers of the Tenth *Bolgia* concerns the island of Aegina in the Saronic Gulf. Juno sent a plague to the island, which killed all the inhabitants except Aeacus. Aeacus prayed to Jupiter to repopulate the island, and Jupiter did so by turning ants into men. See Ovid, *Metamorphoses* VII, 523.

The confusion of this image, which piles one phrase on top of another, imitates stylistically the confusion of the pile of diseased bodies which are described immediately afterwards.

67–139

In the last of the *Malebolge*, at the end of the largest segment of the *Inferno* (*Malebolge* began in Canto XVIII), Dante stylistically summarizes much of the journey so far. Here, for instance, we have a return of the grotesque humor of the *bolgia* of the Barrators presided over by the *Malebranche* (XXI, XXII): there is what we would call "sick" humor in Virgil's remark to the alchemists (88–89), there is the comedy of crude sarcasm in Capocchio's words (125–32), and even the "cooking" imagery in the *bolgia* of the Barrators is repeated in his words (128–29) and in the picture of Griffolino and Capocchio (74). Another example of the condensation in this canto of elements from the journey up to this point is Virgil's summary of the journey's purpose (94–96). The *largo* movement of the *bolgia* of the Hypocrites is found here, too (70–71), and the comparison with monks in a cloister, which Dante had used for the Hypocrites, is also in evidence (40–42). This summarizing technique continues in the next canto. Note, for instance, the immobility of the Counterfeiters and the speed of the Impersonators, and compare with the scene in the Wood of Suicides (XIII) where the immobility of Pier delle Vigne is in contrast to the mad dash of Lano and Giacomo da Sant'Andrea.

109–117. *"I'm from Arezzo," one of them replied*: Most of the commentators identify this man as Griffolino da Arezzo. The story was that Griffolino had led the doltish Alberto da Siena to believe that he could teach him how to fly. Alberto paid him well but, upon discovering the fraud, he denounced Griffolino to the bishop of Siena as a magician, and the bishop had him burned. The expression "the one whose child he [Alberto] was," applied to the bishop, could mean either that he was Alberto's father or his protector.

122. *people as silly as the Sienese*: The Florentines made the citizens of rival Siena the butt of many jokes.

124–26. *With that the other leper who was listening*: Capocchio (see below, n. 136) makes several ironic comments here about the foolishness of the Sienese. Stricca (probably Stricca di Giovanni dei Salimbeni of Siena) was evidently renowned as a spendthrift. The old commentators hold that he was a member of the "Spendthrifts' Brigade" (see line 130), a group of young Sienese who wasted their fortunes carelessly. Compare XIII, n. 115–21.

127-29. *and Niccolo, the first to introduce*: Niccolò de' Salimbeni was another member of the Spendthrifts' club and was possibly the brother of Stricca. He introduced to Siena the use of cloves, then a very expensive spice. Some of the early commentators claim that he roasted pheasants on beds of flaming cloves. In any case Capocchio is referring to Niccolò's careless extravagance as another example of the silliness of the Sienese. The "choice garden" is Siena itself, where any fashionable custom, no matter how foolish, could gain acceptance.

131. *where Caccia squandered all his woods and vineyards*: Caccia d'Asciano was another member of the "Spendthrifts' Brigade" (that "fashionable club," 130), who squandered his inheritance.

132. *and Abbagliato flaunted his great wit!*: Abbagliato has been identified as one Bartolomeo dei Folcacchieri, who held office in Siena up to 1300. He was another member of this "fashionable club."

136. *and you will recognize Capocchio's shade*: Capocchio is the name (or nickname) of a man who in 1293 was burned alive in Siena for alchemy. Apparently Dante had known him; according to the early commentators, it was in their student days.

CANTO XXX

CAPOCCHIO'S REMARKS *are interrupted by two mad, naked shades who dash up, and one of them sinks his teeth into Capocchio's neck and drags him off; he is* GIANNI SCHICCHI *and the other is* MYRRHA *of Cyprus. When they have gone, the Pilgrim sees the ill-proportioned and immobile shade of* MASTER ADAMO, *a counterfeiter, who explains how members of the Guidi family had persuaded him to practice his evil art in Romena. He points out the fever-stricken shades of two infamous liars,* POTIPHAR'S WIFE *and* SINON *the Greek, whereupon the latter engages Master Adamo in a verbal battle. Virgil rebukes the Pilgrim for his absorption in such futile wrangling, but his immediate shame wins Virgil's immediate forgiveness.*

In ancient times when Juno was enraged
   against the Thebans because of Semele
   (she showed her wrath on more than one occasion),   3

she made King Athamas go raving mad:
   so mad that one day when he saw his wife
   coming with his two sons in either arm,   6

he cried: "Let's spread the nets, so I can catch
   the lioness with her lion cubs at the pass!"
   Then he spread out his insane hands, like talons,   9

and, seizing one of his two sons, Learchus,
   he whirled him round and smashed him on a rock.
   She drowned herself with the other in her arms.   12

And when the wheel of Fortune brought down low
   the immeasurable haughtiness of Trojans,
   destroying in their downfall king and kingdom,   15

Hecuba sad, in misery, a slave
  (after she saw Polyxena lie slain,
  after this grieving mother found her son   18

Polydorus left unburied on the shore),
  now gone quite mad, went barking like a dog—
  it was the weight of grief that snapped her mind.   21

But never in Thebes or Troy were madmen seen
  driven to acts of such ferocity
  against their victims, animal or human,   24

as two shades I saw, white with rage and naked,
  running, snapping crazily at things in sight,
  like pigs, directionless, broken from their pen.   27

One, landing on Capocchio, sank his teeth
  into his neck, and started dragging him
  along, scraping his belly on the rocky ground.   30

The Aretine spoke, shaking where he sat:
  "You see that batty shade? He's Gianni Schicchi!
  He's rabid and he treats us all that way."   33

"Oh," I answered, "so may that other shade
  never sink its teeth in you—if you don't mind,
  please tell me who it is before it's gone."   36

And he to me: "That is the ancient shade
  of Myrrha, the depraved one, who became,
  against love's laws, too much her father's friend.   39

She went to him, and there she sinned in love,
  pretending that her body was another's—
  just as the other there fleeing in the distance,   42

contrived to make his own the 'queen of studs,'
  pretending that he was Buoso Donati,
  making his will and giving it due form."   45

Now that the rabid pair had come and gone
  (from whom I never took my eyes away),
  I turned to watch the other evil shades.   48

And there I saw a soul shaped like a lute,
    if only he'd been cut off from his legs
    below the belly, where they divide in two.   51

The bloating dropsy, disproportioning
    the body's parts with unconverted humors,
    so that the face, matched with the paunch, was puny,   54

forced him to keep his parched lips wide apart,
    as a man who suffers thirst from raging fever
    has one lip curling up, the other sagging.   57

"O you who bear no punishment at all
    (I can't think why) within this world of sorrow,"
    he said to us, "pause here and look upon   60

the misery of one Master Adamo:
    in life I had all that I could desire,
    and now, alas, I crave a drop of water.   63

The little streams that flow from the green hills
    of Casentino, descending to the Arno,
    keeping their banks so cool and soft with moisture,   66

forever flow before me, haunting me;
    and the image of them leaves me far more parched
    than the sickness that has dried my shriveled face.   69

Relentless Justice, tantalizing me,
    exploits the countryside that knew my sin,
    to draw from me ever new sighs of pain: 72

I still can see Romena, where I learned
    to falsify the coin stamped with the Baptist,
    for which I paid with my burned body there;   75

but if I could see down here the wretched souls
    of Guido or Alexander or their brother,
    I would not exchange the sight for Branda's fountain.   78

One is here already, if those maniacs
    running around this place have told the truth,
    but what good is it, with my useless legs?   81

If only I were lighter, just enough
   to move one inch in every hundred years,
   I would have started on my way by now   84

to find him somewhere in this gruesome lot,
   although this·ditch winds round eleven miles
   and is at least a half a mile across.   87

It's their fault I am here with this choice family:
   they encouraged me to turn out florins
   whose gold contained three carats' worth of alloy."   90

And I to him: "Who are those two poor souls
   lying to the right, close to your body's boundary,
   steaming like wet hands in wintertime?"   93

"When I poured into this ditch, I found them here,"
   he answered, "and they haven't budged since then,
   and I doubt they'll move through all eternity.   96

One is the false accuser of young Joseph;
   the other is false Sinon, the Greek in Troy:
   it's their burning fever makes them smell so bad."   99

And one of them, perhaps somewhat offended
   at the kind of introduction he received,
   with his fist struck out at the distended belly,   102

which responded like a drum reverberating;
   and Master Adam struck him in the face
   with an arm as strong as the fist he had received,   105

and he said to him: "Although I am not free
   to move around, with swollen legs like these,
   I have a ready arm for such occasions."   108

"*But* it was *not* as free and ready, was it,"
   the other answered, "when you went to the stake?
   Of course, when you were coining, it was readier!"   111

And he with the dropsy: "*Now* you tell the truth,
   but you were not as full of truth that time
   when you were asked to tell the truth at Troy!"   114

"My words were false—so were the coins you made,"
    said Sinon, "and *I* am here for one false act
    but *you* for more than any fiend in hell!"   117

"The horse, recall the horse, you falsifier,"
    the bloated paunch was quick to answer back,
    "may it burn your guts that all the world remembers!" 120

"May your guts burn with thirst that cracks your tongue,"
    the Greek said, "may they burn with rotting humors
    that swell your hedge of a paunch to block your eyes!" 123

And then the money-man: "So there you go,
    your evil mouth pours out its filth as usual;
    for if *I* thirst, and humors swell me up,   126

you burn more, and your head is fit to split,
    and it wouldn't take much coaxing to convince you
    to lap the mirror of Narcissus dry!"   129

I was listening, all absorbed in this debate,
    when the master said to me: "Keep right on looking,
    a little more, and I shall lose my patience."   132

I heard the note of anger in his voice
    and turned to him; I was so full of shame
    that it still haunts my memory today.   135

Like one asleep who dreams himself in trouble
    and in his dream he wishes he were dreaming,
    longing for that which is, as if it were not,   138

just so I found myself: unable to speak,
    longing to beg for pardon and already
    begging for pardon, not knowing that I did.   141

"Less shame than yours would wash away a fault
    greater than yours has been," my master said,
    "and so forget about it, do not be sad.   144

If ever again you should meet up with men
    engaging in this kind of futile wrangling,
    remember I am always at your side;   147

to have a taste for talk like this is vulgar!"

NOTES

1–12. *In ancient times when Juno was enraged*: Jupiter's pre-dilection for mortal women always enraged Juno, his wife. In this case her ire was provoked by her husband's dalliance with Semele, the daughter of Cadmus, King of Thebes, who bore him Bacchus. Having vowed to wreak revenge on her and her family, Juno not only had Semele struck by lightning, but also caused King Athamas, the husband of Ino (Semele's sister), to go insane. In his demented state he killed his son Learchus. Ino drowned herself and her other son, Melicertes.

16–21. *Hecuba sad, in misery, a slave*: Having triumphed over the Trojans, the Greeks returned to their homeland, bearing with them as a slave Hecuba, wife of Priam, King of Troy. She was also to make some tragic discoveries: she saw Polyxena, her daughter, slain on the grave of Achilles (17) and she discovered her son Polydorus dead and unburied on the coast of Thrace (18–19). So great was her grief that she became insane.

25. *as two shades I saw, white with rage and naked*: See below, n. 32 and n. 37–41.

31. *The Aretine*: He is Griffolino d'Arezzo. See XXIX, 109–20.

32. *You see that batty shade? He's Gianni Schicchi!*: A member of the Florentine Cavalcanti family, Gianni Schicchi was well known for his mimetic virtuosity. Simone Donati, keeping his father's death a secret in order that he might change the will to his advantage, engaged Gianni to impersonate his dead father (Buoso Donati, 44) and alter the latter's will. The plan was carried out to perfection, and in the process Gianni willed himself, among other things, a prize mare ("the 'queen of studs,' " 43).

33. *He's rabid and he treats us all that way*: Gianni Schicchi, then, is insane, as must be also his companion in the mad flight through this *bolgia*. These are the only two sinners in *The Divine Comedy* who are mentally deranged, so that it is most fitting that the canto should open with a reminder of two famous cases of insanity in classical mythology.

37–41. *That is the ancient shade / of Myrrha*: The other self-falsifier darting about the *bolgia* with Gianni Schicchi is Myrrha, who, overpowered by an incestuous desire for her father, King Cinyras of Cyprus, went *incognita* to his bed, where they made love. Discovering the deception, Cinyras vowed to kill her; however, Myrrha escaped and wandered about until the gods took pity on her and transformed her into a myrrh tree, from which Adonis, the child conceived in the incestuous union, was born. See Ovid's *Metamorphoses* X.

52–53. *The bloating dropsy, disproportioning*: In other words, Adamo's dropsy was caused by the failure of the humors in his body to follow a natural course of change.

61–75

Although the early commentators disagree concerning Master Adamo's birthplace (Brescia? Casentino? Bologna?), it is now generally believed that he was not an Italian. He plied his art, the falsifying of gold florins ("the coin stamped with the Baptist," 74, i.e., with the image of John the Baptist, the patron saint of Florence), throughout northern Italy, encouraged to do so by the Conti Guidi, the lords of Romena (73). He was arrested by the Florentine authorities and burned to death in 1281.

64–66. *the green hills / of Casentino*: The Casentino is a hilly region southeast of Florence where the headwaters of the Arno river spread out.

76–78. *I would not exchange the sight for Branda's fountain*: Master Adamo, as much as he craves a "drop of water" (63), would forgo that pleasure if only he could see here in Hell the Conti Guidi (Guido, Alexander, Aghinolfo, and Ildebrando), who encouraged him in crime. "Branda's fountain" (78) is the name of a spring that once flowed near Romena. Often confused with it is the still-functioning fountain of the same name at Siena.

79. *One is here already*: Guido (d. 1292) is the only one of the four Conti Guidi who died before 1300.

90. *whose gold contained three carats' worth of alloy*: The florin

was supposed to contain twenty-four-carat gold; those of Master Adamo had twenty-one carats.

92. *close to your body's boundary*: Note the dehumanization suggested by this phrase, which accords well with the advanced state of bodily deterioration in the *bolgia*; Master Adamo is more a land mass than a human being.

97. *One is the false accuser of young Joseph*: Potiphar's wife falsely accused Joseph, son of Jacob and Rachel, of trying to seduce her, while in reality it was she who made improper amorous advances. See Genesis XXXIX.

98. *the other is false Sinon, the Greek in Troy*: Sinon was left behind by his fellow Greek soldiers in accordance with the master plan for the capture of Troy. Taken prisoner by the Trojans, and misrepresenting his position with the Greeks, he persuaded them to bring the wooden horse (XXVI, 59) into the city.

100. *And one of them, perhaps somewhat offended*: Sinon.

129. *the mirror of Narcissus*: Water. According to the myth, Narcissus, enamoured with his own reflection in a pond, continued to gaze at it until he died.

136–41. *Like one asleep who dreams himself in trouble*: The confusing complexity of this closing image is in accordance with the theme of insanity that runs throughout the canto. At first reading, we are disoriented by both the structure and the sense of Dante's comparison. Thus it could be said that the lines cause the reader to experience the Pilgrim's confusion and not just to witness it. In order to understand the mental state of the Pilgrim at this moment, the reader is forced to pause, reread the passage, and consider carefully its meaning and effect.

The idea conveyed by the comparison is difficult because it has to do with perception of reality. The Pilgrim's desire is to beg pardon, but he feels incapable of doing so. Even as he contemplates his apparent inability to convey his message, he discovers that, in fact, it has been done. In this way, he says, he is not unlike the sleeper who dreams he is in trouble and, in his dream, wishes he were dreaming. The desire, then, in each case, is for something that already *is*.

The language of the comparison is in itself confusing; it goes beyond mere definition—it actually reflects the situation. Heavy use of repetition, particularly of the present participle, locks the reader in a kind of spiral, or perhaps a series of concentric circles. The geometrical aspect of the language is a device used elsewhere in the poem: in *Inferno* XIII, 25, for example, the geometrical configuration suggested by the language is a linear one.

*   *   *   *

Canto XXX is unique in that the suffering undergone by the sinners is caused not by something outside of them, some factor in this physical environment, but by something within them, by their own disease—mental or physical. The Alchemists are afflicted with leprosy, the Impersonators are mad, the Counterfeiters suffer from dropsy and the Liars are afflicted with a fever that makes them stink. In this, the last of the *Malebolge*, we see Simple Fraud at its most extreme; and because of the miscellaneous nature of the sins of the Falsifiers, we see perhaps the essence of the sin of Simple Fraud in general. In that case, Dante would be telling us that Fraud in general is a disease: the corrupt sense of values of the Fraudulent is here symbolized, in the case of the Falsifiers, by the corrupt state of their minds and bodies.

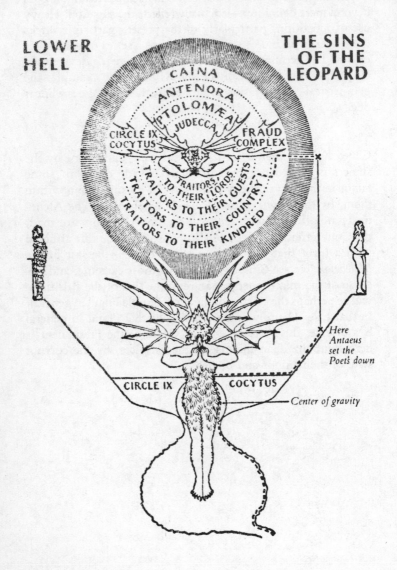

LOWER HELL

THE SINS OF THE LEOPARD

CAÏNA
ANTENORA
PTOLOMÆA
JUDECCA
CIRCLE IX
COCYTUS
FRAUD COMPLEX

TRAITORS TO THEIR LORDS
TRAITORS TO THEIR GUESTS
TRAITORS TO THEIR COUNTRY
TRAITORS TO THEIR KINDRED

CIRCLE IX   COCYTUS

Here
Antaeus
set the
Poets down

Center of gravity

CANTO XXXI

Through the murky air they move, up across the bank that separates the Malebolge *from the pit of Hell, the Ninth (and last) Circle of the* Inferno. *From a distance is heard the blast of a mighty horn, which turns out to have been that of the giant* Nimrod. *He and other giants, including* Ephialtes, *are fixed eternally in the pit of Hell; all are chained except* Antaeus, *who, at Virgil's request, lifts the two poets in his monstrous hand and deposits them below him, on the lake of ice known as* Cocytus.

The very tongue that first spoke—stinging me,
   making the blood rush up to both my cheeks—
   then gave the remedy to ease the pain,   3

just as, so I have heard, Achilles' lance,
   belonging to his father, was the source
   of pain, and then of balm, to him it struck.   6

Turning our backs on that trench of misery
   gaining the bank again that walls it in,
   we cut across, walking in dead silence.   9

Here it was less than night and less than day,
   so that my eyes could not see far ahead;
   but then I heard the blast of some high horn   12

which would have made a thunder-clap sound dim;
   it drew my eyes directly to one place,
   as they retraced the sound's path to its source.   15

After the tragic rout when Charlemagne
   lost all his faithful, holy paladins,
   the sound of Roland's horn was not as ominous.   18

Keeping my eyes still turned that way, I soon
   made out what seemed to be high, clustered towers.
   "Master," I said, "what city lies ahead?"   21

"Because you try to penetrate the shadows,"
   he said to me, "from much too far away,
   you confuse the truth with your imagination.   24

You will see clearly when you reach that place
   how much the eyes may be deceived by distance,
   and so, just push ahead a little more."   27

Then lovingly he took me by the hand
   and said: "But now, before we go on farther,
   to prepare you for the truth that could seem strange,   30

I'll tell you these aren't towers, they are giants;
   they're standing in the well around the bank—
   all of them hidden from their navels down."   33

As, when the fog begins to thin and clear,
   the sight can slowly make out more and more
   what is hidden in the mist that clogs the air,   36

so, as I pierced the thick and murky air,
   approaching slowly, closer to the well,
   confusion cleared and my fear took on more shape.   39

For just as Montereggion is crowned with towers
   soaring high above its curving ramparts,
   so, on the bank that runs around the well,   42

towering with only half their bodies out,
   stood the terrible giants, forever threatened
   by Jupiter in the heavens when he thunders.   45

And now I could make out one of the faces,
   the shoulders, the chest and a good part of the belly
   and, down along the sides, the two great arms.   48

Nature, when she cast away the mold
   for shaping beasts like these, without a doubt
   did well, depriving Mars of more such agents.   51

And if she never did repent of whales
   and elephants, we must consider her,
   on sober thought, all the more just and wary: 54

for when the faculty of intellect
   is joined with brute force and with evil will,
   no man can win against such an alliance.   57

His face, it seemed to me, was about as long
   and just as wide as St. Peter's cone in Rome,
   and all his body's bones were in proportion,   60

so that the bank which served to cover him
   from his waist down showed so much height above
   that three tall Frisians on each other's shoulders   63

could never boast of stretching to his hair,
   for downward from the place men clasp their cloaks
   I saw a generous thirty hand-spans of him.   66

"Raphel may amech zabi almi!"
   He played these sputtering notes with prideful lips
   for which no sweeter psalm was suitable.   69

My guide called up to him: "Blathering idiot,
   stick to your horn and take it out on that
   when you feel a fit of anger coming on;   72

search round your neck and you will find the strap
   it's tied to, you poor muddle-headed soul,
   and there's the horn so pretty on your chest."   75

And then he turned to me: "His words accuse him.
   He is Nimrod, through whose infamous device
   the world no longer speaks a common language.   78

But let's leave him alone and not waste breath,
   for he can no more understand our words
   than anyone can understand his language."   81

We had to walk still farther than before,
   continuing to the left, a full bow's-shot,
   to find another giant, huger and more fierce.   84

What engineer it took to bind this brute
   I cannot say, but there he was, one arm
   pinned to his back, the other locked in front,   87

with a giant chain winding around him tight,
   which, starting from his neck, made five great coils—
   and that was counting only to his waist.   90

"This beast of pride decided he would try
   to pit his strength against almighty Jove,"
   my leader said, "and he has won this prize.   93

He's Ephialtes, who made his great attempt
   when the giants arose to fill the Gods with panic;
   the arms he lifted then, he moves no more."   96

And I to him: "If it were possible,
   I would really like to have the chance to see
   the fantastic figure of Briareus."   99

His answer was: "Not far from here you'll see
   Antaeus, who can speak and is not chained;
   he will set us down in the very pit of sin.   102

The one you want to see is farther off;
   he too is bound and looks just like this one,
   except for his expression, which is fiercer."   105

No earthquake of the most outrageous force
   ever shook a tower with such violence
   as, suddenly, Ephialtes shook himself.   108

I never feared to die as much as then,
   and my fear might have been enough to kill me,
   if I had not already seen those chains.   111

We left him and continued moving on
   and came to where Antaeus stood, extending
   from the well a good five ells up to his head.   114

"O you who in the celebrated valley
   (that saw Scipio become the heir of glory,
   when Hannibal with all his men retreated)   117

once captured a thousand lions as your quarry
  (and with whose aid, had you chosen to take part
  in the great war with your brothers, the sons of earth   120

would, as many still think, have been the victors),
  do not disdain this modest wish: take us,
  and put us down where ice locks in Cocytus.   123

Don't make us go to Tityus or Typhon;
  this man can give you what all long for here,
  and so bend down, and do not scowl at us.   126

He still can spread your legend in the world,
  for he yet lives, and long life lies before him,
  unless Grace summons him before his time."   129

Thus spoke my master, and the giant in haste
  stretched out the hands whose formidable grip
  great Hercules once felt, and took my guide.   132

And Virgil, when he felt the grasping hands,
  called out: "Now come and I'll take hold of you."
  Clasped together, we made a single burden.   135

As the Garisenda looks from underneath
  its leaning side, at the moment when a cloud
  comes drifting over against the tower's slant,   138

just so the bending giant Antaeus seemed
  as I looked up, expecting him to topple.
  I wished then I had gone another way.   141

But he, most carefully, handed us down
  to the pit that swallows Lucifer with Judas.
  And then, the leaning giant immediately   144

drew himself up as tall as a ship's mast.

NOTES

  4–6. *just as, so I have heard, Achilles' lance*: Dante aptly com-
pares the nature of Virgil's words at the end of Canto XXX
(first rebuking, then comforting) to the spear of Achilles and

THE DIVINE COMEDY: INFERNO

his father, Peleus, which reputedly could heal the wounds it had inflicted.

16–18. *After the tragic rout when Charlemagne*: In the medieval French epic *La Chanson de Roland*, Roland, one of Charlemagne's "holy paladins" (17), was assigned to the rear guard on the return from an expedition in Spain. At Roncevalles in the Pyrenees the Saracens attacked, and Roland, proud to the point of foolishness, refused to sound his horn until total extermination was imminent.

19–127

From afar, the Pilgrim, who has mistaken the great giants for towers, asks Virgil, "what city lies ahead?," a question that should recall the scene before the gates of the walled city of Dis in Cantos VIII and IX. By this device not only are we introduced to a new division of Hell (the Pit of the Giants and Cocytus: Complex Fraud), but also the unified nature of Lower Hell (i.e., from the City of Dis to Cocytus) is underscored. And the Fallen Angels perched on the wall who shut the gate to the City in Virgil's face (VIII) are analogous to the Giants here, who stand at the boundary of the lowest part of Hell. The fact that the Giants—in terms of pagan mythology—and the Fallen Angels—in terms of the Judeo-Christian tradition— both rebelled against their respective gods not only links the parts of Lower Hell together, but also suggests that the bases for all the sins punished in Lower Hell (Heresy, Violence, and Fraud) are Envy and Pride, the sins of both groups of rebels.

Canto XXXI revolves around the pride of the Giants, exemplified by Nimrod's mumbling gibberish through his "prideful lips" (68), and even by Virgil's flattering Antaeus about his hunting exploits (115–18) in order to persuade him to transport Dante and himself down to the pit's floor. Of course the greatest evidence of Envy and Pride on the part of the giants is their rebellion against their gods. Nimrod, envious of God's dominion, tried, in his pride, to build a tower to Heaven, and the Titans (save Antaeus, who took no active part) rebelled against Jove. The Fallen Angels, of course (spurred on by their pride and envy), also rebelled against God.

In lines 55–57 is described the terrible combination of qualities represented by the extreme evil of the Giants, as well as of the others in the Ninth Circle:

> for when the faculty of intellect
> is joined with brute force and with evil will,
> no man can win against such an alliance.
>
> (55–57)

The difference between the sins of Incontinence (the first five of the Seven Capital Sins) and the sins punished in the Lower Hell is that the former are sins of the appetite, not the product of an "evil will," while the sins of Heresy, Violence, and Fraud are all inspired by a will to do evil. (That Heresy is caused by intellectual pride and its inseparable companion, envy, seems obvious; see IX, note 127–31.) Violence is an alliance of "evil will" and "brute force," while Simple Fraud (in the *Malebolge*) is the product of "evil will" allied with "the faculty of intellect." But Complex Fraud, exemplified by the Giants, the Fallen Angels, Lucifer, and the other figures in the Ninth Circle, is a combination of simple frauds and violence (all of the figures in this circle are here for violent rebellion or treacherous murder), that is, of "the faculty of intellect . . . joined with brute force and with evil will." It can be seen that the key to the sins in Lower Hell is the "evil will," that is, an active willing of evil ends; and of all the capital sins, only pride and envy could cause such a will to evil.

40–41. *For just as Montereggion is crowned with towers*: In 1213 the Sienese constructed Montereggioni, a fortress on the crest of a hill eight miles from their city. The specific allusion here is to the fourteen high towers that stood on its perimeter like giant sentries.

44–45. *forever threatened / by Jupiter*: When the Titans rebelled against Heaven, Jupiter struck them down with lightning bolts (see XIV, 51–60). Here in Hell they continue to fear his vengeance, suggested by his thundering.

49–57. *Nature, when she cast away the mold*: Dante praises the wisdom that Nature showed in discontinuing the race of giants, for Mars (51), the god of war, with the help of the giants could have effectively destroyed mankind. A clear distinction is made between brute animals ("whales / and elephants," 52–53), which Nature rightly allows to live, and giants, whom she made extinct, in that the former do not possess a rational faculty, and therefore are easily subjugated by man.

59. *and just as wide as St. Peter's cone in Rome*: This bronze pine cone measuring over seven feet in height, which now stands in an inner courtyard of the Vatican, was, at Dante's time, in the courtyard of St. Peter's.

63. *that three tall Frisians on each other's shoulders*: The inhabitants of Friesland, a northern province of the Netherlands, were renowned for their height.

67. *"Raphel may amech zabi almi!"*: Although there have been numerous attempts to interpret these words, I, along with most modern commentators, believe that they are gibberish—the perfect representation of Nimrod's role in the confusion of languages caused by his construction of the Tower of Babel (the "infamous device," 77).

77. *He is Nimrod, through whose infamous device*: Orosius, Saint Augustine, and other early Christians believed Nimrod to be a giant; and his "infamous device," the Tower of Babel, through which he tried to ascend to Heaven, certainly equates him with the giants who besieged Jupiter. In both cases the dominant sin is pride; this, in addition to their gigantic proportions, makes them prefigurations of Lucifer.

78. *the world no longer speaks a common language*: Before the construction of the Tower of Babel all men spoke a common language; it was as a punishment for building the Tower that God confused their tongues. See Genesis XI, 1 (where, however, Nimrod is not mentioned).

94. *He's Ephialtes, who made his great attempt*: Ephialtes was the son of Neptune and Iphimedia. At the age of nine, together with his brother Otus, he attempted to put Mt. Pelion on top of Ossa in order to ascend to the gods and make war on them. But Apollo slew the brothers.

99. *the fantastic figure of Briareus*: The son of Uranus and Gaea (Earth), the Titan Briareus joined the rebellion against the Olympian deities.

101. *Antaeus, who can speak and is not chained*: See below, n. 123.

102. *he will set us down in the very pit of sin*: Cocytus, the ninth and last circle of the Inferno.

123. *and put us down where ice locks in Cocytus*: Antaeus was the son of Neptune and Gaea (Earth) and consequently one of the Titans; but since he did not take part in the insurrection against the gods (119–20) he is not chained (101). Had he taken part, it is quite possible that the Titans ("sons of earth," 120) would have conquered the Olympians. An inhabitant of Libya, he performed great feats of hunting in the valley of the Bagradas, where Scipio later defeated Hannibal (115–17).

124. *Don't make us go to Tityus or Typhon*: Also members of the race of Titans, Tityus and Typhon were slain by Jupiter, the former for his attempted rape of Diana and the latter for his rebellion against the gods. Both were cast down to earth and buried under Mt. Aetna.

131–32. *stretched out the hands whose formidable grip*: Antaeus derived his great strength from constant contact with the earth (Gaea, his mother). In a wrestling match with Hercules, the latter lifted him off the ground, thus killing him.

136–38. *As the Garisenda looks from underneath*: Of the two leaning towers in Bologna, the Garisenda, built c. 1110, is the shorter. The passage of a cloud "against the tower's slant" (138) would make the tower appear to be falling.

CANTO XXXII

They descend farther down into the darkness of the immense plain of ice in which shades of Traitors are frozen. In the outer region of the ice-lake, Caïna, are those who betrayed their kin in murder; among them, locked in a frozen embrace, are Napoleone and Alessandro of Mangona, and others are Mordred, Focaccia, Sassol Mascheroni, and Camicion de'Pazzi. Then the two travelers enter the area of ice called Antenora, and suddenly the Pilgrim kicks one of the faces sticking out of the ice. He tries to force the sinner to reveal his name by pulling out his hair, and when another shade identifies him as Bocca degli Abati, the Pilgrim's fury mounts still higher. Bocca, himself furious, names several other sinners in Antenora, including Buoso da Duera, Tesauro dei Beccheria, Gianni de' Soldanier, Ganelon, and Tibbald. Going farther on, the Pilgrim sees two heads frozen in one hole, the mouth of one gnawing at the brain of the other.

If I had words grating and crude enough
  that really could describe this horrid hole
  supporting the converging weight of Hell,   3

I could squeeze out the juice of my memories
  to the last drop. But I don't have these words,
  and so I am reluctant to begin.   6

To talk about the bottom of the universe
  the way it truly is, is no child's play,
  no task for tongues that gurgle baby-talk.

But may those heavenly ladies aid my verse
  who aided Amphion to wall-in Thebes,
  that my words may tell exactly what I saw.   12

O misbegotten rabble of all rabble,
    who crowd this realm, hard even to describe,
    it were better you had lived as sheep or goats!   15

When we reached a point of darkness in the well
    below the giant's feet, farther down the slope,
    and I was gazing still at the high wall,   18

I heard somebody say: "Watch where you step!
    Be careful that you do not kick the heads
    of this brotherhood of miserable souls."   21

At that I turned around and saw before me
    a lake of ice stretching beneath my feet,
    more like a sheet of glass than frozen water.   24

In the depths of Austria's wintertime, the Danube
    never in all its course showed ice so thick,
    nor did the Don beneath its frigid sky,   27

as this crust here; for if Mount Tambernic
    or Pietrapana would crash down upon it,
    not even at its edges would a crack creak.   30

The way the frogs (in the season when the harvest
    will often haunt the dreams of the peasant girl)
    sit croaking with their muzzles out of water,   33

so these frigid, livid shades were stuck in ice
    up to where a person's shame appears;
    their teeth clicked notes like storks' beaks snapping shut.

And each one kept his face bowed toward the ice:
    the mouth bore testimony to the cold,
    the eyes, to sadness welling in the heart.   39

I gazed around awhile and then looked down,
    and by my feet I saw two figures clasped
    so tight that one's hair could have been the other's.   42

"Tell me, you two, pressing your chests together,"
    I asked them, "who are you?" Both stretched their necks
    and when they had their faces raised toward me,   45

their eyes, which had before been only glazed,
  dripped tears down to their lips, and the cold froze
  the tears between them, locking the pair more tightly.   48

Wood to wood with iron was never clamped
  so firm! And the two of them like billy-goats
  were butting at each other, mad with anger.   51

Another one with both ears frozen off,
  and head still bowed over his icy mirror,
  cried out: "What makes you look at us so hard?   54

If you're interested to know who these two are:
  the valley where Bisenzio's waters flow
  belonged to them and to their father, Albert;   57

the same womb bore them both, and if you scour
  all of Caïna, you will not turn up one
  who's more deserving of this frozen aspic—   60

not him who had his breast and shadow pierced
  with one thrust of the lance from Arthur's hand;
  not Focaccia; not even this one here,   63

whose head gets in my way and blocks my view,
  known in the world as Sassol Mascheroni,
  and if you're Tuscan you must know who he was.   66

To save me from your asking for more news:
  I was Camicion de' Pazzi, and I await
  Carlin, whose guilt will make my own seem less."   69

Farther on I saw a thousand doglike faces,
  purple from the cold. That's why I shudder,
  and always will, when I see a frozen pond.   72

While we were getting closer to the center
  of the universe, where all weights must converge,
  and I was shivering in the eternal chill—   75

by fate or chance or willfully perhaps,
  I do not know—but stepping among the heads,
  my foot kicked hard against one of those faces.   78

Weeping, he screamed: "Why are you kicking me?
  You have not come to take revenge on me
  for Montaperti, have you? Why bother me?"   81

And I: "My master, please wait here for me,
  let me clear up a doubt concerning this one,
  then I shall be as rapid as you wish."   84

My leader stopped, and to that wretch, who still
  had not let up in his barrage of curses,
  I said: "Who are you, insulting other people?"   87

"And you, who are *you* who march through Antenora
  kicking other people in their faces?
  No living man could kick as hard!" he answered.   90

"I am a living man," was my reply,
  "and it might serve you well, if you seek fame,
  for me to put your name down in my notes."   93

And he said: "That's the last thing I would want!
  That's not the way to flatter in these lowlands!
  Stop pestering me like this—get out of here!"   96

At that I grabbed him by his hair in back
  and said: "You'd better tell me who you are
  or else I'll not leave one hair on your head."   99

And he to me: "Go on and strip me bald
  and pound and stamp my head a thousand times,
  you'll never hear my name or see my face."   102

I had my fingers twisted in his hair
  and already I'd pulled out more than one fistful,
  while he yelped like a cur with eyes shut tight,   105

when someone else yelled: "What's the matter, Bocca?
  It's bad enough to hear your shivering teeth;
  now you bark! What the devil's wrong with you?"   108

"There's no need now for you to speak," I said,
  "you vicious traitor! Now I know your name
  and I'll bring back the shameful truth about you."   111

"Go away!" he answered. "Tell them what you want;
　　but if you do get out of here, be sure
　　you also tell about that blabbermouth,　　　　　114

who's paying here what the French silver cost him:
　　'I saw,' you can tell the world, 'the one from Duera
　　stuck in with all the sinners keeping cool.'　　　117

And if you should be asked: 'Who else was there?'
　　Right by your side is the one from Beccheria
　　whose head was chopped off by the Florentines.　　120

As for Gianni Soldanier, I think you'll find him
　　farther along with Ganelon and Tibbald,
　　who opened up Faenza while it slept."　　　　123

Soon after leaving him I saw two souls
　　frozen together in a single hole,
　　so that one head used the other for a cap.　　126

As a man with hungry teeth tears into bread,
　　the soul with capping head had sunk his teeth
　　into the other's neck, just beneath the skull.　　129

Tydeus in his fury did not gnaw
　　the head of Menalippus with more relish
　　than this one chewed that head of meat and bones.　　132

"O you who show with every bestial bite
　　your hatred for the head you are devouring,"
　　I said, "tell me your reason, and I promise,　　135

if you are justified in your revenge,
　　once I know who you are and this one's sin,
　　I'll repay your confidence in the world above　　138

unless my tongue dry up before I die."

NOTES

1. *If I had words grating and crude enough*: Dante fulfills his
wish with the very words he speaks in uttering it ("grating
and crude").

10–12. *But may those heavenly ladies aid my verse*: The Muses ("those heavenly ladies," 10) helped Amphion, the son of Jupiter and Antiope, construct a wall around Thebes. As the legend has it, Amphion played upon his lyre and so charmed the stones on Mt. Cithaeron that they came of their own accord and formed the wall.

27. *nor did the Don beneath its frigid sky*: The river Don, which has its source in the heart of Russia, would naturally be ice-bound in the frigid Russian winter. In the Italian, Dante uses the classical name for the Don, the *Tanai*.

28–30. *Mount Tambernic / or Pietrapana*: Tambernic has never been successfully identified. The older commentators place it in the Balkans. Pietrapana is probably a rocky peak in the northwest corner of Tuscany, today called Pania della Croce.

35. *up to where a person's shame appears*: the face.

55–58. *If you're interested to know who these two are*: The two brothers were Napoleone and Alessandro, sons of Count Alberto of Mangona, who owned part of the valley of the Bisenzio near Florence. The two quarrelled often and eventually killed each other in a fight concerning their inheritance.

59. *all of Caïna*: The icy outer ring of Cocytus is named Caïna after Cain, who slew his brother Abel. Thus, in the first division of this, the Ninth Circle, are punished those treacherous shades who murderously violated family bonds.

61–62. *not him who had his breast and shadow pierced*: Mordred, the wicked nephew of King Arthur, tried to kill the king and take his kingdom. But Arthur pierced him with such a mighty blow that when the lance was pulled from the dying traitor a ray of sunlight traversed his body and interrupted Mordred's shadow. The story is told in the Old French romance *Lancelot du Lac*, the book which Francesca claims led her astray with Paolo in *Inferno* V, 127.

63. *not Focaccia*: He was one of the Cancellieri family of Pistoia and a member of the White party. His treacherous murder of his cousin, Detto de' Cancellieri (a Black), was possibly the act which led to the Florentine intervention in Pistoian affairs.

65. *known in the world as Sassol Mascheroni*: The early com-

mentators say that Sassol Mascheroni was a member of the Toschi family in Florence who murdered his nephew in order to gain his inheritance.

68–69. *I was Camicion de' Pazzi, and I await*: Nothing is known of Camicion de' Pazzi except that he murdered one Ubertino, a relative. Another of Camicion's kin, Carlino de' Pazzi (69) from Valdarno, was still alive when the Pilgrim's conversation with Camicion was taking place. But Camicion already knew that Carlino, in July 1302, would accept a bribe to surrender the castle of Piantravigne to the Blacks of Florence.

80–81. *You have not come to take revenge on me*: See below, n. 106.

88. *And you, who are you who march through Antenora*: Dante and Virgil have passed into the second division of Cocytus, named Antenora after the Trojan warrior who, according to one legend, betrayed his city to the Greeks. In this round are tormented those who committed acts of treachery against country, city, or political party.

106. *What's the matter, Bocca?*: Bocca degli Abati was a Ghibelline who appeared to side with the Florentine Guelfs. However, while fighting on the side of the Guelfs at the battle of Montaperti in 1260, he is said to have cut off the hand of the standard bearer. The disappearance of the standard led to panic among the Florentine Guelfs, who were then decisively defeated by the Sienese Ghibellines and their German allies under Manfred.

116–17. *the one from Duera*: Buoso da Duera, a chief of the Ghibelline party of Cremona, was a well-known traitor. When Charles of Anjou marched against Naples in 1265, Manfred sent troops under the command of Buoso to stop them. But Buoso accepted a bribe from Charles (the "French silver," 115) and allowed the French troops to pass unmolested.

119–20. *Right by your side is the one from Beccheria*: Tesauro dei Beccheria of Pavia was an Abbot of Vallombrosa and a papal legate to Alexander IV in Tuscany. He was tortured and finally beheaded in 1258 by the Guelfs of Florence for carrying on secret intercourse with Ghibellines who had been exiled.

121. *As for Gianni Soldanier, I think you'll find him*: Gianni de' Soldanier was an important Ghibelline of Florence who, when the Florentines (mostly Guelf) began to chafe under Ghibelline rule, deserted his party and went over to the Guelfs.

122–23. *farther along with Ganelon and Tibbald*: Ganelon is the treacherous knight who betrayed Roland (and the rear guard of Charlemagne's army) to the Saracens. See XXXI, 16–18.

Tibbald is one of the Zambrasi family of Faenza. In order to avenge himself on the Ghibelline Lambertazzi family (who had been exiled from Bologna in 1274 and had taken refuge in Faenza), he opened his city to their Bolognese Guelf enemies on the morning of November 13, 1280.

130–31. *Tydeus in his fury did not gnaw*: Tydeus, one of the Seven against Thebes (see XIV, 68–70), slew Menalippus in combat—who, however, managed to wound him fatally. Tydeus called for his enemy's head, which, when brought to him by Amphiaraus, he proceeded to gnaw in rage.

CANTO XXXIII

COUNT UGOLINO is the shade gnawing at the brain of his one-time associate ARCHBISHOP RUGGIERI, and Ugolino interrupts his gruesome meal long enough to tell the story of his imprisonment and cruel death, which his innocent offspring shared with him. Moving farther into the area of Cocytus known as TOLOMEA, where those who betrayed their guests and associates are condemned, the Pilgrim sees sinners with their faces raised high above the ice, whose tears freeze and lock their eyes. One of the shades agrees to identify himself on condition that the ice be removed from his eyes. The Pilgrim agrees, and learns that this sinner is FRIAR ALBERIGO and that his soul is dead and damned even though his body is still alive on earth, inhabited by a devil. Alberigo also names a fellow sinner with him in the ice, BRANCA D'ORIA, whose body is still functioning up on earth. But the Pilgrim does not honor his promise to break the ice from Alberigo's eyes.

Lifting his mouth from his horrendous meal,
   this sinner first wiped off his messy lips
   in the hair remaining on the chewed-up skull,   3

then spoke: "You want me to renew a grief
   so desperate that just the thought of it,
   much less the telling, grips my heart with pain;   6

but if my words can be the seed to bear
   the fruit of infamy for this betrayer,
   who feeds my hunger, then I shall speak—in tears.   9

I do not know your name, nor do I know
   how you have come down here, but Florentine
   you surely seem to be, to hear you speak.   12

First you should know I was Count Ugolino
   and my neighbor here, Ruggieri the Archbishop;
   now I'll tell you why I'm so unneighborly.   15

That I, trusting in him, was put in prison
   through his evil machinations, where I died,
   this much I surely do not have to tell you.   18

What you could not have known, however, is
   the inhuman circumstances of my death.
   Now listen, then decide if he has wronged me!   21

Through a narrow slit of window high in that mew
   (which is called the tower of hunger, after me,
   and I'll not be the last to know that place)   24

I had watched moon after moon after moon go by,
   when finally I dreamed the evil dream
   which ripped away the veil that hid my future.   27

I dreamed of this one here as lord and huntsman,
   pursuing the wolf and the wolf cubs up the mountain
   (which blocks the sight of Lucca from the Pisans)   30

with skinny bitches, well trained and obedient;
   he had out front as leaders of the pack
   Gualandi with Sismondi and Lanfranchi.   33

A short run, and the father with his sons
   seemed to grow tired, and then I thought I saw
   long fangs sunk deep into their sides, ripped open.   36

When I awoke before the light of dawn,
   I heard my children sobbing in their sleep
   (you see they, too, were there), asking for bread.   39

If the thought of what my heart was telling me
   does not fill you with grief, how cruel you are!
   If you are not weeping now—do you ever weep?   42

And then they awoke. It was around the time
   they usually brought our food to us. But now
   each one of us was full of dread from dreaming;   45

then from below I heard them driving nails
   into the dreadful tower's door; with that,
   I stared in silence at my flesh and blood.   48

I did not weep, I turned to stone inside;
   they wept, and my little Anselmuccio spoke:
   'What is it, father? Why do you look that way?'   51

For them I held my tears back, saying nothing,
   all of that day, and then all of that night,
   until another sun shone on the world.   54

A meager ray of sunlight found its way
   to the misery of our cell, and I could see
   myself reflected four times in their faces;   57

I bit my hands in anguish. And my children,
   who thought that hunger made me bite my hands,
   were quick to draw up closer to me, saying: 60

'O father, you would make us suffer less,
   if you would feed on us: you were the one
   who gave us this sad flesh; you take it from us!'   63

I calmed myself to make them less unhappy.
   That day we sat in silence, and the next day.
   O pitiless earth! You should have swallowed us!   66

The fourth day came, and it was on that day
   my Gaddo fell prostrate before my feet,
   crying: 'Why don't you help me? Why, my father?'   69

There he died. Just as you see me here,
   I saw the other three fall one by one,
   as the fifth day and the sixth day passed. And I,   72

by then gone blind, groped over their dead bodies.
   Though they were dead, two days I called their names.
   Then hunger proved more powerful than grief."   75

He spoke these words; then, glaring down in rage,
   attacked again the wretched skull with his teeth
   sharp as a dog's, and as fit for grinding bones.   78

O Pisa, blot of shame upon the people
   of that fair land where the sound of "sì" is heard!
   Since your neighbors hesitate to punish you,   81

let Capraia and Gorgona move and join,
   damming up the River Arno at its mouth,
   and let every Pisan perish in its flood!   84

For if Count Ugolino was accused
   of turning traitor, trading-in your castles,
   you had no right to make his children suffer.   87

Their newborn years (O newborn Thebes!) made them
   all innocents: Brigata, Uguiccione,
   and the other two soft names my canto sings.   90

We moved ahead to where the frozen water
   wraps in harsh wrinkles another sinful race,
   with faces not turned down but looking up.   93

Here, the weeping puts an end to weeping,
   and the grief that finds no outlet from the eyes
   turns inward to intensify the anguish: 96

for the tears they first wept knotted in a cluster
   and like a visor made for them in crystal,
   filled all the hollow part around their eyes.   99

Although the bitter coldness of the dark
   had driven all sensation from my face,
   as though it were not tender skin but callous,   102

I thought I felt the air begin to blow,
   and I: "What causes such a wind, my master?
   I thought no heat could reach into these depths."   105

And he to me: "Before long you will be
   where your own eyes can answer for themselves,
   when they will see what keeps this wind in motion."   108

And one of the wretches with the frozen crust
   screamed out at us: "O wicked souls, so wicked
   that you have been assigned the ultimate post,   111

break off these hard veils covering my eyes
and give relief from the pain that swells my heart—
at least until the new tears freeze again."   114

I answered him: "If this is what you want,
tell me your name; and if I do not help you,
may I be forced to drop beneath this ice!"   117

He answered then: "I am Friar Alberigo,
I am he who offered fruit from the evil orchard:
here dates are served me for the figs I gave."   120

"Oh, then!" I said. "Are you already dead?"
And he to me: "Just how my body is
in the world above, I have no way of knowing.   123

This zone of Tolomea is very special,
for it often happens that a soul falls here
before the time that Atropos should send it.   126

And that you may more willingly scrape off
my cluster of glass tears, let me tell you:
whenever a soul betrays the way I did,   129

a demon takes possession of the body,
controlling its maneuvers from then on,
for all the years it has to live up there,   132

while the soul falls straight into this cistern here;
and the shade in winter quarters just behind me
may well have left his body up on earth.   135

But you should know, if you've just come from there:
he is Ser Branca D'Oria; and many years
have passed since he first joined us here, icebound."   138

"I think you're telling me a lie," I said,
"for Branca D'Oria is not dead at all;
he eats and drinks, he sleeps and wears out clothes."   141

"The ditch the Malebranche watch above,"
he said, "the ditch of clinging, boiling pitch,
had not yet caught the soul of Michel Zanche,   144

when Branca left a devil in his body
  to take his place, and so did his close kinsman,
  his accomplice in this act of treachery.   147

But now, at last, give me the hand you promised.
  Open my eyes." I did not open them.
  To be mean to him was a generous reward.   150

O all you Genovese, you men estranged
  from every good, at home with every vice,
  why can't the world be wiped clean of your race?   153

For in company with Romagna's rankest soul
  I found one of your men, whose deeds were such
  that his soul bathes already in Cocytus   156

but his body seems alive and walks among you.

NOTES

13–14. *First you should know I was Count Ugolino*: Ugolino
della Gherardesca, the Count of Donoratico, belonged to a
noble Tuscan family whose political affiliations were Ghibel-
line. In 1275 he conspired with his son-in-law, Giovanni Vi-
sconti, to raise the Guelfs to power in Pisa. Although exiled
for this subversive activity, Ugolino (Nino) Visconti took over
the Guelf government of the city. Three years later (1288) he
plotted with Archbishop Ruggieri degli Ubaldini to rid Pisa
of the Visconti. Ruggieri, however, had other plans, and with
the aid of the Ghibellines, he seized control of the city and
imprisoned Ugolino, together with his sons and grandsons,
in the "tower of hunger" (23). The two were evidently just
at the boundary between Antenora and Tolomea, for Ugolino
is being punished for betraying his country (in Antenora), and
Ruggieri for betraying his associate, Ugolino (in Tolomea).

25. *I had watched moon after moon after moon go by*: Impris-
oned in June of 1288, they were finally starved to death in
February 1289.

28–36. *I dreamed of this one here as lord and huntsman*: Ugolino's dream was indeed prophetic. The "lord and huntsman" (28) is Archbishop Ruggieri, who, with the leading Ghibelline families of Pisa ("Gualandi . . . Sismondi and Lanfranchi," 33) and the populace ("skinny bitches," 31), runs down Ugolino and his offspring ("the wolf and the wolf cubs," 29) and finally kills them; the phrase "up the mountain" (i.e., up San Giuliano, which lies between Pisa and Lucca) is probably meant to suggest the high tower in which they were imprisoned.

50. *they wept, and my little Anselmuccio spoke*: Anselmuccio was the younger of Ugolino's grandsons; according to official documents, he must have been fifteen at the time.

68. *my Gaddo fell prostrate before my feet*: Gaddo was one of Ugolino's sons.

75. *Then hunger proved more powerful than grief*: Whether in this line Ugolino is confessing to an act of cannibalism or whether it simply relates the cause of his death (hunger instead of grief) Dante has left to the reader's imagination. It cannot be denied that he allows us to think in terms of the first possibility; moreover, he has chosen to present Ugolino as chewing on the skull of Ruggieri.

79–90

Dante inveighs against Pisa for having killed the four innocent offspring of Count Ugolino, not for having punished him as he deserved. He calls upon the islands of Capraia and Gorgona, both of which lie in the Tyrrhenian Sea not far from the mouth of the Arno River, to come block the Arno, thereby flooding Pisa and killing its evil inhabitants (82–84). By referring to Pisa as the "newborn Thebes" (88), Dante evokes the horrendous and scandalous events that characterized the history of that Greek city. For previous allusions to Thebes, see XIV, 69; XX, 59; XXV, 15; XXX, 22; XXXII, 11.

80. *of that fair land where the sound of "sì" is heard!*: Italy. It was customary in Dante's time to indicate a language area by the words signifying "yes." Compare XVIII, 61 and note.

89–90. *Brigata, Uguiccione / and the other two*: Brigata was Ugolino's second grandson and Uguiccione his fifth son. For the "other two" (90), see above, n.50 and n.68. Dante, in mentioning "their newborn years," departs from historical fact—which reports that all except Anselmuccio were grown men.

91–93. *We moved ahead to where the frozen water*: Virgil and the Pilgrim have now entered the third division of Cocytus, called Tolomea (124) after Ptolemy, the captain of Jericho who had Simon, his father-in-law, and two of his sons killed while dining (see I Maccabees XVI, 11–17). Or possibly this zone of Cocytus is named after Ptolemy XII, the Egyptian king who, having welcomed Pompey to his realm, slew him. In Tolomea are punished those who have betrayed their guests.

105. *I thought no heat could reach into these depths*: Wind, according to the science of Dante's time, is produced by varying degrees of heat; thus, Cocytus, being completely icebound, lacks all heat, and should be free of winds. In the next canto the Pilgrim will see for himself that Lucifer's giant wings cause the wind. See XXXIV, 46–51.

115–17. *may I be forced to drop beneath this ice!*: The Pilgrim, fully aware that his journey will indeed take him below the ice, carefully phrases his treacherous promise to the treacherous shade, and successfully deceives him (149–50). The Pilgrim betrays a sinner in this circle, as the latter does one of his companions there with him in the ice (by naming him).

118–20. *I am Friar Alberigo*: One of the Jovial Friars (see XXIII, 103–108), Alberigo di Ugolino dei Manfredi was a native of Faenza. In 1285, in the midst of a family feud, Alberigo invited his principal opponents, Manfred (close relative) and Alberghetto (Manfred's son), to dinner as a gesture of good will. During the course of the meal, Alberigo, using a prearranged signal, called for fruit, at which his men murdered the dinner guests. Continuing the "fruit" imagery, Alberigo laments his present anguish by saying ironically that "here dates are served me for the figs I gave" (120), which is to say that he is suffering more than his share (since a date is more valuable than a fig).

124–35. *This zone of Tolomea is very special*: According to Church doctrine, under certain circumstances a living person may, through acts of treachery, lose possession of his soul before he dies ("before the time that Atropos [the Fate who cuts man's thread of life] should send it," 126). Then, on earth, a devil inhabits the body until its natural death.

137–47. *he is Ser Branca D'Oria*: A prominent resident of Genoa, Branca D'Oria murdered his father-in-law, Michel Zanche (see XXII, 88), after having invited him to dine with him. Although this treacherous act occurred in 1275, Branca (or at least his earthly body) did not die until 1325. Alberigo tells Dante that the soul of Branca, together with that of a close relative who helped him carry out his acts of treachery, fell here, to Tolomea, even before Michel Zanche's soul reached the *bolgia* of the Barrators (142–47).

154. *For in company with Romagna's rankest soul*: Friar Alberigo. Faenza, his home town, was in the region of Romagna (now called Emilia).

155. *I found one of your men, whose deeds were such*: Branca D'Oria.

CANTO XXXIV

*FAR ACROSS the frozen ice can be seen the gigantic figure of LU-
CIFER, who appears from this distance like a windmill seen through
fog; and as the two travelers walk on toward that terrifying sight,
they see the shades of sinners totally buried in the frozen water. At
the center of the earth Lucifer stands frozen from the chest downward,
and his horrible ugliness (he has three faces) is made more fearful by
the fact that in each of his three mouths he chews on one of the three
worst sinners of all mankind, the worst of those who betrayed their
benefactors: JUDAS ISCARIOT, BRUTUS, and CASSIUS. Virgil, with
the Pilgrim on his back, begins the descent down the shaggy body of
Lucifer. They climb down through a crack in the ice, and when they
reach the Evil One's thighs, Virgil turns and begins to struggle
upward (because they have passed the center of the earth), still holding
on to the hairy body of Lucifer, until they reach a cavern, where
they stop for a short rest. Then a winding path brings them eventually
to the earth's surface, where they see the stars.*

"*Vexilla regis prodeunt Inferni*,"
   my master said, "closer to us, so now
   look ahead and see if you can make him out."   3

A far-off windmill turning its huge sails
   when a thick fog begins to settle in,
   or when the light of day begins to fade,   6

that is what I thought I saw appearing.
   And the gusts of wind it stirred made me shrink back
   behind my guide, my only means of cover.   9

Down here, I stood on souls fixed under ice
   (I tremble as I put this into verse);
   to me they looked like straws worked into glass.   12

Some lying flat, some perpendicular,
   either with their heads up or their feet,
   and some bent head to foot, shaped like a bow.   15

When we had moved far enough along the way
   that my master thought the time had come to show me
   the creature who was once so beautiful,   18

he stepped aside, and stopping me, announced:
   "This is he, this is Dis; this is the place
   that calls for all the courage you have in you."   21

How chilled and nerveless, Reader, I felt then;
   do not ask me—I cannot write about it—
   there are no words to tell you how I felt.   24

I did not die—I was not living either!
   Try to imagine, if you can imagine,
   me there, deprived of life and death at once.   27

The king of the vast kingdom of all grief
   stuck out with half his chest above the ice;
   my height is closer to the height of giants   30

than theirs is to the length of his great arms;
   consider now how large all of him was:
   this body in proportion to his arms.   33

If once he was as fair as now he's foul
   and dared to raise his brows against his Maker,
   it is fitting that all grief should spring from him.   36

Oh, how amazed I was when I looked up
   and saw a head—one head wearing three faces!
   One was in front (and that was a bright red),   39

the other two attached themselves to this one
   just above the middle of each shoulder,
   and at the crown all three were joined in one: 42

The right face was a blend of white and yellow,
   the left the color of those people's skin
   who live along the river Nile's descent.   45

Beneath each face two mighty wings stretched out,
    the size you might expect of this huge bird
    (I never saw a ship with larger sails):   48

not feathered wings but rather like the ones
    a bat would have. He flapped them constantly,
    keeping three winds continuously in motion   51

to lock Cocytus eternally in ice.
    He wept from his six eyes, and down three chins
    were dripping tears all mixed with bloody slaver.   54

In each of his three mouths he crunched a sinner,
    with teeth like those that rake the hemp and flax,
    keeping three sinners constantly in pain;   57

the one in front—the biting he endured
    was nothing like the clawing that he took:
    sometimes his back was raked clean of its skin.   60

"That soul up there who suffers most of all,"
    my guide explained, "is Judas Iscariot:
    the one with head inside and legs out kicking.   63

As for the other two whose heads stick out,
    the one who hangs from that black face is Brutus—
    see how he squirms in silent desperation;   66

the other one is Cassius, he still looks sturdy.
    But soon it will be night. Now is the time
    to leave this place, for we have seen it all."   69

I held on to his neck, as he told me to,
    while he watched and waited for the time and place,
    and when the wings were stretched out just enough,   72

he grabbed on to the shaggy sides of Satan;
    then downward, tuft by tuft, he made his way
    between the tangled hair and frozen crust.   75

When we had reached the point exactly where
    the thigh begins, right at the haunch's curve,
    my guide, with strain and force of every muscle,   78

turned his head toward the shaggy shanks of Dis
 and grabbed the hair as if about to climb—
 I thought that we were heading back to Hell.   81

"Hold tight, there is no other way," he said,
 panting, exhausted, "only by these stairs
 can we leave behind the evil we have seen."   84

When he had got me through the rocky crevice,
 he raised me to its edge and set me down,
 then carefully he climbed and joined me there.   87

I raised my eyes, expecting I would see
 the half of Lucifer I saw before.
 Instead I saw his two legs stretching upward.   90

If at that sight I found myself confused,
 so will those simple-minded folk who still
 don't see what point it was I must have passed.   93

"Get up," my master said, "get to your feet,
 the way is long, the road a rough climb up,
 already the sun approaches middle tierce!"   96

It was no palace promenade we came to,
 but rather like some dungeon Nature built:
 it was paved with broken stone and poorly lit.   99

"Before we start to struggle out of here,
 O master," I said when I was on my feet,
 "I wish you would explain some things to me.   102

Where is the ice? And how can he be lodged
 upside-down? And how, in so little time,
 could the sun go all the way from night to day?"   105

"You think you're still on the center's other side,"
 he said, "where I first grabbed the hairy worm
 of rottenness that pierces the earth's core;   108

and you *were* there as long as I moved downward
 but, when I turned myself, you passed the point
 to which all weight from every part is drawn.   111

Now you are standing beneath the hemisphere
   which is opposite the side covered by land,
   where at the central point was sacrificed   114

the Man whose birth and life were free of sin.
   You have both feet upon a little sphere
   whose other side Judecca occupies;   117

when it is morning here, there it is evening.
   And he whose hairs were stairs for our descent
   has not changed his position since his fall.   120

When he fell from the heavens on this side,
   all of the land that once was spread out here,
   alarmed by his plunge, took cover beneath the sea   123

and moved to our hemisphere; with equal fear
   the mountain-land, piled up on this side, fled
   and made this cavern here when it rushed upward.   126

Below somewhere there is a space, as far
   from Beelzebub as the limit of his tomb,
   known not by sight but only by the sound   129

of a little stream that makes its way down here
   through the hollow of a rock that it has worn,
   gently winding in gradual descent."   132

My guide and I entered that hidden road
   to make our way back up to the bright world.
   We never thought of resting while we climbed.   135

We climbed, he first and I behind, until,
   through a small round opening ahead of us
   I saw the lovely things the heavens hold,   138

and we came out to see once more the stars.

NOTES

1. *"Vexilla regis prodeunt Inferni"*: The opening lines of the hymn "Vexilla regis prodeunt"—"The banners of the King advance" (written by Venantius Fortunatus, sixth-century bishop

of Poitiers, this hymn belongs to the liturgy of the Church)
—is here parodied by the addition of the word *Inferni* ("of
Hell") to the word *regis* ("of the King"). Sung on Good Friday,
the hymn anticipates the unveiling of the Cross; Dante, who
began his journey on the evening of Good Friday, is prepared
by Virgil's words for the sight of Lucifer, who will appear
like a "windmill" in a "thick fog." The banners referred to
are Lucifer's wings. The ironic nature of the parodied line and
its effect are evident: with the first three words the reader is
prepared to think in terms of the Cross, the symbol of man's
redemption through Christ; but with the fourth he is abruptly
recalled to the present reality of Hell and, moreover, to the
immediate presence of Lucifer, the personification of Evil and
the antithesis of Christian Love.

   10. *Down here, I stood on souls fixed under ice*: These sinners
in various positions fixed rigidly in the ice present a picture
of complete immobility and incommunicability, as though
they have been entombed a second time. Silence reigns in this
fourth division of Cocytus (named Judecca, 117, after the trai-
tor Judas), the gelid abode of those souls in whom all warmth
of love for God and for their fellow man has been extinguished.

   18. *the creature who was once so beautiful*: Before his fall Lucifer
was held by God to be the fairest of the angels. Pride caused
Lucifer's rebellion against his Maker and precipitated his ex-
pulsion from Heaven. The arch-traitor is, like the other sin-
ners, fixed and suffering in the ice. He weeps.

   20. *This is he, this is Dis; this is the place*: In antiquity Pluto,
god of the Underworld, was often referred to as "Dis," a
name here applied to Lucifer.

   38–45. *and saw a head—one head wearing three faces!*: Dante
presents Lucifer's head as a perverted parallel of the Trinity.
The symbolic value of the three single faces has been much
debated. Although many commentators believe that the colors
(red, yellow, black) represent the three known continents (Eu-
rope, Asia, Africa), it seems more logical that they should be
antithetically analogous to the qualities attributed to the Trin-
ity (see Canto III, 5–6). Therefore, Highest Wisdom would

be opposed by ignorance (black), Divine Omnipotence by impotence (yellow), Primal Love by hatred or envy (red).

46. *Beneath each face two mighty wings stretched out*: The entire figure of Lucifer is a parody of the angelic. Originally belonging to the order of the Cherubim, he retains his six wings even in Hell, though here, devoid of their heavenly plumage, they appear as those of a bat (the standard depiction of the Devil's wings in the Middle Ages). Satan's huge but impotent figure in the darkness might also be contrasted with the image of God (in the *Paradise*) as a small, indivisible point of light in movement.

61–63. *That soul up there who suffers most of all*: Having betrayed Christ for thirty pieces of silver, Judas endures greater punishment than the other two souls. His position in Lucifer's mouth recalls that of the Simonists in Canto XIX. Moreover, Lucifer himself will appear in the same manner ("his two legs stretching upward," 90), when Dante and Virgil have passed the center of the earth and are about to leave Hell. The Simonists, then, prefigure the principal traitors against God and Christ, both in act (treachery to Christ's Church) and spatial disposition of their bodies. See XIX, final note.

65. *the one who hangs from that black face is Brutus*: Marcus Brutus, who was deceitfully persuaded by Cassius (67) to join the conspiracy, aided in the assassination of Julius Caesar. It is fitting that in his final vision of the Inferno the Pilgrim should see those shades who committed treacherous acts against Divine and worldly authorities: the Church and the Roman Empire. This provides the culmination, at least in this canticle, of the basic themes: Church and Empire.

67. *the other one is Cassius, he still looks sturdy*: Caius Cassius Longinus was another member of the conspiracy against Caesar. By describing Cassius as "still looking sturdy," Dante shows he has evidently confused him with Lucius Cassius, whom Cicero calls *adeps*, "corpulent."

79–81. *turned his head toward the shaggy shanks of Dis*: Virgil, carrying the Pilgrim on his back, slowly makes his way down Lucifer's hairy body and, upon reaching a certain point (the

386 THE DIVINE COMEDY: INFERNO

center of the universe and, consequently, of terrestrial gravity), where Lucifer's thighs begin, he must turn his head in the direction of Lucifer's legs and begin to climb "upward"—thus confusing the Pilgrim on his back. The way in which Virgil executed his own shift of position on Lucifer's body must have been as follows: when he reached the thigh he moved his head to the side and downward until (still holding on with one hand to the hair of the chest) he could reach with his other hand to grasp the hair on the thigh—then (aided now by the shift of gravitational pull) to free the first hand and complete the half-circle he had initiated, proceeding henceforth as a man climbing.

Incidentally, of all the translations of this passage that I have read (including not only translations in English but also those in French, Spanish, Portuguese, German, Dutch, Latin, Greek, Welsh), none translates line 79 as I do, attributing the "shanks" to Lucifer; all give them to Virgil, presenting him as turning his head toward his own shanks. This is not because the line is difficult (*"Volse la testa ov'elli avea le zanche,"* "he turned the head to where *he* had the shanks"); in fact, it is not even ambiguous, if the translator bears in mind the use of subject pronouns in Italian. What must have happened is that every translator has copied unthinkingly translations that have preceded. As it is, by attributing the *zanche* ("shanks") to Virgil they have not only sinned on aesthetic grounds (this derisive, pejorative term applied to the noble body of Virgil!), but have blurred the clear symbolism here intended: *zanche* is used only twice in The Divine Comedy, once in reference to the legs of Nicholas (Canto XIX) and once in this canto. Surely, the two pairs of legs thus verbally linked must be those not of Nicholas and Virgil but those of Nicholas and Lucifer—both of whom present to the Pilgrim's eyes their legs protruding from the ground.

96. *already the sun approaches middle tierce!*: The time is approximately halfway between the canonical hours of Prime and Tierce, i.e., 7:30 a.m. The rapid change from night ("But soon it will be night," 68) to day (96) is the result of the travelers' having passed the earth's center, thus moving into

the Southern Hemisphere, which is twelve hours ahead of the Northern.

107–108. *the hairy worm of rottenness*: Compare VI, 22; n. 13–22.

112–15. *Now you are standing beneath the hemisphere*: Lucifer's body, falling head first from Heaven to the Southern Hemisphere, bored through to the earth's center, where he remains imprisoned. Before he fell through the Southern Hemisphere ("this side," 121), it was covered with land, but the land, "alarmed by his plunge," sank beneath the sea and shifted to the Northern Hemisphere ("our hemisphere," 124). But the land at the center of the earth "rushed upward" at once, leaving the "cavern" above Lucifer's legs and forming the Mount of Purgatory, the only land in the Southern Hemisphere.

127–32. *Below somewhere there is a space*: Somewhere below the land that rushed upward to form the Mount of Purgatory "there is a space" (127) through which a stream runs, and it is through this space that Virgil and Dante will climb to reach the base of the Mount. The "space" is "as far/from Beelzebub [Lucifer] as the limit of his tomb" (127–28); that is, at the edge of the natural dungeon that constitutes Lucifer's "tomb," there is an opening, a "space," serving as the entrance to the passage from the earth's center to its circumference, created by Lucifer in his fall from Heaven to Hell.

139. *and we came out to see once more the stars*: The Pilgrim, denied sight of the celestial bodies in Hell, now looks up at them again. The direction his journey will now take is upward, toward that Divine Realm of which the stars are the signal for us on earth. That all three canticles end with the word "stars" symmetrically reinforces the concept of movement upward toward God, the central theme and motive force of *The Divine Comedy*.

GLOSSARY AND INDEX OF
PERSONS AND PLACES

────────

PERSONS and places mentioned by name in the text are listed as they appear in this translation. For example, Ugolino della Gherardesca is entered under "Count Ugolino." If variant names are used in the text, the listing is by title, if any, or by first name, and cross-references to the main listing are given under the variant names. For example, King Frederick is entered under "King Frederick," and cross-references are given under "Frederick" and "Second Frederick." Persons and places not mentioned by name in the text, and those whose identification is questionable, are listed by the first word of the name.

All references are by canto and line; those within parentheses indicate the passages in the text where the person or place is mentioned.

ABBAGLIATO: a nickname meaning "Muddlehead." See note XXIX, 132 (XXIX, 132).

ABEL: second son of Adam and Eve (IV, 56).

ABRAHAM: the patriarch (IV, 58).

ABSALOM: a prince of Israel. See note XXVIII, 137–38 (XXVIII, 138).

ACHERON: a river in Hell. See note III, 78 (III, 78).

ACHILLES: Greek warrior, the hero of the *Iliad*. He was the son of Peleus and the Nereid Thetis. See notes V, 65–66; XXVI, 61–62; XXXI, 4–6 (V, 65; XII, 71; XXVI, 62; XXXI, 4).

ACHITOPHEL: the Gilonite. See note XXVIII, 137–38 (XXVIII, 138).

ACQUACHETA: a river of Italy. See note XVI, 94–101 (XVI, 97).

ACRI (ACRE): a city of Palestine. See note XXVII, 85–90 (XXVII, 89).

ADAM: father of mankind (III, 115; IV, 55).

ADIGE: a river of Italy. See note XII, 4–10 (XII, 6).

AEGINA: an island off the coast of Greece. See note XXIX, 58–66 (XXIX, 58).

AENEAS: a Trojan prince, son of Anchises and Venus, the hero of Virgil's *Aeneid*. After the fall of Troy, Aeneas escapes with his father, his young son Ascanius, and a number of followers, his wife, Creusa, having been lost in the confusion. During his subsequent wanderings over the sea, Anchises dies and Aeneas's fleet is wrecked by the spite of Juno, but he and seven of his ships are saved by Neptune and are brought to the coast of Africa. Here the Trojans are hospitably received by Dido, queen of Carthage, who, breaking her oath of fidelity to her dead husband, Sichaeus, falls in love with Aeneas, and when he sails for Italy at the bidding of Mercury, kills herself. At Cumae, Aeneas, guided by the Sibyl, makes the descent into Hades, where he sees the punishment of the wicked and the placid afterlife of the virtuous. Among the latter he meets Anchises and learns from him that he is destined to be the ancestor of the Roman people, who are to possess the empire of the world. (This is the famous Book VI of the *Aeneid*, from which Dante derived so much of the geography and machinery of his *Inferno*.) Aeneas then sails up the mouth of the Tiber and lands in Latium. Latinus, the king of the country, welcomes Aeneas and offers him the hand of his daughter Lavinia, previously betrothed to Turnus. Juno stirs up war between the Trojans and the Latins. Turnus challenges Aeneas to single combat; and Juno at length comes to an agreement with Jupiter that Aeneas shall be the victor, on condition that Latium shall keep its own name. Thus in Aeneas and Lavinia the Trojan and Latin lines are united and the way is open for the foundation of the city and empire of Rome. See notes II, 10–48, IV, 122, and XXVI, 92–93 (II, 32; IV, 122; XXVI, 93).

AESOP: a Greek fabulist. See note XXIII, 4–9 (XXIII, 4).

AGHINOLFO DA ROMENA: a member of the Conti Guidi family. See note XXX, 76–78 (XXX, 77).

AGNÈL: See note XXV, 68 (XXV, 68).

ALARDO (ÉRARD DE VALÉRY): constable of Champagne (c. 1200–77). He accompanied Saint Louis (Louis IX of France) on his crusading expeditions of 1248 and 1265; on his way home in 1268 he passed through Italy and there assisted Charles of Anjou to win the Battle of Tagliacozzo. See note XXVIII, 15–18 (XXVIII, 18).

ALBERIGO, FRIAR: See Friar Alberigo.

ALBERT (OF MANGONA): See note XXXII, 55–58 (XXXII, 57).

ALBERT OF SIENA: See note XXIX, 109–17 (XXIX, 110).

ALESSANDRO DEGLI ALBERTI: son of Count Alberto of Mangona. See note XXXII, 55–58 (XXXII, 55).

ALESSIO INTERMINEI: See note XVIII, 122 (XVIII, 122).

ALEXANDER: (1) Alexander da Romena, a member of the Conti Guidi family. See note XXX, 76–78 (XXX, 77). (2) Alexander the Great, of Macedon (356–23 B.C.). He ascended the throne in 336 B.C. after the assassination of his father, Philip II. After having subdued Greece, he vanquished Darius the Persian at the Battles of Granicus and Issus, and took most of the cities of Phoenicia. He next received the submission of Egypt and founded Alexandria; then he marched into Mesopotamia, where he decisively overcame the Persians at the Battle of Arebela (331 B.C.). After taking Babylon, Susa, and Persepolis and subduing the northern provinces of Asia, he invaded India, crossing the Urdas and advancing as far as the Hydaspes. He died of a fever at Babylon at the age of thirty-two. See note XIV, 33–36. For the identification of the Alexander mentioned in XII, 107, see note XII, 107–108 (XIV, 31).

ALI (ALI IBN-ABU TALEB): See note XXVIII, 32 (XXVIII, 32).

ALICHIN(O): a devil. See notes XXI, 118–23, XXII, 97–132 (XXI, 118); (XXII, 112).

ALPS: mountains of Europe. See note XX, 64–66 (XX, 64).

ALTAFORTE (HAUTEFORT): castle in the Limousin district of France near Périgueux, belonging to Bertran de Born. See note XXIX, 29 (XXIX, 29).

AMPHIARAUS: one of the seven kings who fought against Thebes. See note XX, 34–36 (XX, 34).

AMPHION: son of Zeus and Antiope. See note XXXII, 10–12 (XXXII, 11).

ANASTASIUS: Pope Anastasius II, from 496 to 98. See note XI, 8–9 (XI, 8).

ANAXAGORAS: Ionian philosopher (500–428 B.C.). He rejected the materialist explanation of the universe and held that mind or intelligence (*nous*) was the cause of all things. See note IV, 137 (IV, 137).

ANCHISES: father of Aeneas (I, 74).

ANDREA DE' MOZZI: bishop of Florence from 1287 to 1295. See notes XV, 16–114, 112–14 (XV, 112).

ANGIOLELLO: Angiolello da Carignano, nobleman of Fano. See note XXVIII, 77–90 (XXVIII, 77).

ANNAS: a high priest of the Jews, the father-in-law of Caiaphus. See note XXIII, 115–24 (XXIII, 121).

ANSELMUCCIO: grandson of Count Ugolino della Gherardesca. See note XXXIII, 50 (XXXIII, 50).

ANTAEUS: a giant, son of Neptune and Terra. See note XXXI, 19–127 (XXXI, 101).

ANTENORA: a region of Hell. See note XXXII, 88 (XXXII, 88).

APENNINES: a mountain range of Italy. See note XVI, 94–101 (XVI, 94).

AQUARIUS: "the water-carrier," sign of the zodiac; the sun is in Aquarius from mid-January to mid-February (XXIV, 2).

ARACHNE: daughter of Idom of Colophon in Lydia. See note XVII, 18 (XVII, 18).

ARBIA: a river near Siena. See note X, 85–86 (X, 86).

ARETHUSA: a nymph who, being pursued by the river-god Alpheus, was changed by Artemis (Diana) into a fountain. See note XXV, 94–102 (XXV, 97).

ARETINE, THE: Griffolino da Arezzo. See notes XXIX, 109–17, XXX, 31 (XXIX, 109; XXX, 31).

ARETINES: citizens of Arezzo. They were strongly Ghibelline and continually feuding with the Florentines. See note XXII, 5 (XXII, 5).

AREZZO: an Italian city in the southeast of Tuscany. See note XXIX, 109–17 (XXIX, 109).

ARGIVES: citizens of Argos, Greece (XXVIII, 84).

ARIADNE: the daughter of Minos. See note XII, 12–21 (XII, 20).

ARISTOTLE: Greek philospher, born in 384 B.C. in Stagira, a town in Chalcidice in Macedonia. In 367 B.C. he went to Athens to pursue his studies, and there became the pupil of Plato. He was Plato's most brilliant pupil, but later diverged considerably from his n   ter's teaching. His writings were rediscovered and translated in the Middle Ages (largely through the work of Arabian scholars), and became enormously influential. Saint Thomas Aquinas incorporated the Aristotelian system of philosophy into Catholic theology. All Western philosophy derives ultimately from the twin Platonic and Aristotelian traditions. The works of Aristotle were voluminous, and covered every branch of learning known in his day: Dialectics and Logic (the *Organon*); Philosophy (the *Physics* and other works on natural science, the *Metaphysics*, two treatises on *Mathematics*); Politics (the *Ethics*, the *Politics*, the *Economics*); Art (the *Poetics*, the *Rhetoric*). Dante was well acquainted with all the writings of Aristotle that were available in Latin translation in his time, and refers to them often. See notes IV, 131, and XI, 79–84, 101–105 (IV, 131; XI, 79; XI, 101).

ARLES: a city in the south of France at the mouth of the Rhone. See note IX, 112–17 (IX, 112).

ARNO: river that runs through Florence, Italy. See notes XIII, 143–50, XXX, 64–66 (XIII, 146; XV, 113; XXIII, 95; XXX, 65; XXXIII, 83).

ARRIGO: See note VI, 79–87 (VI, 80).

ARTHUR: mythical king of Britain, hero of the romances of the Round Table, the husband of Guinevere. See note XXXII, 61–62 (XXXII, 62).

ARUNS: Etruscan augur. See note XX, 46–51 (XX, 46).

ASDENTE: soothsayer of Parma. See note XX, 118–20 (XX, 118).

ATROPOS: in Greek and Roman mythology, one of the Fates, or deities, who preside over the destinies of mankind. According to the Greek poet Hesiod, there were three Fates, later distinguished as: Clotho, who spun the thread of a man's life; Lachesis, who wove it on the loom; and Atropos, who cut it at death. See note XXXIII, 124–35 (XXXIII, 126).

ATTILA: chieftain of the Huns (406?–53). He made himself master of all the peoples of Germany and Scythia, and with his hordes overran Illyria, Thrace, Macedon, Greece, etc. In 451 he invaded Gaul, but was checked by Theodoric and finally routed by Thorismond the Goth. The following year he descended upon Italy, devastating Aquileia, Milan, Padua, and other places. Temporarily restrained by Pope Leo I, he was preparing for a fresh invasion when he died, or was murdered, in the following year. See notes XII, 134 and XIII, 143–50 (XII, 134; XIII, 149).

AUGUSTUS: (1) Caius Julius Caesar Octavianus, first Roman emperor (63 B.C.–A.D. 14). He was the great-nephew of Julius Caesar and adopted by him as his heir. After the assassination of Julius, he assumed the name of Caesar and became, with Lepidus and Mark Antony, one of the triumvirs who took over the government of the republic. He gradually gathered all the great offices of state into his own hands, and in 32 B.C. he accepted the title of imperator. The defeat of Antony at Actium (31 B.C.) and the death of Lepidus (12 B.C.) left him in fact and in name sole master of the Roman Empire. The epithet "Augustus," conferred on him by the Senate in 27 B.C., was borne by his successors as part of the imperial title. The "Augustan Age" was marked by a brilliant flowering of Latin literary genius. (2) Imperial title denoting Emperor Frederick II. See notes XIII, 58–78, 62–72 (XIII, 68).

AVENTINE: See Mount Aventine.

AVERROËS (IBN-RUSHD): Arabian physician and philosopher, born at Cordova and died at Morocco (1126–98). See note IV, 144 (IV, 144).

AVICENNA (IBN-SINA): Arabian physician and philosopher (980–1037). See note IV, 143 (IV, 143).

AZZOLINO: Ezzelino III da Romano (1194–1259). See note XII, 110 (XII, 110).

BACCHIGLIONE: a river in Venetia, Italy, on which Vicenza stands (XV, 113).

BACCHUS: in Greek mythology, the god of wine (XX, 59).

BACCHUS' CITY: Thebes. See note XX, 52–60 (XX, 59).

BAPTIST, THE: Saint John the Baptist, the patron saint of Florence See notes XIII, 143–50, XXX, 61–75 (XIII, 143; XXX, 74).

BARBARICCIA: a devil. See note XXI, 118–23 (XXI, 120; XXII, 29, 59, 145).

BEATRICE: daughter of Folco Portinari, born in Florence, 1266. In the *Vita nuova* (*New Life*) Dante says that he first saw and fell in love with her when both of them were about nine years old. She was married to Simone dei Bardi, and died in 1290. See Introduction and notes II, 49–142, 74, 76–78 102, X, 129–32, XV, 89–90 (II, 53 ff.; X, 131; XII, 88; XV, 90).

BECCHERIA: Tesauro dei Beccheria of Pavia. See note XXXII, 119–20 (XXXII, 119).

BEELZEBUB: the Devil, or Lucifer. See note XXXIV, 127–32 (XXXIV, 128). See also Dis, Lucifer, and Satan.

BENACO: see Lake Benaco.

BERGAMESE: citizens of Bergamo, a city in northern Italy (XX, 71).

BERTRAN DE BORN: lord of Altaforte (Hautefort), soldier and troubadour. See notes XXVIII, 134–36, 142 (XXVIII, 134).

BISENZIO: a river of Italy, tributary of the Arno. See note XXXII, 55–58 (XXXII, 56).

BOCCA: Bocca degli Abati, Florentine traitor. See note XXXII, 106 (XXXII, 106).

BOLOGNA: an Italian city, in the Romagna. See note XXIII, 103–108 (XXIII, 103, 142).

BOLOGNESE: citizen of Bologna (XVIII, 58).

BONIFACE: Pope Boniface VIII (Benedict Caietan) (c. 1217–1303; Pope, 1294–1303). See notes XIX, 53, XV, 112–14, XXVII, 67–71, 85–90 (XIX, 53).

BONTURO: Bonturo Dati, the head of the popular party in Lucca, notorious for his barratry. Benvenuto da Imola says that he "controlled the whole commune, and promoted or excluded from office whomever he chose." He was eventually (1314) expelled from Lucca and fled to Florence, where he died. See note XXI, 38–42 (XXI, 41).

BRANCA D'ORIA (BRANCA, SER BRANCA D'ORIA): of Genoa. See note XXXIII, 137–47 (XXXIII, 137, 140, 145).

BRANDA'S FOUNTAIN: a spring near Romena. See note XXX, 76–78 (XXX, 78).

BRENTA: a river of Italy. See note XV, 7 (XV, 7).

BRESCIA: a city of northern Italy. See note XX, 67–69.

BRESCIANS: citizens of Brescia (XX, 71).

BRIAREUS: a Titan, or giant. See note XXXI, 99 (XXXI, 99).

BRIGATA: Nino della Gherardesca. See note XXXIII, 89–90 (XXXIII, 89).

BRUGES: a city of Flanders. See note XV, 4–6 (XV, 6).

BRUNETTO LATINI (SER BRUNETTO): Florentine politician and man of learning. See notes XV, 16–114, 30, 48, 61–78, 85, 89–90, 99, 119–20 (XV, 30, 31, 101).

BRUTUS: (1) Lucius Junius. See note IV, 127–29 (IV, 127). (2) Marcus Junius (85–42 B.C.), son of M. Brutus the Tribune and Servilia, half-sister of Cato of Utica. He was trained by his uncle Cato in the principles of the aristocratic party, and when the civil war broke out in 49 B.C., he joined Pompey, although the latter had put his father to death. After the Battle of Pharsalia in 48 B.C., Julius Caesar not only pardoned him but raised him to high favor, making him governor of Cisalpine Gaul (46 B.C.) and praetor (44 B.C.), and promising him the governorship of Macedonia. Persuaded, however, by Cassius, he took part in the conspiracy to murder Caesar in the hope of re-establishing the Republic (Ides of March, 44 B.C.). After Caesar's death, he took possession of Macedonia, and was joined by Cassius, who commanded in Syria. In 42 B.C. their united forces were defeated by Octavian (afterward Augustus) Caesar and Mark Antony at the Battle of Philippi, and Brutus committed suicide. See note XXXIV, 65 (XXXIV, 65).

BULICAME: a hot spring near Viterbo, Italy. See note XIV, 79–80 (XIV, 79).

BUOSO: See note XXV, 140–41 (XXV, 140).

Buoso Donati: member of the great Florentine family to which belonged Corso dei Donati, the Black Guelf leader, and Dante's wife, Gemma. See note XXX, 32 (XXX, 44). He is, perhaps, also the Buoso mentioned in XXV, 140. See note XXV, 140–41.

Caccia (Caccia d'Asciano): Sienese spendthrift. See notes XXIX, 127–29, 131 (XXIX, 131).

Cacus: a centaur. See note XXV, 25–33 (XXV, 25).

Cadmus: son of Agenor, king of Phoenicia. Jupiter in the form of a white bull carried away his sister Europa; and Cadmus, in searching for her, became the founder of Thebes. Having killed a dragon sacred to Mars, he was changed into a serpent. See note XXV, 94–102 (XXV, 97).

Caesar: (1) Caius Julius, dictator of Rome (100–44 B.C.). Son of C. Julius Caesar, the praetor, he liked to claim descent from the Trojan hero Aeneas, founder of Rome. A brilliant general and strong adherent of the democratic party, he was made consul in 59 B.C.; his conquest of Gaul (59–51 B.C.) made him the idol of the people and the army. His rival, Pompey, jealous of his rising power, joined the aristocratic party and headed an armed opposition against him; but Julius, crossing the Rubicon, which separated his own province from Italy, marched upon Rome, and, being everywhere received with acclamation, made himself master of all Italy (49 B.C.). After defeating Pompey's adherents in Spain, he crossed over into Greece and decisively overthrew Pompey at the battle of Pharsalia (48 B.C.). He was made dictator and, after a period of further military triumphs, was offered the kingship; this, however, he reluctantly refused for fear of offending the people. On the Ides of March, 44 B.C., he was assassinated in the Capitol by a band of conspirators led by Brutus and Cassius. His successor, Augustus, was the first Roman emperor, and the name Caesar became part of the imperial title. See notes, I, 62, IV, 123, XXVIII, 97–102 (I, 70; IV, 123; XXVIII, 97). (2) imperial title denoting Emperor Frederick II. See note XIII, 58–78 (XIII, 65).

CAGNAZZO: a devil. See notes XXI, 118–23; XXII, 97–132 (XXI, 119; XXII, 106).

CAHORS: a city of France. See note XI, 50 (XI, 50).

CAIAPHAS: the high priest of the Jews who condemned Christ. See note XXIII, 115–24 (XXIII, 115).

CAIN (WITH HIS THORN-BUSH): the Man in the Moon. See note XX, 124–26 (XX, 124).

CAÏNA: a region in Hell. See notes V, 107; XXXII, 59 (V, 107; XXXII, 59).

CALCABRINA: a devil. See notes XXI, 118–23; XXII, 97–132 (XXI, 118; XXII, 133).

CALCHAS: an augur who accompanied the Greeks to the siege of Troy. See note XX, 106–12 (XX, 110).

CAMICION DE' PAZZI: See note XXXII, 68–69 (XXXII, 68).

CAMILLA: a warrior-maiden who vowed service to Diana. See note I, 107 (I, 107; IV, 124).

CAMONICA: See Val Camonica.

CAMPALDINO: a plain in the Casentino, Italy. See note XXII, 1–12 (XXII, 4).

CAPANEUS: one of the seven kings who fought against Thebes. See notes XIV, 51–60, 68–69 (XIV, 51, 63).

CAPOCCHIO: a name or nickname meaning "Blockhead." See note XXIX, 136 (XXIX, 136; XXX, 28).

CAPRAIA: an island near the mouth of the Arno. See note XXXIII, 79–90 (XXXIII, 82).

CAPRONA: a fortress of Pisa. See note XXI, 94–96 (XXI, 95); Intro., p.16.

CARDINAL, THE: Cardinal Ottaviano degli Ubaldini, papal legate in Lombardy and Romagna. See note X, 119–20 (X, 119).

CARLIN: Carlino de' Pazzi, from Valdarno. See note XXXII, 68–69 (XXXII, 69).

CARRARA: a town and hills in Tuscany, Italy. See note XX, 46–51 (XX, 48).

CASALODI: Alberto da Casalodi. See note XX, 95–96 (XX, 95).

CASENTINO: a district in Tuscany, Italy. See note XXX, 64–66 (XXX, 65).

CASSIUS: Caius Cassius Longinus, Roman statesman and general. In 49 B.C. he was tribune of the plebs, but when civil

GLOSSARY

war broke out, he joined the aristocratic party and fled from Rome with Pompey, whose fleet he commanded in 48 B.C. After the Battle of Pharsalia he went to the Hellespont and, accidentally falling in with Julius Caesar, surrendered to him. Caesar not only pardoned him but made him praetor and promised him the governorship of Syria. Cassius, however, repaid this generosity by heading a conspiracy to murder Caesar and persuading M. Brutus to join it. After Caesar's death (Ides of March, 44 B.C.) he claimed the governorship of Syria according to Caesar's promise, although the Senate had given it to Dolabella. He defeated Dolabella and, after plundering Syria and Asia, joined Brutus in Macedonia in opposition to Octavian (Augustus) Caesar and Mark Antony. At the Battle of Philippi (42 B.C.) Cassius was defeated by Antony and took his own life. See note XXXIV, 67 (XXXIV, 67).

CASTEL SANT' ANGELO: the castle of St. Angelo on the Tiber at Rome, originally the Moles Hadriani. See note XVIII, 28–33 (XVIII, 32).

CATALANO: See Friar Catalano.

CATO (MARCUS PORCIUS CATO THE YOUNGER): Roman statesman (95–46 B.C.) from Utica, a strict republican of the old school, nurtured in Stoic philosophy. See note XIV, 15 (XIV, 15).

CATTOLICA: a town of Italy on the Adriatic. See note XXVIII, 77–90 (XXVIII, 80).

CAURUS: Northwest Wind. See note XI, 113–15 (XI, 114).

CAVALCANTE DE' CAVALCANTI: a Florentine nobleman and father of Guido Cavalcanti. See notes X, 42, 53, and 68–72 (X, 53).

CECINA: a river of Italy. See note XIII, 8–9 (XIII, 8).

CELESTINE V: Pietro Angeleri da Isernia, pope from July 5 through December 13, 1294. See notes III, 60; XXVII, 104–105 (XXVII, 104).

CEPRANO: a town in southeastern Latium, Italy. See note XXVIII, 15–18 (XXVIII, 16).

CERBERUS: the three-headed hound of Hell. See notes VI, 13–22, 26–27; IX, 98–99 (VI, 13, 23, 32; IX, 98).

CERVIA: a town near Ravenna. See note XXVII, 41–42 (XXVII, 42).

CESENA: a northern-Italian town on the Savio. See note XXVII, 52–54 (XXVII, 52).

CEÜTA: a city in Morocco. See note XXVI, 110–11 (XXVI, 111).

CHARLEMAGNE: emperor of the West (742–814), son of Pépin le Bref, king of the Franks. He received the Imperial Crown from Pope Leo III on Christmas Day in the year 800. His wars and his Twelve Peers, of whom his nephew Roland and Roland's friend Oliver are best known, became legendary and were celebrated in the early *Chansons de geste* and many later epics. See note XXXI, 16–18 (XXXI, 16).

CHARLES: Charles (I) d'Anjou, king of Naples and Sicily, son of Louis VIII of France and Blanche of Castile (1220–84). Invited by Pope Urban IV to assume the crown of Naples, and urged by Pope Clement IV to take possession of the kingdom, he entered Italy in 1265, was crowned king of Sicily and Apulia in 1265, and defeated Manfred at Benevento in 1266. The Sicilians, revolting against French rule, invited Conradin (son of Emperor Conrad IV) to expel him. He defeated Conradin at Tagliacozzo in 1268, but in 1282 the Sicilian "underground movement" (surreptitiously aided, as was believed, by Pope Nicholas III and others) broke out into open insurrection, leading to a fearful massacre of the French (the "Sicilian Vespers") and the end of their rule in Sicily. Charles died in 1284, while trying to regain the kingdom. See notes XIX, 98–99 and XXVIII, 15–18 (XIX, 99).

CHARON: in classical mythology, the ferryman of the dead, the son of Erebus (Darkness) and Nox (Night). See notes III, 83, 91–93 (III, 83, 94, 109, 128).

CHARYBDIS: an eddy or whirlpool. In the *Odyssey*, the ship of Ulysses (Odysseus) has to pass through a narrow strait between two rocks, which are inhabited by two sea-monsters: Scylla, who devours the sailors with her teeth, and Charybdis, who thrice a day sucks down the sea into a fearful whirlpool and thrice spews it out again. In later legend, both Scylla and Charybdis are women, changed into these shapes for having wittingly or unwittingly offended the gods. Ovid

(*Metamorphoses* xiii, 749ff.) tells the story of Scylla and locates the perilous passage between Scylla and Charybdis in the Straits of Messina (VII, 22).

CHIARENTANA: a mountainous district in north Italy. See note XV, 9 (XV, 9).

CHIRON: a centaur. See notes XII, 65, 67–69 (XII, 65, 71, 77, 97).

CHRIST: He is referred to by various periphrases: "my Lord," by Beatrice (II, 73); "Highest Wisdom," inscription on Hellgate (III, 6, and note III, 5–6); "a mighty Lord," by Virgil (IV, 53), see note IV, 49–50; "the unfriendly Judge," by Virgil (VI, 96); "our Lord," by Dante (XIX, 91); "her bridegroom," by Dante (XIX, 111); "the Man whose birth and life were free of sin," by Virgil (XXXIV, 115) and see note IV, 34 (IV, 37).

CIACCO: a Florentine. See note VI, 52 (VI, 52, 58).

CIAMPOLO: See note XXII, 48–54 (XXII, 44).

CIANFA: a member of the Donati family. See note XXV, 43 (XXV, 43).

CIRCE: daughter of the Sun and Perse, she dwelt on the island of Aeaea, on the northern side of the Gulf of Gaëta. See note XXVI, 90–92 (XXVI, 91).

CIRIATTO: a devil. See note XXI, 118–23 (XXI, 122; XXII, 55).

CLEOPATRA: queen of Egypt (68–30 B.C.). See note V, 63 (V, 63).

CLUNY: a city of France. See note XXIII, 61–63 (XXIII, 63).

COCYTUS: a Circle and river of Hell. See notes XIV, 94–119, XXXI, 19–127, XXXIV, 10 (XIV, 119; XXXI, 123; XXXIII, 156; XXXIV, 52).

COLCHIANS: citizens of Colchis, an ancient country of Asia, below the Caucasus, between Iberia and the Euxine (Black Sea). See note XVIII, 86–96 (XVIII, 87).

CONSTANTINE: Constantine the Great, emperor of Rome from 306 to 337, born in 272, son of Emperor Constantius Chlorus. See note XIX, 115–17 (XIX, 115; XXVII, 94).

CORNELIA: daughter of Scipio Africanus Major, wife of Tiberius Semptonius Gracchus, and mother of the two famous tribunes Tiberius and Caius. She is celebrated as a model Roman mother of the old school, who brought up her sons in the utmost rectitude; after her death, the people of Rome erected a statue to her inscribed: "The Mother of the Gracchi." See note IV, 127–29 (IV, 128).

CORNETO: an Italian town. See note XIII, 8–9 (XIII, 8).

CORYBANTS: the priests or servants of Rhea or Cybele, who celebrated her worship with dances and music. See note XIV, 94–119 (XIV, 102).

COUNT UGOLINO: Ugolino della Gherardesca, of Pisa. See notes XXXIII, 13–14, 28–36ff. (XXXIII, 13ff.).

CRETE: island in the Mediterranean, the fabled birthplace of Jupiter. See notes XII, 12–21; XIV, 94–119 (XII, 12; XIV, 95).

CURIO: Caius Scribonius Curio, Tribune of the Plebs, 50 B.C. See note XXVIII, 97–102 (XXVIII, 102).

CYPRUS: an island in the Mediterranean (XXVIII, 82).

DAEDALUS: "the craftsman" of Minos, and father of Icarus. See notes XII, 12–21; XVII, 109–11 (XVII, 111; XXIX, 116).

DAMIETTA: a seaport of Egypt. See note XIV, 94–119 (XIV, 104).

DANUBE: a river of Europe (XXXII, 25).

DAVID (DAVID THE KING): a king of Israel. See note XXVIII, 137–38 (IV, 58; XXVIII, 138).

DEÏDAMIA: the daughter of Lycomedes, king of Scyros. See note XXVI, 61–62) XXVI, 62).

DEJANIRA: the wife of Hercules. See note XII, 67–69 (XII, 68).

DEMOCRITUS: a Greek philosopher, was born in and lived in Abdera in Thrace (c. 460–361 B.C.). See note IV, 136 (IV, 136).

DIDO: queen of Carthage, daughter of Belus, king of Tyre, and sister of Pygmalion; she married her uncle Sichaeus, who was murdered by Pygmalion for the sake of his wealth, whereupon she fled from Tyre and landed in Africa, where, according to legend, she founded Carthage. Virgil makes her a contemporary of Aeneas. See Aeneas and note V, 61–62 (V, 61, 85).

DIOGENES: a Greek Cynic philosopher (c. 412–323 B.C.). See note IV, 137 (IV, 137).

DIOMED (DIOMEDES): king of Argos, son of Tydeus and Deiphyle. See note XXVI, 55–57 (XXVI, 55).

DIONYSIUS: See note XII, 107–108 (XII, 107).

DIOSCORIDES: a Greek natural scientist and physician. See note IV, 140 (IV, 140).

DIS: in ancient mythology, the Underworld (Hades) itself, and also the god or king of the Underworld (otherwise called Pluto). He was the son of Cronos and Rhea, and brother of Zeus (Jupiter); his queen was Proserpina. For Dis's meaning in the Comedy see notes XI, 65, and XXXIV, 20 (XI, 65; XXXIV, 20).

DIS, CITY OF: the fortified city moated by the river Styx and enclosing lower Hell. See notes VIII, 68, 130, and IX, 61–105 (VIII, 68, 130).

DON (TANAÏ): a river that flows from its source in the heart of Russia to the Sea of Azov. See note XXXII, 27 (XXXII, 27).

DRAGHIGNAZZO: a devil. See note XXI, 118–23 (XXI, 121; XXII, 73).

DUERA: Buoso da Duera, a Ghibelline traitor. See note XXXII, 116–17 (XXXII, 116).

DUKE OF ATHENS: See Theseus.

ELECTRA: daughter of Atlas and Pleione. See note IV, 121 (IV, 121).

ELIJAH: a prophet of Israel who was taken up to Heaven in a fiery chariot (II Kings ii, 11). See note XXVI, 34–39 (XXVI, 35).

ELISHA: a prophet of Israel. See note XXVI, 34–39 (XXVI, 34).

EMPEDOCLES: a Greek philosopher of fifth century B.C., born in Agrigentum, Sicily. See note IV, 138 (IV, 138).

EPHIALTES: a giant, the son of Neptune and Iphimedia. See note XXXI, 94 (XXXI, 94).

EPICURUS: a Greek philosopher (c. 342–270 B.C.). See note X, 14–15 (X, 14).

ERICHTHO: a witch. See note IX, 22–30 (IX, 23).

ERINYES: the Greek name of the Furies, the avenging deities of classical mythology, usually represented as women stained with blood and with snakes for hair. In the late writers their number is given as three: Alecto, Megaera, and Tisiphone. See notes IX, 38–48, and 44 (IX, 45).

ETEOCLES: the son of Oedipus. See note XXVI, 52–54 (XXVI, 54).

ETHIOPIA: ancient country west of the Red Sea, northeastern Africa; in the ancient sources, thought to extend from the Atlantic to India. See note XXIV, 85–90 (XXIV, 89).

EUCLID: a Greek mathematician who lived in Alexandria (fl. 300 B.C.). Besides the *Elements of Geometry*, with which his name is so firmly associated, he wrote treatises on music, optics, etc. See note IV, 142 (IV, 142).

EURYALUS: a companion of Aeneas. See note I, 108 (I, 108).

EURYPYLUS: See notes XX, 106–12 and 113 (XX, 112).

EVANGELIST, THE: Saint John the Evangelist. See note XIX, 106–11 (XIX, 106).

FAENZA: an Italian town on the Lamone, between Forlì and Imola near Bologna. See notes XXVII, 49, and XXXII, 122–23 (XXVII, 49; XXXII, 123).

FANO: an Italian town on the Adriatic coast. See note XXVIII, 77–90 (XXVIII, 76).

FARFARELLO: a devil. See note XXI, 118–23 (XXI, 123; XXII, 94).

FARINATA: Farinata degli Uberti, Ghibelline leader of Florence. See notes VI, 79–87; X, 16–18, 22–27 ff. (VI, 79; X, 32).

FELTRO: a town in the Piave valley in northeastern Italy in Venezia Euganea. See note I, 101–11 (I, 105).

FIESOLE: an Italian town near Florence. See note XV, 61–78 (XV, 62).

FILIPPO ARGENTI: a Florentine, member of the Adimari family. See notes VIII, 32, 36–63 (VIII, 32, 61).

FISH (PISCES): sign of the zodiac; the sun is in Pisces from mid-February to mid-March. See note XI, 113–15 (XI, 113).

FLEMINGS: citizens of Flanders. See note XV, 4–6 (XV, 4).

FLORENCE: a city of Italy, the chief city of Tuscany, on the Arno, birthplace of Dante. See notes VI, 50, 65–75, 73, X, 88–93, XIII, 143–50, 151, XVI, 73–75, XXIV, 143–50, XXVI, 1–6, 7–9 (VI, 49 ff.; X, 92; XIII, 143; XVI, 75; XXIV, 144; XXVI, 1).

FLORENTINES: citizens of Florence. See notes VIII, 36–62, XVII, 70, XXXII, 119–20 (VIII, 62; XVII, 70; XXXII, 120; XXXIII, 11).

FOCACCIA: of the Cancellieri family. See note XXXII, 63 (XXXII, 63).

FOCARA: a headland on the Adriatic coast between Fano and La Cattolica. See note XXVIII, 77–90 (XXVIII, 90).

FORLÌ: an Italian town, in the Marches. See notes XVI, 94–101; XXVII, 43–45 (XVI, 99; XXVII, 43).

FORTUNE: the guide appointed by God to reign over the sublunar world, which she administers as her own sphere. See notes II, 76–78, VII, 22–66, 73–96, XV, 95–96 (II, 61; VII, 62, 67; XV, 93, 95; XXX, 13).

FRA DOLCINO: leader of a heretical sect. See note XXVIII, 56–60.

FRANCESCA: Francesca da Rimini, the wife of Gianciotto da Verruchio, and the lover of his brother Paolo. See notes V, 73–142, 74 ff. (V, 116).

FRANCESCO CAVALCANTI: a Florentine nobleman. See note XXV, 151 (XXV, 151).

FRANCESCO D'ACCORSO: a Florentine lawyer (1225–93). See note XV, 110 (XV, 110).

FRANCE'S KING: Philip IV of France, Philip the Fair (Philippe le Bel) (1285–1314). See notes XIX, 82–84, 85–87 (XIX, 87).

FREDERICK: See King Frederick.

FRIAR ALBERIGO: member of the Manfredi family. See note XXXIII, 118–20 (XXXIII, 118).

FRIAR CATALANO: Catalano de' Malavolti; *podestà* of Florence. See note XXIII, 103–108 (XXIII, 104, 114).

FRISIANS: inhabitants of Friesland. See note XXXI, 63 (XXXI, 63).

FURIES: See Erinyes.

GADDO: Gaddo della Gherardesca, son of Count Ugolino. See note XXXIII, 68 (XXXIII, 68).

GAËTA: a town on the south coast of Italy. See note XXVI, 92–93 (XXVI, 92).

GALEHOT (GALEHALT OR GALEHAUT): In the romance of *Lancelot du Lac*, Galehot acted as intermediary between Lancelot and Guinevere, and so in the Middle Ages his name became a synonym for a go-between. See note V, 17–142 (V, 137).

GALEN: A Greek physician and highly skilled anatomist (c. 130–200). See note IV, 143 (IV, 143).

GALLURA: a district of Sardinia. See note XXII, 81–87 (XXII, 81).

GANELON: the father-in-law of Charlemagne's nephew Roland. See note XXXII, 122–23 (XXXII, 122).

GARDA: a town on the southeastern shore of Lake Garda, Italy. See note XX, 64–66 (XX, 65).

GARDINGO: quarter of Florence near Palazzo Vecchio, site of the present Piazza di San Firenze. See note XXIII, 103–108 (XXIII, 108).

GARISENDA: one of the two leaning towers of Bologna. See note XXXI, 136–38 (XXXI, 136).

GAVILLE: a small town in the Arno Valley. See note XXV, 151 (XXV, 151).

GENOVESE: citizens of Genoa (XXXIII, 151).

GERI DEL BELLO: son of Bello degli Aligheri, who was a brother of Dante's grandfather Bellincione. See note XXIX, 27–35 (XXIX, 27).

GERYON: a monster of Hell. See notes XVI, 106–108, XVII, 1–27, 21–22, 35–36, 136 (XVI, 130 ff.; XVII, 1–3, 97; XVIII, 20).

GHISOLABELLA: the sister of Venedico Caccianemico. See note XVIII, 50–57 (XVIII, 55).

GIACOMO DA SANT' ANDREA: of Padua. See notes XIII, 115–21, 125–29 (XIII, 133).

GIANFIGLIAZZI: a Florentine family who, according to Villani, were members of the Black Guelf party. See note XVII, 55–56 (XVII, 59–60).

GIANNI SCHICCHI: a Florentine of the Cavalcanti family. See note XXX, 32, 33 (XXX, 32).

GIANNI SOLDANIER: a Florentine. See note XXXII, 121 (XXXII, 121).

GIOVANNI BUIAMONTE: of the Florentine Becchi family. See note XVII, 72–73 (XVII, 72).

GOMITA: Fra Gomita, from Gallura. See note XXII, 81–87 (XXII, 81).

GORGON: See Medusa.

GORGONA: an island near the mouth of the Arno. See note XXXIII, 79–90 (XXXIII, 82).

GOVERNOL: a town of northern Italy. See note XX, 78 (XX, 78).

GRAFFIACAN(E): a devil. See note XXI, 118–23 (XXI, 122; XXII, 34).

GREYHOUND: See note I, 101–11 (I, 101).

GUALANDI: a Ghibelline family of Pisa. See note XXXIII, 28–36 (XXXIII, 33).

GUALDRADA: the daughter of Bellincione Berti of Florence. See note XVI, 37–39 (XVI, 37).

GUGLIELMO BORSIERE: See note XVI, 70–72 (XVI, 70).

GUIDO: (1) Guido Cavalcanti, the son of Cavalcante dei Cavalcanti (c. 1255–1300). See notes X, 53, 63 (X, 63). (2) Guido da Romena, a member of the Conti Guidi family. See notes XXX, 76–78, 79 (XXX, 77).

GUIDO BONATTI: an astrologer from Forlì. See note XX, 118–20 (XX, 118).

GUIDO DA MONTEFELTRO: count of Montefeltro, the great Ghibelline captain (1223–98). See notes XXVII, 29–30, 52–54, 67–71, 81, 92–93, 102, 108–109, 113 (XXVII, 29ff.).

GUIDO GUERRA: a Florentine nobleman (1220–72), grandson of "the good Gualdrada." See notes XVI, 37–39, 41–42 (XVI, 38).

GUY DE MONTFORT: son of Simon de Montfort, earl of Leicester, who was killed at the Battle of Evesham (1265). See note XII, 120 (XII, 119).

HANNIBAL: a Carthaginian general (c. 247–183 B.C.), son of Hamilcar Barca; the great adversary of Rome. Having overrun Spain, he entered Italy and, in the Second Punic War, defeated the Romans at the battles of Lake Trasimene (217 B.C.) and Cannae (216 B.C.) (cf. XXVIII, 10–11). He was eventually defeated by Scipio Africanus Major and killed himself to avoid capture. See notes XXVIII, 7–12, XXXI, 123 (XXXI, 117).

HARPIES: originally personifications of the storm-winds, the Harpies are described by Hesiod as beautiful winged maidens; but in later myth they became hideous two-formed monsters. See note XIII, 10–15 (XIII, 10).

HECTOR: the son of Priam, king of Troy, chief of the Trojan heroes in the *Iliad*. See note IV, 122 (IV, 122).

HECUBA: the wife of Priam, king of Troy. See note XXX, 16–21 (XXX, 16).

HELEN: the wife of Menelaus, king of Sparta. See note V, 64 (V, 64).

HERACLITUS: a Greek philosopher (fl. 500 B.C.). See note IV, 138 (IV, 138).

HERCULES: a demi-god, renowned for his enormous strength; the son of Zeus and Alcmene, the wife of Amphitryon. Of the famous twelve labors that he had to perform in the service of King Eurytheus, two are alluded to in the *Inferno*: the capture of the oxen of Geryon, which the monster Cacus stole from him as he was driving them back (XXV, 25ff.) and the carrying off of Cerberus from Hades (VI, 18). After his death at the hand of his wife, Dejanira (XII, 67–69), he was taken up to Olympus and became one of the Immortals. See notes XII, 67–69, XXV, 25–33, XXVI, 108, XXXI, 131–32 (XXV, 32; XXVI, 108; (XXXI, 132).

HIPPOCRATES: a Greek physician (c. 460–377 B.C.). He was born and practiced on the island of Cos, whose medical school he made famous. His name survives today in the "Hippocratic oath," which prescribes the ethical duty of physician to patient. See note IV, 143 (IV, 143).

HOLY FACE: a wooden crucifix at Lucca. See note XXI, 46–51 (XXI, 48).

HOMER: the great epic poet of Greece, probably of 9th or 10th century B.C.; author of the *Iliad* (siege of Troy) and the

Odyssey (wanderings of Odysseus, or Ulysses). He is said to have been blind; seven cities dispute the honor of being his birthplace. See note IV, 86–88 (IV, 88).

HORACE (QUINTUS HORATIUS FLACCUS): Latin poet (65–8 B.C.). Born in Apulia, he was educated and lived in Rome until he earned enough to retire to a small Sabine farm in Ustica. See note IV, 89 (IV, 89).

HYPSIPYLE: daughter of Thoas, king of Lemnos. See note XVIII, 86–96 (XVIII, 92).

ICARUS: the son of Daedalus. See note XXVII, 109–11 (XXVII, 109).

IDA: a mountain of Crete. See note XIV, 94–119 (XIV, 97).

ILIUM (GREEK, ILION): See Troy.

IMOLA: an Italian town in Emilia near the Santerno. See note XXVII, 49–51 (XXVII, 49).

INDIA: See note XIV, 33–36 (XIV, 32).

ISRAEL: Jacob, the patriarch (IV, 59).

JACOPO RUSTICUCCI: See notes VI, 79–87, XVI, 44–45 (VI, 80; XVI, 44).

JASON: (1) a Greek hero, leader of the Argonauts. See note XVIII, 86–96 (XVIII, 86). (2) a high priest of Israel. See note XIX, 85–87 (XIX, 85).

JEHOSHAPHAT: a valley in Palestine. See note X, 11–12 (X, 11).

JOSEPH: the son of Jacob, the patriarch, and Rachel. See note XXX, 97 (XXX, 97).

JOVE (JUPITER): the Roman deity; identified with the Greek Zeus, the son of Cronos and Rhea, "father of the gods and men," and chief of the Olympian deities. His spouse was Juno (Greek, Hera), and his weapon the thunderbolt. See notes XIV, 51–60, XXXI, 19–127, 44–45, 77, 124 (XIV, 52; XXXI, 45, 92).

JOVIAL FRIARS: See note XXIII, 103–108 (XXIII, 103).

JUBILEE: in the Christian Church, a period of remission from penal consequences of sin; first instituted by Pope Boniface VIII, who in 1300 issued a bull granting plenary indulgence to all pilgrims visiting Rome in that year, on condition of confession, penitence, and prescribed attendance at St. Peter's. The name is taken from the Hebrew institution, for which see Leviticus xxv. See note XVIII, 28–33 (XVIII, 28).

JUDAS: Judas Iscariot, the disciple who betrayed Christ. See note XXXIV, 61–63 (IX, 27; XXXI, 143; XXXIV, 117).

JUDECCA: a region of Hell. See note XXXIV, 10 (XXXIV, 117).

JULIA: the daughter of Julius Caesar and wife of Pompey. See note IV, 127–29 (IV, 128).

JUNO (GREEK, HERA): the daughter of Saturn and Rhea, the wife and sister of Jupiter. See note XXX, 1–12 (XXX, 1).

JUPITER: See Jove.

KING ATHAMAS: the husband of Ino, the sister of Semele. See note XXX, 1–12 (XXX, 4).

KING FREDERICK (FREDERICK, THE SECOND FREDERICK): Emperor Frederick II (1194–1250) of the Hohenstaufen dynasty, grandson of Frederick Barbarossa, son of Emperor Henry VI and Constance of Sicily; he was born at Jesi, near Ancona, Italy. He was called by his contemporaries "Stupor Mundi" (the Wonder of the World) for his multifarious and eccentric brilliance. See notes X, 119–20, XIII, 58–78, 68–72, XXIII, 64–66 (X, 119; XIII, 59; XXIII, 66).

KING THIBAULT: Thibault II, Count of Champagne, later King of Navarre. See note XX, 53 (XX, 53).

LAERTES: the father of Ulysses, or Odysseus. See note XXVI, 94–96 (XXVI, 95).

LAKE BENACO: a lake in northern Italy, now Lake Garda. See notes XX, 63, 64–66, 67–69, 70–72 (XX, 63, 73, 77).

LAMONE: a river of Italy. See note XXVII, 49–51 (XXVII, 29).

LANCELOT: the hero of the romance Lancelot du Lac, the most famous of the knights of the Round Table, son of Ban, king of Benoic (Brittany); he was brought up by Merlin, the enchanter, and Vivien, the Lady of the Lake. At the court of King Arthur he became enamored of Queen Guinevere. See note V, 73–142 (V, 128).

LANFRANCHI: a leading Ghibelline family of Pisa. See note
XXXIII, 28–36 (XXXIII, 33).

LANO: from Siena. See note XIII, 115–21 (XIII, 120).

LATERAN: a palace in Rome; in Dante's time the usual residence
of the popes. See note XXVII, 85–90 (XXVII, 86).

LATIAN KING: Latinus, king of Latium. See note IV, 124–26
(IV, 125).

LAVINIA: the daughter of Latinus. See Aeneas, and note IV,
124–26 (IV, 126).

LEARCHUS: the infant son of King Athamas and Ino. See note
XXX, 1–12 (XXX, 10).

LEMNOS: an island in the Aegean. See note XVIII, 86–96 (XVIII,
88).

LETHE: in antiquity, the river of the lower world from which
the shades drank and thereby were granted forgetfulness of
the past (cf. Servius on *Aeneid* VI., 703, 705, 714). See note
XIV, 136–38 (XIV, 131, 136).

LIBBICOCCO: a devil. See note XXI, 118–23 (XXI, 121; XXII,
70).

LIBYA: in ancient Greek geography, the name for north Africa
outside of Egypt; later, divided into Marmarica and Cyre-
naica, which became part of the Roman colony of Africa.
See note XXIV, 85–90 (XXIV, 85).

LINUS: a mythical Greek poet. See note IV, 141 (IV, 141).

LIVY (TITUS LIVIUS): a Roman historian (57 B.C.–A.D. 17).
Born at Padua, he passed most of his life at Rome, where,
under the patronage of Augustus Caesar, he wrote his great
History of Rome (from the landing of Aeneas to the death of
Drusus in 9 B.C.) in 142 books. Of these, the greater part
were lost before Dante's time, but we still possess 35, to-
gether with epitomes of most of the rest. See note XXVIII,
7–12 (XXVIII, 12).

LODERINGO: Loderingo degli Andalò, a Bolognese friar. See
note XXIII, 103–108 (XXIII, 104).

LOGODORO: a province of Sardinia. See note XXII, 88–89 (XXII,
89).

LOMBARD: (1) the dialect of Lombardy. See note XXVII, 20
(XXVII, 20). (2) a citizen of Lombardy (XXII, 97).

LOMBARDY: the northern part of Italy, between the Alps and the Po River, bounded by Venice to the east, and Piedmont to the west (I, 68).

LUCAN (M. ANNAEUS LUCANUS): a Roman poet (A.D. 39–65). Born at Cordova, he was educated at Rome and lived there until, having joined the conspiracy of Piso against the Emperor Nero, he was condemned to death and committed suicide. See notes IV, 90, XXV, 94–102 (IV, 90; XXV, 94).

LUCCA: a town in Tuscany, Italy. See notes XVIII, 122, XXI, 38–42, XXXIII, 28–36 (XVIII, 122; XXI, 42; XXXIII, 30).

LUCIA (SAINT LUCY): See note II, 49–142 (II, 97).

LUCIFER: the Devil. See notes XXXI, 19–127, XXXIV, 1, 18, 20, 38–45, 46, 61–63, 79–81, 112–15, 127–32 (XXXI, 143; XXXIV, 89). See also Beelzebub, Dis, and Satan.

LUCRETIA: the wife of Lucius Tarquinus Collatinus. See note IV, 127–29 (IV, 128).

LUNI: an Italian city, near Carrara. See note XX, 46–51 (XX, 47).

MAGHINARDO PAGANO: Lord of Faenza, Forlì, and Imola. See note XXVII, 49–51 (XXVII, 50).

MAHOMET (MOHAMMED): (c. 570–632) born at Mecca, founder of the Mohammedan religion (Islam). See notes XXVIII, 31, 32 (XXVIII, 31).

MALACODA: a devil. See notes XXI, 76, 118–23 (XXI, 76, 79).

MALEBOLGE: a region of Hell. See note XVIII, 1–20 (XVIII, 1).

MALEBRANCHE: the overseer-devils of the fifth *bolgia*. See note XXI, 37, 118–23, XXII, 97–132 (XXI, 37; XXII, 100; XXIII, 23; XXXIII, 142).

MALLORCA: an island in the western Mediterranean, off the Spanish coast (XXVIII, 82).

MANTO: a prophetess, the daughter of Tiresias. See note XX, 52–60 (XX, 55).

MANTUA (MANTOVA): a city in north central Italy, the birth-place of Virgil. See notes XX, 52–60, 61–99 (XX, 93).

MANTUAN: a citizen of Mantua (I, 69; II, 58).

MARCABÒ: a castle in the territory of Ravenna, near the mouths of the Po, at the eastern extremity of Lombardy. See note XXVIII, 73 (XXVIII, 75).

MARCIA: the second wife of Cato of Utica. See note IV, 127–29 (IV, 128).

MAREMMA: a swampy district along the coast of Tuscany, Italy. See notes XXV, 19–20, XXIX, 47–49 (XXV, 19; XXIX, 47).

MARS: the Roman god of war, son of Jupiter and Juno. See notes XIII, 143–50, XXXI, 49–57 (XIII, 144; XXIV, 145; XXXI, 51).

MASTER ADAM(O): a counterfeiter. See notes XXX, 52–53, 61–75, 76–78, 90, 92 (XXX, 61, 104).

MATTHIAS: the apostle who was elected to fill the place of Judas Iscariot. See note XIX, 94–96.

MEDEA: a sorceress, the daughter of Aeëtes, king of Colchis. See note XVIII, 86–96 (XVIII, 96).

MEDUSA: one of the three Gorgons, daughter of Phorcys and Ceto; she alone of the Gorgons was mortal. See notes IX, 52, 56, 61–105 (IX, 52, 56).

MEGAERA: one of the Furies, or Erinyes. See Erinyes (IX, 46).

MENALIPPUS: a Theban warrior. See note XXXII, 130–31 (XXXII, 131).

MENCIO: a river of Italy. See note XX, 78 (XX, 77).

MESSER GUIDO: Guido da Cassero, a citizen of Fano. See note XXVIII, 77–90 (XXVIII, 77).

MICHAEL: the archangel, chief of the angelic host. See note VII, 11–12 (VII, 11).

MICHAEL SCOT: a Scottish philosopher. See note XX, 116–17 (XX, 116).

MICHEL(E) ZANCHE, (DON): See notes XXII, 88–89, XXXIII, 137–47 (XXII, 88; XXXIII, 144).

MINOR FRIARS: Franciscans. See note XXIII, 3 (XXIII, 3).

MINÒS: the legendary king of Crete, the son of Zeus and Europa. See note V, 4 (V, 4; XX, 36; XXVII, 124; XXIX, 120).

MINOTAUR: the offspring of Pasiphaë and a bull. See note XII, 12–21 (XII, 12, 25).

MONGIBELLO: Mount Aetna. See note XIV, 51–60 (XIV, 56).

MONTAGNA: Montagna de' Parcitati, head of the Ghibelline party in Rimini. See note XXVII, 46–48 (XXVII, 47).

MONTAPERTI: a hill near Siena. See notes X, 85–86, XXXII, 106 (X, 85; XXXII, 81).

MONTE GIORDANO: a hill in Rome. See note XVIII, 28–33 (XVIII, 33).

MONTEREGGION (MONTEREGGIONI): a fortress near Siena. See note XXXI, 40–41 (XXXI, 40).

MONTE VESO: a peak of the Alps in Piedmont, the source of the Montone (XVI, 95).

MONTONE: a river of northern Italy, rises in the Tuscan Apennines, above the monastery of San Benedetto dell'Alpe. See note XVI, 94–101 (XVI, 94).

MORDRED: the traitorous nephew of King Arthur. See note XXXII, 61–62 (XXXII, 61).

MOROELLO MALASPINA: a captain and member of the Guelf party. See note XXIV, 143–50 (XXIV, 145).

MOSCA: member of the Lamberti family of Florence. See notes VI, 79–87, XXVIII, 106–108 (VI, 80; XXVIII, 106).

MOSES: the law-giver of Israel (IV, 57).

MOUNT AVENTINE: one of the seven hills of Rome, legendary site of the cave of Cacus. See note XXV, 25–33 (XXV, 27).

MOUNT OF PURGATORY: See notes XXVI, 133, XXXIV, 112–15, 127–32 (XXVI, 133).

MOUNT SORACTE: a mountain near Rome on which stand the church and monastery of San Silvestro. See note XIX, 115–17 (XXVII, 95).

MOUNT TAMBERNIC: See note XXXII, 28–30 (XXXII, 28).

MUSES: the nine Muses, who are represented as having been born in Pieria, at the foot of Mount Olympus, their father being Zeus and their mother Mnemosyne (Memory). Apollo was their chief guardian and leader. Their favorite haunts in Boeotia were Mount Helicon and the sacred fountains of Aganippe and Hippocrene; Mount Parnassus was also sacred to them, with the Castalian spring. The Muses were invoked by the poets as the inspirers of song. See notes II, 7–9, XXXII, 10–12 (II, 7; XXXII, 10).

MYRRHA: the daughter of Cinyras, king of Cyprus. See note XXX, 37–41 (XXX, 38).

NAPOLEONE DEGLI ALBERTI: the son of Count Alberto of Mangona. See note XXXII, 55–58 (XXXII, 55).

NARCISSUS: a beautiful Greek youth, the son of the river-god Cephisus and the nymph Liriope. See note XXX, 129 (XXX, 129).

NASIDIUS: a soldier in Cato's army in Africa. See note XXV, 94–102 (XXV, 95).

NAVARRE: a kingdom on both sides of the Pyrenees, consisting of French and Spanish Navarre. See notes XXII, 48–54 (XXII, 48).

NAVARRESE: an inhabitant of Navarre. See notes XXII, 48–54, 97–132 (XXII, 121).

NEPTUNE (GREEK POSEIDON): the god of the sea (XXVIII, 83).

NESSUS: a centaur. See note XII, 67–69 (XII, 67, 98).

NICCOLO: Niccolò de' Salimbeni, a Sienese spendthrift. See note XXIX, 127–29 (XXIX, 127).

NICHOLAS III: Gian Gaetano degli Orsini, pope from 1277 to 1280. See notes XIX, 67–72, 74, 98–99, 115–17 (XIX, 67).

NILE: a river of Egypt. See note XXXIV, 38–45 (XXXIV, 45).

NIMROD: commonly supposed to have been the builder of the Tower of Babel. See note XXXI, 77 (XXXI, 77).

NINUS: a warrior king, who with his wife, Semiramis, is said to have founded the Assyrian empire of Nineveh (c. 2182 B.C.) and conquered the greater part of Asia (V, 59).

NISUS: a Trojan companion of Aeneas. See note I, 108 (I, 108).

NOAH: the patriarch (IV, 56).

NOVARESE: citizens of Novara, a town in the northeast of Piedmont, Italy. See note XXVIII, 56–60 (XXVIII, 59).

OPIZZO D'ESTE: Opizzo II d'Esti, Marquis of Ferrara and the March of Ancona (1264–93), a Guelf nobleman who assisted the army of Charles of Anjou to cross the Po in the campaign against Manfred. See notes XII, 111–14, XVIII, 50–57 (XII, 111; XVIII, 56).

ORDELAFFI: the tyrannical ruling family of Forlì. See note XXVII, 43–45 (XXVII, 45).

ORPHEUS: a mythical Greek poet and musician. See note IV, 140 (IV, 140).

OVID (PUBLIUS OVIDIUS NASO): Roman poet, born at Salmo, 43 B.C.; exiled by Augustus (in A.D. 8) from Rome to Tomi, near the Black Sea, where he remained until his death, A.D. 17; of his extant works the best known is his *Metamorphoses*, a collection of legends narrating the transformations of human beings into other shapes, knit into a connected story from the Creation to the time of Julius Caesar. See notes IV, 90, XXV, 94–102 (IV, 90; XXV, 97).

PADUANS: citizens of Padua, a town in Venetia, Italy. See notes XV, 7, XVII, 70 (XV, 7; XVII, 70).

PALESTRINA: the ancient Praeneste, a town in Latium, Italy, situated 25 miles east of Rome. See note XXVII, 102 (XXVII, 102).

PALLADIUM: a statue of the goddess Athena. See note XXVI, 63 (XXVI, 63).

PAOLO MALATESTA: lover of Francesca da Rimini; third son of Malatesta da Verrucchio, lord of Rimini. See notes V, 73–142, 74, 82–84 (V, 101).

PARIS: the son of Priam, king of Troy, and Hecuba. When Jupiter refused to judge who was the fairest of the three goddesses, Juno, Minerva, or Venus, Paris was chosen to decide to whom the golden apple inscribed "To the Fairest" should be awarded. Juno offered him riches, Minerva conquest, but Venus promised him the love of the most beautiful woman in the world, so he gave the apple to her. Aided by Venus, he carried off the beautiful Helen, wife of King Menelaus of Sparta, and took her to Troy. After a ten-year siege, in the course of which Paris was killed, the Greeks, under Agamemnon, sacked Troy and recovered Helen. See note V, 67 (V, 67).

PAUL: an apostle and saint. See notes II, 10–48, 28–30 (II, 28, 32).

PELEUS: the father of Achilles. See note XXXI, 4–6 (XXXI, 5).

PENELOPE: the wife of Ulysses, or Odysseus. See note XXVI 94–96 (XXVI, 96).

PENTHESILEA: the daughter of Mars, and Queen of the Amazons. See note IV, 124–26 (IV, 124).

PERILLUS: the maker of the Sicilian bull commissioned by Phalaris. See note XXVII, 7–15 (XXVII, 8).

PESCHIERA: a town and fortress at the southern end of Lake Benaco (Garda). See note XX, 70–72 (XX, 70).

PETER: See Saint Peter.

PHAËTHON: the son of Apollo and Clymene. See note XVII, 106–108 (XVII, 106).

PHLEGETHON: a river of Hell. See notes XII, 47–48, XIV, 94–119, 134–35 (XII, 47; XIV, 116, 131).

PHLEGRA'S BATTLE: the scene of the battle in which Jupiter, with Hercules, defeated the Giants who attempted to storm Olympus. See note XIV, 51–60 (XIV, 58).

PHLEGYAS: the son of Mars and Chryse, king of the Lapithae. See note VIII, 18 (VIII, 19, 24).

PHOLUS: a centaur. See note XII, 72 (XII, 72).

PHOTINUS: a deacon of Thessalonica. See note XI, 8–9 (XI, 9).

PICENO: See note XXIV, 143–50 (XXIV, 148).

PIER DA MEDICINA: See note XXVIII, 73 (XXVIII, 73).

PIER DELLE VIGNE: a minister of Emperor Frederick II, and a poet (c. 1190–c. 1249). See notes XIII, 58–78 and 84 (XIII, 58).

PIETRAPANA: See note XXXII, 28–30 (XXXII, 29).

PINAMONTE: Pinamonte de' Bonaccolsi, a Ghibelline lord of Mantua (1272–91). See note XX, 95–96 (XX, 96).

PISA: a city in Tuscany, Italy, on the Arno. See note XXXIII, 79–90 (XXXIII, 79).

PISANS: citizens of Pisa. See note XXXIII, 28–36 (XXYIII, 30).

PISTOIA: a town in Tuscany, Italy, near Florence. See notes XXIV, 125–29, 143–50 (XXIV 126, 143).

PLATO: Greek philosopher (c. 428–347 B.C.), born in Athens. In his youth he became a pupil of Socrates, and later founded the Academic school. His extant writings consist of a large number of works on various philosophical subjects, in the form of dialogues. See note IV, 134 (IV, 134).

PLUTUS: the god of wealth, the son of Iasion and Demeter (Ceres). See note VII, 2–15, 8 (VI, 115; VII, 2).

PO: a river of northern Italy. See note XX, 78 (V, 98; XX, 78).

POLA: a seaport near the southern extremity of the Istrian peninsula celebrated for its Roman remains. See note IX, 112–17 (IX, 113).

POLENTA: a castle in Emilia, Italy, a few miles south of Forlì, from which the Guelf Polenta family took their name. See note XXVII, 41–42 (XXVII, 41).

POLYDORUS: son of Priam, king of Troy, and Hecuba. See note XXX, 16–21 (XXX, 19).

POLYXENA: the daughter of Priam, king of Troy, and Hecuba. See note XXX, 16–21 (XXX, 17).

POTIPHAR'S WIFE: See note XXX, 97 (XXX, 97).

PRATO: a town in Tuscany, Italy, about ten miles northwest of Florence. See note XXVI, 7–9 (XXVI, 9).

PRINCE HENRY: (1) the son of Richard, Earl of Cornwall. See note XII, 120 (XII, 120). (2) the son of Henry II, King of England. See note XXVIII, 134–36 (XXVIII, 135).

PRISCIAN (PRISCIANUS CAESARIENSIS): a famous Latin grammarian, born at Caesarea in Cappadoccia in the sixth century after Christ (XV, 109).

PROSERPINA (GREEK, PERSEPHONE): the daughter of Ceres (Greek, Demeter) the Earth-Mother. She was stolen away by Dis (Pluto) while gathering flowers in the vale of Enna, Sicily, and carried off to be his queen in Hades. She is identified with the moon, as one of the manifestations of the "Triple Goddess" Hecate-Luna in Heaven, Diana on earth, and Proserpina in Hades. See notes IX, 44, X, 79–81 (IX, 44; X, 80).

PTOLEMY (CLAUDIUS PTOLEMAEUS): Greek mathematician, astronomer, and geographer, born in Egypt about the end of the first century after Christ. See note IV, 142 (IV, 142)

PUCCIO SCIANCIATO: a member of the Galigai family of Florence. See note XXV, 148 (XXV, 148).

PUGLIA: a region of southeastern Italy. See note XXVIII, 7–12 (XXVIII, 8).

PUGLIANS: citizens of Puglia. See note XXVIII, 15–18 (XXVIII, 16).

PYRRHUS: See note XII, 135 (XII, 135).

QUARNERO'S GULF: the Gulf of Quarnero at the head of the Adriatic on the eastern side of the Istrian peninsula. See note IX, 112–17 (IX, 113).

RACHEL: the wife of the Patriarch Jacob and mother of Joseph and Benjamin. See note II, 102 (II, 102; IV, 60).

RAVENNA: a town in Italy on the Adriatic, near the mouth of the Po. See notes V, 97–99, XXVII, 41–42 (V, 97; XXVII, 40).

RED SEA: a body of water that separates the Arabian peninsula from Africa. See note XXIV, 85–90 (XXIV, 90).

RENO: a river of northern Italy. See note XVIII, 61 (XVIII, 61).

RHEA (CYBELE): the daughter of Uranus (Heaven) and Ge (Earth), and the wife of Saturn. See note XIV, 94–119 (XIV, 100).

RHÔNE: a river of France. See note IX, 112–17 (IX, 112).

RINIER DA CORNETO: a highway robber. See note XII, 137–38 (XII, 137).

RINIER PAZZO: a highway robber. See note XII, 137–38 (XII, 137).

ROBERT GUISCARD: Duke of Apulia and Calabria (c. 1015–85); born at Hauteville in Normandy; one of the twelve sons of Tancred. See note XXVIII, 14 (XXVIII, 14).

ROLAND: the French epic hero who was represented as the nephew of Charlemagne and one of the twelve peers; according to the poetical account, he was slain at Roncesvalles by the Saracens in league with the traitor Ganelon. See note XXXI, 16–18 (XXXI, 18).

ROMAGNA: a province of Italy lying between Bologna and the Adriatic, now called Emilia. See note XXXIII, 154 (XXVII, 37; XXXIII, 154).

ROMAGNOLS: the inhabitants of Romagna. See note XXVII, 28 (XXVII, 28).

ROMANS: citizens of Rome. See notes XV, 61–78, XXVI, 58–60 (XV, 77; XVIII, 28; XXVI, 60).

ROME: city in Latium, Italy, on the Tiber. See notes II, 15–21; XIV, 94–119; XXXI, 59 (I, 71; II, 21, 27; XIV, 105· XXXI, 59).

ROMENA: a village in the Casentino, a hilly region southeast of Florence, Italy. See notes XXX, 61–75, 76–78 (XXX, 73).

RUBICANTE: a devil. See note XXI, 118–23 (XXI, 123; XXII, 40).

RUGGIERI THE ARCHBISHOP: Ruggieri degli Ubaldini, Archbishop of Pisa (1278–95), nephew of Cardinal Ottaviano degli Ubaldini mentioned in X, 119. See note XXXIII, 13–14 (XXXIII, 14).

SABELLUS: a Roman soldier in Cato's army in Africa. See note XXV, 94–102 (XXV, 95).

SAINT FRANCIS (GIOVANNI FRANCESCO BERNADONE): (c. 1181–1226) the son of Pietro Bernadone, a wool merchant of Assisi. In 1209 he drew up the rules of his order, the members of which were called *frati minori* (minor friars) in token of humility, and which received the sanction of Pope Innocent III. He was canonized in 1228 by Gregory IX (XXVII 112).

SAINT PETER: one of the twelve apostles. See notes I, 133–35, XIX, 94–96 (I, 134; II, 24; XIX, 91, 94).

SAINT PETER'S: the cathedral in Rome. See note XVIII, 28–33 (XVIII, 32).

SAINT PETER'S CONE: a bronze pine cone. See note XXXI, 59 (XXXI, 59).

SALADIN (SALAH-ED-DIN YUSSUF IBN-AYUB): Sultan of Egypt and Syria (1137–93). See note IV, 127–29 (IV, 129).

SAN BENEDETTO DELL' ALPE: a monastery on the upper reaches of the Montone. See note XVI, 94–101 (XVI, 100).

SAN GIOVANNI: the Baptistery of Florence (XIX, 17).

SANTA ZITA: the patron saint of Lucca. See note XXI, 38–42 (XXI, 38).

SANTERNO: a river of northern Italy, in Emilia. See note XXVII, 49–51 (XXVII, 49).

SARDINIA: an island off the northwest coast of Italy. See notes XXII, 81–87, 88–89, XXIX, 47–49 (XXII, 90; XXVI, 104; XXIX, 47).

SASSOL MASCHERONI: See note XXXII, 65 (XXXII, 65).

SATAN: the Evil One, or Lucifer or the Devil. See note VII, 1 (VII, 1). See also Beelzebub, Dis, and Lucifer.

SATURN: a mythical king of Crete and afterward of Italy, identified by the Romans with the Greek god Kronos (time). Having been dethroned by his son Jupiter, he retired to Italy, where he became king and introduced agriculture and civilization; hence his reign is looked upon as the Golden Age of Italy. See note XIV, 94–119 (XIV, 96).

SAVENA: a river of northern Italy, in Emilia. See note XVIII, 61 (XVIII, 61).

SAVIO: a river of northern Italy, which rises in the Etruscan Apennines and flows north past Cesena, falling into the Adriatic. See note XXVII, 52–54 (XXVII, 52).

SCARMIGLIONE: a devil. See note XXI, 118–23 (XXI, 105).

SCIPIO (PUBLIUS CORNELIUS SCIPIO AFRICANUS MAJOR): a Roman general (c. 234–183 B.C.). He fought against Hannibal at Cannae (cf. note XXVIII, 7–12) and defeated Hannibal at the Battle of Zama (202 B.C.). See note XXXI, 115–18 (XXXI, 116).

SCROVEGNI: a family of Padua, Italy, notorious for its usury. See note XVII, 55–56 (XVII, 64–65).

SECOND FREDERICK: See King Frederick.

SEMELE: the daughter of Cadmus, king of Thebes, and the sister of Ino. See note XXX, 1–12 (XXX, 2).

SEMIRAMIS: a legendary queen of Assyria, the wife and successor of Ninus. See note V, 58 (V, 58).

SENECA (LUCIUS ANNAEUS SENECA): Roman philosopher and tragic poet, born at Cordova (4 B.C.–A.D. 65). He was appointed tutor to the youthful Domitius Nero, afterward emperor, under whom he amassed an enormous fortune, and was for a time practically the administrator of the empire. He committed suicide by command of Nero, who accused him of complicity in the conspiracy of Piso (A.D. 65). Seneca was a voluminous writer; his philosophical works consist of treatises on ethics, moral letters, and discussions of natural philosophy from the point of view of the Stoical system; he was also the author of tragedies, written in imitation of the Greek, nine of which are extant. See note IV 141 (IV, 141).

SER BRANCA D'ORIA: See Branca D'Oria.

SER BRUNETTO: See Brunetto Latini.

SERCHIO: a river in Tuscany, Italy, near Lucca. See note XXI, 46–51 (XXI, 49).

SEVILLE: a city on the southern coast of Spain. See notes XX, 124–26, XXVI, 110–11 (XX, 126; XXVI, 110).

SEXTUS: See note XII, 135 (XII, 135).

SICHAEUS: a wealthy Phoenician of Tyre, the uncle and husband of Dido. See note V, 61–62 (V, 62).

SICILIAN BULL: an instrument of torture. See note XXVII, 7–15 (XXVII, 7).

SICILY: an island in the Mediterranean off the southwest coast of Italy. See note XII, 107–108 (XII, 108).

SIENA: city in Tuscany, Italy, stronghold of the Ghibelline party. See notes XXIX, 109–17, 127–29 (XXIX, 110).

SIENESE: citizens of Siena. See notes XXIX, 122, 124–26, 127–29 (XXIX, 122, 134).

SILVESTRO: Pope Sylvester I (314–35). See note XIX, 115–17 (XIX, 117; XXVII, 94).

SIMON MAGUS: a magician. See note XIX, 1–6 (XIX, 1).

SINON: a Greek soldier of the Trojan War. See note XXX, 98 (XXX, 98).

SISMONDI: a leading Ghibelline family of Pisa. See note XXXIII, 28–36 (XXXIII, 33).

SOCRATES: Greek philosopher, born near Athens (c. 469–399 B.C.). He wrote nothing, and made no attempt to found a school or system of philosophy. He is famous for the method of argument that proceeds by questions so framed as to elicit from opponents an admission of the confusions and self-contradictions that their opinions involve (the "Socratic Dialectic"). He held that all vice was ignorance, and that rightly to understand virtue would enable men to live virtuously. Accused of blasphemy against the gods and of perverting the morals of the young, he was condemned to death by drinking hemlock. He is best known to us in the "Socratic Dialogues" of his pupil Plato. See note IV, 134 (IV, 134).

SODOM: an ancient city of Palestine. See note XI, 50 (XI, 50).

STRICCA: a spendthrift. See note XXIX, 124–26 (XXIX, 126).

STROPHADES: islands in the Ionian Sea, off the coast of Messenia. See note XIII, 10–15 (XIII, 11).

SULTAN: (1) the sultan in 1300 was El-Melik En-Násir Muhammad (1299–1309). See note V, 60 (V, 60). (2) the sultan mentioned by Guido da Montefeltro is El-Melik El-Mansoor La' geen (1296–99). See note XXVII, 85–90 (XXVII, 90).

STYX: a river of Hell, one of the nine rivers of the ancient underworld. See notes VII, 108, IX, 61–105 (VII, 108; IX, 81; XIV, 116).

SYLVIUS: the son of Aeneas and Lavinia. See note II, 13–21 (II, 13).

TAGLIACOZZO: a town in central Italy, in the Abruzzi, about twenty miles south of Aquila. See note XXVIII, 15–18 (XXVIII, 17).

TARQUIN (LUCIUS TARQUINIUS SUPERBUS): the seventh and last of the Tarquinian kings of Rome. See note IV, 127–29 (IV, 127).

TARTARS: the name applied to certain roving tribes which inhabited the steppes of central Asia and descended upon eastern Europe in the early part of the thirteenth century. See note XVII, 16–17 (XVII, 16).

Tegghiaio Aldobrandi: a Florentine Guelf nobleman. See notes VI, 79–81, XVI, 41–42 (VI, 79; XVI, 41).

Telemachus: the son of Ulysses (Odysseus) and Penelope. See note XXVI, 94–96 (XXVI, 94).

Thaïs: the whore in Terence's *Eunuchus*. See note XVIII, 135 (XVIII, 133).

Thales: Greek philosopher, born at Miletus (c. 635–c. 545 B.C.). See note IV, 137 (IV, 137).

Thames: river that flows through London. See note XII, 120 (XII, 120).

Thebans: citizens of Thebes. See notes XX, 34–36, XXX, 1–12 (XX, 32; XXX, 2).

Thebes: a city of Boeotia, Greece. See notes XIV, 68–69, XX, 52–60, XXV, 15, XXXII, 10–12, XXXIII, 79–90 (XIV, 69; XX, 59; XXV, 15; XXXII, 11; XXXIII, 88).

Theseus (Duke of Athens): a legendary king of Athens, a Greek hero, son of Aegeus, king of Athens, and Aethra, daughter of Pittheus, king of Troezen. See notes IX, 54, XII, 12–21 (IX, 54; XII, 17).

Tibbald: member of the Zambrasi family of Faenza. See note XXXII, 122–23 (XXXII, 122).

Tiber: river on which Rome stands. See note XXVII, 29–30.

Tiresias: a famous soothsayer of Thebes. See note XX, 40–45 (XX, 40).

Tisiphone: one of the Erinyes, or Furies. See Erinyes (IX, 48).

Tityus: a member of the race of Titans. See note XXXI, 124 (XXXI, 124).

Tolomea: a region of Hell. See notes XXXIII, 91–93, 124–35 (XXXIII, 124).

Toppo: the name of a ford near Arezzo. See note XIII, 115–21 (XIII, 121).

Trent: a city in northern Italy on the Adige. See notes XII, 4–10, XX, 63, 67–69 (XII, 4; XX, 68).

Tristan: a knight of Arthurian legend, the lover of Isolt, wife of King Mark of Cornwall. See note V, 67 (V, 67).

Trojans: inhabitants of Troy. See note XIII, 10–15 (XIII, 11; XXX, 14).

Troy: an ancient coastal town in Asia Minor, taken and sacked by the Greeks under Agamemnon, after ten years of siege, for the recovery of Helen. The siege is described in Homer's *Iliad*, and the sack in Virgil's *Aeneid*. See note XXX, 98 (I, 74; XXX, 22, 98, 114).

TULLY (MARCUS TULLIUS CICERO): celebrated Roman orator, writer, philosopher, and statesman (106–43 B.C.), the author of various rhetorical and philosophical works. His discourses on *Friendship* (*de Amicitia*) and *Old Age* (*de Senectute*) were well known to Dante, and the arrangement of sins in the *Inferno* is partly derived from his essay *On Duty* (*de Officiis*). See notes IV, 141, XI, 23 (IV, 141).

TURNUS: a king of the Rutulians to whom Latinus had promised his daughter Lavinia, before the arrival of Aeneas. See note I, 108 (I, 108).

TUSCAN: (1) an inhabitant of Tuscany. See notes X, 22–27, XXVIII, 106–108 (X, 22; XXII, 97; XXIII, 91; XXVIII, 108; XXXII, 66). (2) the dialect of Tuscany (XXIII, 76).

TUSCANY: district of Italy that lies, for the most part, between the Apennines and the Mediterranean, extending roughly from the Gulf of Genoa in the north to Orbitello in the south. The Arno is its major river, and Florence, Dante's birthplace, was its chief city (XXIV, 123).

TYDEUS: a king of Chalydon, one of the Seven against Thebes. See note XXXII, 130–31 (XXXII, 130).

TYPHON: a member of the race of Titans. See note XXXI, 124 (XXXI, 124).

TYROL: the mountainous district drained by the Inn and the Etsch (the Italian Adige) and their tributaries, and bounded on the north by Bavaria, on the west by Switzerland, and on the east by Salzburg and Carinthia, on the southwest by Lombardy and on the southeast by Venetia. In the twelfth century the Tyrol was ruled by counts (XX, 63).

UBRIACHI: a family of Florence notorious for their usury. See note XVII, 55–56 (XVII, 62).

UGUICCIONE: Uguiccione della Gherardesca, son of Count Ugolino. See note XXXIII, 89–90 (XXXIII, 89).

ULYSSES (ODYSSEUS): a prince of Ithaca, the son of Laertes, the husband of Penelope, and the father of Telemachus. He was one of the principal Greek heroes of the Trojan War. See notes XXVI, 55–57 (XXVI, 55).

URBINO: a town in central Italy, in the northern corner of the Marches. See note XXVII, 29–30 (XXVII, 29).

VAL CAMONICA: a valley in northeastern Lombardy. See note XX, 64–66 (XX, 65).

VALDICHIANA: the valley of the Chiana, in Tuscany, Italy, notorious for its malarial and unhealthy climate. See note XXIX, 47–49 (XXIX, 47).

VALDIMAGRA: the valley of the Magra river, which flows through Lungiana, Italy, the territory of the Malaspina family. See note XXIV, 143–50 (XXIV, 145).

VANNI FUCCI: the illegitimate son of Fuccio de' Lazzari. He was a militant leader of the Blacks in Pistoia and a thief. See notes XXIV, 125–29, 138–39, 143–50 (XXIV, 125).

VENEDICO CACCIANEMICO: a Guelf nobleman of Bologna, born c. 1228, head of the Guelfs in that city from 1260 to 1297. See note XVIII, 50–57 (XVIII, 50).

VENETIANS: citizens of Venice, a city in northern Italy on the Adriatic. See note XXI, 7–15 (XXI, 7).

VERCELLI: an Italian town at the western extremity of Lombardy. See note XXVIII, 73 (XXVIII, 75).

VERONA: an Italian city, in Venetia. See notes XV, 123–24, XX, 67–69 (XV, 122; XX, 68).

VERRUCCHIO: a castle and village near Rimini, seat of the Malatesta family. See note XXVII, 46–48 (XXVII, 46).

VERRUCCHIO'S NEW ONE: Malatestino, son of Malatesta da Verrucchio, Lord of Rimini from 1312 to 1317. See notes XXVII, 46–48, XXVIII, 77–90 (XXVII, 46; XXVIII, 85).

VERRUCCHIO'S OLD MASTIFF: Malatesta da Verrucchio, Lord of Rimini from 1295 to 1312. See note XXVII, 46–48 (XXVII, 46).

VIRGIL (PUBLIUS VERGILIUS MARO): Roman poet (70–19 B.C.), born in the village of Andes near Mantua. He was educated first at neighboring Cremona, then at Milan, Rome, and Naples. The poet Horace was a close friend, and among his patrons was Augustus. His great epic, the *Aeneid*, tells the story of Aeneas and celebrates the origins of the Roman people and empire (see Aeneas). Constantine, Eusebius, and Augustine accepted Virgil's *Fourth Eclogue* as a prophecy of Christ's birth. Throughout the Middle Ages he assumed in the popular imagination the character of a wizard and magician. See notes I, 62, and passim (I, 79, and passim).

VIRGIN MARY: See note II, 49–142, 94 (II, 94).

VITALIANO: See note XVII, 68–69 (XVII, 68).

VULCAN: the Roman god of fire, and the blacksmith of the gods. See note XIV, 51–60 (XIV, 57).

WAIN: the Great Bear. See note XI, 113–15 (XI, 114).

WISSANT: a port city between Calais and Cape Gris-Nez, in what was formerly part of Flanders. See note XV, 4–6 (XV, 5).

ZENO: See note IV, 138 (IV, 138).

SELECTED BIBLIOGRAPHY

I. REFERENCE BOOKS AND BIBLIOGRAPHICAL SOURCES

Barbi, Michele. *Life of Dante*. Edited and translated by Paul Ruggiers. Gloucester, Mass.: Peter Smith, 1962.

Cosmos, Umberto. *Handbook to Dante Studies*. Oxford, 1950.

Dante Studies. Edited by Anthony L. Pellegrini. Cambridge, Mass.

Dinsmore, Charles Allen. *Aids to the Study of Dante*. Boston and New York, 1903.

Enciclopedia Dantesca. Edited by Umberto Bosco. 5 vols. Rome, 1970.

Esposito, Enzo. *Gli studi danteschi dal 1950 al 1964*. Rome Centro Editoriale Internazionale, 1965.

Gardner, Edmund G. *Dante*. London, 1905.

Toynbee, Paget. *A Dictionary of Proper Names and Notable Matters in the Works of Dante*. Revised by Charles S. Singleton. Oxford, 1968.

II. CRITICAL WORKS

Auerbach, Eric. *Dante: Poet of the Secular World.* Translated by Ralph Manheim. Chicago, 1961.

Bergin, Thomas. *Dante*. Boston: Houghton Mifflin, 1965.

Brandeis, Irma. *The Ladder of Vision: A Study of Dante's Comedy*. New York, 1961.

Carroll, John S. *Prisoners of Hope*. Port Washington, N.Y.: Kennikat Press, 1971.

Davis, Charles Till. *Dante and the Idea of Rome*. Oxford, 1957.

Demaray, John I. *The Invention of Dante's "Commedia."* New Haven, Conn., 1974.

d'Entrèves, Passerini. *Dante as a Political Thinker*. Oxford, 1952.

Dunbar, H. Flanders. *Symbolism in Medieval Thought and Its Culmination in the Divine Comedy*. New York, 1961.

Fergusson, Francis. *Dante's Drama of the Mind, A Modern Reading of the "Purgatorio."* Princeton, N.J., 1952.

Fletcher, Jefferson Butler. *Dante*. Notre Dame, Ind., 1965.

Gardner, Edmund G. *Dante and the Mystics*. London, 1913.

Gilson, Etienne. *Dante the Philosopher*. New York, 1949.

Lansing, Richard H. *From Image to Idea: A Study of the Simile in Dante's Commedia*. Ravenna: Longo Editore, 1977.

Mazzeo, Joseph Anthony. *Structure and Thought in the "Paradiso."* Ithaca, N.Y., 1958.

Mazzotta, Giuseppe. *Dante, Poet of the Desert*. Princeton, N.J., 1979.

Montanari, Fausto. *L'Esperienza poetica di Dante*. Florence, 1959.

Montano, Rocco. *Storia della poesia di Dante*. Naples, 1962.

Musa, Mark. *Advent at the Gates: Dante's Comedy*. Bloomington, Ind., 1974.

———. "Essay on the *Vita nuova*." In Musa, *Dante's Vita nuova: A Translation and an Essay*. Bloomington, Ind., 1973.

———. *Essays on Dante*. Bloomington, Ind., 1964.

Nardi, Bruno. *Nel mondo di Dante*. Rome, 1944.

Nolan, David, ed. *Dante Commentaries*. New Jersey, 1977.

Orr, M. A. *Dante and the Early Astronomers*. Rev. ed. London, 1956.

Sayers, Dorothy. *Introductory Papers on Dante*. New York, 1959.

———. *Further Papers on Dante*. New York, 1957.

Singleton, Charles S. *Dante Studies I*. Cambridge, 1954.

Thompson, David. *Dante's Epic Journeys*. Baltimore, Md., 1974.

FOR THE BEST IN PAPERBACKS, LOOK FOR THE

In every corner of the world, on every subject under the sun, Penguin represents quality and variety—the very best in publishing today.

For complete information about books available from Penguin—including Penguin Classics, Penguin Compass, and Puffins—and how to order them, write to us at the appropriate address below. Please note that for copyright reasons the selection of books varies from country to country.

In the United States: Please write to *Penguin Putnam Inc., P.O. Box 12289 Dept. B, Newark, New Jersey 07101-5289* or call 1-800-788-6262.

In the United Kingdom: Please write to *Dept. EP, Penguin Books Ltd, Bath Road, Harmondsworth, West Drayton, Middlesex UB7 0DA.*

In Canada: Please write to *Penguin Books Canada Ltd, 10 Alcorn Avenue, Suite 300, Toronto, Ontario M4V 3B2.*

In Australia: Please write to *Penguin Books Australia Ltd, P.O. Box 257, Ringwood, Victoria 3134.*

In New Zealand: Please write to *Penguin Books (NZ) Ltd, Private Bag 102902, North Shore Mail Centre, Auckland 10.*

In India: Please write to *Penguin Books India Pvt Ltd, 11 Panchsheel Shopping Centre, Panchsheel Park, New Delhi 110 017.*

In the Netherlands: Please write to *Penguin Books Netherlands bv, Postbus 3507, NL-1001 AH Amsterdam.*

In Germany: Please write to *Penguin Books Deutschland GmbH, Metzlerstrasse 26, 60594 Frankfurt am Main.*

In Spain: Please write to *Penguin Books S. A., Bravo Murillo 19, 1° B, 28015 Madrid.*

In Italy: Please write to *Penguin Italia s.r.l., Via Benedetto Croce 2, 20094 Corsico, Milano.*

In France: Please write to *Penguin France, Le Carré Wilson, 62 rue Benjamin Baillaud, 31500 Toulouse.*

In Japan: Please write to *Penguin Books Japan Ltd, Kaneko Building, 2-3-25 Koraku, Bunkyo-Ku, Tokyo 112.*

In South Africa: Please write to *Penguin Books South Africa (Pty) Ltd, Private Bag X14, Parkview, 2122 Johannesburg.*